Your Country, Our War

The Press and Diplomacy in Afghanistan

KATHERINE A. BROWN

OXFORD
UNIVERSITY PRESS

OXFORD
UNIVERSITY PRESS

Oxford University Press is a department of the University of Oxford. It furthers
the University's objective of excellence in research, scholarship, and education
by publishing worldwide. Oxford is a registered trade mark of Oxford University
Press in the UK and certain other countries.

Published in the United States of America by Oxford University Press
198 Madison Avenue, New York, NY 10016, United States of America.

Library of Congress Cataloging-in-Publication Data
Names: Brown, Katherine A., author.
Title: Your country, our war : the press and diplomacy in Afghanistan /
Katherine A. Brown.
Description: New York, NY, United States of America : Oxford University
Press, [2019] | Includes bibliographical references and index.
Identifiers: LCCN 2018031175 (print) | LCCN 2018045038 (ebook) |
ISBN 9780190879426 (Updf) | ISBN 9780190879433 (Epub) |
ISBN 9780190879419 (pbk. :acid-free paper) | ISBN 9780190879402 (hbk.)
Subjects: LCSH: Afghan War, 2001—Press coverage—United States. |
Afghan War, 2001—Press coverage—Afghanistan. |
Journalism—Afghanistan—History—21st century. |
Press and politics—Afghanistan.
Classification: LCC DS371.4135 (ebook) | LCC DS371.4135 B76 2019 (print) |
DDC 958.104/72—dc23
LC record available at https://lccn.loc.gov/2018031175

9 8 7 6 5 4 3 2 1

Paperback printed by Sheridan Books, Inc., United States of America
Hardback printed by Bridgeport National Bindery, Inc., United States of America

Your Country, Our War

For my parents, John and Christine Brown,
who gave me the world.

Contents

Preface

THE FIRST TIME I met Hamid Karzai was on December 15, 2003. My colleagues from the American embassy and I waited for him in a white, airy tent on the grounds of the Polytechnic University in western Kabul, a few feet away from where 502 delegates gathered for the *Constitutional Loya Jirga*. The men, and some women, from each of Afghanistan's 32 provinces were working to forge the country's first democratic constitution in its 5,000-year history via a massive, grand version of the traditional assembly known as a *jirga*.[1] As an optimistic 25-year-old, I had arrived in Afghanistan a month before to serve as a junior press aide.

The U.S. news media version of Afghanistan depicted a country full of rapid progress after bleak decades of war and fundamentalism. A new constitution was one of the many firsts in Afghanistan that would happen in the next year, including the first paved highway from Kabul to Kandahar, the first presidential election, and the first independent television station. My colleagues and I were eager to continue to pitch these hopeful news stories to the American press. While U.S. embassies' public affairs officers normally target local press, the Afghan media were so nascent, and the concept of free speech was so foreign, that local journalists looked to their American and other Western counterparts for content and editorial guidance. But by late 2003, the majority of Western broadcast stations had shifted their attention 1,800 miles away to Iraq, the other U.S.-led post-9/11 war. With the communications infrastructure still weak in Afghanistan, and no U.S. television reporters stationed in the country, we purchased satellite time so that news anchors in New York could directly interview the Afghan President about the *jirga* as a historic milestone.

We turned the tent into a miniature, barebones television studio. It was winter in Kabul and we all shivered as we waited for Karzai to arrive. Around 8 p.m., the U.S. east coast 9.5 hours behind, he swept in wearing his signature green and blue striped cape and lamb's wool hat.

In impeccable English, he spoke excitedly of the day's deliberations and what that meant for Afghanistan's future. We guided him to a chair and placed an "IFB" (interruptible foldback) that provided an audio feed into his ear. Then we stood and watched as he spoke to Tom Brokaw of NBC News about the progress taking place in America's "good war," which also was already being referred to as a forgotten one.[2] Karzai often smiled as he spoke, his rapport with the anchor already firmly established during the previous two years. His tone was easy and relaxed.

To the West, Karzai was a symbol of optimism, unification, and progress—even elegance. Acclaimed fashion designer Tom Ford called him in 2002 "the chicest man on the planet"; *Esquire* magazine later anointed him one of the best-dressed men in the world, alongside Tom Brady and Jay-Z.[3] He was not just a darling of the American government, but also of the American press.

That cold December night was at the top of my mind on October 24, 2016, as I was escorted into Karzai's residence in the former United Nations compound in the center of Kabul, around the corner from the presidential palace he had occupied for nearly 13 years. It was the same compound where, in 1996, the Taliban castrated former president Mohammad Najibullah Ahmadzai and his brother, and then tied them to trucks and dragged them to their deaths through the streets of Kabul. The same compound that, nearly five years later, hosted a fresh generation of UN employees who believed the new international coalition was accelerating advancement in a country that desperately deserved it.

After passing through three waves of security, where women patted me down and took away all but my notebook and voice recorder, I entered the familiar space. The compound was an oasis from the haze of car exhaust on the streets. Four one-floor buildings lined the perimeter of a lush green courtyard with vibrant rose bushes holding on to the last warmth of the year. Delegations of Afghans from throughout the country walked through the compound daily to see Karzai, to still consult with him about their problems and ask for his help. I passed one delegation, and one of Karzai's young male assistants escorted me to a waiting room. Two elders from Nangarhar, an eastern province that borders Pakistan, were already there. "She is writing a book," an aide must have said to them in Pashto as I sat down. The elder closest to me turned and said in English, "You are writing a book!" It was more of a statement than a question, but I nodded anyway.

After more than a dozen years of traveling to Afghanistan for work and research, I went to Kabul in fall 2016 to finish writing this book. I completed my doctoral dissertation in 2013 on the Afghan, American, and Pakistani news media's storytelling during the U.S.-led war. I then sat on the research for years, chipping away at rewrites for no more than a couple hours a week. I decided to focus exclusively on the U.S.–Afghan relationship for the book and realized that the nearly four-year pause was necessary to see what had become of the country after the 2014 deadline President Barack Obama had set for American troop withdrawal—and soon after the U.S.-led war entered its sixteenth year on October 7, 2016.

"We are here to talk about Daesh!" the elder proclaimed, using the Arabic term for the Islamic State of Iraq and the Levant (ISIL). Daesh's activities in Iraq and Syria and its encroachment into Europe and the United States had become the dominant foreign news story in the American press in 2015 and 2016, far surpassing any mention of al Qaeda and/or the Taliban. "You know about Daesh?" he asked me with a smile.

"Yes," I replied. "I'm an American. We know about Daesh." I smiled back.

Both of the elders laughed, likely amused that I thought I knew about the apocalyptic death cult they were trying to keep from invading their homes when they weren't busy trying to keep the Taliban at bay.

Graciously, they insisted I speak with the former president first. I was escorted outside. Karzai was there, waving me over. He had traded his cap and cape for a simple *khet partug*, the traditional Pashtun dress of a beige flowy tunic and wide-legged pants with a black vest. We walked together to another building, which housed his library. One of his small daughters ran to him and he stopped to introduce me. A lifetime had elapsed between the 2003 Constitutional Loya *Jirga* and the present day, and he understandably didn't remember me. I explained briefly who I was, why I had come to Afghanistan in the first place, and why I had requested to see him.

As an administrative aide to President Bush's National Security Advisor in 2002–2003, I believed in the U.S. mission in Afghanistan and volunteered to be a public affairs assistant at the embassy in Kabul. Unlike the tightly controlled environment of 2016, I was fairly mobile when I lived in the American compound. I traveled to Mazar-e-Sharif, Jalalabad, Kandahar, Kunar, Sheberghan, Bamiyan, and Herat, and I embraced a country seemingly unrivaled in its ability to combine beauty with tragedy. The long history it had with the United States, its centrality to centuries of great power politics, and the devastation it suffered along the way both fascinated and horrified me. After I stopped working for the U.S. government in late 2004, I sought reasons to return. The chaos and complexity of the place drove many Americans and Westerners from there, mad and frustrated. But for some of us, trying to understand Afghanistan and the region became an addiction, as we felt inexplicably connected to the people and their enduring struggle for a life of peace. We felt we could do something to help.

But this time in 2016, more than any other visit, the city felt starkly different, and the American media's coverage reflected that. Setbacks in the Afghan economy, its security, its democratic governance, and nationwide respect for human rights—especially for women—were well documented despite a progressive technocrat, Ashraf Ghani, serving as president of a shaky national unity government that was engineered by the United States in 2014. Wazir Akbar Khan—the neighborhood with Karzai's current compound as well as the presidential palace, U.S. and other Western embassies, and the International Security Assistance Force—was now heavily fortified. I could barely recognize the area; its once familiar buildings were now locked up behind high, armored walls with coils of barbed wire. Some Westerners began to refer to the neighborhood as the "Green Zone," a term from the U.S.-led Iraq War that meant the space was secured from outside threats. We had never used that term in Kabul before. Nestled in the middle of it was the *New York Times* house, where I stayed for this trip. I woke up each morning to the sound of helicopters flying overhead. They were moving not troops but U.S. embassy civilians between their offices and the airport—which was only a mile away; the short stretch of road was deemed to be too dangerous to drive. The idea that American officials were living in Afghanistan was only by time zone; more than ever before, the U.S. embassy felt frighteningly isolated.

The deteriorating situation had been reflected in the American media's shifting portrayal of the country over the years as well as their shifting portrayal of Karzai himself. By the end of his presidency, he too was isolated, rarely leaving the palace grounds, preferring instead that Afghan provincial leaders come to him, as they still do today. He and his country watched nearly 200,000 American soldiers, diplomats, and aid workers who tried to provide security and development support for the country come and go. When security did not improve, when the war dragged on, when corruption worsened, when infrastructure deteriorated, Karzai became increasingly vocal about his aggravation with his American and other Western partners. By 2009, he began to openly clash with the Obama administration, accusing U.S. officials of interference and hypocrisy. In August 2016, he had told the press that "the Americans, whose primary slogan is democracy, are making a sham of democracy in Afghanistan."[4] He thought that the American free press was also a sham, voicing a belief held by the leaders of many other developing countries: that in the same way the American government has the power to shape the international system, the American news media have the power to fix people's perceptions of countries that operate within that system. If the country is not a Western one, the image Western journalists often bestow upon it is of a failed and conflict-ridden state.

As we finished our interview, which is the subject of Chapter 1, I thanked him for his time. I explained how a generation of American public servants and aid professionals—my generation, the one that professionally came of age post-9/11—had spent years in the country he once led and how fondly we think of Afghanistan and the Afghan people. I started to stand up, but he gestured for me to sit down. He asked:

> But how do the *common* Americans see Afghanistan? How do they understand Afghanistan? What perception do they have of us? As a violent people? As a people with a history, with a culture, or a people simply with guns and violence? What we see in the Western press . . . it is not the story in Afghanistan, in many ways. We are affected by violence, of course. But we are also a people, a country with weddings, with life, with people meeting. There's music, there's culture, there's history, there's niceties in life. Do they recognize that? Because the American media has not given that picture to the American people . . . Or has it? Have they? No.

There was sincerity in his voice, a nostalgia for the time when American journalists expressed nothing but respect for his country and his leadership, as Tom Brokaw and so many others had. Years after that cold night in 2003, Karzai would try to dilute the Western media's portrayal of him as corrupt and his country as backward by discrediting the sources, but the reputation of his country in the West remained as a violent and failed nation.

"No," I confirmed. "They mostly have not."[5]

THIS BOOK IS about the storytelling and framing of modern Afghanistan and of America's longest war from the perspectives of two nations' media systems. It reviews how news intersects with international politics and discusses the global power and reach of the U.S. news media, especially within the context of the post-9/11 era. It is based on years of interviews conducted between 2009 and 2017, in Kabul, Washington, and New York. It also draws from two bodies of communications scholarship that are analogous yet rarely linked together. The first is on hegemony and the U.S. news media's relationship with American society and the government. This includes literature on indexing and cascading; agenda-building and agenda-setting; framing; and conflict reportage. The second is on the American news media's relationship with the world and how *national bias*—defined as creating and maintaining a shared sense of identity—and *ethnocentrism*—defined as evaluating other people's cultures according to the standards of one's own culture—are fixed phenomena in international news. This includes examining the different kinds of press systems that exist globally, and how they interact with each other. In addition, the book examines the sociology of journalism development in Afghanistan since its news media became independent in 2001, and the habits and underlying philosophies its journalists have developed, including their tendency to look to U.S. news to make sense of the volatility, policies, and politics affecting their everyday lives.

It is broken into eight chapters. Chapter 1 acquaints the reader with the impact of the U.S. and Western news media in Afghanistan through the story of how President Hamid Karzai banished *New York Times* reporter Matthew Rosenberg in August 2014, during the final weeks of his presidency. The chapter uses this story as an entry point to the perceived hegemony U.S. news has in international affairs by foreign actors. It explains how news and nationalism intersect with international politics and introduces the reader to the groundbreaking yet nascent community of Afghan journalists who saw American and other Western journalists as their professional guides.

The second chapter discusses U.S. news reportage in the wake of 9/11 and how certain habits and norms in American national security journalism drove the coverage. It reviews scholarship on the U.S. news media's relationship with U.S. government and society, especially in the context of international issues and events. The chapter establishes that the foreign policy narrative in Washington is set by a small cohort of U.S. government officials, in addition to international news reporters and editors for elite news agencies, like the *New York Times* and *Washington Post*. Through interviews with U.S. officials and reporters, it also examines the roles the American government and news play in setting the agenda and framing events for the American public and how the U.S. press maintains an ethnocentric bias in its foreign reportage.

The third chapter examines how the American public was reintroduced to Afghanistan after the events of 9/11 and how the U.S. broadcast and print media began to frame "the good war" in October 2001. It analyzes the American news media's relationship with Afghanistan beginning in the 1980s; the reality it has constructed since 2001 about Afghanistan and the conflict; the waning coverage of Afghanistan during the Iraq War from 2003 to 2009; its increased coverage when President Barack Obama took office in 2009; and its coverage since 2014, as the United States began to prepare to disengage militarily from the country. It also reviews some U.S. officials' perceptions about their responsibilities to the press. During these 15 years, the news coverage, especially that of the broadcast news media, was tightly indexed to the degree of White House attention to the war and the intensity of conflict for American soldiers. Yet some American print news agencies, especially the Associated Press, *New York Times*, and *Washington Post*, have stayed committed to the Afghanistan news story despite decreased American presidential attention.

Having established the attitudes and norms of American national security news, Chapter 4 introduces the reader to the history of the Afghan news media, which was under either authoritarian or hyperpartisan control throughout the 20th century. This chapter explores the political and sociocultural factors that have contributed to the state of modern Afghan journalism, and how Afghan government officials have treated their press since 2001. Through the perspectives of more than 30 elite Afghan journalists, the chapter also examines the habits and norms local journalists have created, in addition to the impact of Western aid money and the presence of Western journalists in the country. The chapter also introduces the reader to the independent news media organizations that have helped to drive dramatic change in Afghan politics and society, often at a seemingly breakneck speed. In sum, it explains the patchwork media landscape of present-day Afghanistan and how it reflects the various power struggles between the country's politicians, extremists, strongmen, and progressives—and foreign actors.

Chapter 5 describes the various sociological constraints modern Afghan journalists have to work within, not the least of which is a highly volatile security environment within which they are often targeted with threats, in addition to a high degree of economic instability that jeopardizes their organizations' sustainability. Based on the interviews, it explores the ways in which they think of themselves, their relationships with Afghan government officials, and their roles in Afghan society. (Some of the journalists were interviewed on the record and are quoted by name, while others—due to Institutional Review Board [IRB] requirements for my dissertation research—were interviewed on background and are not named.) It also surveys the dense networks that Afghan journalists have created with American and other Western journalists to report news stories. Afghan journalists have an inherent national bias and are proud that U.S. elite news professionals find Afghanistan newsworthy as this confers legitimacy on Afghanistan's importance in the world. Yet given their nascent state, they acknowledged that they depend on Western journalists' reportage to hold Afghanistan's powerful accountable.

Chapter 6 focuses on the correspondents in Afghanistan who report for American news agencies, most, but not all, of whom are American. It reflects the views of more than a dozen news professionals who reported for elite news organizations on Afghanistan on how they perceived their roles. (As with the Afghan reporters interviewed, some of them were interviewed on the record, while others were interviewed on background and will not be named.) It discusses their agenda-setting power and their hegemonic role as purveyors of information to their primary and intended audience, Americans, and to the secondary audiences, such as Afghan journalists. The chapter explores these journalists' relationship with Afghan officials and explores what they believe the future of Afghan journalism will be.

Chapter 7 reviews how Afghan journalists perceive the "reality" journalists for American news organizations have constructed about Afghanistan, and how Afghan journalists make meaning from it. While reporters for U.S.-based news agencies saw Afghanistan through an American, or Western, lens, they rarely had the kind of access to U.S. officials' secret information that Karzai, and many others, assumed they had. The actual day-to-day mechanics of U.S. press–state relations is embroiled in an infuriating state of mistrust and dysfunction for both parties. Afghan journalists and a majority of Afghan officials assume that U.S. journalists are advocates for the U.S. government's foreign policies and are sometimes chauvinistically nationalistic, even jingoistic. The U.S. journalists vehemently reject this notion and the suggestion that their coverage is blindly patriotic. Yet they agree that they are largely aligned with U.S. officials in protecting and advancing America's general interests abroad. This is natural. The majority of journalists writing for American agencies are American; they have a built-in worldview and sense of identity that is difficult to abandon when they are writing primarily for American audiences. But Afghan journalists also are emotionally affected by the news stories they read that reduce their country to being shattered and hopeless. Consuming U.S. news about Afghanistan can be an affront to their Afghan identity and can inspire intense feelings of nationalism and frustration within them.

WHILE THERE IS a detailed methodology section in Appendix I, there are a few issues I'd like to emphasize about how I constructed this book. First, I chose Afghanistan because of my professional history with the country and my ability to travel there with relative ease. In many ways, not the least of which is the sheer duration of the U.S. government and news media's engagement in the country, Afghanistan provides an exceptional new case study, a microcosm for press–state relations from two perspectives. While my initial research had included Pakistan as another case study for comparison, I chose to focus solely on the Afghanistan case study because of its richness.

Second, I use "the United States" and "the West" interchangeably. This is because, in Afghanistan especially, the United States is seen as a leader of other Western countries and a creator of liberal international institutions that currently give some structure to global affairs. The Afghan journalists and officials would also speak of the United States and the West interchangeably in their interviews. I also focus on reporters who work for U.S. news agencies, but not all of them are American. This is the case, for instance, with the *New York Times*' Carlotta Gall and Associated Press's Kathy Gannon, who are English and Canadian, respectively. For this reason, when speaking about U.S. correspondents, I sometimes do not simplify them as Americans but as "U.S. journalists" or "U.S. reporters" to indicate that they work for U.S. news agencies.

Third, the qualitative research reflected in the second half of the book focuses on three years in U.S.–Afghan relations and the U.S.-led war: 2010, 2012, and 2016. This corresponds with the years when I conducted my fieldwork in Kabul. My interviews therefore are focused mainly on Afghan and U.S. correspondents who were in Kabul at the same time that I was. I realize this does not cover the entire universe of correspondents, but

I believe the overall sample is strong. Since this research was originally initiated for my doctoral dissertation at Columbia University, it was subject to their IRB processes, which deemed all of the journalists I was interviewing to be vulnerable subjects. As mentioned earlier, all of the interviews from 2010 and 2012 are anonymous and, to curb confusion, I did not give them pseudonyms in the text. My interviews in 2016, and the few I completed from Washington and New York in 2017, were on the record and their names are noted accordingly. Those interviewed in 2016 and 2017 also included U.S. officials. All of them are public officials and gave consent to speak on the record. In addition, because of the permanence of U.S. print bureaus in the country and the parachute nature of broadcast journalism, I conducted few interviews with U.S. broadcast reporters, yet since most Afghan news agencies are broadcast, the strong majority of Afghan journalists I interviewed were broadcasters.

Last, I would be remiss if did not acknowledge the limitations of my own identity as an American researcher in Afghanistan as well as the biases journalists may have had toward me because of my nationality, gender, and past professional history as a U.S. government official. While I believe that I captured their unfiltered opinions on the issues I asked about during the interviews, it is not entirely unlikely that they felt they could not be completely candid. Also, to a certain extent, my own research was a sort of parachute journalism. For the sake of this research project, my time in Afghanistan amounted to approximately six months. Collectively, however, I have spent two years in the country over the course of 13 years, which gives me some long-term perspective on the place and the ability to filter out the most salient issues worthy of exploration.

AMERICANS AREN'T THE only ones paying attention to U.S. news about the world; those affected by U.S. foreign policy rarely live within American borders. The people who often care the most about U.S. foreign policy are the government officials, journalists, and publics who are directly affected by the policies created at a distance in Washington. American news has been largely accessible to interested foreign audiences for more than a century, yet technology has accelerated a media boomerang pattern for foreign correspondence: News written abroad for an American audience travels almost instantaneously back to the government officials, journalists, and citizens of the nation U.S. correspondents are talking about.

To most foreign citizens interested in the United States—if not to most Americans—Washington is an intangible place. But a surefire way to get a sense of a nation and its priorities and worldview is to consume its news. People who speak English and have access to digital media can turn to U.S. news—normally, elite and mainstream agencies—to make their own meaning of U.S. intentions toward their country or region, and to see how America is projecting their country's image across a global media landscape. While people can use the news of another nation to gain a sort of intelligence about its intentions in the world, it can also provoke strong nationalistic feelings when they see themselves through foreign citizens' eyes. Contrary to those who hoped that a digital infrastructure would increase two-way flows of respectful dialogue, a greater flow of news and information does not necessarily bring understanding and peace between people and nations. National identity and bias can be maintained and reinforced through their national press, which travels internationally. And news content is both reported and understood ethnocentrically.

In foreign affairs, journalists are not merely observers to a story; they are participants in it. The stories they choose to tell, and how they tell them, can become dominant narratives in global politics. And America's news narratives provide a national representation. Journalists who report about the world for U.S. news agencies are profoundly important liaisons. In developing countries, they can even be official and unofficial mentors to local press cohorts.

Given the longevity of the U.S. presence in Afghanistan and the Afghan news media's dramatic proliferation since 2001, Afghanistan provides a fascinating case study for the role of journalists in conflict and diplomacy. By identifying, framing, and relaying narratives that affect the normative environment, U.S. correspondents have played unofficial diplomatic and developmental roles. They have negotiated the meaning of war and peace. Indirectly and directly, they have supported Afghan journalists in their professional growth. The impact they have had on Western public perceptions of the war and in the country's development have been profound: They did not just provide the first draft of history on this enduring post-9/11 entanglement between the United States and Afghanistan—they actively shaped it.

Acknowledgments

THIS BOOK WAS an exceptionally long project, which I put together in pieces from 2007 to 2018. I have a tremendous amount of people to thank, which I'll try to do here.

I'm extremely grateful that Angela Chnapko at Oxford University Press saw this book's potential in 2016, and was so patient with me the last two years as I finished it. Thank you to her and her wonderful production team, including Alexcee Bechthold and Shalini Balakrishnan, who made this process so much easier.

The book began to take shape while I pursued my doctorate at the School of Journalism at Columbia University. I'm forever indebted to the Ph.D. faculty there who pushed me to finish the dissertation and the book, especially Andie Tucher, Todd Gitlin, and Michael Schudson. They were wonderful advisors and editors and, at times, therapists. Thank you, Todd, for encouraging me to focus on Afghanistan for my dissertation research and for regularly challenging me. Thank you also to Brigitte Nacos from Columbia University's School of International and Public Affairs (SIPA), to Sean Aday from George Washington University, and to Hassan Abbas from the National Defense University who all served on my dissertation committee. I'm also thankful for my fellow cohorts in Columbia's Communications Ph.D. program and for my colleagues at SIPA, who gave support and friendship over the years: Ruth Palmer, Chris Anderson, Tom Glaisyer, Rasmus Nielsen, Ri Pierce Grove, Julia Sonnevend, Soomin Seo, Gabrielle Oliveira, and Dan McIntyre. And I'll always be grateful to the late David Klatell, who pushed me to take risks and taught me how to be a better teacher. Deepest thanks as well to Sam Freedman, who taught me how to write and structure a book—and believed in this one's possibility long before I did.

I feel very lucky to have witnessed firsthand the beauty of life in Afghanistan, beyond the headlines. Thank you to Jen Easterly and Steve

Hadley for helping me make the leap from the middle desk to Kabul, and to Mike Hammer for putting me on a career trajectory to make everything happen. Thanks also to Jennifer Betti, Debbie Felix, and Nancy Yuan at The Asia Foundation who helped ensure I had reasons to go back to Afghanistan—and for being wonderful colleagues and friends. And to Shannon Green who gave me residency at the Center for Strategic and International Studies (CSIS) for a brief period and helped me return to Kabul one last time for this book in 2016.

I'm grateful for all of my incredible Kabul colleagues, friends, and housemates over the years, from the U.S. embassy to "Timur's House": George Abi-Habib, Maria Abi-Habib, Joan Ablett, Jason Aplon, Kim Barker, Caroline Chung, Shane Christensen, Chris Del Corso, John Dempsey, Bay Fang, Sarah Gordon Gonzales, Jayne Howell, Gelareh Kiazand, Jamshid Mangal, Patt Maney, Siobhan Oat-Judge, Ashley Kushner Orbach, Shirin Pakfar, Farah Pandith, Michelle Parker, Josh Partlow, Jeff Raleigh, Amandine Roche, Matt Rosenberg, Beth Sanzone, Kevin Sieff, Marin Strmecki and Sarah Takesh. Thank you very much to the Afghan journalists and friends who spoke so candidly with me over the years—especially to Bilal Sarwary, Mujib Mashal, Sami Mahdi, Ahmad Mukhtar, and Lotfullah Najafizada. With much gratitude to Saad Mohseni, and all of the other Kabul-, New York, and Washington-based sources for this book who took the time to speak with me.

I'll never really be able to thank Scott Shadian, who I first met in 2005 and helped me to find ways to return to Kabul multiple times thereafter for research. I'll be similarly, perpetually indebted to Kay McGowan, the first friend I made in Kabul in 2003, who has looked out for me ever since, no matter where we are in the world.

To friends who read drafts of this book, helped to shape academic papers along the way, and/or helped to identify additional data points and research, thank you very much to: Amelia Arsenault, Kate Bateman, Nicholas Cull, Danny Gaynor, Chris Hensman, Kathryn McGarr, Nick Schifrin, Philip Seib, Jay Wang, Anne Wedner, and Rebecca Zimmerman.

I'm lucky to have had other extraordinary friends in New York, San Francisco, and Washington the last decade who all encouraged me to get this project done despite multiple things getting in the way. Thank you to the inimitable Camille Eiss and Sarah Arkin, who always help me exhale, as do the wonderful Miriam Magdieli, Emily Tavoulareas, Gwen Camp, Rose Jackson, Katherine Maher, Sidney Olinyk, Katherine Finnerty, Shilpa Nadhan, Eguiar Lizundia, Amit Magdieli, Erik Woodhouse, Mike

Masserman, Gordon Griffin, Meredith Gloger, and Lane Edwards. They've helped to keep me sane the last couple years in DC. Thanks also to Jenna Arnold, Kim Barker, Lisa Beyer, Reah Johnson Bravo, Dan D'Lauro, Niki Ganz, Tanya Gallo, Jeremy Goldberg, Alex Rossmiller, Jennifer Rosenbaum and Jennifer White who made graduate school life in New York so much easier; and to Chris Anderson, Melanie Bariso, Bill and Julie Coleman, Holly Clune, Rachel Hagen, Karl Rectanus, Mona Rowghani, and Victoria Wheeler for always being such wonderful touchstones, no matter the distance. A special thanks to Dena Lazarova, who convinced me at age 18 that I actually would have a career in international affairs and has been one of my biggest cheerleaders since. And to her daughter, my goddaughter, Gia Lazarova, who will run the world one day.

I also need to add this to the list: My high school loves—Adrienne Sletten, Erin Meyer Krupsaw, Katy Moore, Lindsey Dazel Nichols, Melissa Skrabo Munster, and Robin Remmel Henrich—who've always reminded me that California is home.

And I'll always be grateful to my love, Jim Arkedis, for helping me to cross the finish line.

And thank you to my magnificent family, who've encouraged this book and everything I've ever done: my sisters, Judy McEntee and Colleen Brown Swan; my brothers-in-law, Dan McEntee and Padraig Swan; my nieces and nephews, Briana and Patrick McEntee, and Saoirse and Sean Brown Swan; my cousins Maria Breber, Chris Carson, Tim Carson, RJ Bannister, Kristen Bannister, Mary Pat Cain Weidner, and their families; and my Aunt Mary and Uncle Tom Carson, who've always showed up for me.

Last, to my parents, John and Christine Brown, who've passed onto me their curiosity about the world, continue to give me unconditional love and support, and always want to hear my stories: Thank you.

1

Hamid Karzai vs. the *New York Times*

We are fully committed to the freedom of the press. It is just to stop the evil in the *New York Times'* reporting

—AIMAL FAIZI, presidential palace spokesman, August 20, 2014, on the expulsion of *New York Times* reporter Matthew Rosenberg from Afghanistan[1]

HAMID KARZAI BEGAN nearly every day of his presidency with two books of news clips from his palace press office. One was filled with Western news about Afghanistan; the other was filled with Afghan news reports. He rarely touched the latter.

Karzai was fixated on how Western journalists framed his country, himself, and his family for global audiences. Fairly early into his tenure as president he had become deeply suspicious of American intentions in the country and determined that the elite U.S. press was a channel for the American government. He began to rant about Western, especially American, news coverage in public, believing the media were waging a psychological war against him. He explained in open forums to local reporters that he had studied the American news media and had concluded that U.S. journalists were trying to convince Afghans they would suffer without the U.S.'s sustained financial and military support, which was set to expire at the end of 2014.[2]

Journalists for American news agencies, Karzai believed, were U.S. government agents. He was first convinced of this in November 2004. At the time, he was in a fierce disagreement with American and British officials over how to counter the increasing proliferation of poppy fields in the country, which narco-traffickers were cultivating into 90 percent of the world's heroin supply. Poppy was one of the few cash crops Afghanistan's arid land could produce and it provided a lifeline for the country's rural class. But the heroin flooded Europe's streets. The Americans and British proposed eradicating the supply by spraying the fields from the air, which could efficiently kill vast amounts of crops. Karzai refused to subject his citizens to mass chemicals and pesticides. He said in an October 2016 interview: "The second day of that serious argument between me and the U.S. government, I saw an article in the *New York Times* accusing my brother of involvement in drug dealing. I thought, 'How was it that I just had an argument with the American government about this the day before yesterday and a day or two later the *New York Times* publishes an article saying that my brother was involved with drugs?' "[3]

That November 19, 2004 article, written by *Times* correspondent Carlotta Gall, who is a British national, reported on the United Nations Office on Drugs and Crime's (UNODC) conclusion that 321,236 acres of land in all of Afghanistan's 32 provinces had been planted with poppy in 2004—a 64 percent increase since 2003. The head of the UNODC said that Afghanistan was deteriorating into a "narco-state."[4] Near the bottom of the article, Gall included this line: "Diplomats say there are even reports linking Mr. Karzai's brother, Ahmed Wali Karzai, an influential figure in the southern city of Kandahar, to the trade." She also stated that the presidential palace dismissed the allegation as "propaganda" against the president and his brother.

Gall had been hearing news about Ahmed Wali Karzai's involvement in the drug trade for years. "That wasn't leaked from the Americans," she explained in a 2017 interview. When she was writing the article, she had thought, "We should just be saying this," so she added the allegation into the story. "I shouldn't have done it like that because the paper regretted it afterwards," she reflected. "We named people and we should've done a more rigorous investigation. But I had known this stuff for years. I actually had very good sources, but I didn't spell it all out in that piece."[5]

The timing, however, was too convenient for President Karzai. He recalled in 2016 that, as a result of that story, "I recognized that either the U.S. press and the U.S. government was working hand in hand in what they deemed to be in the national interest of the United States, or that it was worse than that—and that the press was controlled by and was an arm of U.S. policy vis-à-vis countries like us. And I still hold that second view."[6]

After believing for a decade that the U.S. government and the American news industry were united in a cabal that was determined to destabilize Afghanistan and undermine his rule so that the United States could stay in Afghanistan indefinitely, reading the American press had become all but unbearable.[7]

The American public, however, the primary audience for U.S. news, had no interest in helping Karzai realize his suspicion. Americans wanted out of Afghanistan. In June 2010, Afghanistan became the U.S.'s longest continuous, modern war with troops actively deployed. By June 2014, Gallup found that 49 percent of Americans thought starting the war was a mistake; in 2002, only 6 percent had. Despite nearly $1 trillion of U.S. tax-payer funds, more than 1 million American troops and diplomats serving in the country, and more than 2,000 dying and 20,000 Americans wounded there, Afghanistan had largely failed to capture America's imagination.

But in Karzai's mind, the Western press was writing "the 2014 movie," an American horror show about a dystopian Afghanistan without Western troops and aid. In 2009, President Barack Obama had created a five-year timeline to end U.S.-led combat operations in the country. For years, American officials had been trying to reach a bilateral security agreement (BSA) that would ensure U.S. troops' immunity within Afghanistan if they continued to support the fledgling Afghan National Security Forces (ANSF) beyond 2014. Without one, all remaining U.S. ground troops— roughly 16,000 down from a peak of 100,000 in 2010—would leave.[8] Karzai believed the United States wanted to stay in a country that bordered Iran, China, Pakistan, and the former Soviet Central Asian states to grow its sphere of influence. He declared publicly that the U.S. news media were working with the U.S. government to intentionally undermine the Afghan people's faith in their own government and bolster their need for American assistance.[9] The U.S. government, he later said in October 2016, "were manufacturing things and telling the press to say things that were not there . . . It was absolute disinformation. It was psychological warfare, launched by the U.S. press."[10]

By August 2014, Karzai, physically isolated in a heavily fortified palace in the Wazir Akbar Khan neighborhood of Kabul, deeply suspicious of the Americans, and citing the history of Western powers colonizing Afghanistan, had refused to sign the BSA. He was politically isolated as well: While the two presidential candidates running to succeed him that year, Abdullah Abdullah and Ashraf Ghani, conflicted on many issues, they both emphatically pledged to sign a BSA if elected.

On August 18, the *New York Times* ran a story by reporter Matthew Rosenberg titled "Amid Election Impasse, Calls in Afghanistan for an Interim Government."[11] It discussed an idea brewing for a temporary government to bring stability to Kabul and end Abdullah and Ghani's feud over a deeply flawed election. The stopgap measure, Rosenberg reported, would give the two candidates more time to compromise and perhaps time to sign the BSA before the end-of-2014 deadline. He compared the plans to a "soft coup, though one . . . [that] would later lead to a return to democratic rule" when the final outcome of the election was determined.[12]

Talk of an interim government was pervasive among the Kabul elites, according to the correspondents in the *Times* bureau in Kabul at the time. Afghan officials were actively reaching out to them about its potential, seemingly hoping that they would report it so they could gauge American government officials' reaction to the possibility. The Minister of Interior, Umer Daudzai, and the National Security Advisor to Karzai, Rangin Dadfar Spanta, were quoted on the record in the news story. Rosenberg had filed it in mid-August with his New York-based editor. Yet he was unsure when it would run, not because of any potential controversy, but because Afghanistan wasn't at the top of the U.S. news agenda. By this time, the war's 12th summer, political infighting between Afghanistan's leaders was barely newsworthy.[13]

To Karzai, the news story was another fabricated rumor, an American government plot designed to sow disruption and destroy Afghanistan's decade-old democratic experiment. He had determined that it was no longer enough to just make public statements against the U.S. news media in Afghanistan.

A few hours after the story ran on the *Times* webpage, Rosenberg received a call from the presidential palace's deputy spokesman. The official asked about the quotation by National Security Advisor Spanta. Having had no complaints from Spanta himself, Rosenberg didn't think twice about the call. Later, as he was sitting down for lunch, the phone of one of his colleagues rang. It was the Afghan Attorney General's office, asking Rosenberg to come to his office to meet with "junior officials." Rosenberg and his colleagues agreed to go later that afternoon.

Upon arriving at the Attorney General's office, which was just minutes from their office by car, Rosenberg and his two colleagues were taken to a conference room with General Noorullah, the senior prosecutor and the general director of the Crimes Against External and Internal Security unit. At first, the tone was friendly. They requested the names of Rosenberg's sources; while Daudzai and Spanta had been quoted on the record, Rosenberg quoted other Afghan officials anonymously. He refused to name his sources. The mood changed. The meeting continued for a tense two hours. Eventually, the Afghan officials presented Rosenberg with a piece of paper with writing in the Dari language and requested he sign it. Rosenberg exchanged glances with his colleagues, and then said he would return with a lawyer. The Afghan officials allowed him to walk out of the ministry.

As they were returning to the *Times* bureau, a tweet by Tolo News, Afghanistan's most popular news agency, delivered the message that the Afghan officials didn't deliver to their faces. "BREAKING," the tweet read. "Afghan Att. Gen. bans Matt Rosenberg of the NYTimes from leaving the country b/c of a controversial story."[14] News quickly spread through the small journalism community in Kabul. Minutes later, the Associated Press called Rosenberg to try to confirm the report.

Rosenberg called his parents to explain the situation before they would have to read about it and to assure them he was safe. As far as he knew, he would be: The Afghan Media Law, enacted in 2009, protected him from imprisonment. The story was also multisourced and sound. *Times* editor Doug Schorzman later explained in a 2016 interview, "We had every reason to believe that this was a serious thing going on. It was not predictive. It was a serious discussion of an emergency government and we cross referenced it in a serious way."[15] Rosenberg's Kabul bureau colleague Rod Nordland also agreed that "It was an important story and it was a true story."[16]

That night, Nordland published a piece about Rosenberg's interdiction, the first known one of a Western journalist by the Afghan government since the overthrow of the Taliban. The story, "Afghan Officials Interrogate a Times Correspondent," included a quote from Adela Raz, the deputy spokeswoman for President Karzai. He said:

Such baseless reports by the *New York Times* are in violation of all the recognized principles of journalism, or they are politically motivated. Since the beginning of the [2014] presidential election the *New York Times* newspaper has sought to sow disunity among the Afghans by publishing several reports of this nature. We have notified the administration of the newspaper in writing several times about the publication of reports that encourage disunity, but they have repeatedly published such reports, and therefore we must take serious action in accordance with appropriate Afghan law.[17]

The next evening, August 20, the *Times* bureau was preparing to host a dinner in honor of Rebecca Corbett, a senior editor who had flown in for the scheduled interview that week with President Karzai. Around 8 p.m., two white Toyota pickup trucks with armed Afghan police officers arrived outside the barbed-wire fence in front of the bureau's compound, which was around the corner from the presidential palace. Unsure if they were coming to take him into custody, Rosenberg hid in the bureau's safe room. The Afghan police didn't come in but handed a *Times* employee a piece of paper at the gate with a statement from the Afghan government. It read that the ban had been lifted, but now Rosenberg had to leave the country within 24 hours or else he would be arrested.[18] They had also cancelled the *Times'* scheduled interview with the president.

The Afghan news media had been technically free since 2001, which made Karzai immensely proud. Article 34 of the Afghan constitution, which was heavily influenced by the U.S. government, calls for freedom of expression and of the press; and, as mentioned, the 2009 Mass Media Law prohibits censorship and guarantees the right of citizens to obtain information. Yet the country's first democratically elected president expelled an American journalist for his reporting.

The decision, though, had been easy for Karzai. Before announcing it, he had called both presidential candidates, Ghani and Abdullah. He explained in an October 2016 interview, "I told them that a story like that, that I see it as very wrong." He continued:

> And they agreed with me. And I said the only way that I can express my anger at this and the anger of the Afghan people, that we express that we remain committed to democracy and that we are not a country of fools is to have Rosenberg leave . . . So that is what I did, to tell him that what he did was wrong.[19]

It was one of his final acts in office.

No one from the Attorney General's office followed through with the *Times* to ensure Rosenberg was leaving. When he arrived at Kabul International Airport, he went through the first round of security, checked his bags, and received his boarding pass. He then walked to another round of security, where an agent checked his name on a list of departing passengers that day. Rosenberg saw a yellow sticky note on the document with his name on it. Minutes later, two policemen arrived to escort him through passport control and the final round of security. They shadowed him in the terminal until his flight to Dubai began to board and then escorted him to the plane. As a farewell token, Rosenberg took a photo with the policemen. "They could not have been friendlier," Rosenberg recalled later. "They were Afghan."

Rosenberg sat in business class, which had the only available seat for a last-minute purchase, and drank the sparkling wine that came with it. He thought: After dedicating six years to reporting Afghanistan, the Karzai administration threw him out over an accurate piece of reporting and accused him of being a spy. He believed the act spoke volumes about President Karzai's final agenda as president and his obsession with the Western press. "Karzai was sick of us," he explained in an interview six months later, with "us" being the entire Western news media corps. Weeks before he stepped down as part of a power-sharing deal for a unity government run by both Ghani and Abdullah, Karzai had seized his last chance to declare his disgust for the Western news media, especially the *Times*. Karzai did not see an accurate report that revealed his own people's doubts about the country's political transition; he saw an attempt by a foreign government to manipulate the country's future.

Reflecting on the matter more than two years later, President Karzai didn't believe that his expulsion of Rosenberg was counter to the values enshrined in the Afghan constitution and the free speech he championed for the Afghan press. The *Times*' reporting, he said, "was not freedom of the press. That was undermining democracy in Afghanistan . . . That was directly an infringement of a most serious type on the democratic transition in Afghanistan from one government to another government." He saw the *Times* as trying to interfere in the state of the country: "This was an effort against a democratic transition of power in Afghanistan." Karzai continued:

> What was sad in it was the fact that we perceived the United States as a democracy. We really believed in the freedom of media and the freedom of speech there. We really thought that the press was free. But actually, they behaved like the *Pravda* of the former Soviet Union. But *Pravda* did not have the mask of democracy on. We all knew that *Pravda* was the propaganda arm of the Soviet Union. But the *New York Times* and others claim to be free, and then for them to serve a governmental purpose—it was revealing.[20]

Karzai was wrong about Rosenberg's intentions—the *New York Times* is not a direct propaganda arm of the U.S. government—but it is understandable why he perceived U.S. journalists as being more dangerous to the stability of his country than they consider themselves to be. Foreign correspondents for U.S. news agencies are not simple purveyors of the facts. They are powerful storytellers who fundamentally shape Americans' and foreigners' perspectives and the information environment within which crucial decisions are made. They represent American society to the world in a form far more tangible than American government officials often do; their stories often fill in the gaps left by misunderstood or poorly explained U.S. foreign policies. Karzai knew that American and other Western news professionals had the power not only to influence narratives and perceptions within the West and inside his own country, but also to shape foreign policy decisions for many potential allies and adversaries, and therefore the conduct of international relations.

In some ways, President Karzai was right about a possible partnership between the U.S. reporters and officials. When it comes to foreign news coverage, the U.S. press and government are generally aligned in protecting and advancing America's interests. A country's news media create and maintain a nation, employing common symbols and language and constructing narratives that resonate with the country's citizens. Journalists intend to be observers of international politics, but unintentionally they are its participants. The majority of journalists writing for American agencies are American; they have a built-in worldview and sense of national bias and ethnocentrism that is difficult to abandon when producing news about the world. Despite the span and interconnectedness of global media, the national security narrative in the U.S. media remains static as news professionals maintain a U.S.-centric worldview with a myopic focus on conflict, disaster, and crisis abroad.

But that doesn't make U.S. journalists employees of the U.S. government. To the contrary, the actual day-to-day mechanics of U.S. media–American diplomatic relations have long been embroiled in an infuriating state of distrust and dysfunction. While reporters for U.S.-based news saw Afghanistan through an American or Western lens, they rarely had the kind of access to U.S. officials' secret information that Karzai and others assumed. The sociological constraints working against them were vast: They were often ignored by government officials, fought for attention from their U.S.-based news editors and producers, worked in understaffed bureaus, were reminded hourly of their foreignness, and often had to cover several countries simultaneously.

Afghans, however, believed that American news stories about their country advanced U.S. policy. Therefore, when U.S. reporters chronicled endless shortcomings of U.S. engagement in the country—war, violence, poverty, corruption, and power grabs—the Kabul elites especially believed they were reading about the opinions of the American government that so profoundly affected their sense of security, government, and way of life. President Karzai looked to it as proof of the U.S. government's true intentions: to ensure Afghanistan was consistently vulnerable and dependent on the United States, perpetuating a sense of colonialism the country had long been subjected to.

But Afghan officials also gravitated toward U.S. reporters when they wanted to make both local and international news simultaneously and to speak directly to Washington. They eagerly chased U.S. reporters in the country and lobbied them to report information that would cater to their agendas; they believed that the press, in particular the *New York Times* and *Washington Post*, strongly affected perceptions within and outside the U.S. government, including the leaders of other countries.

The Afghan journalists also closely observed U.S. reporters in the country. A new, young, and emerging Afghan press corps, wanting to pursue a Western style of journalism, looked to them as their instructors and agenda-setters. Therefore, news about Afghanistan in the American press also reverberated throughout the local media in the early years of the U.S.-led conflict. Karzai and members of his administration knew this, and they deemed it to be dangerous since he believed the U.S. press was out to stain his image in the world under the guise of independent reporting. When Karzai said in October 2016 that the U.S. press "was controlled by and was an arm of U.S. policy vis-à-vis countries like us," one can interpret that to mean that the U.S. press tried to suppress the development of not just Afghanistan but all developing countries.

There has been a widespread, longstanding belief in developing nations that American and other Western news media intentionally seek to undermine their strength and keep them dependent on the West, a sort of neocolonialism. The United States is the most talked about country in the world: According to a comparative study of international news reported by 38 nations' media systems, the United States was referenced and editorialized the most.[21] Reporters, opinion writers, columnists, talk show hosts, headline writers, photo editors, and cartoonists in other countries generate journalistic images and messages of the United States from their respective locations. But few foreign news agencies from developing countries have the budget to dispatch journalists to cover Washington to garner first-hand knowledge of a country that has a profound impact on the rest of the world.[22] U.S. news narratives, however, travel rapidly around the world and can be picked up by another nation's news professionals, who then interpret and relay them through their own lenses.

No matter where they are reporting from, foreign journalists do not always see America and its place in the world as U.S. journalists do. In general, the U.S. media have depicted countries going to war as being aggressive, but for American audiences, U.S. aggression is often rationalized as being in support of U.S. interests.[23] Directly and indirectly, they perpetuate the myth that America is the world's hero, with the world in need of being saved. Some foreigners see this as damaging propaganda against their interests.[24]

WALTER LIPPMANN FAMOUSLY said in *Public Opinion* (1922) that "the only feeling that anyone can have about an event he does not experience is the feeling aroused by his mental image of that event." We all relate to others and the complex world beyond through the "pictures in our heads." And the source for the mental images we construct is, most often, the news media. News about a nation—usually written and edited by fellow Americans—constructs our understanding of that nation, especially when it describes that which is truly foreign for most Americans: war, disaster, and authoritarian societies. As in other countries, Americans who want to understand the world have no choice but to turn to journalists for snapshots of foreign issues and events. In the United States, we can form opinions on domestic events and issues through direct experiences or the experiences of friends, family, colleagues, and acquaintances. News stories about domestic events, in other words, are influential but are only one source of many others available that can help us make sense of an issue or an event.[25] But for most Americans, the world beyond our borders is brought to life only by content creators in the media.

Lippmann also made a second point in *Public Opinion*: Until "we know what others think they know," he said, "we cannot truly understand their acts." How can someone understand the perceptions of another? One method is to consume their news media: to read what they read, to watch what they watch, to listen to what they listen to. Citizens of countries who are affected by America's economy, military, and/or global politics, like

Afghans, can watch and read what U.S. policymakers and citizens watch and read to gain better insight as to how they think—and try to predict how they will act.

Today, the U.S. news media are part of a transnational, instantly available digital media landscape in which information flows within and between nations faster and in more quantities than ever before. News may be created with a national audience in mind, but it is not confined to that audience. Global journalists often use news as source material and can be exposed to several narratives, each of which can represent a distinct version of international compacts and conflicts. The imagery and narratives U.S. journalists provide to Americans are also consumed by anyone in the world who speaks English and has access to the Internet, satellite television, and radio. The questions therefore are not just whether U.S. journalists fairly convey information about the rest of the world, or help legitimize official positions, or create realities for Americans—but also how foreign audiences interpret those constructed narratives.

To understand how the world communicates, it is important to understand the stream of news stories and the way they build an entire nation and its population in outsiders' imaginations. The U.S. news media negotiate meaning not just between the government and the public in the United States, but between governments, between people, and between journalists worldwide. And yet the global effect of American news products is largely unexplored. There are few answers on how U.S.-based news—which normally focuses on episodic, crisis reporting, is ethnocentric, and can lack historical context—is perceived and used abroad, especially in conflict environments. Global audiences for American news are often unintended. But whatever text is written, whatever pictures are taken, whatever words are said about a foreign land for a U.S. audience can travel back to the government officials, journalists, and citizens of the nation American journalists are talking about. What is created for one group of people living in a society can fairly easily be accessed, relayed, and interpreted by its very subjects.

Reporters who work for elite U.S. news organization are powerful but overlooked players in international diplomacy and conflict. Not only can they influence U.S. policymakers and the American public, but they also represent the views of the United States in an accessible package that foreign journalists can recycle for their audiences and foreign officials can interpret for signals on policy. The U.S. experience in Afghanistan from 2001 to 2016, especially, tells an intriguing story of the impact of the U.S. news media on the diplomatic relationship between the United States and Afghanistan, and on an emerging democracy and a nascent free press heavily influenced by the West.

By 2017, Afghanistan's press consisted of more than 60 television channels, 150 radio stations, and 500 newspapers. By Western standards, according to Freedom House's Press Freedom Index, the environment had shifted from "not free" to "partly free."[26] This was considerable progress, but after decades of authoritarian rule, the Afghan journalists were still reluctant to take on the many powerful figures in their country and report about their government without skepticism. The Afghan journalists with the more popular news outlets have relied on the American government's economic support for technical assistance, media training, and program-ming budgets; they also relied on American news reportage on their country for information about the conflict, the United States, and its own government. From the Afghan journalists' perspectives, the U.S. media serve as credible purveyors of what the U.S. government wants the world to know. U.S. journalists' selection and representation of Afghanistan, and the U.S. government's policies toward it, made them effective and widely accessible liaisons for anyone seeking to understand U.S. thought about, and action within, the country and the South Asia region. As U.S. for-eign correspondents are the American public's connection to a world un-known, they also serve as guides for others about an America unknown.

Afghans, however, do not want to understand all of America any more than Americans want to understand all of Afghanistan. They want to put their country at the center and use their worldview as the lens. This ethnocentrism helps manage and simplify complexity like the Afghan–American entanglement. For U.S. journalists, that means maintaining a worldview in which liberal democracies are the ideal form of government and in which American material power must be used to keep the United States safe and also be a force for good. U.S. journalists are working to hold American officials accountable for their words and actions at home and abroad, but Afghans see no humility in U.S. news coverage of their country. They see news media that follow the U.S. government's lead and reduce their country to a one-dimensional, failed, and violent nation. For some Afghans, reading about themselves through a security frame can stir resentment toward America as a nation. Because Afghan news professionals put Afghanistan at the center, they can be frustrated with U.S.-centric news—and the assumed impact that it has on other coun-tries' views of Afghanistan.

Just as the United States exercises global hegemony in a material sense, the U.S. media are powerful in shaping the "pictures in the heads" of American and international publics. Through the U.S. journalists' attempt to inform and educate others, principally Americans, on global events, they often create an image that the residents, journalists, and government officials of those countries can perceive as drastically distorted. The news stories they tell often create more friction than facilitate understanding. But ethnocentrism and national bias in the press is hardly an American phenomenon. Most journalists see themselves as part of a nation they feel responsibility toward, and they want to primarily serve that nation. A global news system in which national news narratives are shared does not foster global consensus: In an international media landscape, news narratives, themes, and frames remain decisively national.

Rosenberg's banishment from Afghanistan was temporary. By October 2014, President Ashraf Ghani, now the head of a national unity government in which Abdullah Abdullah was the chief executive officer, enthusiastically welcomed Rosenberg back to Afghanistan. The palace's improved relationship with the U.S. press was a product of a positive uptick in diplomatic relations. As Rosenberg himself reported from Washington, Ashraf Ghani's first official visit to Washington in March 2015 opened "with a simple message: He is a man with whom the United States can work, and he is thankful for American support and sacrifices."[27] In 2014, Karzai saw an enemy and Ghani saw an ally. They treated the U.S. press accordingly, recognizing the power that it had in conferring status and legitimacy to the country.

But to tell the greater story of the two nations' diplomatic and media entanglement, we begin as the U.S.-led war in Afghanistan did: with 9/11.

9/11 and the American Press

I was reasonably successful in staying steady. But there was a time early on, when the first tower collapsed, that my legs began to shake underneath the anchor chair. I remember saying to myself, "I cannot let that show; that has to stop."

—NBC News Anchor Tom Brokaw on reporting on 9/11[1]

ON SEPTEMBER 11, 2001, Washington- and New York City-based journalists became war correspondents. The scale of death on American soil that day was second only to the Civil War battle of Antietam in 1862.[2] More than 3,000 people were killed: 2,801 in the World Trade Center, 184 at the Pentagon, and 40 in an open field in Shanksville, Pennsylvania. Local and national journalists reported on active trauma scenes and the threats of more looming attacks, which were on a scale previously familiar only to conflict journalists. The reporters also became therapists for a vulnerable nation in deep shock. Primarily, though, they were Americans trying to make sense of devastating events for themselves and their fellow countrymen, who were now addicted to every word they said and wrote. They served as the conduit between the horror and the public, the government and the public, and a way for the public to connect with each other as an American nation.[3]

U.S. journalists often abandon efforts to provide neutral reporting under at least three conditions: tragedy, public danger, and a grave threat to national security.[4] The September 11 attacks, media sociologist Michael Schudson emphasized, represented all three.[5] While crises regularly consume American news organizations, the 9/11 attacks sent journalists, editors, and producers into overdrive. On September 12, 2001, 190 front pages of U.S. newspapers featured the carnage and its aftermath. One hundred nineteen daily newspapers also created extra editions, responding to the public's great demand for information on why the attacks happened and their impact on America's economy, security, and society.[6]

Americans became overwhelmingly hooked on television coverage. "On a day of death," Caryn James of the *New York Times* wrote on September

12, 2001, "television was a lifeline to what was happening."[7] For the next 10 days after 9/11, two-thirds of the American public said they were fixated on news coverage and roughly 75 percent said they were scared by what they had read and heard. Eighty-one percent said they were keeping a television or radio on during waking hours for updates while 46 percent said they were reading the newspaper more closely, according to the Pew Research Center.[8] Terrorism thereafter became a mainstay in U.S. news, drastically altering the public's sense of the threat international terrorists posed and their ability to reach American shores. Networks' news coverage of terrorism alone skyrocketed to 656 percent: From September 2000 to September 2001 there were 178 stories on the topic; from September 2001 to September 2002 there were 1,345 of them.[9] In the three months leading to 9/11, zero Americans told Gallup that terrorism ranked as one of the most important problems facing the country; immediately after the attacks, 46 percent of Americans reported that terrorism was the biggest problem facing the United States.

The American press helped to create a perception that 9/11 represented a global upward trend in terrorism events, but at the time it did not.[10] The 2001 State Department Patterns of Terrorism report, which had tracked global terrorism since 1969, found that the actual dangers from terrorism had fallen since the early 1990s—but since it had happened in the United States with such grisly force, American fears of terrorism had sharply increased.[11] Their perception became the new normal for the American public and news media.[12]

President George W. Bush, commanding the armed forces and diplomatic corps of the United States, soon launched a seemingly endless, so-called Global War on Terror, with American war theaters concentrated in Afghanistan and Iraq. Through favorable news coverage and editorials, the elite U.S. news media embraced a pervasive sense of chauvinistic patriotism as they—at least initially—explicitly and implicitly supported the Afghanistan War, which began on October 7, 2001, and later, the second Iraq War, launched on March 20, 2003. By 2003, one-fifth of the public still believed that terrorism trumped all other economic or social concerns for the nation.[13]

When the World Matters to Americans

Communications scholarship has long established that the idea that the press can provide unfettered, completely objective news is simply an ideal. This is certainly the case for U.S. news about the world. Often, American journalists and editors cover international events with a subjectivity that would not be acceptable in domestic news.[14] Unless the American public follows presidential and congressional speeches and academic analysis, and/or experiences foreign issues and events firsthand, it is often journalists who construct and utilize symbols not just to influence how the public understands realities or how policymakers react to realities, but to create those realities.[15] And, typically, the reality that the U.S. news media construct is based on a consensual way of talking about American society, American culture, and the place of the United States in the larger geopolitical structure.[16]

Americans read about the world through lenses of conflict, disaster, and brewing chaos. In *Deciding What's News*, his influential sociological study of newsrooms in the United States and how foreign news is often selected, Herbert Gans found that American news is primarily about the U.S. nation and society, which means that coverage is largely concerned with depicting the nation as the unit. Therefore, news is U.S.-centric and its aim is to be relevant to Americans and their nation's interests.[17] Because foreign news normally receives the least amount of print space or airtime in the U.S. news media, only the most dramatic events abroad are deemed newsworthy. Since American news agencies believe the United States to be the most valued nation in the world order, international reportage is traditionally episodic, shallow, intermittent, and quick in order to make room for domestic news; it is determined by a sense of ethnocentrism, or evaluating other cultures against American culture, and a focus on American national interests.[18]

While there is not a strong tradition of foreign reporting in the American news media, the small percentage of it dropped further when the Cold War ended in 1989. The Cold War had provided an organizing mechanism for U.S. policymakers and journalists alike: The idea of a bipolar world, the United States versus the Soviet Union, allowed reporters and editors to neatly keep international issues in a dominant frame. According to this worldview, global issues and events were byproducts or manifestations of the Cold War. If the issue in a foreign country wasn't specifically about the United States or the Soviet Union, then it was pegged to the ideological struggle between democracy and communism. By the early 1990s, international news budgets at elite news agencies were slashed. Citing the disinterest of American citizens to learn about the world, the market-driven U.S. news corporations closed foreign bureaus and invested in more popular, inexpensive, and local news stories.[19]

As the bipolar world disintegrated in the 1990s, many journalists and scholars lamented that foreign news coverage was waning.[20] Smaller conflicts plagued countries in Europe, Africa, the Middle East, and Asia, making global events both more complicated and less reported. In the early 1970s, 10 percent of U.S. news among elite broadcast and print news organizations was dedicated to international news; by 1990, less than 3 percent was.[21] In the 1980s, the average number of foreign stories on U.S. network news was four per week; by the 1990s, it decreased to two per week.[22] U.S. news agencies had fewer permanent bureaus overseas—and those that existed were often one-person operations. Even more than before, U.S. news organizations relied on "parachute journalism," meaning that a roving correspondent would spend a limited amount of time in any specific country, yet be responsible for explaining its complications to an American audience in limited time. Journalists need time to build relationships and understand cultures and histories in order to provide in-depth, comprehensive, and/or investigative reporting. With less time to absorb local contexts, such reporting about the world was rare, and America's focus turned inward.[23] In 1994, former *New York Times* editor Max Frankel noted the general disinterest of Americans in what happened beyond U.S. borders:

> A great shroud has been drawn across the mind of America to make it forget that there is a world beyond its borders. The three main television networks obsessively focus their cameras on domestic tales and dramas as if the end of the Cold War rendered the rest of the planet irrelevant. Their news staffs occasionally visit some massacre, famine, or shipwreck and their anchors may parachute into Haiti or Kuwait for a photo op, but these spasms of interest only emphasize the networks' apparent belief that on most evenings the 5 billion folks out there don't matter one whit.[24]

By September 11, 2001, the norm for U.S. news was to mostly ignore the world, especially developing countries, unless there was a disaster, war, riot, massacre, or other shocking atrocity. Rarely did international news feature a country's culture or society, nor did it highlight positive events. Reporting was frequently indexed to foreign crises and it often put the United States at the center of the world, focusing on the details of American diplomacy or military efforts.[25] Factors that determine whether a country makes it into the news include how it ranks on the world stage and its relation to the United States, its degree of economic development and press freedoms, and its cultural and geographic proximity to the United States.[26] It depends on the country's position in post–World War II international institutions (e.g., the United Nations, the World Trade Organization, the International Monetary Fund) and/or the material power the country has—either through nuclear or other weapons of mass destruction, troop levels, or its gross domestic product and how much it exports.[27] It can also depend on issues that violate U.S. or Western norms, such as human rights and a country's poor treatment of women and minorities, or on the role of the United States in the country, especially if there is a U.S. military presence.[28]

While difficult to prove causality, one study in particular showed that U.S. foreign news coverage had a particular impact on the American public's perceptions of foreign nations. A qualitative analysis of newscasts and public opinion polling in 1998 found that U.S. news provided the most negative coverage of Iraq, with 329 negative stories, followed distantly by India (85 stories), Pakistan (83), China (37), Iran (28), North Korea (28), and Mexico (22). The degree of disapproving coverage seems to have been a signal to the public on how to perceive these particular nations: Correspondingly, the American public had the most negative perceptions toward Iraq, India, Pakistan, China, Iran, and North Korea, in addition to Cuba, Turkey, Saudi Arabia, and Russia.[29] From this study, one could surmise that the American news media helped to shape the identities of foreign nations for their primary audience, the American public.

U.S. coverage also firmly focuses on Washington's foreign policy.[30] To American audiences, the United States is often positioned as the international community's sole superpower, prepared to respond militarily to any threat against U.S. national security or the American way of life, or even on behalf of what are deemed to be larger civilizational values, or "enduring values," according to Herbert Gans.[31] U.S. officials also normally guide U.S. news professionals, who are dependent on them for information, to establish the salience of issues, set their news agendas, and frame narratives.[32] While the target audience for news is primarily Americans, the news media also create a tangible, digestible package for anyone curious about America's intentions since it reflects the priorities and concerns of the U.S. government and society.

American Reporters and Officials

Why is U.S. coverage of international news often told through the lens of American diplomacy and the military? One reason is because the image that journalists craft about America's global role depends on their codependence with military and diplomatic officials.[33] The press normally follows the U.S. government's lead on issues of national security, deferring to officials on what Americans should think is most important about the world, especially during the policy formation stage.[34] The relationships journalists maintain with government officials give them some access to information about decisions, processes, gossip, and official intelligence. This contributes to their legitimizing and sustaining the image of American hegemony, defined as "the ruling class's ability to persuade the subordinate class of ideas and assumptions until these ideas become common sense."[35]

Since World War II, and especially during wartime, the press has rarely strayed from amplifying the U.S. government's policy.[36] Journalists prefer to speak with officials and to use them as principal sources in foreign policy stories. The American president is the most central figure in the U.S. press and both benefits and suffers from the constant coverage.[37] In times of crisis, like 9/11, the news media and the public also both look to the president for emotional and psychological support.[38] Reporters normally defer more to the words and views of the president and his executive branch than to those in the legislative branch on foreign policy issues because they trust those closest to executive decision-making processes in Washington to explain them.[39]

This ritual reliance on government officials for source material—and journalists' seeming inability to challenge the initial consensus between executive officials and legislators on foreign policy issues—is called *indexing*.[40] Indexing is particularly relevant to issues that have a larger, global effect, which the public may not know much about without the media's guidance—such as military, diplomacy, trade, and other international economic policy decisions.[41] When news is breaking, government officials who are especially close to the president have a commanding influence.[42] Government representatives can control how the issue is initially framed. While journalists can consult pundits outside of government, White House officials are the most sought after because of their decision-making roles and access to classified information. Officials can then carefully select attributes of a foreign policy to win the support of journalists and the public.[43] And a journalist rarely has access to intelligence or facts that could contest the official line.[44]

Journalists tend to deem few sources in the legislative branch, academia, and think tanks as credible without validation from the executive branch, and noncredible dissenting opinions can be perceived as being deviant. The few people "in the know," those who control and promote policy, are the most credible sources for information; outsiders with dissenting views, who may sometimes give balance to a news story, are not as credible. Journalists trust executive branch officials more especially during wartime and other crises that involve the American military, such as international disasters. Analysis from the 1991 Gulf War found that U.S. reporters and officials were especially codependent: The government wanted to sell its policies, and the commercial media wanted to sell papers or accrue high ratings.[45] Especially during time of conflict, both reporters and officials cater to not just a norm of nationalism to maintain audiences, but a sense of *chauvinistic* nationalism, or patriotism.

To keep their everyday access to government officials, journalists are likely to remain cautious about making judgments against them.[46] The need to protect and foster sources—compounded by the implicit code of conduct for Washington reporters to try to detach themselves from the story and relay the facts—demands that journalists simply report what they are told.[47] This idea of deferential journalism intersects with what Daniel Hallin defined in his analysis of media coverage of the Vietnam War in *The Uncensored War* as journalists' oscillation between a "sphere of legitimate controversy" and a "sphere of consensus." The sphere of legitimate controversy includes the central positions staked out in elections and legislative debates, which are established as credible by political actors; the sphere of consensus is the space within which the journalist is expected to serve as a patriot and an advocate of policy.[48] There is also a "sphere of deviance" for news professionals who fall completely out of the two spaces. For the reporters who cover the discourse over foreign policy issues from Washington, once a foreign policy issue is removed from a sphere of legitimate controversy and inserted into one of consensus, the story can lose its salience, as there is little credible dissent—or skepticism—to index coverage to. If there is political consensus over a foreign policy decision, Washington-based reporters rarely contest it.

The lack of American foreign correspondents abroad means that much U.S. news about the world is pegged to and/or written from Washington.

In 2016, President Barack Obama's White House press and communications team publicly acknowledged that the prominence of Washington-based national security correspondents gave them an advantage to shape the message. As Ben Rhodes, a Deputy National Security Advisor to the president, told the *New York Times*:

> All these newspapers used to have foreign bureaus. Now they don't. They call us to explain to them what's happening in Moscow and Cairo. Most of the outlets are reporting on world events from Washington. The average reporter we talk to is 27 years old, and their only reporting experience consists of being around political campaigns. That's a sea change. They literally know nothing.[49]

While this was largely perceived to be a disparaging comment, it symbolizes the constraints national security reporters face without institutional support to report from abroad, and the power the White House has to set the news agenda and frame stories for the press and the public.

American government officials have good reason to work closely with the press to build their case for policy and action: Throughout the 20th century, governments became more concerned with their own popularity because support from the citizenry meant their actions were legitimate.[50] Michael A. Hammer, former National Security Council Spokesman and Assistant Secretary for Public Affairs at the State Department in the Obama administration, explained in an interview that U.S. government spokespeople "have a responsibility and strong belief in favor of transparency." He continued, "It is important to provide context [for the press and the public] and to develop a greater understanding for the facts, rationale, and thinking that leads to our policies."[51] Marc Grossman, former Undersecretary for Political Affairs at the State Department in the George W. Bush administration, similarly described the responsibility as follows: "If you take the taxpayers' money, you ought to explain to the taxpayers what you are doing . . . in our system, [journalists] are an important part of how our society works."[52] Yet while reporters and officials may feel a shared sense of responsibility to inform the public about policies and their reasons for being, the relationship with officials can still be mired in distrust.

U.S. government officials may have the power to set the global agenda for reporters and initially frame it, but official government messaging rarely sticks. Those officials interviewed for this study insisted that as foreign policies unfold, the journalists create new storylines that often challenge those the officials want amplified. Hammer explained that, as a public affairs official, "you don't get the sense that you are in control of the narrative or in control of what is going to be the actual reporting by the press . . . That is why there's generally a tense relationship between the Washington press corps and spokespeople in any administration, it doesn't matter if it's Democratic or Republican."[53] Daniel Feldman, the former Deputy Special Representative for Afghanistan and Pakistan at the State Department under Obama, also agreed that the relationship between reporters and officials in Washington "is not necessarily an adversarial relationship, but it's a wary one." Reporters often want information that officials cannot share and take little interest in reporting the good news the officials want projected.[54]

Once a policy is in action, governmental control over the narrative can weaken. A policy will receive the most validation or support from the news media when it is first introduced. Hammer explained, "The times that we felt we were successful, at least initially, is when there was a rollout of a new policy initiative or policy approach" because "usually the press doesn't have an opportunity in advance to critique it and to look into where there might be pitfalls."[55] In other words, if the press amplifies government messages, it can provide a straightforward news story on what government officials said or are doing, with little critical analysis or additional context. Yet, because the U.S. press corps is a national one, it still frames the world in relation to U.S. interests.

Framing the World for Americans

How news organizations frame an event or issue affects how the public perceives that issue or event. Frames organize knowledge by assigning issues and events recognizable categories, shaping one's understanding of objects or situations, and then suggesting how one should act toward or within them.[56] Filtering complexity by giving news a simple storyline within a frame is especially common, as foreign events are often too abstract for the public to understand.[57] Frames are both mental images, "the pictures in our heads," and social objects that are embedded in our discourses, routines, institutions, and cultural norms. They are often assumptions taken to be truth. They allow readers to quickly interpret, categorize, and evaluate issues without giving them due analysis.[58] Journalists can select some aspects of a perceived reality—a particular

problem definition, causal interpretation, moral evaluation, and/or treatment recommendation—and make them more prominent.[59] Through
frames, journalists can sort and make meaning of world events quickly
for audiences who often know less than they do.[60]

Foreign affairs news often depends largely on conventional news
frames, or on how similar stories have been explained to the public in the
past, especially news on terrorism, war, and conflict. The news is often
slotted into familiar categories that give meaning and order to complex
problems by assigning familiar storylines. These conventional news frames
include four general categories of international news: security, diplomacy,
the economy, and humanitarianism. Using them allows audiences to receive a snapshot of what the issue is, why it is important, and what the
U.S. role is and should or should not be. Above all, journalists frequently
rely on the security frame to organize the world for Americans. This is
certainly the case for countries that are at war, especially wars where the
U.S. military is involved. If a country is not described in security terms,
then the news story will emphasize its government, economy, overall role
in the international community, or health and well-being (by Western
standards). Rarely does U.S. news include stories about a country's culture or society, unless it is in the travel section or has a direct impact on
U.S. commerce, politics, policy, or culture.[61]

A dominant frame, in which there is no other competing frame,
discourages dissent, therefore further cementing the power of that
frame.[62] Substantive news frames can also define effects or conditions as
problematic, identify causes, convey a moral judgment of those involved
in the issue, and endorse prescriptions for the problem being discussed.[63]
With 9/11, the problem was the slaughter of thousands of U.S. citizens;
the cause was terrorism; the moral judgment was to call the acts and
perpetrators evil; and the remedy became war. This created a cultural logic
for the American public's worldview.[64]

As discussed, the Cold War news frame gave Americans a dichotomous paradigm to explain the world for nearly half a century. But it
fell when the Berlin Wall did in 1991 and most Central and Eastern
European governments turned into electoral democracies.[65] 9/11 gave
American news organizations both a new framework to tidily explain
the world and a reason to expand, however temporarily, foreign news
coverage. The "war on terrorism" frame categorized the world map again
as a collection of either U.S. friends or enemies. Employing this structure, one could lump together different facts and personalities within

diverse stories about international security and simultaneously reinforce the American worldview and priorities of the U.S. government,
even if the stories' content eventually strayed from official U.S. government messages.[66]

The Afghanistan War Begins

President Bush presented this new dichotomous world order in a joint
session to Congress on September 20, 2001, when he declared to a global
audience, "You are *either* with *us*, or *you are with the terrorists.*"[67] Leaders
traditionally select language and symbols that will evoke support, pride,
and public unity for particular political and foreign policy goals. By
highlighting certain events and issues, the American president can define the news agenda and bring drama and urgency to foreign policy.[68]
But the aftermath of 9/11 was also an opportune time for the American
president to encourage a sense of fierce patriotism in the American public
and a belief that America was superior to all other nations. The Bush
administration's strategic communications operation after 9/11 used its
agenda-setting power to describe a war on terrorism in which the invasion
of Afghanistan would be the first step.[69] Zalmay Khalilzad, who was the
Special Presidential Envoy for Afghanistan from 2001 to 2003 (a title he
maintained when he also became U.S. Ambassador to Afghanistan from
2003 to 2005), recalled that at the time the press "didn't do what we would
think. They weren't independent, they weren't questioning in part to inform and encourage debate." However he conceded in a 2017 interview
that "It would've been difficult to be in that mode given what happened."
He continued, "9/11 had a huge impact on American society, American
politics, the American psyche. There was a rallying around the flag. And
the journalists were not immune from that."[70]

Indeed, coverage by the *New York Times* and *Washington Post* gravitated
toward ethnocentric reportage and its editors supported U.S. action.[71]
These elite papers have a more profound effect on the public and
policymakers during times of crisis; they are also less likely to take a critical stance toward the government during them.[72] The news stories in
September 2001 fixated on the material aftermath of the attacks and how
they would affect the U.S. economy and security. According to a qualitative
analysis by Changho Lee, they generally did not try to figure out or explain
why the attacks occurred, or to investigate the social and historical roots
and context of terrorism.[73] They focused on American officials' actions on

behalf of U.S. national security. The *Post* and the *Times*, especially, became platforms to explore war as a response.[74]

This was evident not just in the volume of news coverage, but also in the content of their editorials. Immediately after the attacks, neither of the editorial boards of these newspapers questioned the merits of retaliation, although they urged the Bush administration to be cautious with its plans for war and ensure that they established a link between al Qaeda and the Taliban before invading Afghanistan. The *Washington Post* editorial board wrote on September 23, 2001:

> The United States must make clear to other countries why it is sure that al Qaeda and Osama bin Laden were behind the attacks in New York and Washington, and it must work hard to line up allies for a potential battle with the Taliban . . . in this new kind of war, civilian casualties and suffering probably would strengthen rather than weaken al Qaeda, winning it new recruits in both Afghanistan and elsewhere in the Muslim World.[75]

The *New York Times* editorial board similarly wrote the day before:[76]

> It is a reasonable presumption that the terrorists who attacked New York and Washington aimed not just to kill American civilians, but also to draw the United States into an indiscriminate and brutish military response that might attract Muslims around the world to their cause . . . Washington must be smart in selecting targets and cognizant of the political consequences that its military operations are likely to produce in the Islamic world.[77]

It prescribed that President Bush narrowly target groups that were involved in the World Trade Center and Pentagon attacks in Afghanistan rather than extend "the fight to countries more broadly linked to international terrorism, possibly including Iraq."[78]

In 26 days, both papers ran 24 editorials that addressed the challenges and goals of the country's new war footing that set the agenda for other news organizations in the country.[79] Eventually, both papers' boards fully supported President Bush's declaration of war against the Taliban.[80] The *Times* wrote that the American people "will support whatever efforts it takes to carry out this mission properly . . . Mr. Bush has wisely made providing humanitarian assistance an integral part of the American strategy," but it criticized the U.S. government's focus on building a coalition only with the United Kingdom at the time.[81] There was no criticism about President Bush's intent to go to war in any of the editorials.[82]

News articles also signaled support for the U.S. government and its new foreign policy.[83] They bolstered the government's logic by repeating official talking points.[84] This coverage, Khalilzad later reflected, was "very helpful" for U.S. policymakers and the military at the time in preparing for war in Afghanistan. The press depicted both al Qaeda and the Taliban "in the worst way . . . The Taliban were not responsible for the attack but they represented values that were abhorrent to the American public . . . The image they created of the enemy was very helpful."[85] This led to nearly unanimous American support for the actions the Bush administration was about to take.

On October 7, 2001, President George W. Bush announced that Mullah Omar and the Taliban had refused to hand bin Laden over to the Americans and to stop giving him and all al Qaeda fighters safe haven. American journalists had few dissenting opinions against the war that they could credibly source.[86] Congress had voted overwhelmingly on September 14, 2001—with only one opposing legislator out of 531—to give the president Authorization for Use of Military Force, which said he was authorized to "use all necessary and appropriate force against those nations, organizations, or persons he determine[d] planned, authorized, committed, or aided the terrorist attacks that occurred on September 11, 2001, or harbored such organizations or persons."[87]

President Bush's remarks to the American people explaining the October 7, 2001, invasion of Afghanistan framed the war in both security and humanitarian terms. With absolute policy certainty, President Bush explained the war as not only a direct result of the attacks, but also a humanitarian act, in the sense that U.S. forces would liberate the Afghan people from dire Taliban rule and give them hope for a better life within a democracy. He explained that it was not only the right thing to do to keep America safe, but it was the right thing to do for the Afghan people. The Bush administration used the opportunity, according to Robert Entman, to "propound a line designed to revive habits of patriotic deference, to dampen elite dissent, dominate media texts, and reduce the threat of negative public reaction—to work just as the Cold War paradigm once did."[88] Journalists could adapt to a frame of good versus evil, anti-terrorists versus pro-terrorists, with the United States once again cast as the force for good, as during the Cold War, which had also used Afghanistan as a primary battleground.

A November 16, 2001, Gallup poll found that a strong majority of the American public, 89 percent, approved of the president's performance post-9/11.[89] It also found that 92 percent of the American public supported the war in Afghanistan.[90] This was second only to American support for Congress's declaration of war against Japan after Pearl Harbor, which Gallup found to be 97 percent in December 1941.[91]

But the American public also thought the war in Afghanistan would be quick. In December 2001, 47 percent told Gallup they believed the fighting would last for just a few months; only 15 percent thought it would be more than two years. By the end of 2016, it endured, with more than 8,000 U.S. troops still in the country.

3

Afghanistan in Americans' Imagination

Afghanistan existed before 9/11

—KATHY GANNON, Associated Press reporter in Afghanistan and Pakistan since 1986[1]

EARLY ON SEPTEMBER 11, 2001, the morning edition of the *New York Times* reported the assassination of Ahmed Shah Massoud, a mujahedeen hero of the 1980s and the leader of the Northern Alliance in Afghanistan, the rebel opposition group to the Taliban.[2] *Times* journalist Barry Bearak explained to readers that the Taliban—whom many assumed to be responsible for his death—likely hadn't killed him, but Arabs linked to al Qaeda, which had been nesting in Afghanistan's south for nearly five years, did.[3] The Taliban would have gleefully taken credit for it, they told Bearak, but they insisted it was not them.[4] Massoud was an unknown figure to anyone who wasn't closely following Afghan politics for the previous 20 years, yet he was as a giant for all who did. Massoud was revered as the "Lion of Panjshir," a title he acquired while protecting his home district—the lush, narrow, and nearly impenetrable Panjshir valley—from the Soviets. Upon hearing that Massoud was killed, Hamid Karzai, the future president, reportedly said, "What an unlucky country."[5]

Hours after the story was printed, al Qaeda was again successful—this time, with the largest attack on the United States in nearly 60 years.

By the afternoon of September 11, Afghanistan began to matter to Americans. Since the Cold War ended, few of them, including the policymakers at the White House and the journalists covering them, had personal experience with the country or knew much about its history or modern complexities. The Taliban ran a closed society. There had been no formal American diplomatic presence inside since the Soviets withdrew from Afghanistan on January 31, 1989, and President George H. W. Bush suspended its diplomatic mission days later. Since then, Afghanistan had received scant and sporadic attention from the U.S. press, with the exception of the Associated Press.

In 2001, American reportage about the world had become scarce, and only six newspaper groups—*New York Times, Washington Post, Wall Street Journal, Chicago Tribune/Los Angeles Times, Christian Science Monitor,* and *Baltimore Sun*—had foreign news bureaus; these newspapers represented 20 percent of total U.S. circulation figures.[6] The AP largely served as a linchpin for international coverage for American news organizations, as its foreign news was reprinted in hundreds of local American papers.[7] While reporters for the major elite news agencies visited Afghanistan only on occasion, as acquiring visas from the Taliban was a bureaucratic nightmare, Kathy Gannon, a Canadian reporter for the AP, had been continuously reporting from Afghanistan and Pakistan since 1986. A small bureau of Afghan stringers kept the bureau running when she wasn't in the country.

In 2001, months before the attacks, two stories from Afghanistan especially violated Western norms and shocked the world, therefore garnering U.S. press attention: the kidnapping of Western aid workers and the destruction of globally renowned historical symbols.[8] Gannon and *New York Times* reporter Bearak were both in the country to report them. In March, the Taliban destroyed the Great Buddhas of Bamiyan, statues that were 175 and 120 feet high and more than 1,500 years old. Buddhist monks created them when Bamiyan, located in the center of modern Afghanistan, was part of the Gandhara Kingdom, which existed before the Muslim Saffarids, who were part of the Persian dynasty, conquered the land in the ninth century. People of all faiths had revered them for centuries. Yet the Taliban leader, Mullah Omar, declared in 2001 that the giant statues had been "gods of the infidels" and ordered their destruction.[9] World leaders were outraged, but the Taliban's Minister of Information and Culture told Bearak that he didn't understand what the big deal was: "The statues," he told him, "are objects only made of mud or stone."[10] Then, in August, the Taliban had accused eight Western aid workers, two of them American, affiliated with Shelter Now, a humanitarian organization operating in the country, of preaching Christianity to Muslims, a grave offense to the fundamentalist government that lived by their version of Sharia law.[11] Salim Haqqani, a Taliban official in the Ministry for the Promotion of Virtue and Prevention of Vice, told Gannon, "We want that humanitarian organizations should work here, but they should work here honestly. They should give our religion dignity and not show disrespect by teaching against it."[12]

On 9/11, Gannon and Bearak were still in Afghanistan, and well positioned to help Americans become reacquainted with the country. It was early evening there when the attacks happened in New York, Washington, and Pennsylvania. The Taliban rejected the idea that they or bin Laden had anything to do with them. A foreign ministry spokesman explained it was too sophisticated an operation for the Taliban or even bin Laden to successfully execute. He said to Bearak, "If we want peace for ourselves, we want peace for others. But such coordinated attacks cannot be carried out by one man or by the Islamic Emirate of Afghanistan." In 2001, President Bill Clinton had ordered the launch of 70 Tomahawk cruise missiles at what were suspected to be al Qaeda camps along the Afghanistan–Pakistan border after the network took credit for an assault on the USS *Cole*, a U.S. Navy ship in Yemen. The fear at the time was that the strikes backfired: Bin Laden survived, but Afghan civilians died along-side terrorist fighters, bringing al Qaeda and the Taliban politically and ideologically closer together.[13] In the September 12 article about Afghans' reaction to 9/11 in Afghanistan, Bearak speculated that they may dread an-other strike in retaliation.[14] The reprisal, officially launched 25 days later, was the start of America's longest continuous war.

Afghanistan in Americans' Imagination

By 9/11, Afghans had been living with U.S. foreign policy decisions for more than two decades. On Christmas Eve 1979, the Soviet Union, fearing that the Afghan communist government was too weak to stand on its own, invaded the country and began a nearly 10-year occupation. Earlier that year, President Jimmy Carter ordered the U.S. government to begin to covertly support Afghan freedom fighters, the mujahedeen, in their fight against the increasing Soviet presence. In 1979, due to the February assas-sination of U.S. Ambassador Adolph Dubs by an anticommunist faction in Kabul and the December Soviet invasion, the U.S. mission in Afghanistan had dwindled to just a dozen people; the American embassy became simply a listening post that administered no major programs or consular services. The Reagan administration continued to give the mujahedeen billions of dollars in military and development aid to fight the Soviets. During his radio address to the American people on the Soviet occupa-tion in December 1985, President Reagan called the mujahedeen's fight a battle for "the human spirit" and the U.S. contribution to it "a compel-ling moral responsibility of all free people."[15] The U.S. also gave Pakistan roughly $5 billion in economic and military aid to become a key transit country for U.S. arms supplies to the mujahedeen, and to support the millions of Afghans who took refuge in Pakistan almost immediately after the Soviet invasion.[16] This infusion of weapons and cash seemingly helped U.S. foreign policy: The Soviet military left Afghanistan in February 1989. Nearly 10 months later, due to a host of geopolitical factors, the Berlin Wall fell. By the end of 1991, the Soviet Union was no more.

The Cold War was over and America moved on from Afghanistan and the region. Correctly predicting a power vacuum that mujahedeen leaders would rush to fill, President George H. W. Bush had already suspended all remaining U.S. embassy operations in Kabul on the eve of the Soviet withdrawal, on January 31, 1989. The significantly downsized diplomatic mission was moved across the border to Peshawar, Pakistan. U.S. reporters and officials watched from there as Afghanistan began to plunge into a devastating civil war. With the Soviet enemy no longer uniting them, the mujahedeen fractured into a confusing set of factions, their leaders becoming warlords who scrambled to control territory. With leftover weapons and ammunition from the United States and Soviet Union, they destroyed Afghanistan's infrastructure in the process. Kabul city, which had attracted so many international tourists in the 1960s and 1970s, fell to ruins.[17]

Gannon, alongside her Afghan colleagues in the AP bureau, reported from there at the time. "It was far more dangerous between 1992–96 than it was between 1996–2001 [the Taliban years]," she explained in a 2017 interview. "During the civil war, Kabul was horrific in terms of the bombing, the incoming and outgoing shelling."[18] The violence drove more and more Afghans across the border into Pakistan. Through the 1990s, the Afghan refugee community in Pakistan swelled to roughly 4 million people, putting an enormous strain on Pakistan's resources.[19] Pakistan's military leaders actively sought solutions to quell the chaos in Afghanistan and to control its leadership. At the end of the decade, the Taliban became the Pakistani military's panacea for the tumult that, in their view, America had left behind.

Taliban, by definition, means "students" in Pashto, a language spoken by the Pashtuns who live in southern and eastern Afghanistan and western Pakistan. They were known to be pious Muslims—some of them former mujahedeen—who wanted to create an Islamic state. The Pakistani military's intelligence wing, Inter-Services International, supported their move into southern Afghanistan in 1994. At first, the

Afghan people welcomed the Taliban: They overpowered and uprooted the warlords who had terrorized communities and destroyed much of the country. Their rise to power seemed natural, said Gannon, who was on the frontlines with them as they accumulated power: "They weren't some horrible foreign force; they were Afghans."[20] Gradually, by 1996, the Taliban gained control of most of the country and took over the national government, moving Afghanistan's capital to the southern city of Kandahar.

Only Pakistan, Saudi Arabia, and the United Arab Emirates recognized the Taliban as legitimate rulers.[21] The American government largely ignored them. After being subjected to constant fear and violence from the warlords during the civil war, the Afghans now faced a new kind of cruelty. The Taliban enacted Sharia (Islamic) law; their form of justice was swift and unforgiving. Women were not allowed to venture out of their homes, let alone to work. Music and imagery of the human form were banned. The little television that existed vanished. Radio Television Afghanistan became in service to the Taliban and was renamed Radio Shariat. Life became extraordinarily dull, and Afghanistan seemed to be frozen in time. The Taliban government provided no social services for their citizens, but it welcomed Osama bin Laden and members of his al Qaeda network, who shared a belief in Sharia law, as their guests. They granted them safe haven as the transnational terrorist network planned attacks against the United States and its allies and developed its mission to erect a larger caliphate.[22]

After the Taliban took control of the country in 1996, Afghanistan had warranted only occasional news coverage in U.S. papers during events that editors classified as crises. A review by Beverly Horvit of Afghanistan reportage in eight American newspapers from September 11, 1996, to September 10, 2001, found that the *Los Angeles Times, New York Times,* and *Washington Post* ran an average of 50 stories a year about Afghanistan, or four per month.[23] Sixty-five percent of the stories were about Taliban diplomacy and violence, and 13 percent were about human rights, especially the Taliban's atrocious treatment of women. While the AP and British Broadcasting Corporation (BBC) bureaus provided a steady stream of news about Afghanistan for anyone who looked for it, rarely was there analytical, in-depth reportage to increase American audiences' understanding of issues and events in the country.

As discussed in Chapter 2 and further explored in Chapters 6 and 7, U.S. news about the world is traditionally limited in its depth and breadth.

It often fits within a security frame because conflict attracts readers and viewers. News professionals also rely on official sources for foreign affairs news, are consciously or subconsciously ethnocentric, and face multiple constraints and limitations during the newsgathering process when reporting abroad. In addition, journalists working for U.S.-based agencies often index their international coverage to political discourse in Washington; they largely write with the American audience in mind and the U.S. is regularly promoted as the most significant actor in global issues.[24] Conflict and drama—in Washington or overseas—involving foreign affairs issues drive most global coverage for the U.S. news media. And in 2001, Afghanistan was once again the central theater for a global struggle. It would soon become home for hundreds of international journalists.

Bush's "Good War" Begins

In the days after 9/11, Afghanistan became a focal point for the American public as they anticipated retaliation. On October 7, Operation Enduring Freedom officially began with a North Atlantic Treaty Organization (NATO) coalition called the International Security Assistance Force (ISAF), composed of more than 50 countries. By December 3, 2001, roughly 3,000 foreign journalists were in Afghanistan and the war was the most covered news story in U.S. papers and television.[25]

While wars are inherently dramatic, American-fought wars traditionally receive substantial coverage since they are deemed to be essential to U.S. interests.[26] If American troops are involved, Americans attention to the conflict increases.[27] During the 1991 Gulf War, for instance, 25 American newspapers that were analyzed for a study increased in circulation and CNN (Cable News Network), the only U.S.-based news agency in Baghdad during the time of the initial U.S. attack on Iraq, increased its audience share tenfold.[28] Covering American troops allows U.S. news media to celebrate consensual values and show the public that they are being responsive to the soldiers who are in harm's way. And war not only creates a supply of news, it creates a demand for it: The U.S. public wants imagery and narratives from the frontlines to try to understand the experience.[29] Traditionally, as Thomas Carruthers emphasized, for the U.S. public, it's not any war—it's *our* war: the U.S. news consumer can become invested in the conflict as it appeals to their sense of patriotism and ethnocentrism.[30]

The tradition dates back to the 19th century.[31] A content analysis by Giovanna Dell'Orto of foreign news coverage in the mid-1800s found that the theme of American superiority in the world was dominant, whether it was the "beneficial intervention" of the United States in South America or the United States providing an "enlightening example" to Europe.[32] When President Bush defined in 2001 the reason to go to war in Afghanistan in both security and humanitarian terms, it was framed as yet another beneficial intervention on behalf of the United States that would help enlighten the country—and the American public and news media overwhelmingly embraced the pitch.

After 9/11, elite U.S. media agencies began to dispatch reporters to the region along with hundreds of other Western journalists, as the role of NATO—which invoked Article Five for the first time since the alliance's founding, believing an attack against the United States was an attack against all the allies—helped to amplify the amount of foreign, especially European, coverage of the country. In September and October 2001, the international journalists flocked to Afghanistan's northern and eastern borders with Tajikistan and Pakistan, waiting for the opportunity to enter the country. Two days after September 11, the Taliban had banned all Westerners in the country, including the reporters who were already there.

Kathy Gannon was pushed out as part of the ban, but she lobbied her Taliban contacts to give her a visa to return. She was the only Western reporter the Taliban let back in. She returned on October 23, a couple weeks before the Taliban abandoned their government offices and left Kabul.[33] Other international journalists tried to get in with sponsors other than the Taliban. David Rohde of the *New York Times* waited for the Northern Alliance to give him a chance to enter the country from Tajikistan. The opposition group had maintained diplomatic representation in Dushanbe, and the officials had liked Bearak's reporting, they told Rohde. They offered him a ride on a helicopter with Abdullah Abdullah—the future Foreign Minister and, later, Chief Executive Officer of Afghanistan—to the Northern Alliance's stronghold in the Panjshir Valley.[34] Rohde's colleague Carlotta Gall—who had spent much time in Afghanistan and Pakistan with her father (a reporter) and her sister (an aid worker in the refugee camps in Pakistan)—followed soon after. Her first stop was Mazar-e-Sharif in the north, a city she had visited before. "It was unbelievable," she recalled in an 2017 interview. "Mazar had always been a quite well-off city . . . but when I went in in 2001, it had been under a blockade by the Taliban. It was so poor and shocking. It was Ramadan and you couldn't find a single egg in the city."[35] The *Washington Post*'s Pamela Constable, who had also reported from the region for years, came in from Pakistan. She ultimately joined a gaggle of international journalists in Jalalabad who waited for the roads to open so they could drive to Kabul.

The reporting work was treacherous and unpredictable. In the first two months of the U.S.-led war, eight Western journalists were killed.[36] On November 11, 2001, three of them—French journalists Johanne Sutton and Pierre Billaud and German journalist Volker Handloik—were shot when they were embedded with Northern Alliance fighters who were working with U.S. Special Forces to uproot the Taliban. Six days after the Taliban fell from power, on November 19, Constable and roughly 50 colleagues decided to drive to Kabul together via a convoy from Jalalabad. Her car was in the middle. An hour or so into the trip, the Taliban stopped the first car and removed from it Harry Burton and Azizullah Haidari from Reuters, Julio Fuentes from the Spanish paper *El Mundo*, and Maria Grazia Cutuli from the Italian paper *Corriere della Sera*. They were assassinated on the spot.[37] The Afghan driver was spared. He quickly turned the car around and furiously motioned the other drivers in the convoy to follow him, Constable recalled.[38] Stuck in Jalalabad for weeks afterward and traumatized by the death of their colleagues, they spent a makeshift Thanksgiving there, cooking a scrawny turkey and sharing one bottle of wine that Fox News correspondent Geraldo Riviera had brought with him.[39]

Eventually the journalists made it to Kabul to celebrate the dawn of 2002, a year of tremendous optimism for the country. Constable recalled:

> It was a time of enormous hope and expectation. It was exciting for us; it was exciting for the Afghans. It wasn't as if everyone was suddenly flinging off their burkas and shaving their beards off, but they were coming out of their shells. . . . When it became spring and summer [of 2002] you began to see beauty parlors and restaurants opening up, and the first Nowruz to be celebrated in a long time . . . it was a real awakening.[40]

David Rohde agreed: "It was all very emotional. Afghans were happy that the Taliban had fallen. I felt genuine optimism. People were very excited, Afghans were very excited. The Taliban were not popular," he said.[41] The publics in America and the West, too, were receptive to the reporting, Gall remembered. "Post-9/11, there was a phenomenal desire of the public to read about Afghanistan to understand what the hell 9/11 was about, but there also was a huge amount of interest in everything Afghanistan." The reactions to stories about women in Afghanistan were especially strong, she said.[42]

By fall 2002, however, as the fighting in Afghanistan continued, American news reports diminished, and many of the journalists went home. Washington policymakers were also giving Afghanistan less attention. By the January 2002 State of the Union Address, President Bush defined Afghanistan as a country that was of more humanitarian concern to the United States than a security threat. In the 2003 State of the Union Address, President Bush mentioned Afghanistan only three times, but he spent one-third of the speech building the case for a new war in Iraq.[43] With the Taliban seemingly in retreat, the urgency and crisis associated with Afghanistan had passed and the public's limited attention for foreign news was being directed elsewhere.[44] Many Americans got the impression that the war had been won, and the expectation among them and Afghans alike was that the country would be on a fast track to development, peace, and security, lifting it from the dark days of the civil war and the Taliban.

The second post-9/11, U.S.-led war began in Iraq on March 19, 2003, and the American press shifted its interest accordingly. According to the *Tyndall Report*, in October 2001, Afghanistan received 106 minutes of airtime on network evening news; by January 2003, it received 11 minutes; and by March 2003, when the Iraq War began, it was reduced to a total of 60 seconds.[45] By the end of 2003, Afghanistan had received only 80 minutes of collective coverage from the three networks, and it no longer ranked as one of the 20 most covered stories for the United States.[46] From 2003 to 2009, the majority of American foreign news was focused on Iraq, chronicling the rise of extremism, a civil war, and an American troop surge to battle it. While NPR, the *New York Times, Washington Post*, AP, and other print news bureaus remained open in Kabul, the television networks mostly withdrew and began to rely on stringers and parachute journalists to episodically cover specific events inside the country, despite the fact that U.S. troops were still fighting there.[47]

Overall, Iraq had supplanted Afghanistan on the public agenda, shifting the American public's awareness and ability to make informed opinions about U.S. involvement in the country.[48] The Iraq War became one of the most thoroughly reported ones in U.S. history. More than 600 accredited journalists were embedded in combat, roughly five times that of those embedded with troops in Afghanistan a year before, and more than 2,000 reporters covered the war without being embedded.[49] The U.S. media had largely echoed the Bush administration's case in the buildup and initial execution of the war and were largely seen by academics and critics as being complicit, granting the Bush administration a free pass to open a second front that had no direct connection to the 9/11 attacks. This was especially so with the reporting of Judith Miller for the *New York Times*, who helped make the case that Saddam Hussein represented a threat to the world; she later defended her reporting by saying that she was simply reporting what her sources told her.[50] The U.S. news support for the war in pursuit of Hussein's weapons of mass destruction was so strong that, in 2004— with no weapons found but an insurgency quickly gaining strength—the *Times* apologized to its readers for "coverage that was not as rigorous as it should have been."[51]

Afghanistan had slipped in the agenda for both U.S. officials and reporters. Americans who wanted to receive news about Afghanistan had to deliberately look for it.[52] While the Afghanistan war story began with a national crisis, by 2003 the news coverage hit a plateau and then began to decline by 2005.[53] However, the conflict was about to get much worse.

In September 2005, U.S. Ambassador to Afghanistan Ronald Neumann was reporting in cables to Washington that the Taliban was resurging. He explained later in a 2017 interview, "one of my concerns was that we should talk to the American people about this so it wouldn't come as a major shock," but the administration told him not to and "the press and the administration reinforced one another."[54] He continued that the U.S. press failed to independently investigate a resurging Taliban and forecast what would happen; instead, they waited for the story to explode.[55]

In 2006, with the Taliban dragging U.S. and European soldiers into intensified conflict, Afghanistan erupted again.[56] That spring, the Taliban carried out its biggest offensive since 2001. Forces infiltrated southern Afghanistan in droves; suicide bombings quintupled to 136 from previous years. More than 190 American and NATO troops died, which was 20 percent more than in 2005. The Taliban also freely set up checkpoints, burned schools, and assassinated Afghan officials in the provinces. For the first time since the Iraq War began, Afghanistan was as statistically dangerous for U.S. soldiers as Iraq was.[57]

On February 15, 2007, President Bush gave his first policy speech focused on Afghanistan in years, warning that the Taliban was gaining power again and that the U.S. and NATO needed to intensify their joint military and aid mission there. He announced a new offensive, explaining that the "Taliban and al Qaeda are preparing to launch new attacks."[58] This speech merited some renewed American press attention to Afghanistan, although not much. In 2007, Iraq ranged from 11 to 26 percent of the total U.S. news coverage and 33 percent of Americans thought that Iraq was the most important problem facing the United States.[59] Afghanistan, though, made up less than 1 percent of American news coverage in 2007 and 2008.[60] A new American president, however, would put Afghanistan back on the top of the news agenda.

Obama's "Endless War" Begins

In 2008, then-Senator Barack Obama, the Democratic presidential candidate, made a campaign promise to refocus U.S. diplomatic and military attention on Afghanistan, calling the Iraq War "a dangerous distraction."[61] A fifth of the U.S. news coverage that election year was focused on foreign news and half of it was pegged to policy discussions within Washington and from the presidential race between Senator Obama and his opponent, Republican Senator John McCain.[62] This reinforces the idea of indexing, which is that most foreign news in the United States is based on what the government says and does about a country, and less so about the country itself.[63] Afghanistan mattered again.

In 2009, after President Obama was inaugurated, his decision to take most of the year to decide what to do about U.S. involvement in the country drove the quantity of news coverage. From August to December, Afghanistan was the third biggest U.S. news story, receiving 8 percent of coverage, trailing only health care and the economy—a place it hadn't claimed since October 2001.[64] Like President Bush's decision to dedicate troops to Afghanistan eight years before, the U.S. presence in Afghanistan was noncontroversial, but the details were hotly contested. Several leaks came from the Pentagon, the State Department, and the White House about the new policy and potential troop sizes, which shaped the perceptions of Congress, NATO allies, and the Afghans. It also ensured that nearly half of the news about Afghanistan was tied to the policy debate.

On December 1, 2009, the debate was settled: President Obama announced that he would send 30,000 "surge" troops to Afghanistan on a counterinsurgency mission. The new strategy would also include a dramatic increase in development funding and diplomats from the State Department and the U.S. Agency for International Development, in addition to roughly $7.5 billion to support Pakistan's democracy and development, which was seen as being intricately tied to the fight against al Qaeda and to Afghanistan's success.[65] He decided to deliver the message at the U.S. Military Academy at West Point. Michael Hammer, who was the National Security Council spokesman at the time reflected that President Obama chose West Point because "American service members' lives were at stake in terms of what was going to be announced and the risks they were going to take . . . It was necessary and felt right to find an appropriate venue to convey that."[66] The President told the cadets that this revived and significantly extended mission, born from the horror of 9/11, was consistent with a special responsibility that the United States had in the world:

> Since the days of Franklin Roosevelt, and the service and sacrifice of our grandparents and great-grandparents, our country has borne a special burden in global affairs. We have spilled American blood in many countries on multiple continents. We have spent our revenue to help others rebuild from rubble and develop their own economies. We have joined with others to develop an architecture of institutions—from the United Nations to NATO to the World Bank—that provide for the common security and prosperity of human beings . . . We have not always been thanked for these efforts, and we have at times made mistakes. But more than any other nation, the United States of America has underwritten global security for over six decades—a time that, for all its problems, has seen walls come down, markets open, billions lifted from poverty, unparalleled scientific progress, and advancing frontiers of human liberty.[67]

Obama indicated a five-year timeline, however, signaling to the American public, the Afghan government, the Taliban, and other interested parties that U.S. troops would not stay in Afghanistan forever.

The U.S. news media took their cues from Washington. *Time* magazine wrote in its feature story on October 12, 2009, "The War Up Close": "If it's true that sometimes we've let ourselves lose sight of Afghanistan, then as a start, let's look here."[68] While major print outlets had maintained bureaus in Kabul since 2001, for the television networks, it was almost as if the war had begun in 2001, ended in 2002, and restarted in 2009. When ABC, NBC, CNN, and Fox re-established bureaus in Kabul in 2009, news executives told Brian Stelter of the *New York Times* that they decided to refocus on Afghanistan because Obama signaled it would be a foreign policy priority.[69] The elite print and broadcast outlets were quick to comment on the upsurge in media coverage of Afghanistan and how they had largely overlooked the country for years. Richard Engel of NBC News told Stelter, "It's like the Baghdad class of 2003 is now the Kabul class of 2009."[70] Lara Logan of CBS, an outlier who had more consistently covered Afghanistan since 2001 than her broadcast competitors, explained in the same article that "Afghanistan has always been the poor man's war" that wasn't as exciting to cover for broadcast networks.[71]

Overall, by the end of 2009, news about Afghanistan received five times the coverage it had in 2007 and 2008, and more than double the coverage of Iraq during the year. In their reporting agenda and their language, journalists reflected the administration's new "Af-Pak" paradigm, which determined that the security of Afghanistan and that of Pakistan were so intertwined that any policy needed to take both into consideration. The Pew Center found in 2009 that news coverage of Afghanistan was consistent among the five media sectors (television, radio, newspaper, magazine, and online); it ranged from 4 to 5 percent of the total news coverage in each.[72] Television coverage of Afghanistan peaked in 2009 at 9.26 hours, its highest amount since 2003, while Iraq received only 1.33 hours.[73] How the U.S. news agencies covered Afghanistan in 2009, however, is telling. Forty-six percent of the coverage was devoted to the U.S. policy debate, tightly focused on Washington's deliberations on how many U.S. resources to dedicate to the country; only 14 percent was about actual combat in the country and still less, only 9 percent, was concerned with the internal affairs of Afghanistan. Much of the latter involved the disputed Afghan presidential election in 2009 between President Hamid Karzai and the former Minister of Foreign Affairs, Abdullah Abdullah.[74]

Through 2010, Afghanistan remained the primary foreign news story for the U.S. press. The majority of U.S. elite news organizations continued to have bureaus in Kabul: the New York Times, Washington Post, Los Angeles Times, NPR, CNN, NBC, CBS, Fox News, and the AP all had full-time staff in country. The New York Times, Washington Post, AP, and ABC News also had full-time reporters in neighboring Pakistan, becoming the most reliable sources for daily news coverage on the region. By 2011, however, stories about Afghanistan had fallen back to 2 percent of total U.S. news coverage.[75] And then the news agencies' coverage of Afghanistan fluctuated. In 2012, when the bulk of original research for this study was conducted, journalists anticipated that their bureaus would be shuttered by 2014, the year President Obama said U.S. troops would withdraw, and the year of the third-ever Afghan presidential election, which President Karzai would not run in.

However, as discussed in chapter 1, the war entered its 14th year in October 2014 and U.S. troops remained. Ashraf Ghani, the newly elected president, signed the bilateral security agreement (BSA) that President Karzai had refused to sign, which granted American troops immunity from the Afghan courts. A residual force of 10,000 U.S. troops remained, a tenth of the size of the force in 2010. While American news covered global events in 2014—the most it had since 1990—Afghanistan was largely overlooked in favor of Syria, Iraq, Ukraine, Gaza, Mexico, and the terror inflicted by the emerging Islamic State of Iraq and the Levant (ISIL), or Daesh. Still, the expected U.S. troop withdrawal in Afghanistan gained a relatively considerable amount of news: 144 minutes from the three networks the entire year. By 2015, Afghanistan was tied for news coverage of the rise of ISIL with 76 minutes each, second only to the Obama administration's pursuit of a nuclear deal with Iran, which received 107 minutes in American broadcast news.[76] But by 2016, Afghanistan did not rank among the major domestic or foreign news stories of the year. During one of the most contentious American presidential elections in history, Afghanistan was never mentioned in press conferences or the debates. Neither of the party's candidates—former Senator and Secretary of State Hillary Clinton and businessman and reality show star Donald Trump—discussed it in their foreign policy platforms.[77] But the AP, *New York Times*, NPR, *Wall Street Journal*, and *Washington Post* have kept their Kabul bureaus open.

Throughout 15 years of shifting U.S. news coverage about the region, Afghanistan was mainly a priority for the majority of U.S. news professionals when it was a priority for the White House. Overall, Afghanistan news has been tightly indexed to the degree of presidential attention to it and the intensity of conflict for U.S. troops. This is natural for the American press as a lens that puts your country at the center can bring another country into sharp focus.

Yet, America's version of Afghanistan, seen through the prism of the 9/11 attacks, was largely unfamiliar to Afghans. American journalists' easy access to U.S. officials, and their built-in understanding of American-style democracy and political dynamics, made their reportage an invaluable benchmark and source of information for Afghans, but it also was incredibly aggravating for them to see themselves through an American filter.

American News Flows to the World

To understand the hegemony of Western news—especially American and British—we must first examine their massive reach. Most global news flows from the West; rarely does content from developing countries' news agencies transcend their borders. There exists what Jeremy Tunstall and David Machin call the "US/UK news duopoly" in the sense that both countries' newswires and cable broadcasters—the AP and Reuters, and CNN and BBC World—seem to dominate the trajectory of global news.[78] A dozen years ago, the CNN News Group, with 42 bureaus worldwide, was already available to 160 million homes in 212 countries and BBC World was available to 167 million homes in 200 countries.[79] By 2017, they had more than doubled that reach, with 354 million homes able to access CNN and 372 million homes able to access the BBC, according to the two networks.[80]

English is the lingua franca of international communication, and major Western news institutions have expanded globally via the Internet, wire or satellite services, and/or the international publishing of Western newspapers and magazines to meet a growing demand for news and entertainment.[81] While most independently owned media are in Europe and North America, the developing world's press is mostly under the control of the state. The World Bank found in 2002 that in 97 countries, state governments controlled an average of 29 percent of newspapers, 60 percent of television stations, and 72 percent of radio stations; in 43 countries, the state had complete oversight over television.[82] While the World Bank has not updated that statistic since 2002, the U.S. nongovernmental organization Freedom House found in 2016 that 69 percent of countries had a media environment that was either not free or only partly free, meaning, among other indicators, that the state likely had some control over the majority of the country's press.[83] Governments are most likely to control the news media in poorer countries that have markets too weak to sustain an independent press.

Global elites often look for themselves in U.S. and other Western news. A country's place in the international system depends not just on its material might and clout in the network of international institutions, but also in how it is framed by the Western news media. As described in Chapter 2, there is consensus between the U.S. news media and U.S. government about America's global power. The press believes that the United States is the most valued nation in the world order, and coverage of other countries is traditionally episodic, shallow, intermittent, and quick.[84] U.S. international news prioritizes stories on U.S. foreign policy, and it is infused with a sense of ethnocentrism, nationalism, and, during war or the anticipation of it, fierce patriotism.[85] As a result, foreign leaders often contest and resent the content of American news about them and their nations.

Like President Hamid Karzai, other developing countries' leaders have long complained that Western news agencies socially construct political conditions and events that maintain the national interests of their own countries and lend legitimacy to the international political structure and norms that keep the West in leadership positions.[86] Quantitatively and qualitatively, Western countries' press corps are seen to create and reinforce images and stereotypes that are biased and harmful, as they are absorbed with news of disasters, overall insecurity, acts of corruption and other moral failures of the developing world.[87] Local journalists can be dependent on the Western news narratives that reach their countries for content but are simultaneously frustrated with the agendas and frames of those narratives. In the same way that U.S. journalists tend to amplify American interests, developing countries' press corps also tend to construct news that aligns with their nation's political, economic, and cultural interests.[88] The journalists may need and accept the facts and information from their Western colleagues, but the worldview of the foreigner can conflict with theirs and strengthen their own sense of nationalism and ethnocentrism.

The concept of "international freedom of the press" dates back to 1943, when American First Amendment scholar and Harvard Law School Professor Zechariah Chafee, Jr., and the American Society of Newspaper Editors promoted its inclusion in the United Nations Charter. A subcommittee on the subject was established during the charter's creation, but its participants were stuck on debates over how to define press freedom, press responsibility, and who would qualify as a journalist.[89] On December 10, 1948, the United Nations General Assembly adopted the Universal Declaration of Human Rights, which included Article 19. While avoiding definitions of press responsibility and who qualified as a journalist, it states, "Everyone has the right to freedom of opinion and expression; this right includes the freedom to hold opinions without interference and to seek, receive and impart information and ideas through any media and regardless of frontiers."[90]

Decades later, in the late 1970s and 1980s, many elites and journalists in recently independent Asian, African, and Caribbean countries that subscribed to Western wire services were disturbed by the news they read about their countries, and the debate resurfaced.[91] They openly lamented that the West was still controlling the news inflows and outflows from countries they once controlled under colonialism. Dependency theorists argued that the Western news media's ability to fix narratives and images of developing countries was neocolonialism, as the West was still representing the countries as weak and therefore suppressing their ability to attract global investment and legitimization by international institutions.[92] It was a popular argument that inspired international action.

In 1976, the United Nations Educational, Scientific and Cultural Organization (UNESCO) General Conference in Nairobi published the report *One World, Many Voices*, an overview of communications and society that focused on imbalances between the Western and non-Western world. The report's contributors determined that there was a one-way flow of communication, dominating from the West, or the North, with the newswires AP, Agence France-Presse, United Press International, and Reuters controlling roughly 95 percent of global information. This provoked calls for a New World Information Communication Order.[93] In 1977, the *Washington Post* ran a sympathetic editorial acknowledging the reluctance of letting U.S. journalists serve as the image-makers for a country:

> One does not have to accept the third-world charges that Western news agencies are cultural and political predators in order to understand a country's reluctance to have its picture of the world, and the world's picture of it, drawn entirely by foreigners who are sometimes knowledgeable and sympathetic, sometimes not, but who nevertheless are foreigners.[94]

And, in 1979, the MacBride Commission—chaired by Irish attorney Sean MacBride and sponsored by UNESCO—argued that it's the media's job not to inform, but to assist. Its report stated:

> What communication can do is focus attention, point out opportunities, attack indifference and obstruction, and influence the climate of opinion. Communication thus plays a supporting and participatory role in development, but its contribution can be significant. This applies to the mobilization of public opinion in developing countries, and to the spread of greater understanding in the developed.[95]

Developing countries that supported the commission called for an order to seek "fair and balanced" coverage of the postcolonial states. The idea was that Western news flows should focus on supporting the development of countries and not focus on their shortcomings. It gave public control of the news media more importance than private ownership, which Western news professionals saw as a repudiation of editorial independence and freedom of expression.[96] The news agencies of the United States, United Kingdom, and other European countries responded that this was a kind of pre-censorship and that the commercial and political constraints already made reporting on these countries difficult.[97] They pointed to Article 19 and emphasized that news from the Third World was heavily loaded with government press releases, which reflected the very state-controlled news systems that suppress freedom of information and the pursuit of truth.

The influence that geopolitics has on international news flows reinforces the developed world's hegemony over the developing one.[98] A 1985 follow-up study undertaken for UNESCO found that the richest countries with the most considerable sway over international politics continued to be covered the most in global news, with the United States enjoying a big lead over France and the United Kingdom. The Soviet Union and Africa were covered the least.[99] Indeed, a news organization that is based in a major power, and belongs to a strong military alliance and the G7 and/or G20, has considerably more sway globally than a news agency based in a developing country that is not a member of any exclusive international club.[100] Journalists for elite Western news outlets can also fundamentally misunderstand and misconceptualize dilemmas in developing countries, and therefore offer misleading ideas about the role Western states and institutions can play in supporting them.[101]

This fits with Bella Mody's analysis of the U.S. elite media's coverage of the Darfur crisis in Sudan. She found that American journalists frequently distorted reality by referencing tribalism and "ancient hatreds" to describe the crisis without explaining the role of colonial legacies. Susan Carruthers similarly explained the Western media's lack of context in its reportage on Africa. What she describes as "explanatory impoverishment" lets the West off the hook for setting some of the very conditions during colonialism and unfair trade practices that created or heightened the crises.[102] Stuart Kaufman, too, uses the case of conflict in the Balkans in the 1990s to discuss the oversimplification of relying on "ancient hatreds" to understand modern political dynamics. Some Western policymakers' belief that issues are primordial and fixed can lead them to conclude that the conflicts are intractable and therefore not worth international attention.[103] American press stories rarely delve into the complex sociological issues that contribute to a country in conflict, which can over-simplify U.S. government officials and the public's perceptions of the country.

Through its continued control of the global media market and news flows, the Western press accentuates images and solidify identities around the world. Often, nascent press corps, like Afghanistan's, are dependent on Western-centric media for information, despite the ominous stories that are told of their nation.[104] And foreign journalists tasked with reporting the United States to their audiences regularly seek U.S. news to aid them in their reporting on the country, especially if they do not have bureaus in the United States.

Once news is broken it is a sort of common property that journalists can repeat; they only need to quote another outlet's reportage if they use the exact wording.[105] Stephen Hess found in his survey work on foreign journalists that the *New York Times* and *Washington Post* had the greatest readership, at 89 percent and 70 percent respectively; many of the stories in these papers were reprinted for foreign publications.[106] In one of the few other studies on foreign journalists covering the United States, Philo Wasburn also found that the foreign journalists were especially reliant on the *Times*, which was perceived to be an agenda-setter for American policy.[107] While several more American news sources were available, the *Times* was deemed the most important because it was the most widely read by the American public and policymakers.

U.S. elite news about global events and/or American foreign policy can easily affect bilateral and regional relationships, and the dynamics within international institutions. The American press carries considerable weight abroad and can often send confusing signals. "Any reporting that is done in the mainstream media will be taken to be true even if it's sourced to an unnamed individual, until you provide clarification that it is not the fact," explained former National Security Council and State Department spokesman Michael Hammer. The issues of interest to foreign citizens, businesses, institutions, and governments can range from consular and visa matters to talk of economic sanctions, trade deals, humanitarian aid, peace treaties, and war. Should they report something untrue or leak information the U.S. government is not ready to disclose, journalists can create anxieties abroad and construct a new framework for policymakers to work within. Washington officials and diplomats abroad often have to assuage the concerns of allies on U.S. foreign policy over something they saw in the U.S. press.[108]

This was certainly the case in Afghanistan.

U.S. OFFICIALS AND REPORTERS for this study agreed that President Karzaï's distrust of the United States may have started under President Bush, but it accelerated under President Obama. In February 2008, then-Senator Joseph Biden, who was Chair of the Senate Foreign Relations Committee at the time and not yet Obama's vice-presidential running mate, visited Afghanistan and had dinner with Karzai in the presidential palace. According to Peter Bergen's reporting, at the dinner, Biden tried to talk with Karzai about corruption in the country and the Afghan government's failure to control it. When Karzai reportedly continued to talk around the issue, Biden said, "Look, I think we've come to the point where we're not getting more out of this discussion." He then said, "this dinner is over," and walked out of the palace with his delegation.[109]

This was a "tone-deaf" reaction, according to Ronald Neumann, U.S. Ambassador to Afghanistan from 2005 to 2007. He said:

> No Afghan would treat another Afghan like that in front of his supporters, in this case his cabinet. If you did, it was because you turned against him and you were signaling that you were going to burn him down. By attacking Karzai in that way in that forum, they convinced Karzai they were after him and it had nothing to do with corruption, corruption was only a pretext.[110]

From that dinner in 2008 to President Obama's last trip to Afghanistan in 2014, when he opted only to visit troops at Bagram Air Base and not visit Karzai at his palace, the United States sent signals that were, according to Neumann, "gratuitously insulting" and reflected "at the highest level that we didn't understand the country and we didn't care to."[111] Karzai saw the American press and government alike framing his country as a failed democracy with little respect for him.

With the increasing attention of the U.S. press in 2009 came an influx of leaks from the Obama administration to American reporters, *New York Times* reporter Carlotta Gall remembered. She recalled that it was almost as if the members of the new administration wanted to make their predecessors in the Bush administration look incompetent and their closeness with Karzai short-sighted. One *New York Times* story in 2010 by

Dexter Filkins, "Iran Is Said to Give Top Karzai Aide Cash by the Bagful," was cited by several reporters and officials as being a classic case of a leak from the Obama administration. The story described how Karzai's Chief of Staff Umer Daudzai received "a steady stream of Iranian cash" intended to buy his loyalty and "promote Iran's interests in the presidential palace."[112] The story continued the narrative that Karzai was corrupt and was not being faithful to his main benefactor, the United States.

The story enraged Karzai, who responded the next day, "We are grateful for the Iranians' help in this regard. The United States is doing the same thing. They are providing cash to some of our offices."[113] The *Times* story particularly incensed him, seeing the paper as working hand in hand with the U.S. government to smear him in the eyes of Western donors and publics, and also among his Afghan citizens.

As explored in Chapter 1, Karzai expected that leaks were not episodic, as American reporters and officials insisted they were, but painstakingly orchestrated. While the relationship between reporters and officials was mired in distrust and frustration, he saw a calculated, coordinated, and systemic disinformation campaign to smear him and to undermine the Afghan state. David Ensor, the Director for Communications and Public Diplomacy at the U.S. embassy in Kabul from 2010 to 2011, said in a 2017 interview, "I remember the president having always read the *New York Times* or other publications and be annoyed by them, and quoting them back at us as if somehow it was up to us what was in the newspapers . . . I knew, of course, we could be quoted in those stories, but we didn't get to decide what was in the newspapers."[114] Marc Grossman, the Special Representative to Afghanistan from 2011 to 2012, agreed with other U.S. officials that they never saw American reporters as cheerleaders for U.S. policy, but he believed Karzai's growing frustration with the United States had to be put into context. He explained that it stemmed from "the fact that he felt that American policy had overwhelmed his country" and that was reflected in the U.S. press.[115] As part of the influx of 30,000 American troops and more than 1,000 diplomats, the United States had set up what Karzai called "parallel structures," in which Americans would be doing the jobs of Afghan cabinet officials, governors, and district leaders. Grossman explained that in response to news stories about the work of American diplomats and soldiers, "He would say, 'I should see an Afghan doing that'—and he was right," said Grossman. Karzai was also deeply disturbed by the thousands of civilian deaths and injuries in the country at the hands of coalition forces. Grossman continued:

President Karzai wasn't just frustrated with the press, he was frustrated with all of us. We would go see him to talk about a substantive issue, but on the day before we had bombed some Afghan civilians by mistake, for example, thinking a group of women cutting down trees for firewood were terrorists. That would be all he wanted to talk about. Karzai could not accept that, even in a war zone, Western militaries sometimes killed civilians by mistake. It colored his view of everything that we tried to do . . . So it wasn't the press he was frustrated by, it was the fact that he felt that Americans had overwhelmed his country and we couldn't do what he considered the simplest things, like protect Afghan civilians from being killed by mistake by U.S. and allied forces.[116]

Neumann agreed that not just Karzai, but all Afghans, had difficulty believing that the United States could make such mistakes, given its material and technological power and its mission as articulated by President Obama to underwrite global security. He explained, "There are some things that will not register well with Afghans. Long periods in which America isn't paying attention is incomprehensible to them. Afghanistan is the center of the world to an Afghan." He continued, "There's a huge idea that America knows what it is doing, or it at least has a plan. The idea that a plan could often be incoherent completely doesn't register . . . everything is 'deep state,' everything is part of a plan."[117] Zalmay Khalilzad, who was U.S. Ambassador from 2003 to 2005, similarly stated in a 2017 interview, "I've never gotten instructions from 'the deep state.' There's no secret CIA outfit. Karzai thinks that we're all front men for real people controlling America." While Karzai was angry for being criticized by the U.S. press, blaming the foreign news media for working to psychologically pressure him was "convenient to absolve himself of responsibility," Khalilzad.[118]

Yet each American official interviewed agreed that Afghanistan made much progress during the Karzai years. Part of this was the development of the Afghan news media. This too, however, irked Karzai, because the U.S. news professionals helped to set the agenda for their Afghan peers to follow.

Afghanistan's young press corps has relied on U.S. news to inform them about how the American government and public understands and talks about their country. It has also became source material for them as they tried to make sense of the U.S.-led war for the Afghan public, and the political, economic, and societal impacts it was having on their everyday life. Just as Afghanistan relied on the United States for aid, they depended on the independent U.S. news media narratives to make meaning of America's entanglement in their country, and sometimes their own government. Just as the American military and government had power over Afghanistan's security and development, the American press had power in creating perceptions about Afghanistan's progress, or lack thereof, among Americans, Afghans, and anyone around the world touched by the U.S. news media.

4

Afghanistan's Press

I had a vision for a democratic Afghanistan, for human rights, and for the freedom of the press and freedom of expression

—HAMID KARZAI in 2014[1]

ON OCTOBER 16, 2004, three years after the Taliban fell from power, a new television station named Tolo, meaning "sunrise" in Dari, went on the air. It was the second media venture of Moby Media Group, which was owned by Saad Mohseni, a businessman who returned to Afghanistan with his four siblings after they had left in the 1970s with their diplomat father. They were living in Australia when the Soviets invaded Afghanistan and decided to stay there. When the Taliban fell and the United States and European countries signaled their intent to support Afghanistan's development, the Mohsenis were eager to invest in their homeland and support its new economy. They didn't intend to start a media business, though.[2]

One freezing December night in 2001, Mohseni, at the last minute, joined Ahmed Rashid, a Pakistani author, and Andrew Natsios, the head of the U.S. Agency for International Development (USAID), for dinner in Kabul. When Mohseni was explaining his family's business plans, Rashid suggested that he go into the media business and perhaps start with a radio station. The idea appealed to Mohseni—and to Natsios, whose responsibility was to identify trusted partners to help with Afghanistan's democratic development.

The demand for news and entertainment was staggeringly high in Afghanistan. On November 13, 2001, Kabul residents had heard music on the radio for the first time in five years. Since the United States had invaded on October 7, the Taliban's Radio Shariat had been reduced to white noise in Kabul.[3] In 1996, the Taliban had rebranded the state-run Radio Television Afghanistan as Radio Shariat, which broadcast regular recitations of the Holy Koran and rote statements from the Taliban on its government activities.[4] With the Taliban now out of power, Radio Afghanistan was back on the air via a mobile transmitter. Agence France-Presse (AFP) reported that day: "Shrieks of joy erupted when Radio Afghanistan began broadcasting . . . offering verses from the Koran, music that had been banned under the Taliban, and a woman newscaster."[5] The newscaster, Jamila Mujahid, told her audience:

> You can celebrate this great victory . . . We have to thank God for giving us this opportunity for Afghanistan to move toward unity . . . I don't believe this. I never thought that a time would come when I would be reading the news again. As I read the news this morning it's like a dream.[6]

Two hundred sixty miles north in Mazar-e-Sharif, a large city in Balkh province, Radio Shariat had continued airing through October and early November despite poor broadcasting quality.[7] On November 10, broadcasts had switched from Pashto, the preferred language of the Taliban, to Dari, the preferred language of the Northern Alliance, the main opposition group to the Taliban. A new announcer declared that the local station would now be known as "Radio Balkh." The Taliban, he stated, had fallen from the north: "Dear pious and Muslim compatriots," he said, "peace be with you. We congratulate you from the bottom of our hearts on the victory of the Islamic State of Afghanistan."[8] Afghan and Indian music then filled the airwaves.

A familiar voice to northern Afghanistan's citizens later came on. Abdul Rashid Dostum, the former Soviet general, infamously brutal Uzbek warlord, and future vice president, interrupted the music to announce his triumphant return to the country he had fled in 1997 for Turkey. The United States had asked him to return from exile and help guide U.S. Special Forces in eliminating the Taliban from Afghanistan's north.[9] He proudly announced that they had prevailed.

Afghanistan's media was freed from Taliban controls, but old powerbrokers like Dostum quickly returned to influence it. The country was in deep recovery from a decade of Soviet rule, six years of civil war, and five years of Taliban brutality. The painstaking work to create a viable news system alongside a new democratic government had just begun. Each of Afghanistan's 20th-century rulers had favored an authoritarian style of reportage, so there was no blueprint for an emerging cadre of news professionals on how to build a free and independent news media that informed the Afghan public—and how to hold an emerging new democratic government accountable.[10] But in a country where opportunity had been routinely suppressed, freedom of speech was an exciting prospect. USAID's Natsios and other officials in the U.S. embassy in Kabul, along with the diplomatic and aid missions of other Western governments, saw the news media as a vital component of a transitional democracy and a medium to promote free speech, encourage public discourse, and create a 21st-century Afghanistan.[11]

Over the next decade, the Mohseni family would go on to modernize the Afghan media space. After that dinner in 2001, Natsios gave them $280,000 to apply toward a $500,000 media license from the Ministry of Information and Culture so he could launch Radio Arman, a station that mixed music and news, targeting Afghanistan's youth. It went on the air in April 2003 with a team so small that, at times, Mohseni himself had to DJ. In a symbolic move, he hired Massood Sanjer, the English news broadcaster for the Taliban's Radio Shariat, to be the voice for a new, more open generation of Afghans.[12]

With Radio Arman's early success, Mohseni's Moby Media Group went on to launch Tolo TV in 2004, Lemar TV (in Pashto) in 2006, and the 24-hour ToloNews station in 2009.[13] Saad Mohseni said in a 2016 interview that when Radio Arman launched, he "hadn't fully understood the impact it would have . . . We were lucky in one sense that when it launched, the state wasn't a proper state. Institutions were in place, but they didn't have much authority."[14] The new media industry moved faster than regulations could be made.[15] After its launch, Tolo quickly became Afghanistan's most popular television station. Sami Mahdi, a news anchor for Tolo and for 1TV, another popular independent television station, remembered the first time he saw it in 2004: "It was an amazing new era, you could see amazing energy in the air. On Tolo, you could listen to young guys and girls, you could watch them on TV, they were performing like never before."[16] It was a vast departure from the state-owned network Radio Television Afghanistan (RTA), which had been resurrected but was more conservative in its programming and, by habit, more deferential in its reporting on the government.

A more pluralistic, independent news media began to form, albeit they were heavily backed by special interests representing the United States and European countries, India, Iran, Pakistan, Afghan businessmen, or warlords. Here, independent news agencies are defined as ones that do not have just one benefactor and their editorial bodies do not pay allegiance to the Afghan government or any other foreign government. The West helped the media's early formation in Afghanistan, and governments continue to provide funding and technical assistance, which will be further discussed. But as much as Afghanistan's new independent news media energized the country, residues of the past also stuck. Dostum, the warlord who announced triumph on Radio Balkh's airwaves in November 2001, quickly moved to launch his own television station, Aina, which means "mirror" in Dari, as a sort of warlord reality television channel, which produces a constant stream of official speeches and images of Dostum. Sometimes he is in the trenches with a radio, shouting orders to fight the Taliban; other times he is riding his horses. Other warlords followed his example. Soon, multiple power centers seized this new medium, and a patchwork news media landscape that reflected the fragmentation and various biases of the country quickly became the norm.

Afghanistan's Early Media

A nation's media system is deeply entangled with the worldviews of its government and population; it is profoundly affected by both the ills and successes of its society. The story of the Afghanistan news media is the story of the country's transitions from British occupation to monarchy to communism to civil war to theocracy to democracy. Afghanistan's first newspaper, *Saraj-al-Akhbar* ("Lamp of the News"), was created by Afghan politician and intellectual Mahmud Ber Tarzi in 1906 but produced just one edition. Five years lapsed before he revived the paper after returning to Afghanistan from exile in Europe. He made *Saraj* into a biweekly with the dual purpose of uniting the country under the banner of Islam against British colonial rule and creating an enlightened Afghan public that could reform the country.[17] He seemed to recognize that the media could serve as a tool to simultaneously modernize and consolidate the Afghan nation, and show the British that Afghanistan was strong enough to survive in the international system without a Western patron.[18] The newspaper promoted a sense of nationalism, advocating that Afghanistan should be autonomous and take its place among nations while also coordinating cultural symbols and narratives for the Afghan people.[19]

In 1919, when Afghanistan gained its independence from the United Kingdom, King Amanullah (1919–1929) used the media to unite the Afghan nation under his rule and promote his agenda. This authoritarian style of news media lasted for most of the century. The king created a new publication, *Aman-i-Afghan* ("Afghan Peace"), to replace *Saraj-al-Akhbar* and serve his administration.[20] Later, in 1923, the king allowed the principle of free speech to be part of the 1923 constitution, and various newspapers and magazines began to circulate in Kabul and the provinces. Amanullah's progressive wife, Queen Soraya, who had shocked Afghans by appearing unveiled in public, even sanctioned a short-lived magazine, *Dastoor be Zananengee* ("Instructions for Women"), which encouraged a more liberal path for Afghan women.[21] Later, after Germany provided equipment for a broadcasting system, King Nadir Shah (1929–1933) created the first iteration of Radio Afghanistan, thus expanding the reach of information to illiterate citizens.

Under the reign of Zahir Shah (1933–1973), Afghanistan's last king, the Afghan media became more robust but remained under strong government control until the last few years of his rule. By 1940, Radio Afghanistan had become available nationwide and the public became accustomed to broadcasts of government announcements and policy statements to serve the narrow purposes of particular officials.[22] The Media Law of 1950 allowed for private media, but King Shah banned them just two years later. His administration established the state-run newswire, Bakhtar News Agency (BNA), managed by the Ministry of Information and Culture.[23] While BNA allowed Afghan news to transcend borders and create relationships with the global newswires AFP, Reuters, AP, Deutsche Presse Agentur, the Soviet Union's TASS, and China's Xinhua News Agency in an effort to exchange information with the world, the Afghan news media remained mostly an instrument of the government.[24]

In 1966, a new law allowed for more private news media and by 1973, 24 private newspapers—and various radio stations—surfaced.[25] But those agencies, while independent from the government, largely depended on government officials' tolerance for them.[26] Many of the private newspapers were politically charged, and some advocated strongly for communist rule. The emerging Communist People's Democratic Party of Afghanistan (PDPA), especially, espoused their views through the papers *Khalq* ("Masses") and *Parcham* ("Banner").[27] As a sign of the country's looming fragmentation, PDPA split into two factions in 1967 and organized their diverging ideologies around the two newspapers; the factions become popularly known as Khalq and Parcham.

In 1973, King Shah's 40-year rule dramatically ended when his cousin, the former Prime Minister Daoud Khan, overthrew him. King Shah then left Afghanistan and began a nearly 30-year exile in Rome. Daoud Khan reconstituted Afghanistan as a republic instead of a monarchy, made himself president, and banned most private news media while keeping Radio—and now Television—Afghanistan (RTA) as the country's primary broadcast outlet.[28] By the late 1970s, roughly 15 newspapers and magazines managed to remain, catering to an elite, literate, and urban group.[29] Daoud Khan's presidency lasted five years. On April 27, 1978, Nur Muhammed Taraki, who ran the Khalq faction of the PDPA, which was pro-Soviet Union, overthrew Daoud in a bloody coup known as the Saur Revolution. He assassinated Daoud Khan and most of his family and quickly established the Democratic Republic of Afghanistan.[30]

Afghanistan was now a communist state run by Taraki, who was under the careful watch of the Soviets, but he lasted just 17 months. His introduction of large-scale land reforms and Marxist policies challenged traditional customs and values, infuriating the rural population and igniting mass protests in the countryside. Seeing his rule as a failure, Taraki's prime minister, Hafizullah Amin, directed that Taraki be killed by suffocation. After his murder, Amin then seized power on September 14, 1979.[31] The Soviets, perceiving the Afghan communist regime under Amin as unstable, invaded Afghanistan just two months later, on December 24, 1979, and killed Amin shortly after. They installed Babrak Karmal of the PDPA as president, and Soviet troops proceeded to occupy the country for nearly a decade.

During the Soviet occupation, the trend toward authoritarian-style reporting in Afghanistan solidified. Freedom of speech was further constricted, and the media focused on the actions of the PDPA and Soviet interests in the region and the world. Afghan reporters working for government-run news agencies—notably BNA and RTA—were forced to embrace and maintain a mechanical style of news. The journalism school at Kabul University, established in the early 1980s, taught students to relay the details of government announcements and events with little analysis or investigation. Any traces of Afghan media independence that had survived bouts of government crackdowns through the decades vanished.

However, Afghans with radios could still receive news from the international services such as BBC, Voice of America (VOA), and Deutsche Welle. An opposition media also surfaced with the purpose of resisting Soviet rule and Karmal's "puppet" Afghan government, which answered to Moscow. Seeing Afghanistan as an opportunity to weaken Soviet power, the United States began to covertly aid the mujahedeen, or freedom fighters, who had been forming a resistance since Taraki's 1978 coup. In addition to providing the mujahedeen with millions of dollars in weapons and cash, the United States supported an information campaign to galvanize anti-Soviet sentiment, which included creating newspapers and radio broadcasts in certain pockets of the country and in Afghan refugee camps in Pakistan that favored the rebels.[32]

The mujahedeen, aided by a combination of U.S. military, economic, and humanitarian aid to the Afghans, prevailed. On February 15, 1989, the last Soviet soldiers departed Afghanistan, leaving behind roughly 200 diplomats in the severely weakened Soviet embassy in Kabul.[33] Two weeks before, newly inaugurated U.S. President George H. W. Bush and his Secretary of State James Baker, citing concerns over impending instability in the country, evacuated the U.S. embassy and suspended its already downsized diplomatic mission. The United States stopped providing all but the slightest amount of humanitarian aid to the country, which was now to be overseen through a small Afghanistan office in the U.S. consulate in Peshawar, Pakistan.

The Soviets left behind a communist government run by Mohammed Najibullah. He held on to power for roughly one year, until April 16, 1992, when the Soviet Union had begun to dissolve and Moscow stopped providing him with financial support. Najibullah took refuge in the United Nations compound in Kabul as the now-fractured mujahedeen began to fight each other and plunge the country into a horrifying civil war. Burhanuddin Rabbani, seen as the leader of the mujahedeen, became the country's internationally recognized president. The official Afghan press, which had been under Communist Party control for a decade, most notably RTA, were now under Rabbani's control, but he couldn't stop the fighting, and the opposition media proliferated as militia leaders, popularly known as warlords, used newspapers to advance their own agendas for the country.[34]

During the civil war, which lasted roughly four years, thousands were killed, Kabul and other cities were destroyed, and the countryside was divided into multiple fiefdoms and battlegrounds. In 1994, a movement of young scholars, known as Talibs, began to take on the warlords in the Pashtun-dominated south. At first the Afghan people welcomed their peaceful ways and their ability to control the warlords; as Kathy Gannon said in chapter 3, they were Afghans, their fellow countrymen, and not a foreign force. The Taliban moved into the west and the north and soon took control of most of the country. In late September 1996, Rabbani's government fell to them.[35] One of their first acts was to locate the last communist leader, Najibullah, at the United Nations compound down-town. They found him and his brother there, castrated them, tied them to trucks, and dragged them to their death through the streets of Kabul. They then hung their bodies from cranes in the center of the city so that all residents could see the beginning of the new era of Taliban rule. President Rabbani, however, survived. He fled to Badakhshan, the remote north-east province that borders China, and went on to fight the Taliban for five years through the Northern Alliance, a collection of warlords and militia leaders, all former mujahedeen, again united against a common enemy.

The Taliban used an extremely harsh style of governance. It transformed the media with the goal of imposing a theocracy that strictly adhered to Sharia law. Because images of the human form were now outlawed, RTA television broadcasting was halted completely.[36] Taliban religious police smashed privately owned television sets and strung film from videocassettes in trees. Anyone found to harbor a television set could receive the punishment of flogging and a six-month incarceration.[37] Radio Afghanistan, renamed Radio Shariat, broadcast mainly prayers, official announcements, news of military victories against the Northern Alliance, and criticism of any foreign or Afghan opposition to Taliban rule. The Taliban Ministry of Information and Culture, which managed Radio Shariat, also produced approximately a dozen state-owned print publications, but their circulation rate was limited to 1 percent of the country. Because there were no newsstands and the literacy rate was less than 25 percent, the papers were mainly distributed to political and reli-gious institutions.[38]

There were some alternatives to Taliban-controlled media. The Northern Alliance financed a television station in President Rabbani's province of Badakhshan that broadcast news and old movies for three hours each evening. However, it had only about 5,000 viewers, a minis-cule fraction of Afghanistan's 30 million people, who were both safe from the Taliban's reach and owned a television set and a generator to power it. The station existed primarily to symbolize hope for a post-Taliban society where communication would be less restricted. Yet Afghans throughout the country who tuned into foreign radio stations still felt connected to the world outside.[39] The BBC, VOA, and Deutsche Welle in particular provided a lifeline for news beyond and within Afghanistan's borders.[40] *New York Times* reporter Carlotta Gall traveled to Afghanistan frequently in the 1990s to visit her father, Scottish journalist Sandy Gall, who wrote sev-eral books about the country. She later reflected that whenever she would get out of the car, Afghans would say, "Suzy Price! Suzy Price!" thinking she was the BBC correspondent who had reported from there during the civil war and Taliban rule. "When they saw a foreign woman, they thought it was her. She was just so famous because everyone listed to BBC, VOA, and Deutsche Welle radio programs . . . they would all sit around the one radio at night and listen" to the news.[41]

Afghans had heard of the 9/11 attacks from Radio Shariat, but the Western news agencies gave the information more depth and provided the international reaction to it. They also told Afghans about the death of Northern Alliance leader Ahmad Shah Massoud. When the United States officially began its war in Afghanistan on October 7, 2001, the Afghans also learned what was happening from Western radio stations. "The BBC was all we had," recalled *New York Times* reporter Mujib Mashal, at the time a 13-year-old Kabul resident.[42] The habit of turning to the Western news to understand events inside their country and the world outside is why so many Afghans welcomed the international press into the country in late 2001 with such little suspicion, Gall believes. It was also why so many Afghans like Mashal flocked to journalism: They understood its power.

Afghanistan's 21st-Century Press

On November 13, 2001, the Taliban fell from power and striking change began to take place in Afghanistan yet again. Under the Taliban, women were not permitted to work or even leave their homes, so Jamila Mujahid's broadcast on Radio Afghanistan (rebranded overnight from Radio Shariat) was a powerful symbol of liberty: The Taliban no longer controlled the airwaves or the country. But Mujahid was able to broadcast music and deliver news unfettered by authorities only because there was no Afghan government to stop it. Since 1906, the monarchy, the Soviets, the warlords, and the Taliban had carefully managed the media outlets to ensure they supported their regimes and amplified their messages. The news media now stood on an unstable yet hopeful platform.

Western governments, believing liberal democracy was the best form of governance for the country, became the architects of Afghanistan's new government. In late November, the United Nations convened a meeting between four Afghan opposition groups in Bonn, Germany, to decide what Afghanistan's post-Taliban government should be. Included were representatives of the Northern Alliance; the "Cypress Group," Afghans who lived in exile in Iran; the "Rome Group," Afghans loyal to former King Zahir Shah, who was still living in exile in Rome; and the "Peshawar Group," Afghans who had been living in Pakistan.[43] They made two consequential decisions that would shape Afghanistan's current society and government. First, they agreed that the United Nations should create a multinational peacekeeping force to stabilize the country. The International Security Assistance Force, as it would become known, would operate under the auspices of the United Nations but would soon be led by the United States and member states of the North Atlantic Treaty Organization (NATO).[44] They also agreed to make Afghanistan into a constitutional democracy. It would begin with an interim administration for three to six months until a *loya jirga*, a grand council of tribal leaders, could agree to and legitimize a transitional administration.

There was much debate over who would lead this administration. At first, it looked as if the former king would resume his role.[45] But Burhanuddin Rabbani, the last internationally recognized Afghan president and representative of the Northern Alliance faction, opposed him. The United States wanted Hamid Karzai, a cousin of the king and a Pashtun, the dominant ethnicity in Afghanistan (most Taliban also were Pashtun). Originally from Kandahar, the center of Taliban rule, Karzai had been living in exile in Quetta, Pakistan, since the mid-1990s. He had served as Rabbani's deputy foreign minister from 1992 to 1994 and, for some time, recognized the Taliban as a legitimate force that could quell the violence from the civil war. In 1999, however, the Taliban assassinated Karzai's father and he began to support the Northern Alliance. The Bonn conference representatives ultimately agreed, most reluctantly Rabbani, that all ethnic groups in Afghanistan would accept Karzai. He was selected to lead a 29-member interim administration.[46]

The Bonn Agreement, also known as the Agreement on Provisional Arrangements in Afghanistan Pending the Re-Establishment of Permanent Government Institutions, was established on December 5, 2001. Karzai, who was still living in Quetta and hadn't attended the conference, received a phone call about his selection. Two days later, he crossed into Afghanistan with a team of U.S. Special Forces for the first time in nearly seven years. Two weeks later, he was sworn in as the interim leader of Afghanistan. David Rohde of the *New York Times* wrote of the ceremony:

> Appealing for help from God, his fellow citizens and the outside world to unify and rebuild his war-ravaged nation, Hamid Karzai,

an Afghan tribal leader with a regal bearing and an aristocratic lineage, was sworn in today as chairman of an interim government that replaces the defeated Taliban . . . Resplendent in a purple and green traditional robe, Mr. Karzai bowed his head five times as a diverse array of Afghan leaders and 2,000 spectators applauded his inauguration . . . Adding to the optimism and calm that pervaded the capital today was the show of unity by two Afghan military commanders who had been expected to snub the ceremony: Gen. Rashid Dostum, the dominant commander in northern Afghanistan, and Gen. Ismail Khan, a powerful leader in the west . . . In [Karzai's] speech, in which he struck a plain-spoken, humble tone, Mr. Karzai called on Afghans here and around the world to join in the challenge of reconstructing a nation brought down by decades of conflict. "In this critical time, when our motherland is watching our actions, let us come together and be brothers and sisters," he said. "Let us be good to each other and be compassionate and share our grief. Let us forget the sad past."[47]

The challenge ahead was staggering. Civilization in Afghanistan had been decimated. There were few institutions, schools, or health clinics; little physical infrastructure and electricity. The economy relied exclusively on weak agriculture and an illicit narcotics industry. After such a turbulent 30 years, however, Afghanistan was full of hope. That time, Rohde later reflected in a 2017 interview, "was all very emotional . . . I felt genuine optimism. People were very excited, Afghans were very excited. That was accurate reporting." However, he also thought there was "an exaggerated expectation of what the U.S. could achieve there among Afghans, and probably among us as well as correspondents."[48]

ONE OF AFGHANISTAN'S most exciting prospects was expanding and diversifying the media ecosystem, which received help from U.S. government officials and correspondents alike. The new Afghan press seemed to be its most visible example of how a population could embrace modernity, just as it had a century before with its first newspaper, *Lamp of the News*. In a 2016 interview, Karzai said a free press "was one of the cornerstones of my vision for Afghanistan . . . because it was in my view one of the fundamental rights of the Afghan people."[49] However, tradition runs deep in Afghanistan and, at least in the beginning, an authoritarian style of rote reportage with little investigation or analysis continued.

In 2002, the state-run media outlets RTA and BNA were revived with U.S. funding and technical assistance. RTA resumed television broadcasting in the major cities of Kabul, Jalalabad, Mazar-i-Sharif, and Faizabad, but it did not provide entertainment at first, despite the population's demand for it.[50] Radio Kabul was the lead station in RTA's network, but it initially reached just half of the provinces in the country. It was mostly Afghanistan's urban residents who had access to the national news media; only 24 percent of the rural population could access it early on.[51] In addition to BNA resuming its role as a government information newswire, 35 publications tied to the Afghan government began publication in 2002.[52] Reporters and broadcasters working for these agencies rarely criticized officials and remained loyal to the transitional government under Karzai.[53]

At first there was confusion over whether the interim government even permitted independent media. In February 2002, Karzai signed a new Media Law that closely resembled the last Media Law of 1966 in the sense that it allowed for private news media, though it no longer made reference to a monarchy.[54] The law required that news agencies obtain a license from the Ministry of Information and Culture that cost roughly $500,000, but established no firm criteria by which officials would decide who would get a license. The law did not guarantee public access to information, and it did not ensure the media's independence. It also included a ban on "subjects that could offend Islam and subjects that could dishonor the people or weaken the Army" and warned news professionals that if they offended Islam or the new Afghan National Army, their news agencies would be suspended.[55] Afghan officials, used to a press that blindly accepted the government, sometimes sought to punish the country's cohort of news professionals. In January 2003, the weekly newspaper *Farda* ("Tomorrow") ran a cartoon of an Afghan celebration, with Karzai seemingly leading a song and a dance. The president was out of the country when it was published and his vice president, Mohammed Fahim, who had been a military commander for the Northern Alliance, had *Farda*'s editor, Abdul Ghafoor Iteqad, who approved of the caricature, arrested. When Karzai returned to Afghanistan, someone had told him that Iteqad was in jail.[56] Karzai later reflected in 2016:

> So I immediately intervened, I said, "Who has done this?" And I found out the people responsible and I scolded them. I called the man to my office who was in detention and I apologized to him.

I said, "I'm sorry I wasn't here. This is not the mindset of this administration." . . . I told that man that you should consider me an
opportunity for practice—write anything you want about me, say
anything you want about me, but enjoy your freedom of the press.[57]

While Afghan state-run news media stayed within safe, known
boundaries, Karzai's public support for a free press and the financial
support from Western governments helped bolster a new cohort of independent Afghan journalists. A host of politicians, warlords, and other
foreign governments also moved in to claim their space in the new ecosystem. "It was a fundamentally important thing for me, and a vision. I'm
glad it worked. This is one of the best things that worked," Karzai said in
2016. "The Afghan people took the opportunity very, very well. And the
international community helped with it in a way. Of course, I have a different opinion there too about the role of the international community
and the Afghan press."[58]

The Patchwork Modern Afghan Media Landscape

Since 2001, the Afghan media has reflected the country's struggle to embrace freedom of expression.[59] The presence and span of coverage has expanded dramatically, from being available mainly in the cities to nearly all
of the country, from presenting 15-minute news bulletins to 24-hour news.
But it also reflects the struggle for power in the country. This is a patron-
based media system that heavily depends on people who want the country
to bend in their direction.

For decades, democratic countries in the West have worked to advance
ideas about freedom of the press in developing countries by providing
bilateral or multilateral financial, material, and technical support. Since
the end of the Cold War, media assistance has specifically been pegged to
promoting liberal democracies and the ideas of transparency and accountability.[60] Its goals are normally expressed in the same vein as supporting
civil societies, a culture of free expression, and empowering citizens to
have a voice in their government and society.[61] According to Craig LaMay
in his book *Exporting Press Freedom*:

The sum of it is usually that journalism is a means to an end: to
promote fair elections and universal suffrage; to develop political parties; to guide legal, judicial and administrative reform; to

strengthen civil society; to support public education and social services; and perhaps, most often, to promote free-market economies.[62]

The Western consensus—in governments and academia alike—is that
Western journalistic standards should be the global norm.

Sometimes media assistance—ranging from journalism training
and education to material assistance to developing regulatory and legal
frameworks to creating professional journalism societies—is offered
through international institutions such as the United Nations, the
European Union, or the Organization for Security and Cooperation in
Europe.[63] A host of nongovernmental organizations also promote the
cause, roughly a dozen of which are focused mainly on media and freedom
of speech. These include Internews, IREX, Open Society Institute, the
Committee to Protect Journalists, Freedom House, American Society of
Newspapers, Fairness and Accuracy in Media, and many others. There
is much interplay between governments and nongovernmental organization, especially through funding .

For the U.S. government, media assistance has been central to democracy promotion abroad in the post-9/11 era. As mentioned, its work is
grounded in the moral authority of Article 19 of the Universal Declaration
of Human Rights. USAID has primarily provided assistance through its
Office of Transitional Initiatives, which administered the funding Natsios
promised Mohseni in 2001.[64] Shortly after 9/11, USAID said that the role
of the press is to serve as "a watchdog over government and educating
people about the issues that affect their lives." It continued, "Two hundred
years ago, President Thomas Jefferson said it best: 'The only security of all
is in a free press . . . The force of public opinion cannot be resisted when
permitted freely to be expressed.' "[65]

However, U.S. media development assistance and related public diplomacy efforts to influence foreign audiences are commonly criticized because, according to LaMay, they "export the normative values and practices
of the American media system to countries where they are inappropriate
or of little use."[66] What constitutes a free and independent news media is
contextual. Applying the same model of press freedom to each country
is difficult because values are inherently subjective. Media scholars,
donors and recipients of media assistance use the words "independence,"
"freedom," "responsibility," "professionalism," "diversity," and "sustainability" to mean various things depending on the norms and historical
legacies within a certain place.[67]

The Afghan journalists working for the more popular news agencies have determined that they want their news media to reflect the American and British, or Western, tradition. While technically this may be feasible, creating investigative content and challenging authoritarian figures is not a cultural norm. In its earliest days, Radio Arman of Mohseni's Moby Media Group, one of the first of more than 170 independent radio stations in 2016, mainly faced resistance from warlords and religious leaders. Arman played pop music from throughout South Asia, with short news reports at the top of the hour. In 2003, a mob of people went to the studio in Kabul and demanded that the music stop. Saad Mohseni pressed on, however. With the launch of Tolo TV in 2004, the first of more than 65 independent television stations, his team faced more challenges as it challenged conservative and religious customs. "We had women on television singing in dresses, and there were political discourse openly questioning issues like corruption," Mohseni explained.[68] While there was a history of a political opposition press in Afghanistan, its more conservative leaders were unaccustomed to having their values openly challenged in society— and not just during news programs and talk shows, but through global music, soap operas, crime shows, and mysteries on the air. "Everything offended someone," reflected Mohseni in 2016.[69]

In 2005, Tolo debuted "Afghan Star," a national singing contest similar to the British show "Pop Star," which was later adapted for U.S. television as "American Idol." It helped to create new role models for Afghan youth but also tested the tolerance levels of government, religious, and cultural leaders.[70] Mohseni constantly feared that his stations would get shut down and his journalists locked up. But he explained, "I thought if we're going to go down, we might as well go down . . . It was like a hurricane coming through, but if you could hang on and make it, it meant that you were onto something." He gave his networks even odds that they'd survive.[71] They treated every complaint, every threat, on a case-by-case basis. As the de facto leaders and agenda-setters of the Afghan press corps, Mohseni and his colleagues had to ask tough questions: "How do you lead by example? How do you have women on the television screen? We had to convince parents that their daughters would not become prostitutes. How should women conduct themselves in the presence of men and vice versa?"

Intimidation was pervasive. Thick cultural norms in Afghanistan dictate how information is shaped. Afghan's most powerful officials, businessmen, drug lords, and warlords largely expect journalists to be deferential to their varying objectives. Afghan journalists were hesitant to investigate them for fear of shaming their honor, and for fear that they or their families would be harmed or killed. Government officials, religious leaders, and warlords also threatened Afghanistan's emerging business owners, telling them not to work with the media stations. Starting in 2002, most provincial governors took control of local radio stations. Warlords, some who also held official positions in the Afghan government, also saw opportunities to burnish their individual brands and political agendas by funding their own television stations, as they had with newspapers during the civil war. A sample of them include Abdul Rashid Dostum's Aina ("Mirror"), Haji Mohammad Mohaqiq's Rah-e-Farda ("Future Path"), Burhanuddin Rabbani's Noor ("Light"), and Karim Khoram's Kabul TV. Iran and Pakistan, too, seized the opportunity to influence the young democracy and began to finance Afghan news agencies.[72] The Taliban also became more sophisticated in crafting news narratives and interacting with Afghan journalists via traditional and digital media platforms. Soon, the Afghan media space became maintained by benefactors: Afghan government officials, Americans and other Westerners, Pakistanis, Iranians, warlords and their militias, Taliban members, other extremists. Each wanted the Afghan media to reflect their agendas for the country. While some shaped it by providing funding, others did so by withholding or granting access to information, and others by making threats; these tactics were not mutually exclusive.

Yet even though there were seemingly endless challenges for the Afghan journalists, there was also a sense of adventure and mission that propelled them along, especially those who worked for independent outlets. They began to transform the way in which the larger Afghan public relates to information, expanding their reach beyond the cities. Because Afghans put a high premium on the *source* of the information, news delivered by a member of their community or another trusted group can automatically be accepted as truth.[73] This is partly why most of Afghanistan's media landscape is fragmented along ethno-linguistic lines. Afghans want information from people that they identify with.[74] Those with a Pashtun identity are more likely to trust Pashto-language media; those with other ethnic identities (e.g., Tajik, Uzbek, Hazara) are more likely to trust the Dari-language press. Simultaneously, however, Afghans want to be part of an Afghan nation and know about people outside of their immediate communities. Thus, they consider the state-owned RTA, although it is known to be biased toward the government, as contributing to national unity because of its national reach.[75] By 2016, there were roughly 65 television stations, 150 radio stations, and 500 newspapers, and 64 percent of the public trusted the news media—more than any other Afghan institution.

While the Afghan public deemed anything that was not RTA as being independent, including the Iranian, Pakistani, and warlord-controlled stations, the Kabul elite mainly saw these stations as being disruptive to Afghanistan's democratic progress and a return to days of fiefdoms and division.[76] As former BBC journalist Bilal Sarwary explained in 2016, "What's worrying is that we have the re-emerging of social fragmentation in Afghanistan . . . The media can inflame that and be divisive."[77]

The more than 30 Afghan journalists interviewed for this study—many of whom worked for the most popular, Kabul-based agencies—believed that of all the foreign benefactors of the Afghan press, the United States and European countries supported the development of a free press the most, because they didn't tell the agencies they funded what to report.[78] They were also transparent about which agencies received which funding. This was contrary, they said, to the funding from the Iranians and Pakistanis, who expect journalists to report what they are told to.[79] Yet with the exception of news agencies sanctioned by Western governments, like BBC, Deutsche Welle, VOA, and the U.S.'s Radio Azadi ("Radio Liberty," part of the U.S.-funded Radio Free Europe/Radio Liberty network), Western governments do not underwrite entire news agencies. Consistent with the norms of Western media assistance to help build liberal institutions, they seek to support specific media programs that advance Western ideals and norms, such as human rights, and for Afghans to support their emerging democratic and security institutions.

Since 2001, the U.S. embassy in Kabul has been firmly focused on ensuring that an Afghan press matured into one with Western standards. "In any embassy anywhere," said Ryan Crocker, U.S. Ambassador to Afghanistan from 2011 to 2012, "doing what you can to professionalize the local media is important . . . [and] focusing on the local press was absolutely part of the development of Afghanistan." From 2010 to 2012, during the U.S. civilian surge, public diplomacy funding skyrocketed to $180 million, when it had been far less than $1 million for nearly a decade. The expanded public diplomacy budget helped to complement the millions of dollars in media assistance that USAID was providing. Eileen O'Connor, a former journalist who became the Director of Communications and Public Diplomacy at the U.S. embassy from 2011 to 2012, explained:

> This was public diplomacy on steroids . . . We were really recreating the information space in Afghanistan. We were building cell phone towers, we were trying to help build free and independent media, we were also in charge of working with the Ministry of Education along with USAID on education reform. We really helped to bring in exchanges with U.S. universities that were designed to drive curriculum changes to help critical thinking . . . We worked on countering violent extremism, we had programs where we worked with radical imams. We also had creative programming thinking about what Afghans related to culturally, so poetry and stories.[80]

Most U.S. officials saw Tolo as the network with the most promise to build a culture of transparency and accountability. They supported budgets for specific programming, such as the Afghan version of "Sesame Street" and dramas such as "Eagle Four," about a policeman who worked to keep the country safe from the Taliban. It was created to inspire confidence in the Afghan National Security Forces (ANSF).[81] David Ensor, who was the Director of Communications and Public Diplomacy before O'Connor, also funded training and broadcast equipment for the Pashto-language Shamshad TV to extend its reach in the southern and eastern parts of the country. Ensor saw Shamshad as a moderate, Pashtun voice that filled a gap in an Afghan independent news ecosystem heavily influenced by Dari speakers. "We didn't hand over cash, but we would pay for costly things if it would help the interest of Afghanistan writ large and U.S. foreign policy," he explained in a 2016 interview.[82] The U.S. government also directly subsidized the launch of the Pajhwok newswire in 2004, offered grant funds to the newspaper *Hashteh Sobh*, and supported media training programs implemented via several nongovernmental organizations in the country, among other efforts.

By 2016, however, the U.S. budget for this work had decreased by at least 90 percent from its peak in 2010. With the Afghan economy still weak and dependent on international aid, the future of the Afghan independent news media hinges on the amount of ongoing U.S. and Western financial support. From 2001 to 2011, the Afghan journalists interviewed saw a large injection of Western resources into their professional development.[83] By 2012, however, that assistance sharply decreased, with fewer training programs and fewer advertising dollars to support the news business. The journalists interviewed were disappointed since their work and livelihoods were at risk.[84] As one told me, "It is the West that created this environment for us, but they are not working actively to help sustain that environment."[85] Shah Hussain Murtazawi, *Hashteh Sobh*'s deputy chief editor, similarly told the *Christian Science Monitor* in 2012, "Now we have climbed all the way to the peak and if we fall from here it won't help. I think the international community should realize this and not let go of the Afghan independent media."[86] The Afghan media market, inflated by foreign donor money, is largely unsustainable. There is no norm for advertising in Afghan society, Mujib Mashal of the *New York Times* explained in 2016: "While there's a drive for feeding people information on new platforms, the money in business remains very traditional in Afghanistan."[87] While donor funding decreases, the Afghan market has not adapted to using the media as a vehicle for advertising.

In societies and governments undergoing political transition, it is normal for media professionals to experience a profound shift in purpose. Media that previously existed to support or oppose the government now must grapple with the challenges of keeping the government accountable and also running a business with or without donor support.[88] Often the most overlooked yet essential dimension of media assistance is working to ensure its sustainability. Who will pay the bills of running a media operation?

Craig LaMay, in his history of Western media assistance, emphasized that the press is rooted not just in civil society, but in the economy: "The central dilemma is economic, between the need to find adequate and diverse sources of revenue while also providing a high-quality editorial product, one that contributes to democratic consolidation and maturity." Similar problems in democratic media systems worldwide—too much sensationalism, a focus on breaking news, too little investigation—can often be described in economic terms. In Afghanistan, where the economy is not conducive to independent media, how can they be sustained financially without giving up editorial independence?

This is why hundreds of Afghan television and radio stations and newspapers are not sustainable. Most of the Afghan journalists interviewed for this book believed that the media sponsored by warlords, the Afghan government, and Iranian and Pakistani benefactors are much more likely to continue than the independent press that they prefer and largely work for. The independent press's funding is subsidized in some parts by Western governments and organizations, but the news professionals and journalists have editorial control of the news.[89] Even though warlord station audiences are limited to those warlords' main supporters, cannot attract advertising dollars, and are largely inconsequential to national public opinion, they are backed by powerful elements that will find the funding to maintain the stations to promote their own brands and agendas.[90]

One independent news group well positioned to survive is Saad Mohseni's Moby Media Group, as it has diversified globally. In addition to Tolo, Lemar, and Radio Arman in Afghanistan, the agency has outlets in five other countries, reaching 300 to 400 million people.[91] In 2014, its revenue was estimated to be $60 million. 21st Century Fox, formerly NewsCorp, has a 47.8 percent stake in the company. In a 2016 interview, Mohseni predicted his stations would remain and that there would be a near-term consolidation of Afghan independent television stations. But even with the current Ghani administration's support for a free press, donor money to underpin the country's security and development will be essential to independent journalism's survival. "There will be no economic growth unless there is security," Mohseni explained, "so no one will invest [in the news media]."[92]

Even if Afghanistan does not collapse into civil war and/or fundamentalist rule again, it will not develop a market to solely support independent media for decades and will likely remain reliant on international assistance. But by 2016, the majority of Afghans trusted their press more than their government.[93] More than 60 percent of the Afghan population was under the age of 25 and, as a result of the democratization of media and education, were more informed than past generations. The comfort of entertainment and the empowerment of information provided by the media have been fundamental to the country's democratic development, and U.S. reporters and officials have played a central role in that. Former Kabul-based *Wall Street Journal* reporter Maria Abi-Habib reflected in a 2017 interview:

> One of the things I always thought—for all of Americans' mistakes in Afghanistan—I always thought there were a few good things that came out of the occupation. One of them was an incredibly vibrant civil society . . . The government is very wary of what people think about them and say about them in public. Kabul may be a bubble, but it's very clear that the different protest groups and activist groups

do have an impact. When you think of Afghan journalists, that's one bright spot. People are consuming the media and wanting it— if they can read, they'll read it; if they can get TV reception, they'll watch the news. That is one of the biggest accomplishments of the U.S. or the international occupation, giving the tools to have a civil society, whether it be a women's activist group or a really strong journalist corps.[94]

The cohort of modern, independent Afghan journalists interviewed for this book agree.

5

The Modern Afghan Journalist

The media is the only place where I see democracy in Afghanistan

—SARDAR AHMAD, former Agence France-Presse reporter, 2012. He and members of his family were killed by the Taliban in 2014.[1]

AT THE END of most workdays, employees of Moby Media Group boarded a shuttle bus inside its secure compound in Wazir Akbar Khan to take them home to the outskirts of Kabul city. On the evening of January 20, 2016, it exited the metal gates and drove the equivalent of two city blocks when a Taliban fighter, hidden among end-of-the-day traffic, activated a bomb. It destroyed the bus in front of the Russian Embassy, killing 34 people: seven Tolo employees and 27 civilians who happened to be nearby.[2]

This was the first time the Taliban deliberately attacked a media institution, having labeled the Afghan news agency a "legitimate military target" three months before. Tolo had become a daringly progressive platform in the country, airing soap operas and talent programs alongside news bulletins and talk shows, most of which featured women. It was challenging traditional cultural norms at what some considered to be a breakneck speed and many conservative powerbrokers—national and local officials, warlords, and the Taliban—felt threatened. The Taliban especially deemed Tolo not only to be promoting "obscenity, irreligiousness, foreign culture and nudity" but also to be "an intelligence network opposing our national unity and our religious and national values."[3] They threatened Tolo in October 2015 after it reported that Taliban fighters kidnapped, raped, and executed women during the battle for the northern city of Kunduz.[4] The Taliban had briefly captured Kunduz before the Afghan National Army, with assistance from the U.S. military, uprooted and ran them out of the city, albeit temporarily. The Taliban also threatened Tolo's competitor, 1TV, for its reporting on the siege. The statement had read:

Tolo and iTV channels are . . . propaganda networks tasked with promoting the intellectual, cultural and information invasion of the infidels in Afghanistan. These networks, with the complete backing of the Americans, ridicule our religious and cultural norms, encourage obscenity and lewdness [and] inject the minds of youth with dangerous substances such as irreligiousness, immorality, violence, gambling, intermixing and profanity. Henceforth no employee, anchor, office, news team and reporter of these TV channels holds any immunity.[5]

The Taliban then called out Tolo in particular for what they considered to be exaggerated reports about the Taliban's treatment of Kunduz's citizens.

The reaction among Afghanistan's media leaders to the January 2016 attack was quick and defiant. Saad Mohseni, the CEO of Moby Media Group and creator of Tolo, stated: "The freedom to speak and the right to express ourselves is one that Afghans have fought too long for . . . the voice of Afghanistan will not be silenced by this incident."[6] Sediqullah Tawhidi, the head of Nai, an Afghan nongovernmental organization (NGO) that works to support the development of the Afghan independent news industry, similarly told the *New York Times*, "The Taliban think they can stop the wheel of the free press with such attacks. But our journalists have repeatedly shown that they cannot be stopped."[7]

Nearly two years earlier, the Kabul journalism community had also been rocked by the death of Sardar Ahmad, an entrepreneur who created Pressistan, a small business that helped foreign journalists navigate Afghanistan with local translators and fixers. He was also a reporter for the French international newswire, Agence France-Presse (AFP). On March 20, 2014, he was with his family at the Serena, a luxury hotel in downtown Kabul frequented by foreigners, when the Taliban opened fire on guests in the lobby and dining room, killing nine people. Among them were Ahmad; his wife, Humaira; and two of his children, Omar, age 5, and Nelofar, age 6. Miraculously, his 2-year-old child survived three gunshot wounds.[8]

The Taliban stated repeatedly that they did not target Ahmad and his family but that they were accidentally killed in the crossfire.[9] But it was no less a devastating blow to the Afghan journalism community. Three days after the attack, hundreds of Sardar's friends and media colleagues gathered on a hill overlooking Wazir Akbar Khan for a candlelight vigil to remember him and his family. His friend, Bilal Sarwary, later reflected: "We don't have people like Sardar growing on trees. We're losing people. The more people we lose in the media, the more we are deprived of hearing voices we would otherwise not hear." He continued, "Sardar had a unique way of reporting the news . . . he would talk about the street kids of Kabul and profile widows, and he understood the complexities of Afghanistan. He was not just a journalist; he was a bridge between Afghanistan and the West. He had influence."[10]

Tributes from politicians, including President Hamid Karzai and the warlord and future vice president Abdul Rashid Dostum, also poured in shortly after his death.[11] In his statement about the Serena attack, the president said: "The killing of [Sardar] Ahmad, his wife and two children is the biggest crime, and a painful tragedy. I offer my condolences and sympathies to his family, relatives, and all Afghan press."[12] Perhaps recognizing the symbolism of Sardar's death to the Afghan press and public, it was the only statement he gave about the victims.

Afghan journalists have been on the frontlines of their country's democratic development since 2001, propelled by a buzzing and emerging sense of freedom. While journalists worldwide disagree on what makes their practice professional, they largely agree on what they do not want: editorial interference and manipulation, and punishment for their reporting. They want to tell the truth and to have unfettered access to the publics they want to serve; they also want their institutions to provide the legal infrastructure and support for them to do so. In Afghanistan, news professionals interviewed believe that the media offer a pathway to justice and to modernity by bringing Afghans into contact with each other and with the world outside its borders.[13] They saw the news as an essential device to unify an Afghan nation fragmented by decades of conflict and to hold their new leaders accountable. They have become significant figures in Afghan public life, enough to generate statements of support from major political figures.

Yet to the Afghan journalists, such sentiment feels empty. While the Afghan government has supported them publicly, the journalists interviewed for this study believe it is because it is in their political self-interest to do so: They know that the press is popular with and trusted by the Afghan public, much more than the Afghan government. They also know that such government rhetoric is popular with the leaders of Western donor countries. But while they laud journalists' work and presence in Afghan society, officials have made slow efforts to institutionalize and regularly protect their freedoms.

The bulk of the Afghan journalists interviewed for this study felt powerless in making choices that will meaningfully change their lives.[14] They had high professional expectations of themselves, which they often had difficulty in meeting. Many of them received journalism training and education from Western organizations and agreed with the norms and philosophies that make up a professional press by those standards. They agreed, though, that they largely did not currently meet them.

In part, they cannot. They operate within a media landscape of warlord television, Taliban public relations professionals, payoffs from the Iranian and Pakistani governments, the disdain of Afghan officials, and fluctuating support and overall confusing signals from Western government officials who wanted to build a liberal democracy that included a strong civil society and a solid fourth estate. They found it difficult to stick to professional principles in such a complicated environment and to reverse the habits of rote, authoritarian-like reportage.[15] They wanted to hold power accountable, yet they felt consistently vulnerable toward it. Remarkably, however, they have made progress in creating new norms in Afghan government and society and are one of the most trusted institutions in the country.

Press Freedoms in Afghanistan

Nominally, the Afghan constitution and government institutions provide journalists with freedom of speech and legal safeguards to protect it.[16] The American and other Western governments helped to shape the contents of the Afghan constitution in 2003–2004 and, consistent with democratization norms, insisted on the promotion and protection of free speech. While President Hamid Karzai and President Ashraf Ghani have also lauded free speech as a basic human right, the news professionals have consistently lobbied the Afghan government to support their work.[17]

In the Afghan constitution, Article 50 grants citizens the right to access information from the government; Article 34 provides for freedom of speech and expression. However, while Afghanistan's Media Law permits anyone who can afford a license to establish media agencies, free speech is largely up for interpretation.[18] For instance, the law prohibits journalists from publishing "matters contrary to the principles of Islam and offensive to other religions and sects."[19] The ambiguity of this rule has allowed the Ministry of Information and Culture to order the detention of Afghan journalists, the shuttering of several privately owned media outlets, and the banning of radio and television programs.[20] This includes the 2010 government shutdown of Emrooz TV, a privately owned Dari-language station based in the western city of Herat that was well known for its fierce criticism of the Iranian government.[21] The ministry also banned the Pashto-language news website Benawa.com after it erroneously reported that former Vice President Mohammad Qasim Fahim had died in 2012.[22]

In early fall 2012, after a struggle between conservative elements in the government and more progressive journalists and civil society leaders, Afghan parliamentarians considered some amendments to the Media Law. One of them wanted to further increase government control over the media through a complicated set of regulatory bodies that would diminish free speech and ban foreign programming.[23] In response, a group of concerned journalists and civil society representatives, coordinated by Nai, drafted an alternative version that allowed for even greater transparency, more legal protection, and better libel laws. They prevailed and the more liberal amendment was adopted in 2013.

Despite the shaky legal foundation, Afghan journalists initially found encouragement from Karzai. Saad Mohseni offered that it was true the president would say, "Let them ridicule me; this is what a free press is all about." While he was tolerant of the Afghan news media, however, he would often become frustrated with Tolo, which spoke frequently about Karzai's lack of leadership over the economy, corruption, judiciary reform, and the bilateral relationship with Pakistan, Mohseni said. Karzai would not, however, actively interfere with the Afghan press's work nor would he try to control the content of the independent press.[24] Journalist Mujib Mashal explained in 2014, "Under Karzai, a relatively free press blossomed, but every time threats against it have emerged, they have been blunted not by the institutions or laws Karzai put in place, but by the president's personal intervention."[25] When officials in Karzai's government, however, challenged the Afghan press, Karzai did not always step in. As a result, heavy-handed government controls on radio, television, and newspapers continued and the progress remained uneven. This included his own chief of staff, Karim Khoram, maintaining his anti-Western television station, Kabul TV, while in office.

When Karzai left office in October 2014, the new national unity government made moves to further institutionalize press freedoms. Two months later, however, President Ghani signed the Access to Information Law, similar to the U.S. Freedom of Information Act (FOIA), which President

Karzai did not sign when it had been passed by Parliament in June. The law stated that government-held information should be available to the public except for information that would harm "national security, privacy, or interfere with a criminal investigation."[26] Ghani and the CEO of the Afghan government, Abdullah Abdullah, also endorsed a 12-point pledge of commitment that promised to support investigations and punish violence against journalists; in addition, they introduced a law addressing job security for journalists.[27] Remarkably, Parliament accepted that version with only minor changes.[28] In January 2015, further amendments to the Media Law created a new Media Complaints and Violations Investigation Commission that allowed for journalists and media freedom advocates to be represented alongside representatives from the Ministry of Information and Culture (MoIC). The older commission, which was directed only by government officials, was dissolved.[29] But much of the media's ability to operate will continue to depend on the personalities within the MoIC and the High Council, on the cooperation of the Afghan government, and on the overall security and economic situation.

By 2016, Afghanistan had not yet developed a norm and culture of press freedoms despite the rapid progress in building independent news media. Journalists did not work in a free environment and their work became increasingly dangerous.[30] As Sami Mahdi, a journalist who had worked for 1TV and Tolo, said in 2016: "It's complicated to be a journalist in Afghanistan. The rules of journalism are clear. But the rules of the game in Afghanistan are not very clear."[31] Afghan politicians and officials, warlords, and the Taliban regularly harass and intimidate reporters.[32] Roughly 50 Afghan and foreign media professionals were killed between 2001 and 2016: 67 percent of them were foreign, 33 percent of them were Afghan. Of the 50, 33 percent were killed in crossfire, like Sardar Ahmad; 22 percent while on assignment; and 44 percent were targeted, like the Tolo TV employees killed in January 2016, according to the Committee to Protect Journalists (CPJ).[33] Over these 15 years, there were 742 cases of violence against Afghan news professionals, which ranged from making threats against them to killing them. With the Taliban attack on Tolo, 2016 was the most dangerous year, with 114 cases, as documented by Nai.[34] The most cases were against Tolo TV (47), Ariana TV (32), 1TV (15), and the Pajhwok newswire (15).[35] In a listing of countries where journalists are killed regularly and governments fail to solve the crimes, CPJ ranked Afghanistan seventh, between Mexico and Pakistan, on its Impunity Index.[36]

For Afghan journalists, each day of work requires an extraordinary amount of courage. Western journalists in the country are at least afforded some sense of protection from discriminate killings due to the passports they carry. While they can be seriously injured or killed during larger attacks, government officials, warlords, and members of the Taliban and other extremist groups do not target them as much as they do Afghan journalists. They live in a climate of fear, restraint, and uncertainty, but they also often thrive within it. To be a modern, independent Afghan journalist means struggling to find truth within a complicated terrain of fundamentalists, strongmen, and corrupt officials, but also the gratification that you are helping to improve the quality of life for your fellow Afghans, increasing transparency and accountability, and legitimizing and socializing universal human rights norms of free speech.

Generating Change in Afghan Society and Government

For young Afghans eager to have a greater role in their country besides military service, journalism has provided a pathway. As Sami Mahdi explained, "It's not like the past where you had to wait until you were 40 or 45 years old to make an impact on Afghan society. This new media provides an opportunity for the new generation."[37] Yet the journalists are unsatisfied with their progress thus far and have worked vigorously to try to improve it. In 2016, at just 28 years old, Lotfullah Najafizada was Tolo's news director. "Afghans use the news media as a basis for their everyday [lives]," he explained, so he felt a great responsibility to provide them with information that could help them. Najafizada moved 30 news packages a day, relying on seven bureaus and 20 reporters and stringers throughout the country. He said, "We explain current events that matter to Afghans and want to look into Afghans' lives beyond the security situation," which is what the U.S. and other Western news media are more focused on.[38] And the Afghans trust them in return. As mentioned, 64 percent of the public has faith in the press—more than their elected officials, police, military, and even religious leaders. According to the Asia Foundation's surveys of the country, that trust was consistently high between 2011 and 2016.[39] "Afghans were silent for three decades," Najafizada said, but now "more than 1,000 people come on Tolo programs a year . . . They knock on Tolo's door when there is a problem, and we take this trust seriously. We do not want to abuse this power."[40]

To be informed about politics and society in Afghanistan no longer requires a formal education, the journalists agreed; the news media have educated a new generation and made information accessible to all, including the illiterate population, who make up roughly 30 percent of the country.[41] It's the news media's job, the Afghan journalists believed, to help their fellow citizens make sense of their government, their economy, and their nation. Since Afghans are vulnerable to politics and conflict, they take information very seriously.[42] They want their news media to monitor the government, promote a national identity, provide education, and give them hope that the country is progressing.[43] With the news media, Afghans can learn what it means to be a citizen, learn about their rights living within a democratic society, and learn how to seek justice within it, which they could never do before.[44] Through the press, the Afghan people see an opportunity to hold their leaders accountable, which they do not see in other institutions.[45] Because there is no nationwide, reliable justice system, one reporter explained in 2012, the press "has become a voice of the people."[46] Saad Mohseni's further explained in 2016, "Over time, we noticed that people saw the media as the pillar of society that ensured there were checks and balances. In essence, we were doing what Parliament should've been doing."

One indicator of the Afghan press's growing maturity is how they approached the country's elections between 2004 and 2014 and prepared the Afghan electorate for them. During the 2004 presidential election, Afghan journalism was too nascent to actively inform voters of candidates' platforms and to encourage them to vote.[47] In 2009, the press had improved but still provided few checks on the core candidates, Hamid Karzai and his former foreign minister, Abdullah Abdullah. By 2014, the most-watched television stations—Tolo, 1TV, and Ariana—planned voter education programming well in advance. In 2009 there was just one televised presidential debate, and Hamid Karzai did not attend. In 2014, Tolo alone planned three debates with Ashraf Ghani and Abdullah Abdullah on the economy, domestic issues, and foreign affairs. Since there was no precedent for debates inside the country and therefore no manual on how to conduct them, Najafizada and his colleagues wrote one.[48] The network also ran town halls across the country for a full year before the 2014 presidential election so that common Afghans could raise their concerns about the state of the country to inform candidates' platforms. In addition, the stations supported the Independent Election Commission's communication efforts to get information to the public. By vetting the candidates more thoroughly, challenging them to articulate their views and policies, and highlighting the concerns of the electorate, the journalists have become better guides to the democratic process.[49]

The journalists also work to inform citizens of their basic human rights.[50] Many of the television and radio journalists described their work as scouring the countryside to find people who will discuss their concerns publicly. Most concurred that journalists can steer the country in the right direction by reminding the Afghan public that they deserve not just competent elected representatives, but basic security and freedoms in their daily lives.[51] When asked about examples of their impact, roughly half of the journalists interviewed believed that the mere existence of the press acts as a deterrent against politicians' bad behavior.[52] Without the empirical evidence to prove it, the journalists agreed that the level of corruption in the government would be much higher without independent journalists, as Ministers of Parliament are wary of what the press could expose to the public.[53] As another Afghan reporter said in 2012, the media have acted as an "agent of change" since warlords, the Taliban, drug lords, and Afghan politicians are worried about the image-making power of the press and its popularity with the public. The fact that they have developed this fear and feel a sense of accountability is a positive in itself, they say.[54]

Despite this perceived impact, the Afghan journalists are also incredibly self-critical, hyperaware of their general lack of professionalism by the Western standards they see as being universal. They also attribute it, however, to the near-absence of a professional, independent press in the country for generations before and the scrupulous work of intentionally creating new norms toward transparency, accountability, and free speech.

Early into their development, the Afghan reporters would often use their interview time with Afghan officials to vent, even rant, about their problems and not probe the dignitaries for information, some of the Afghan journalists explained.[55] Over time, however, they have become increasingly adept at interviewing Afghan and Western officials; once timid in challenging authority, they have also become bolder in press conferences. In addition, they have learned to report breaking news and some have become particularly adroit in using social media platforms, especially Twitter, to report on suicide attacks, bombs, and shooting, providing a cable to foreign journalists everywhere reporting on the country.

Their core weakness in their work, the journalists believed, is the lack of analysis and investigative reporting. Many Afghan reporters think they need to strike parity, or balance, in a "he said, she said" style. As a result, news content can often echo official statements. The complicated worlds of the Taliban and other militant factions, which are all involved in some kind of organized crime to fund their activities, can be opaque and dizzyingly complicated to make sense of for the public.[56] If Afghan journalists do not investigate a story, it is often because they do not have the skills or resources to do so—or because they fear to try.[57] Investigative reports therefore tend to focus on safe topics, such as consumer issues like Afghanistan's traditionally costly weddings. Stories on the Taliban, warlords, drug lords, corrupt businessmen, and powerful officials are regularly off limits. The journalists felt the most frustrated with their inability to report on systemic levels of corruption, especially on the national and subnational levels. They explained that Afghan powerbrokers take accusations of corruption deeply personally, seeing them as affronts to their honor, and will not hesitate to intimidate and threaten the reporters in return.[58] While there are sparks of deep, investigative journalism on corruption and other issues, it is rarely consistent because reporters do not see their work as making an impact in terms of how society, business, and/or government runs. The newspaper *Hashteh Sobh* ("8 a.m.") and networks Tolo, 1TV, and Ariana especially have taken risks in exposing wrongdoings, but no officials or strongmen were arrested as a result, and policies did not change. They are therefore putting their social capital, credibility, personal safety, and professional security at enormous risk with little return.[59] As will be discussed in Chapter 7, this is why they value American and other Western reporting in the country.

There is also the issue of credible sources. During decades of conflict in Afghanistan, general lying became necessary for one's survival.[60] Dishonesty on issues of security and governance can therefore seem pervasive and finding facts is an immense challenge. Afghan journalists must identify sources who tell the truth and don't seek to manipulate them to advance their individual agendas. But since such sources are rare, many Afghan journalists sometimes rely on practices that Western journalists might not. For instance, and as will be explored more later, when reporting on the actions and motivations of the extremist factions like the Haqqani network, it is nearly impossible to verify the identity of people who claim to be spokespeople or leaders. Afghan reporters who choose to film interviews with those claiming to represent the networks often allow them to cover their faces with scarves and use names that could be fake.[61] The journalists usually know Taliban representatives only by their phone numbers or screen names on social media platforms, which means that they reach a collective of spokespeople instead of consistent individuals. And despite frequent statements of support from the Afghan government for the press as an institution, Afghan officials often lie to journalists, expecting them to report and disseminate their statements without question—or they ignore reporters altogether.

Press–State Relations in Afghanistan

Although Afghan officials frequently boast that the development of the Afghan press has been one of the country's greatest accomplishments since 2001, the journalists interviewed thought their reality was far from the image Afghanistan's statesmen wanted to project to the West. As previously established, President Hamid Karzai was the government's most vocal supporter of free speech and a free press during his tenure.[62] He reflected in 2016:

> I announced the freedom of the press to let them flourish and work.
> The laws were not quite there, just the decision to have the press
> work totally free. Whatever administration we had [in 2001] was
> still in the mindset of controlling the press and while there are still
> some limits, overall the trend is toward freedom and the courage
> to speak.[63]

The Afghan journalists agreed that they have had remarkable freedoms compared with the situations of their colleagues in the central and south Asian regions—especially neighboring Turkmenistan, Uzbekistan, Iran, and China. Unlike those countries, there is no official form of censorship in Afghanistan.[64] The Afghan constitution, Media Law, and Access to Information Act grant journalists some protection when they criticize the Afghan government, and indeed some of those interviewed said they were free to criticize the government as they like.[65] Yet there was broad consensus among the reporters interviewed that their president and members of the cabinet and Parliament—while often stating the importance of a free press to Western donors—simply didn't respect their role in government or their work.[66]

As Sami Mahdi explained, "The Afghan government celebrates press freedom, but they don't like it."[67] While Afghan officials "did their best to censor," press freedoms remained in the country because it was important to the Western donor countries.[68] Afghan government officials were often indifferent to actually engaging with Afghan journalists; they did not make an effort to explain their politics, policies, or laws.[69] Karzai himself rarely granted interviews, giving roughly four interviews to Afghan news stations during his tenure.[70] In 2004, when Tolo TV originally launched and did not yet have a reputation, Karzai granted them one interview; then he never met with them again.[71] The few interviews Karzai granted to Afghan news stations included one with Barhanuddin Rabbani's Noor TV, after Rabbani was assassinated in September 2011, and a 2012 roundtable interview with reporters from state-owned RTA; independent outlets Ariana and Shamshad TV; and Kabul News, which was owned by Karzai's chief of staff, Karim Khoram.[72]

In many ways, the interplay between Afghan reporters and officials is analogous to those in other countries with an independent press. It is not normal for reporters and officials to trust one another; while they both have missions to serve the public, the journalists' mission to keep government officials accountable can naturally create a defensive dynamic. When government spokespeople do communicate with Afghan reporters, they seek out the journalists who have proven to be the most deferential to government, or the reporters for the most popular outlets for legitimization and exposure to the public. Most journalists have to settle for simple and vague statements from government officials and are not offered the opportunity to ask questions outside of press conferences.[73] "If you are a journalist with good ties to an Afghan official, then you get better stories," one Afghan print journalist said in a 2012 interview, "and if you don't, you're treated like shit."[74] When officials do take the time to speak with journalists, they feel as if they are owed favorable coverage. When they are displeased with the reportage, they cut off journalists' access.[75]

With more than $10 million of U.S. government support, the Afghan government created the architecture for press–state relations with dozens of press offices and spokespeople within various Afghan government ministries.[76] The problem, many of the journalists concurred, is that the offices serve more as aspirational symbols for free speech, transparency, and accountability than as actual forums for substantive discourse.[77] The Afghan Government Media and Information Center (GMIC), for instance, which was created in 2007 with the help of Western consultants, was designed to make Afghan officials more accessible to Afghan and international press.[78] Over time, however, the officials working there became less responsive.[79] Press conferences were routine, but they were just platforms to deliver statements; officials rarely took and/or answered questions.[80] One Afghan journalist gave the example of the 2012 North Atlantic Treaty Organization (NATO) conference in Chicago about the military alliance's future involvement in Afghanistan. In preparation for it, the Afghan government delivered a statement that officials would be attending, but they did not share their agenda with Afghan reporters, nor did they allow them to ask any questions about the government's objectives for the meeting.[81] Then, closer to the end of the Karzai administration, Karzai's chief of staff Khoram used the GMIC to publicly denounce the United States. After Khoram downsized the GMIC staff from 130 to roughly 22 people, the U.S. embassy—which had renovated the center's building, complete with a state-of-the-art television studio, and subsidized the staff—pulled its funding.[82]

This institutionalized dismissal of the news media also extended to a disregard for the Afghan journalists' safety. When it came to protecting the reporters' basic rights and physical security, the Afghan journalists believed that officials deemed them to be unworthy.[83] Journalists described occasions when they or their colleagues felt intimidated by officials.[84] In contrast, as one Afghan reporter pointed out, American journalists feel safe with their government sources, and those sources feel safe with the journalists because they know they have a judicial system they can trust.[85] In Afghanistan, government officials don't just openly intimidate journalists, they also cannot protect them from warlords, the Taliban, and other extremists in the country. This contributes to the Afghan journalists' hesitation to investigate any malfeasance.[86] "If you are an Afghan journalist and you do investigative work, you come back in a coffin," one radio broadcaster said simply in 2012.[87] Despite the death of 17 Afghan journalists between 2001 and 2016, no one had properly investigated how they were killed.[88] The Afghan journalists' frustration with their government is in part an emotional reaction: They are angry because they don't feel as if their leaders recognize their value to society through their actions. At worst, officials and strongmen will threaten them physically, making them personally vulnerable; at best, they will cut off their access, making them professionally vulnerable, or ignore them altogether.

By 2017, Afghan reporters and officials had yet to settle into a constructive dynamic where information from the government was routinely provided and the journalists routinely were given opportunities to question it.[89] The strong legacy of authoritarianism and a persistent culture of deference to power are such that officials think questioning them is improper.[90] As mentioned earlier, however, the national unity government run by President Ashraf Ghani and CEO Abdullah Abdullah has worked more actively through a series of laws to institutionalize press freedoms. In 2015, Ghani also appointed Nader Nadery, a former activist and civil rights leader, as a Special Envoy to Press Freedoms, and many journalists noted improvements in palace press operations as a result. Yet severe distrust between reporters and officials remained and access to officials was still strictly controlled.[91] The Afghan officials and reporters regularly complained about each other's lack of professionalism and the disregard they show to one another.[92]

The Taliban, however, was very eager to engage with the Afghan press. Since 2006 in particular, the journalists agreed, the Taliban has been in closer contact with them than most Afghan government officials. They also were incredibly well focused with their messaging, crafting narratives and poetry that strongly and emotionally appealed to Afghans' pride and sense of national identity.[93] In the early days of the Afghan news media, the Taliban would appear on Afghan television.[94] While they rarely do so now, the spokespeople have become sophisticated in breaking news and have made themselves so accessible to the Afghan news media, the journalists largely agreed, that the Afghan government should be embarrassed.[95] "If something happens and I want to reach government officials and spokespeople I can't catch them, but if I want to reach Taliban they are always available through What's App, through Twitter, and you can call them," explained broadcast journalist Ahmad Mukhtar in 2016.[96] When an attack takes place, Taliban representatives send journalists messages via multiple platforms to take credit for it. While it's difficult to get spokespeople from the Ministries of Defense or Interior to talk about casualties, the Taliban spokesmen are eager to give their versions of the story.[97] For a response from the Afghan government, one print journalist pointed out in 2012, "you have to wait and wait and wait until the end of the day until they have a press release or send a spokesman to talk."[98] The twisted perception, the Afghan journalists said, is that the Taliban values them more than the International Security Assistance Force/NATO, the Western embassies, and the Afghan government do.[99]

But most Afghan journalists recognized that the Taliban communicated with them only on their own terms.[100] Their representatives make themselves accessible, but also regularly threaten and harass the reporters. "They will release a statement, and then call to ask why we are not releasing it right away. They do not understand that we are not their mouthpieces, that we need to have some balance," one radio broadcast journalist explained in 2012.[101] But the capacity of Taliban spokespeople to appear as polished media professionals can be chilling for the reporters: they are polite; they use good English in press releases; their website has a complete summary of news for the week, which they also email to journalists; and they refer to the (male) journalists as "sir" and ask them about their families.[102] Afghan government officials, on the other hand, do not convey their messages with the same efficiency and personal touch.[103] The journalists also point out, however, that while the Taliban representatives want to communicate with them, they also want to kill them. "I can see an increasing self-censorship in media now, more than before," Sami Mahdi explained in 2016. "Not just because of the change in the government but the pressure the Taliban is putting on the news media." He continued, "The Taliban inflicting violence on us is not a threat anymore, it is a reality. They are going to kill, as we saw on January 20th [2016]" with the attack on the Moby Media Group employees.[104]

Since Afghan journalists are constantly under threat and feel unprotected by the Afghan government, they habitually self-censor their work as they believe it protects their lives and those of their colleagues, while also sustaining their news agency as a business.[105] Self-censorship, however, has been regularly reinforced in Afghan culture for decades as the journalists are used to working within clear boundaries of authoritarian societies. One journalist explained in a 2012 interview, "There is a general belief [in the family and the tribe] that just a very select group of people should be informed, as too much freedom of information will interfere with security and progress."[106] In a 2016 interview, Sami Mahdi agreed: "When it comes to culture—religion, ethnicity, women's issues—we have much self-censorship. You feel more under threat and need to be careful about your own survival."[107]

By 2016, the daily act of reporting had become increasingly difficult as security deteriorated. News reports on sensitive issues—such as religious and ethnic rivalries, human rights abuses, corruption, or the drug trade—were often described in general terms, and journalists often opted not to pursue investigative reports that could get them jailed or killed.[108] One radio broadcaster emphasized that the best way to work around these limitations was to maintain the trust of the people and to prove to them that "our responsibility is to provide them with information without fearing anyone, or without biases."[109] The reporters interviewed overwhelmingly agreed that they are able to do with assistance from the U.S. government and U.S. reporters.

Contribution of the U.S. Government and U.S. Journalists to Afghan Journalism

Afghan news professionals insisted that they have received considerable support from U.S. and other Western reporters in the country. Bilal Sarwary, a longtime reporter who worked for the BBC, said in a 2016 interview, "The West has given us a generation of Afghan journalists. If the West had never come, we wouldn't have a press."[110] They have helped them both directly (by conducting trainings through NGOs or hiring Afghans as local reporters or fixers) and indirectly (by coming into contact with Afghan reporters at press conferences and other media events, and by producing information Afghan journalists can use as source material).

As discussed in Chapter 4, in order to meet the West's goals to develop a stronger Afghan civil society that contributes to a liberal democracy, a sizeable portion of aid money has gone to assisting the media. While the exact number is unavailable, the U.S. government spent more than $100 billion on reconstruction assistance, a tenth of which has gone to strengthening civil society between 2001–2016.[111] This is on top of the considerable U.S. public diplomacy funding that provided equipment, technical assistance, and program production support; in 2011, the public diplomacy money that funded such efforts peaked to roughly $180 million for that year, later trailing off and settling around $60 million in 2016. At least some of this funding has been distributed to NGOs or journalism schools in the country.[112] NGOs like the Institute for War and Peace Reporting, Internews, and Aina, a French photojournalism group, also contributed significantly to developing the local press corps, supplementing the subpar journalism education that was available at Kabul University, which was heavily influenced by the Soviets during their 10-year occupation of the country. Some foreign journalists who have never reported from Afghanistan have come to conduct media training through these NGOs. There is also on-the-job direct training for translators, fixers, and local reporters who work in international news bureaus. These local professionals have for decades been linchpins for foreign coverage of Afghanistan, as they feed news stories to the agencies when Western reporters are absent.

The local journalists for U.S. news agencies who were interviewed insisted that they were taught to be objective. As one said in 2012, "We were trained, we were not influenced. We were never told to do something that was in the interest of the American government or American media, and not the Afghan government or Afghan media. We were told to be impartial, to not take sides, and to tell the truth."[113] Yet there are few examples of Afghan reporters who have worked directly with the Western press and then moved on to work in the Afghan news media, meaning that their impact has not largely cascaded into the direct development of the local news media.

The Western press has, however, indirectly impacted the Afghan news media. By consuming U.S. news, the Afghan journalists have learned how to script a television segment and produce news stories. The Western reporters taught them "the rules and regulations of journalism. They taught us how to be precise and tell the story," another Afghan broadcaster said in 2012.[114] Many of the sensitive stories the Afghan press does run about tribal affiliations, language, and Islam—topics that were once off limits— are inspired by the Americans, the majority concurred.[115] As Lotfullah Najafizada emphasized in an October 2016 interview, "We shouldn't forget one fact: We have learned a lot from American journalists . . . They have inspired us with their audacity for questioning people, with their bravery. That is something we have inherited from them."[116]

Should American and other Western news bureaus be shuttered, though, Afghan journalists believed that the degree of self-censorship would increase and Afghans would be less likely to break news without the larger support network of the international news media.[117] While Afghan news agencies may continue, Afghan journalists also relied on their U.S. counterparts for agenda-setting, content, and moral support; they depended on the cover that the American and other Western outlets gave them to report on issues of corruption and other abuses of power.[118] "The Afghan media is an easy target, so we will lose momentum if we don't have the American media by our side," one Afghan print reporter explained in 2012.[119] Another agreed that year: "I cannot imagine Afghanistan without the *New York Times*, the *Washington Post*, and some of the British outlets. If they leave Afghanistan, journalism will die."[120] Without sustained Western media attention on the country, the consensus was that journalism would slip back under authoritarian controls as power brokers would feel emboldened to intimidate journalists and the press would become less progressive.[121]

The 12 Kabul-based U.S. journalists who have reported for U.S. news agencies over the years and were interviewed for this book largely congratulated the Afghan reporters for their accomplishments. Given that Afghanistan has a GDP of just $18 million and a per capita income ranking of 216 out of 228 countries in the world, they concurred that it was astonishing how many media outlets are in the country. With the Afghan journalists from Tolo TV, 1TV, Ariana, *Hashteh Sobh*, and Pajhwok doing particularly groundbreaking work, their counterparts believed that the Afghans have become increasingly powerful voices in their society.[122] However, the U.S. reporters had serious doubts about Afghan journalists' professional development and long-term sustainability. While they appreciate Afghan journalists' ability to quickly break news and offer story ideas, they tend to see them as in need of continued professional development. "Democracy is a novel concept in Afghanistan," one American print journalist explained in 2012. "Leaders don't know how to operate in a democracy, citizens don't know how to operate in a democracy, the media doesn't know how to operate in a democracy, and institutions are still in raw form."[123] They also agreed that the conditions they work within, most importantly the economy, need to substantially improve if the Afghan journalists are to make the impact on their government and society they are capable of.

The Afghan journalists' worldview, the U.S. journalists agreed, is also limited by their experience and the history of heavy government interference with the news media. Afghans journalists can fear breaking the cultural taboo of discrediting their elders. The American foreign correspondents stressed that Afghan journalists often accept certain information as truth without investigating or validating it, and their standard of proof can be different from that of American and Western journalists. For example, some local reporters for U.S. agencies often raise objections about the stories their peers are running about malfeasances committed by Afghan figures, saying that such stories will ruin their reputations. In turn, the American reporters must spend time explaining to their local staff, repeatedly, why the criticism is merited. "It's in Afghan culture that you don't put people on the spot," one U.S. print reporter explained in 2012.[124] Given that these conversations were happening within a Western news bureau, American journalists question whether Afghan reporters at local agencies will be willing to hold influential officials accountable without regular encouragement.

The majority of the journalists reporting for U.S. agencies agreed, however, that their Afghan peers were in a much more challenging position to report on their government and society than they were. Societal norms and the pervasive culture of intimidation and fear strongly affect their work.[125] The U.S. journalists, on the other hand, are entitled to laws and protections that their Afghan peers are not. In many developing countries, an American radio reporter emphasized, governments fear journalists and threaten them with harm; in the West, governments may see journalists as nuisances but they do not threaten them.[126] "Afghan journalists get in a lot of trouble," said Pamela Constable of the *Washington Post* in 2016. "They've been arrested and run into problems with blasphemy laws . . . most of the deaths of journalists in any country are war-related, but some are also targeted because they've been writing things that anger radical religious groups."[127] Carlotta Gall of the *New York Times* recalled being asked to appear on Afghan radio and television news shows to discuss stories about corruption and human rights that they could not physically or financially cover themselves:

> They were fairly frank, they said they couldn't report [a story] but they could report on my reporting. That's an old trick . . . In any country where there is censorship or heavy influence on media, that's how you broach sensitive subjects. Do a news roundup of Western media on issues, that's how you get around the censorship. You can still criticize the story, but your main aim is to air it.

The *Post*'s Joshua Partlow agreed that for emerging Afghan news agencies, "If you're going out on the limb to say the president's brother is corrupt, you're taking a big risk." It is therefore understandable that "they look to the Western press to cover this first and let them absorb some of the initial shock."[128] Maria Abi-Habib, who reported in Kabul for years with the *Wall Street Journal*, often received threats from powerful Afghans. "And if I got threats with the weight of being an American citizen and having an American newspaper behind me, I think a lot of Afghan journalists would have disappeared. I don't think it was very plausible for them to do hard-hitting investigative pieces . . . It's not because they're not good reporters," she explained.[129]

With the exception of India, Afghanistan's neighborhood does not offer examples of a pluralistic, free press that is socially responsible and challenges authority with impact. The American reporters concurred that the future of the Afghan press simply hinges on the Afghan economy and how the Afghan government continues to treat them and the legal infrastructure and protections they provide. If they crack down on freedom of speech and an independent press, then it will disappear; if they protect them, they will survive.

Still, however, the Afghan journalists have become bolder with time. One American print reporter believed that the best of the Afghan journalists "feel like their leaders ought to be criticized and held accountable the way we do when we cover Washington or any state capital." Rod Nordland of the *New York Times* agreed in 2016 that the Afghans have become "a little less intimidated by authorities and more willing to ask questions. They've demanded more access to the American authorities, military and otherwise, and I think they've gotten that."[130]

While the U.S. journalists did not think that the democratically elected Afghan government would revoke press freedoms after U.S. troops leave the country, the U.S. and other Western bureaus will likely dwindle, which could affect the quality of the Afghans' reporting. With the lack of a sustained, full-time Western news media presence in the country, there could be significantly less investigative news about the Afghan government or the country's strongmen. In many ways, the Afghan news media have pushed society to reform too quickly, the U.S. journalists concurred; Afghanistan's more popular television stations are "too American" and will likely regress into more government-friendly stations.[131] Constable predicts a reversal toward more conservative traditions, seeing the last 15 years as a "Western interlude" that was "somewhat artificial, not really wanted, and more of a money-making venture than a successful effort to reform and modernize." It will likely be remembered as an American-manufactured moment in time.[132]

By the end of 2016, much of Afghanistan was still embroiled in conflict, and a transition from fundamentalist to democratic rule was still under way. If security and the economy improve and the government remains democratic, then the quality and breadth of Afghan news could also continue to improve. However, if the Taliban returns or a civil war erupts again, then the independent news media will likely weaken, if not entirely collapse.[133] Afghanistan and its journalists are still deeply dependent on the West, especially the United States, for its financial and security support. What the U.S. government decides in terms of security assistance and funding for the media will considerably impact the course of the young Afghan independent press corps. The majority of the Afghan journalists agreed with their U.S. counterparts on this point.[134]

Despite the uncertainty, however, the Afghan journalists have helped to foster a new national identity, one that the Afghan people reinforce and respect.[135] A majority of the Afghan reporters were cautiously optimistic that the quality of the news media is moving in the right direction; they predict that journalists will become more professional with experience and, as Mohseni predicted, fewer—but higher-caliber—news organizations will survive.[136] The new generation of Afghan journalists is "very tired of conflict. They are very tired of wars," Ahmad Mukhtar explained in 2016. "They are trying to bring peace through their work. They are trying to overcome conflict."[137] While being a journalist in Afghanistan is difficult, one broadcaster said in 2012, "It is up to us to take opportunities and rise to challenges. It is not easy, but we can do it."[138] Sami Mahdi agreed, saying that this more progressive era of Afghan journalism is a "source of inspiration that our generation has a chance to show ourselves, to prove to ourselves that we can be part of the change, that we could play a role in shaping the country. It gave us room to breathe."[139]

Yet there is a concern that, despite the optimism and clear successes the Afghan news professionals have enjoyed, the press is helping to create expectations for a secure and prosperous Afghanistan that the Afghan government and the international community cannot meet.[140]

Tolo TV on-air reporter and anchor Shakila Ebrahimkhil overcame a lot to become one of Afghanistan's most recognized journalists. Married as a teenager during the Taliban years, her husband died young and she looked after her elderly parents and children at home. After 2001, she got a formal education and pursued journalism in part to expose the pervasive human rights abuses in the country, especially toward women. She produced features on child brides, like she once was, and focused on the victims of suicide attacks. "I suffer a lot," she told the BBC in April 2016. "Maybe it's because I am a mother. I try to control my emotions, but it's not possible. I'm a mum, too, you know. I'm worried about the future of these kids. When I see these kids, I think of my own children. I understand that the future won't be good for any of them."[141]

She reported on the January 20, 2016, suicide attack against her colleagues at Moby Media on the air. "I wanted to scream and cry with each name I read," she later said.[142] But she added, "We believe the suppression of Tolo means the suppression of freedom of speech in Afghanistan. And we won't let the people of Afghanistan feel that."

A few months later, Ebrahimkhil left Afghanistan to raise her children in Turkey. One cannot blame her, and she is in good company: According to Nai, between mid-2015 and mid-2016, 300 Afghan journalists, 60 of them female, left Afghanistan.[143] Others see the reporting constraints to be too stifling but are staying in Afghanistan and choosing more lucrative government appointments or jobs with Western NGOs instead.[144] Some insist that because of the popularity of the news media in the country, droves of young Afghans stand ready to take their place.[145] Ryan Crocker, a former U.S. ambassador to Afghanistan from 2011–2012, noted how important it is to remember "how long it took the U.S. to develop the media as an institution with safeguards and protections and also to develop a media that was independent, that was not being pressured to fly the flag for one side or another."[146] The U.S. correspondents have impacted the development of Afghan reporters. But ultimately, as longtime AP reporter in the region Kathy Gannon emphasized, the continued story of journalism in Afghanistan "depends on Afghans, not outsiders."[147]

6

U.S. Correspondents in Afghanistan

As the crisis in the country deepened, the Westerners would segregate themselves and retreat into their compounds, building a separate world in Kabul, free of the hassles of Afghanistan, free of Afghans

—kim barker, former *Chicago Tribune* correspondent in Afghanistan and Pakistan, 2003–2009, as quoted in her book, *The Taliban Shuffle* [1]

ON FEBRUARY 22, 2010, the *Washington Post* broke a story that the leaders of Afghanistan's first private bank, Kabul Bank, were essentially running a Ponzi scheme. The bank's founder and chairman, Sherkhan Farnood, Andrew Higgins reported, was giving multimillion-dollar loans to members of Karzaï's family, his administration, and his supporters to buy luxury villas in Dubai.[2] "What I'm doing is not proper, not exactly what I should do. But this is Afghanistan," Farnood told him.[3]

The bank, which had President Karzaï's brother Mahmoud Karzai as a shareholder and a board member, grew rapidly from $5 million to more than $980 million in assets in five years. By 2010, it had big plans to grow its presence within and outside of Afghanistan, especially in central Asia. Higgins found that most of the bank's shareholders had multiple properties in Dubai, with Farnood alone having 16. The city, however, had been suffering a financial crisis that began in 2009. Each property was highly exposed and vulnerable to Dubaï's faltering housing market. Kabul Bank's investment in helping Afghan's richest and most powerful find comfort outside of Afghanistan was, Higgins wrote, evidence of "a crony capitalism that enriches politically connected insiders and dismays the Afghan populace."[4]

The story initiated a firestorm. After it initially broke, the *Post*, along with the AP, *New York Times*, and *Wall Street Journal* covered the fallout consistently for nearly two years, ensuring that it was repeated in Afghan news as well.

Higgins had spent months investigating the story, working to follow the money from Kabul to Dubai. Once the Obama administration began its tenure in 2009, the relationship between the United States and Afghanistan had become thick with tension. After President Karzai emerged heavily scathed from the 2009 election, corruption became the principal news story for the U.S. press. *Washington Post* reporters, including Higgins and Joshua Partlow, had heard whispers of wrongdoing at Kabul Bank from U.S. officials. However, it was the reporters who told the officials the extent of the corruption.[5]

On January 23, a month before the article was published, the U.S. Department of Treasury attaché at the U.S. Embassy in Kabul met with Higgins, who alarmed him about the scope of Kabul Bank's activities and the amount of money involved. A February 2010 cable from the embassy, later released by WikiLeaks, warned other American officials about the upcoming *Post* article:

> Depending on the severity of the article, its publication could significantly shake the public's confidence in the Afghan financial sector and lead to backlash from international coalition partners . . . A failure of either bank would have a significant negative impact on the development of the country's economy, in turn severely undermining the U.S. Mission's goals in Afghanistan.[6]

By 2010, the United States had invested more than $40 billion in the country to keep the economy afloat. It's been estimated that through the Kabul Bank alone, more than $900 million left the country. Later, Afghan officials were able to recover just 10 percent of it. "It was a big amount of money that had been stolen, compared to how much money Afghanistan had," Partlow later said in a 2017 interview. Further investigation by Partlow found that the bank was a Ponzi scheme from the outset.

Over time, the story faded, but then Afghan officials and businessmen affected by the bank's pending collapse started to talk openly to U.S. journalists with the hope that the U.S. government would come to their rescue. In 2012, Mahmood Karzai approached U.S. reporters in Kabul, an American print reporter recalled, and said: "Write this down—the Americans need to bail us [the Kabul Bank] out." His rationale was that the U.S. government had saved America's major banks in 2008 during the

U.S. financial crisis and should do the same for the Kabul Bank. The story was almost dead, the reporter explained, "but then the corrupt brother of the president called for an American bailout of the bank . . . so that kept the story alive" in the U.S. news media.[7]

The Special Representative to Afghanistan and Pakistan, Marc Grossman, at the time reflected that the scandal changed U.S. policy: "If Kabul Bank hadn't been exposed, we might never have focused so closely on it. . . . This made the Kabul Bank story important and therefore made corruption even more important to the policy agenda."[8] To make sure the economy stayed afloat, the U.S. government kept investing in the country, but there wasn't even an argument among U.S. officials about whether they should directly bail out the bank.

In 2012, a partner in the Kabul Bank, Khalilullah Frozi, shooed away *New York Times* reporters Matthew Rosenberg and Graham Bowley, who had approached him as he was having lunch at an upscale restaurant in Kabul. The American press, Frozi said, had "destroyed the bank."[9] The U.S. press eventually moved on, but in 2014, days after taking office, President Ashraf Ghani ordered the Supreme Court to reopen the Kabul Bank case, sending a signal that his new administration was taking corruption seriously, and ensuring the issue received continuous coverage in the Afghan and U.S. news media.[10]

This is the kind of investigative story, the Afghan journalists said, they could not report without the small cohort of correspondents for U.S. news agencies. As mentioned in Chapters 2 and 3, U.S. investigative reporting about the world is rare, but the protracted U.S. presence in Afghanistan has meant some U.S. correspondents have been exceptionally dedicated to the Afghanistan story. With the dearth of U.S. news agencies' foreign bureaus—for instance, between 1998 and 2011, 20 print agencies shuttered theirs—it is impressive that at least five U.S. news agencies (*New York Times, Washington Post*, NPR, *Wall Street Journal*, and AP) kept Kabul bureaus open with full-time senior correspondents by 2016.[11] The quantity of reporters for U.S. agencies in the country has oscillated between roughly six and 30, depending on where Afghanistan ranked in priorities for the American president. Over the years, they have been responsible for reporting on more than 1,000 American diplomats, 100,000 American soldiers, and 30 million Afghan citizens. By deciding what's news primarily for the American people, and secondarily for Afghans and other foreign publics, they became a small but powerful community of storytellers.

We know from scores of communications studies that U.S. foreign affairs reportage is likely be periodic, to have a dramatic quality, to promote U.S. interests, and to contrast a country's values with American values. The developing world is largely left off the news agenda, unless there is a disaster or an atrocity that shocks the world, or if U.S. troops are involved in a war in the country.[12] And when it comes to wartime, journalists' definition and framing of foreign events and issues can largely reflect the sociological constraints they face in trying to do their jobs.[13] Given that sometimes the best way to see a war up close is under the protection of the U.S. military, it can also provide for nationalistic, sometimes patriotic, news coverage.

The post-9/11 war in Afghanistan, though, provides a unique case. There are few examples of a robust, steady presence of Western correspondents in a country where professional journalism and an independent news media ecosystem were simultaneously emerging for the first time. As noted in Chapter 5, correspondents for American news agencies have directly and indirectly helped to shape the habits and practices of the Afghan press. Just as the American news media reflect the American nation, the Afghan press has reflected the Afghan nation. To better understand it, the U.S. reporters and their local colleagues often looked to Tolo, 1TV, Ariana, Pajhowk, and *Hashteh Sobh* for story ideas, and the Twitter accounts of specific journalists for breaking news. But correspondents for U.S. news agencies in Afghanistan had more influence with both Afghan and American officials than their local peers, and they were more likely to create the information environment that helped to shape relations between the United States and Afghanistan. This chapter explores how the U.S. journalists influenced Afghan news, while looking more deeply at how the Afghans have followed American news about their country.

Being a U.S. Correspondent in Afghanistan

Finding truth in Afghanistan as a foreigner is incredibly difficult work. As in any modern conflict environment, correspondents already face a host of limitations, such as restrictions on their travel and movement, language and cultural barriers, and the pressures of delivering content for a 24-hour digital news cycle.[14] Journalists also must stay relevant to both their subjects in the field and their editors and producers back home, often having to abide by what Mark Pedelty described in his study of foreign correspondence as "two clocks."[15] These are formidable constraints, and efforts to overcome them require resources and time that they often do not have.

Since 2001, the U.S. news bureaus in Afghanistan have traditionally included one to three foreign correspondents, with the *New York Times* consistently having the largest presence. No reporting could happen without their Afghan colleagues. Local Afghan reporters, also referred to as fixers or stringers, support the full-time staff reporters at the bureaus by helping them to gather and translate information, arrange travel, coordinate interviews, check facts, and draft copy. Many U.S. foreign correspondents must also cover two countries or entire regions for their news agency, as was the case with many journalists covering Afghanistan and Pakistan at once. For them—and the parachute journalists who are based in the United States or another region entirely—their local colleagues are indispensable. But even with this assistance, foreign correspondents mostly convey what they can determine in a haze; the inevitable murkiness and uncertainty of conflict can yield confused reports throughout large swaths of the country. The final copy is not necessarily a full, accurate representation of reality but rather represents highlights of the attributes that are available to the reporter.[16]

A reporter can physically be in only one place at one time.[17] In Afghanistan, reporters are largely based in Kabul, but news stories, especially security ones, often unfold in the countryside, which can be difficult to access. Several print journalists for major U.S. newspapers emphasized for this study that while they could travel frequently around Afghanistan in earlier years, by 2012 they were less able to do so, especially in the volatile south and east, due to threats to their personal security. Leaving the relative safety of Afghanistan's major cities demands meticulous and time-consuming planning with local staff and, if resourced well, their security detail. Therefore, much coverage of this enduring conflict is not based on what writers observe firsthand or who they can interview in person, but what they can derive from their sources and local colleagues at a distance.[18]

Traditionally, U.S. journalists focus on events in the capital and thus can deliver a narrow definition of the country to consumers, often filing a news story about a part of the country they have never visited.[19] One example was the March 11, 2012, story of the murder of 16 Afghan civilians by Army Staff Sergeant Robert Bales. He killed them in their sleep in Panjwai, a dangerous district in Kandahar province.[20] The massacre made global news, yet no U.S. correspondents traveled to Panjwai to get a firsthand perspective of its aftermath. "I don't blame anyone for not going to the place," an American print journalist explained in 2012, as it would have been especially dangerous for an American to visit there at the time. "It was good that American readers had a rough idea of what was happening, but the great stories that could've been done if they went to Panjwai just weren't done. No one could write the human stories of the families and people who were affected," he lamented.[21] The Kabul-based U.S. journalists interviewed believed that despite their restricted movement they could still report on the facts, but they felt very limited in providing any further analysis without witnessing the local impact events have. And Afghan journalism did not provide enough color on these issues for them to expand their reporting. A majority said they wanted to give as much depth to Afghanistan as they could, but the war is different from other modern wars in the sense that it is a low-intensity, chronic conflict.[22] It can be maddening for the journalists to decipher, independent of the U.S. military, who is winning and who is losing, and the totality of the impact it is having throughout the country and the region and on U.S.–Afghan relations.

The U.S. journalists are also not necessarily the final decision-makers on what they publish. They pitch stories to their U.S.-based editors or producers, who are removed from the foreign correspondent's day-to-day reality, before writing them; the editors and producers also must review the stories before they go to print or are broadcast. Since the editors and producers need to pick from a mosaic of domestic and global content for a news agency, the correspondents also need to be able to argue why a certain story matters more than another.[23] Sometimes foreign correspondents can be told not to bother with a certain story because of the limited space available for foreign news reporting and/or because it is not seen to be relevant or important for the agency's audience.[24] Editors or producers can also be influenced by their competitors' coverage, which is also known as inter-media agenda-setting. They may not accept news stories offered by their correspondents unless they have already been reported by other prestigious organizations, the *New York Times* in particular, and deemed by the journalistic community to be salient.[25] Rod Nordland, the *Times*' Kabul bureau chief in 2016, agreed, saying, "frankly the Times has become so dominant . . . I don't think about what the [Washington] *Post* is doing or what the *Wall Street Journal* is doing." He mainly thinks about what will play well for his editors.[26]

However, the Kabul-based U.S. journalists agreed that their U.S.-based editors largely did not restrict their story choices.[27] Debates between the reporters and their editors often focus on the salience of a news story and how to frame it. As one print journalist for an elite newspaper explained in 2012, her conversations with her editor are about:

> What are we really trying to tell? Is this a corruption story, or a favoritism story? If it is corruption, to what extent is the U.S. complicit? It's a fairly sophisticated conversation over how to tell the story. It is rare that a story is ordered up. It happens once in a while; [the editors] will say, for instance, that we need an analysis on why Karzai is going after Pakistan. But it's mostly a topic, and not what the story should say. There is a distinction there.[28]

The pressures involved with selecting and framing a news story are also palpable in the newsroom back home. Doug Schorzman, a foreign editor at the *New York Times*, explained that there can be "a lot of error and misjudgment and complete wrong-headedness that enters at the editing level."[29] He said that editing global news stories is a humbling experience, and he often stays awake at night wondering if his edits did harm to the reporters and/or the story's subjects.[30] Editors must adjust not only for the reporter's potential bias, but also for editorial bias that can happen. They must also try to address their blind spots, especially those that derive from their own sense of national identity and how they are influenced by U.S. officials and the American public. To get closer to the truth, Schorzman explained, they must work to identify their unconscious bias and focus on the story's substance and frame with reporters.[31]

The Afghan journalists who consume U.S. news about their country appreciate the dilemmas foreign news professionals face. The on-the-ground realities of Afghanistan compel U.S. and other Western journalists to make quick calculations and analyses of the small slice of Afghan life they experience. When Afghan journalists are disappointed by U.S. reporting (which will be mainly explored in Chapter 7), they largely understand that there are security and time constraints that are outside of the reporters' control. Afghanistan's instability makes journalists highly immobile, and those U.S. reporters who venture into combat areas are often embedded with American troops.[32] The experience of being embedded with the U.S. military, an Afghan broadcast journalist said in 2012, offers only a "filtered version of reality" for the American correspondents. But he also sympathized with them: "How else do they get the coverage? It's better than nothing."[33] While they do not face the regular barrage of threats Afghan journalists do, U.S. journalists can't travel as freely as their Afghan peers, another Afghan radio reporter noted, because "It is dangerous for them to go to the villages and really find the reality. Because they will become kidnapped, they will be arrested, they will be killed."[34]

While the majority of attacks on Western correspondents happened in 2001, there were a few that have considerably affected the small Western press corps since then. In November 2008, the Taliban kidnapped *New York Times* reporter David Rohde, whose work was featured in Chapter 3, along with his Afghan reporting colleague Tahir Ludin, and their driver, Asadullah Mangal, and held them in captivity in Pakistan. In June 2009, Rohde and Ludin escaped; Mangal escaped a month later.[35] In June 2016, NPR photojournalist David Gilkey and Zabihullah Tamanna, his Afghan colleague, were killed when their convoy was targeted by Taliban attackers in the southern Helmand province. They had traveled there to assess the effectiveness of the Afghan National Army, which had recently taken over from U.S. forces for the security of southern Afghanistan. Gilkey had been traveling to Afghanistan nearly every year since 2001.

On April 4, 2014, the AP's Kathy Gannon and Anja Niedringhaus were in Khost, an eastern province, covering the Afghan presidential election. They were accompanying a convoy of ballots from Khost to a Taliban stronghold on the outskirts. They were under the protection of Afghan National Security Forces and sitting in a car when an Afghan policeman yelled "Allahu Akbar" and fired on them with an AK-47. Niedringhaus died immediately. Gannon was hit with six bullets in her left arm and shoulder, in addition to her right hand. Hamid Karzai called in a helicopter to medevac her to Kabul. "Honestly, I've thought it through so many times—I know neither Anja nor I would have done anything differently . . . Neither Anja nor I would ever accept to be forced out by some crazy gunman," Gannon said in an October 2014 interview. "There's history still to be told there."[36] In January 2016, while taking a break from the multiple reconstruction surgeries she needed for her arm and hand, she returned to Afghanistan for the first time since the attack. She explained in a 2017 interview, "I needed to go back and make sure they knew that I didn't look at the country any differently."[37]

Afghan journalists acknowledge the limitations U.S. correspondents face and the exceptional commitment some have had to reporting on the country. They reserve their criticism for reporters who do not seem to try very hard to immerse themselves in the language and culture of Afghanistan. Foreign correspondents need time to build relationships, but they also need to try to understand the culture, history, and language—essentially, what makes Afghanistan a nation—to provide in-depth and comprehensive reporting. Bilal Sarwary, a local reporter who has worked for both ABC News and the BBC, explained it like this:

> I'm very positive about [the U.S. foreign correspondents]. I like them. But few of them had made an effort to learn the language, and if you don't speak the language, there is not much you can do. Then, once they know the country better, they have to leave . . . In Afghanistan, your biggest asset is people and relationships matter significantly, yet the Western journalists did not believe in contact development, in building relationships. They socialized among themselves, not with Afghans.[38]

The other Afghan journalists agreed that Americans and Western news professionals in Kabul foster their networks in the expatriate community and use them for stories and quotes that may resonate best with their audiences. As one Afghan broadcaster said in 2012, "they are not valuable in explaining Afghan society . . . they cannot explain the ordinary Afghan."[39] This is particularly the case for parachute journalists who drop into the country episodically, or national security beat reporters who often write from New York or Washington. Those reporters, the Afghan journalists interviewed concurred, have the comfort of writing thousands of miles away, in safe cities, and as a result they make many mistakes about Afghanistan.[40] The journalists who come the closest to understanding the country are the ones who have lived there consecutively for years, and/or who continue to return to Afghanistan for long stretches of time.[41]

Many of the journalists for U.S. news agencies agree that this is a weakness of their press corps. "I've never had much time for the people who said, like Karzai is now saying, that we're the mouthpiece for the West," said Carlotta Gall of the *New York Times* in an interview. "I think I've always tried to avoid being the voice of America, because I don't see that as my job. But I do feel quite a lot of foreign reporters, or reporters who come to a country for a short stint, they rely on briefings [from Western governments or the UN] so much or they come with an idea in their head already."[42] This became especially grating for her in 2009, when a sudden influx of reporters had arrived after she had been reporting from there for nearly eight consecutive years. Like Gannon, Gall is also a non-American reporter working for a U.S. agency, and had spent years trying to "give a voice to the Afghans." Gall continued, "I spent an awful lot of time going around the country and talking to ordinary Afghans. It's partly because the officials weren't so easy to get to but also because you started to get bored with the difficulties or the briefings, which didn't always match what you were seeing. I was always slightly on the Afghan side anyway."[43]

NPR's Anand Gopal was another U.S. journalist mentioned by some of the reporters who went to extraordinary lengths to understand the Afghan point of view. Gopal spent years writing *No Good Men Among the Living: America, the Taliban and the War Through Afghan Eyes*, and embedded himself with the Taliban. The ability to write with that kind of empathy comes from experience, the *Washington Post*'s Joshua Partlow emphasized: "You need people to take the time to see things from Afghans' eyes rather than just go on a U.S. military embed." He continued:

> There are definitely a million layers of Afghan society I didn't understand and that I wasn't privy to. You hardly ever get to interview women, for example . . . I didn't speak the language, I relied on translators. Obviously, as a foreign correspondent you're not going to be as in tune with all the different nuances of Afghan life. What you can do, whether U.S. or Afghan, is try to be empathetic to what's happening to Afghan civilians in a war zone.[44]

Former *Wall Street Journal* reporter Maria Abi-Habib similarly reflected, "For me, my biggest regret was not trying to understand Afghans from their own point of view but a foreign point of view, which I think was unfair." It was also difficult, she said, because "I wrote for an American audience that wanted things from a very specific perspective or lens."[45]

Afghan Journalists Newsgathering Habits with American News

Since 2001, Afghans have had firsthand experience with members of the U.S. military, diplomatic corps, and aid workers representing western nongovernmental organizations (NGOs). But to understand the larger political game at play, elite Afghan journalists have also developed perceptions of the United States from American newspapers and television agencies, mostly delivered via the Internet. They look daily to U.S. news websites to gather information directly related to Afghanistan, Pakistan, or the larger South Asia region. Afghan reporters are not normally looking to cover

America as a country, though, and therefore do not pay much attention to U.S. domestic news.

The *New York Times* and *Washington Post* hold a prominent place in Afghan journalists' newsgathering routines.[46] The Afghan reporters also said that they rely on the AP, the *Wall Street Journal*, and magazines like *Time* and *Newsweek*.[47] This is consistent with Stephen Hess's findings in the 1990s that to understand U.S. government attitudes toward the world, foreign reporters most often turn to the *Post* or the *Times* because they believe U.S. government officials talk to these papers the most, and because the reporters from these institutions are so comparatively well resourced. In addition, because most journalists who work for them are American or hold a passport from another Western country, they are protected by their government officials as citizens and can therefore publish what Afghan reporters are afraid to.[48]

The Afghan journalists began this habit in 2001. As noted in Chapter 3, the frequency of U.S. news in Afghanistan has oscillated significantly since then. The influx of U.S. news in 2009, indexed to President Obama's decision to increase the troop levels and funding for the war, was especially helpful for the Afghan reporters in making sense of the U.S. government's intentions.[49] Between 2009 and 2013, Afghans also looked to broadcast news outlets, CNN, NBC, CBS, and ABC, because they were reporting on the country more regularly and therefore had more content on their digital sites and social media platforms.[50] Several of the Afghan journalists interviewed mentioned that they would also occasionally follow Fox News to get a sense of conservative voices in the United States, and the opposition view to President Obama's administration, but they would not look to it for coverage of Afghanistan.[51] The Afghan reporters continued to follow the U.S. news for stories about Afghanistan in 2016, but with increasingly less coverage, the Afghan news media had less to quote from. When the elite U.S. press reports on the country, however, Afghan journalists continue to repeat it in Afghan news.[52]

Directly and indirectly, the Afghan public has learned about U.S. military initiatives, regional diplomacy, their own Afghan government, and the actions of various power brokers inside the country and the South Asia region from the U.S. news media. When it comes to local issues, Afghan journalists set the news agenda, but for issues at the national or regional level, the Western—mainly the U.S.—press has had more influence.[53] Even news reports on debates about Afghanistan and Pakistan in Washington, such as think tank and U.S. government reports, which tend to matter mostly to the wonky policy community in the United States, make their way to the country.[54] Stories about the Afghan government, drug lords and warlords, and U.S. government decisions and politics about Afghanistan and Pakistan have all been required reading. Sometimes news about NATO's International Security Assistance Force's (ISAF) military offensives are too, although stories focused narrowly on U.S. troops are not, according to the Afghan journalists interviewed.[55]

As the independent Afghan press was beginning to take shape, U.S. news stories would often be relayed verbatim in Afghan broadcast and print news.[56] At one point, the Afghan journalists said, roughly 50 percent of the content in local newspapers was from foreign sources, especially the *Times* and the *Post*.[57] Radio broadcasters would similarly read aloud from translated versions of the same papers. Several of the Afghan journalists interviewed emphasized that Tolo TV especially would routinely report on U.S. news.[58] One Afghan radio broadcaster explained, "Half of the leading news on Afghanistan's most-watched stations is from Western media. Like, 'Karzai spoke with the *New York Times* and he said this'."[59] American news was also of value not just because it conveyed the views of their officials, but because it indicated how U.S. foreign policy would affect their country and their lives in the future.[60]

American news agencies have influenced the wording and imagery of Afghan news, with Afghan television receiving raw imagery from television wire services like Associated Press Television (APTV) and then rebroadcasting it. "We literally get our picture of the war from Western media outlets, because Afghan journalists don't go—or don't dare—visit battlefields," an Afghan broadcaster emphasized in 2012.[61] Imagery created for an American or other Western audience can be recycled for an Afghan one with little adaptation. With APTV, "some of the footage shows patriotic images of American soldiers in combat." Some is reshown legally, through subscriptions; some is pirated. As a result, an Afghan reporter said, "the picture of the war that the American media want the American public to see ends up being shown to the Afghan public." By 2016, as Afghan broadcast journalists, producers, and cameramen became more skilled, they increasingly generated their own coverage. Western-shot B-roll footage of the war, however, was still known to be used on Afghan television.[62]

Most Afghan journalists said they would use the facts American journalists reported as the foundation and/or inspiration for a story, but then, through local angles, they would produce follow-up stories that they felt safe pursuing.[63] This has especially been the case with investigative news reports like the Kabul Bank story.[64] If the reporters saw news broken by the *Post* or the *Times* especially, they would try to verify it with their local sources and then highlight the facts, discard the U.S. news frame, and frame it with an Afghan perspectives.[65]

Other times, U.S. news can be used to launch editorials or, more commonly, become fodder for the talk shows, which are inexpensive to produce and have become popular programming for Tolo, 1TV, Ariana, and multiple other networks, including the warlord stations. One broadcast journalist explained that if there was a negative story in the *New York Times* about an Afghan official, then producers for a major channel would often collect experts to talk about it during a televised roundtable.[66] The Afghan journalists also pay attention to U.S. news agencies' editorials, columns, and op-eds to gauge U.S. public sentiment about their country and the war, and then tell the Afghan public what "America" is thinking.

Yet this reliance on the American and other Western press was more prominent between 2001 and 2014. By 2016, while the U.S. press still had some agenda-setting power, the Afghan press had become more competent and relied less on Western content. Tolo News anchor Sami Mahdi explained, "Earlier, whenever there was an article from the *Washington Post* or the *New York Times* on Afghanistan, it would affect not just media in Afghanistan but Afghan politics as well." By 2016, however, the American news media had less of an impact. Mujib Mashal, an Afghan citizen who is a full-time senior correspondent for the *New York Times*, believed that the *Times* still had an agenda-setting function with the local press in 2016, but television did not relay its direct content (although radio, print, and digital media often would). As an Afghan national, sometimes he would catch mistakes in translations and call the reporters personally to correct them. Because of its habitual citation, Mashal said, many in the Afghan public know what the *New York Times* is even though they have never directly read it themselves.[67]

Yet while Afghan journalists were becoming even more independent and capable in 2016, the U.S. press still had more access to information from policymakers than the Afghan journalists did. Mahdi said in 2016, "Maybe because of their experience and techniques to convince parties to give up information to them, maybe because of their credibility. But Afghan officials who want to leak information still prefer to give it to the Western press."[68] And Afghan reporters still counted on these news stories for a different perspective on their country, America, and the entanglement of both.[69]

Afghan Officials' Pursuit of U.S. Journalists

As long as they relied on Western donors for the country's stability, the Afghan and American journalists agreed that Afghan government officials would remain fixated on the attitudes of the U.S. news media toward them. They gravitate toward U.S. journalists when they want to make news internationally and at home. At times, they chased U.S. reporters in the country and pressed them to report information that would cater to their political agendas. The Afghan journalists emphasized that their Western peers had far greater access to Afghan government representatives than they did; the U.S. journalists acknowledged that they indeed often had unfettered access to Afghan politicians and cabinet officials. In 2012, an American broadcaster said that the preference for speaking to Western reporters is common throughout the developing world:

> When you go to these events and all you see is Western media, you think that they are intentionally bypassing their local media because they know the local population won't be the primary consumers of the media they are talking to. They want to talk to the West. They want to be seen as talking at the table internationally.[70]

Rod Nordland of the *Times* said in 2016 that he and his colleagues continued to "get privileged access to information from Afghan officials that they [Afghan journalists] don't get." His bureau had direct phone numbers of major officials in Kabul and in all 34 provinces; most of the time, the reporters could reach them quickly for comments and interviews.[71] The *Washington Post*'s Joshua Partlow believed that while it was not always a given that he could land an interview with a high-level official, he would normally have access to mid- and low-level presidential palace and ministry officials for background information and on-the-record interviews. "Compared to other countries where I worked, the Afghan government was very open and people were much more willing to talk. There was this feeling that everyone was in this conflict together and everyone had something to say about it. It was all fast-moving, so people were happy to put in their two cents."[72]

Afghan officials were more open to U.S. and other Western reporters than Afghan ones from 2002 to 2016 often for three overlapping reasons: because of the status that international reporters could confer on Afghan officials; because of the distrust they may have had in Afghan reporters' abilities to report truth accurately; and because officials wanted to send direct messages to Washington.

First, the U.S. elite news media offers Afghan officials international prestige, which they cannot acquire with the Afghan news media.[73] "Nobody here takes the Afghan media seriously," an Afghan print journalist explained in 2010.[74] If officials speak with the *Washington Post, New York Times*, AP, or *Wall Street Journal*, another offered, "then all the world is reading about them." If they just want to speak to Afghans, they go to Afghan news—if they want to speak with both Afghans and the world at once, then they go to American news.[75] The U.S. journalists agreed with their Afghan peers. One American print reporter emphasized in 2012 that the "idea of 'social betters' is very strong in Afghanistan," meaning that Afghan officials would rather talk to U.S. reporters, because it is a legitimization of their status on the world stage.

Second, Afghan officials trust that American and Western reporters are more professional than their Afghan peers and therefore will represent their words accurately.[76] Afghan officials go to Western and U.S. journalists because they keep off-the-record interviews off the record and do not fabricate or modify quotes, the Afghan journalists conceded.[77] The complexity of the political situation and the patron-based media system in the country also means that Afghan officials can perceive international media to be the most neutral medium: They know Western journalists' biases are blatantly toward their respective countries and not to a particular ethnic Afghan faction, such as Pashtuns, Tajiks, Hazaras, Aimaqs, Turkmen, Balochs, Nuristanis, and many others. The American journalists agreed that Afghan officials do not trust Afghan journalists to handle information professionally, but they are also naturally suspicious of Afghan reporters.[78] One elite print journalist for an American paper explained in 2012 that this too is a dynamic in the Middle East and a hallmark of any authoritarian society:

> Especially in closed societies like Afghanistan, people are constantly worried about who you are connected to. It's not like Afghanistan is a small nation; there are 30 million people here. But people are very aware of where you're from, what tribe you could be affiliated with,

what political party you could be affiliated with, what ethnicity you are—and that plays into a lot whether or not they trust you.[79]

This is a legitimate concern, U.S. journalists believed, because the elite Afghan news media ecosystem is politically charged and influenced by powerful Afghans. Even within the news media, agencies that are perceived to be more independent and professional—such as Tolo, 1TV, Ariana, Shamshad, Pajhwok, and *Hashteh Sobh*—reporters, editors, producers, and owners are of different ethnic heritages, which by fact alone can cause distrust. But such suspicions about journalists' underlying agendas were also an excuse, one American print reporter said, for Afghan officials to ig- nore their country's journalists. This is especially frustrating, since those officials often tout Afghan's news media as one of the greatest success stories in the country to the West.[80] At times, the officials approached the Western press because they wanted to take advantage of the U.S. press's lack of sociopolitical knowledge. As former *Wall Street Journal* reporter Maria Abi-Habib explained, "Sometimes it was genuine and sometimes it was about settling scores because somebody pissed them off. You had to go through what was genuine and what was petty."[81]

Third, Afghan officials prefer to speak with U.S. reporters because they want to send a message to Washington. This is a fairly reasonable strategy. Afghan officials sometimes need the support of the U.S. government, and the U.S. press can be a logical conduit to convey a message soliciting such support.[82] An American print journalist explained in 2012 that Afghan officials approached her frequently and could be "a little more open in the way they think they can manipulate the press to get their story out" than American officials, which will be explored in Chapter 7. Often, middle- to low-ranking Afghan officials approached the U.S. foreign correspondents with information about high-level officials' corruption. In one American newspaper reporter's words, they "are horrified with how people at the top behave, the nepotism and the patronage," but they are too poor to leave Afghanistan, so exposing it to try to generate change is their only option.[83] Another U.S. print journalist explained in 2012 that when she speaks with Afghan palace officials, they often say to her, " 'We know that the [American] ambassador takes you and whispers things into your ear.' And I want to say, 'Actually, it's Afghans who are whispering into my ear because they are so sick of corruption here'."[84] Those lower-ranking Afghan officials have been valuable sources for U.S. reportage on government corruption, which, consequently, considerably damaged the journalists' relationship with President Hamid Karzai and his administration. In sum, one Afghan journalist argued in 2012 that "The Western media criticizes the Afghan government and elites, and they in turn criticize Western media because it thinks the Western media has great influence on the U.S. government."[85] The Kabul Bank story exemplified this.

The U.S. journalists, however, believed that Afghan reporters and officials alike had an exaggerated sense of their impact on U.S. foreign policy. One newspaper reporter explained in 2012 that Afghan officials see him more as an advisor to the American president than as an independent journalist:

> There are folks that when you talk to them about a story you are working on or in the process of interviewing people, it is very clear that they are saying things they want the American president to hear. And they think you are the conduit between this person in the palace and the White House. That's a very grandiose way of viewing our role here. I'm not sure that's the case.[86]

President Hamid Karzai had an even more extreme view: He believed that journalists reporting for the American press were agents of the U.S. government. The Afghan and U.S. journalists concurred that he was much more concerned with what elite Western news media, especially the *New York Times* and *Washington Post*, thought about him than what the Afghan press did.[87] This is in part why he could celebrate the Afghan news media's progress publicly while also routinely keeping them at a distance. Karzai would strongly react to U.S. daily news reports, especially those that addressed his relationship with western diplomats, ISAF military leadership, and his family. One American newspaper journalist explained in 2012 that Karzai's spokesman's office called him regularly to make clear that the president was unhappy with a news story, even fairly insignificant ones.[88] Often the officials couldn't articulate their specific concerns and they rarely asked for corrections, but they wanted to at least register their anger and disapproval with the foreign correspondents.

During the George W. Bush administration, U.S. reporters' relationships with Afghan officials, especially members of President Karzai's senior staff at the palace, were fairly open and functional. But that relationship deteriorated considerably after the Obama administration assumed power in 2009. Much of the U.S. news coverage was indexed to the rocky relationship between the two governments, fueled by statements that Karzaï's victory in the 2009 election was fraudulent and unwanted by the American government.[89] As the U.S. journalists in the country increased their reporting on corruption and began to publish more investigative stories on the Afghan government, including ones on President Karzaï's brothers Ahmed Wali and Mahmood Karzai, the palace began to restrict their access, particularly that of the *Times*.[90]

As discussed in earlier chapters, the Karzai administration also blamed the American news media for projecting a hopeless image of Afghanistan, and believed they did so with the U.S. government's encouragement.[91] The same is true for the U.K. government and British news. In fall 2009, at the height of accusations of election fraud, Karzai told a gathering that the *New York Times*, the BBC, *The Times of London*, and CNN "know the election was right, but on a daily basis they call me a fraudulent president in order to pressure me."[92] In October and November 2012, he said in press conferences that the American media were waging a "psychological war" against Afghanistan, one in which they were fixing in the minds of the global public that Afghanistan's economy would collapse, and that civil war and the Taliban would return once U.S. troops leave.[93] They were doing so, he hinted, because U.S. reporters and officials together wanted to pressure him publicly to concede to America's vision of Afghanistan so that U.S. troops could stay in perpetuity.[94] Great powers—Alexander the Great, Mongols, Arab armies, Genghis Khan, the United Kingdom, the Soviet Union—had invaded Afghanistan, or attempted to do so, in the past for long periods of occupation, and he believed the United States, already in the country for 11 years at that point, was just settling in.

The U.S. journalists saw and reported another story. Since the U.S. government had invested more than $100 billion into Afghanistan through development funding, they associated the Afghan government's successes and failures with the successes and failures of U.S. foreign policy.[95] *New York Times* editor Doug Schorzman stated that the stories they published about President Karzai were ones the *Times* normally does, "because we're fascinated with power and its uses." He explained, "It's the same reason why we do a big piece on [billionaire businessman] Carlos Slim after he became a top shareholder in the *New York Times*. We always want to bite the hand."[96] A U.S. print reporter similarly said that it is part of their job to report Karzaï's words and actions, because he was "the president of the country that we [the U.S.] are essentially occupying and we're very interested in the stability of the country moving forward . . . we helped install President Karzai and we helped perpetuate his term as president," she explained in 2012. Examining Karzai and his actions in depth was a way to hold U.S. officials accountable for their extraordinary investment in the country with American taxpayer dollars.[97]

Pamela Constable of the *Washington Post* similarly explained in 2016 that the U.S. press did not make a decision to turn against President Karzai in 2009. The "souring of the relationship between President Karzai and the United States . . . [was] a reflection of the reality, it wasn't something [the press] had an agenda about," she said. U.S. news coverage about Afghanistan was more positive in Karzai's first term because events were more positive: "Schools were opening, clinics were opening, the currency was stable, violence was down, girls were going to school—there was so much good news during Karzai's first term that it lent itself to coverage about a country in recovery, that was stabilizing and increasing its capacity to modernize." Karzai's second term, however, was more tenuous. The 2009 election, "was much more fraught and controversial. He took office in a more controversial way." When the relationship between him and the United States and other Western countries by association began to deteriorate, "he became much more nationalistic and much more harsh and critical with his rhetoric. And that was reflected in what was written," Constable said. She agreed with the U.S. officials in Chapter 3 who said that Karzai was genuinely horrified by civilian and military deaths and uncomfortable with the terms of the 2014 bilateral security agreement. However, "I couldn't add any of them up to an understandable explanation for why things [the bilateral relationship] fell apart so badly." The journalists didn't set out to cause psychological harm against President Karzai and were not in cahoots with the U.S. government.[98]

Nonetheless, the distrust was so deep between the presidential palace and the U.S. reporters during Karzai's final years in office that even when they wanted to report good news, their efforts were usually rebuffed. As a result, the palace's suspicion and rejection of U.S. journalists often worked against the government's interests, the U.S. reporters interviewed thought. One print reporter explained how a palace spokesman, Aimal Faizi, ignored her when she wanted to write a story on the progress of Afghan women. She called, texted, and emailed him to no avail: "It was in his interest to tell me that Afghan women are doing incredibly well—and he never answered."[99] Another U.S. reporter said that while she actively worked to hold Karzai accountable, she also had a great deal of empathy for the position he was in: "He was up against a lot . . . he has a really troubling, corrupt family that he cannot completely abandon as an Afghan. And he had a lot of people around him who are a terrifying combination of being corrupt and bullies, and they are also armed. And he couldn't get rid of any of them." She wanted to be more sympathetic in her news reports but still thought he didn't try hard enough to overcome these barriers. When she would write positive news stories, the palace would wonder out loud why she also still wrote negative ones. "They did not understand the concept of balanced reporting," she said in 2012.[100]

While President Ashraf Ghani was not known to make public statements railing against the American news media, he was known to be resentful of the *Times* and other Western coverage of him, some of the Afghan and American journalists explained in 2016. He seemingly expected a certain amount of deference and favorable coverage, given that he inherited a chaotic government from Karzai.[101] Ghani shares power with his election opponent, Abdullah Abdullah, through a unity government that was negotiated by the Obama administration. According to Mujib Mashal of the *New York Times*, "Ghani's frustration with the coverage here is that when he goes to Washington, he can communicate very well because he says things that are tangible and easy to digest," a reference to Ghani's decades in the United States and his attainment of a doctoral degree from Columbia University. "But the Western press reports what he says differently. Ghani thinks they have made it tough for him and he wants to keep the Washington audience happy" as he cares about American government officials' opinion of his performance and wants continued U.S. and other Western financial assistance. It is difficult, however, when the U.S. news media criticizes his work and reflects the disorder of his government, because that coverage continues to reverberate through the Afghan news media. The difference between Ghani and Karzai, Mashal explained, was that while Ghani cares what the world thinks about his work, Karzai cared what the world thought of his family. But both felt personally and professionally discouraged, as if the U.S. news media and governments should cheerlead for them and choose to project Afghanistan more optimistically around the globe. Since Afghan leaders will continue to rely on development aid and military support for the near future, they will likely remain keenly sensitive to U.S. news coverage.[102]

Afghan officials believed U.S. journalists are an extension of the U.S. government, and/or representatives of the American nation; they work to amplify U.S. government rhetoric and action. Even if you are not an American but work for a U.S. news agency you still, indiscriminately, represent America. Often, the perception among Afghan officials, and the Afghan public, has been that the United States owes them both material and moral support after launching this war in pursuit of al Qaeda in 2001.[103] Afghans want economic and development assistance, in addition to praise and reassurance that they are successfully moving toward democracy in light of extremely difficult conditions. Because Afghan officials felt that they were aligning themselves with the United States—which made them suspicious to their neighbors in Iran, China, and Pakistan—they were entitled to favorable U.S. news coverage. They believe that not just U.S. officials but the U.S. journalists as well should be grateful to them for their sacrifices to help the United States in its post-9/11 war. As one U.S. print reporter sympathized:

> It has not been easy for [Afghan officials] to be an ally of the Americans. It is not a popular stand to take in this country. Even though people will say that they need the Americans privately, being seen standing next to them is a fraught position. And they have been out there doing that. And we've never given them credit for that . . . So then when anything or anyone is American in a country where honor and image and face is so terribly important comes out and criticizes them, they feel really insulted. And that's why they feel betrayed. They say, "We stood up for you, we let you come into our country." That's become the narrative: Here you are just saying we are blemished in every possible way.

This is compounded by the fact that U.S. journalists see the Afghan government through an American and Western filter, with expectations for liberal institutions that operate without endemic corruption and threats of violence. In Afghanistan, that can be interpreted, one print reporter said, "as a betrayal on some moral level. After all, the U.S. is an ally of Afghanistan." So why is the United States criticizing an ally? Why are U.S. reporters making them look inefficient? For Karzai and others, it must be because U.S. reporters and officials are in sync to undercut Afghan democracy and the country's sovereignty. It did not help that U.S. news content rippled through Afghanistan's most-watched, most-listened-to, and most-read media outlets.

Why Afghan Journalists Want U.S. News

A consensus among communications scholars is that global news outlets routinely examine and relay U.S. news about American politics and celebrity culture to keep their audiences informed about the health of the U.S. government, and entertained by Hollywood. In Afghanistan, there are three fundamental, often intersecting, reasons why local journalists have specifically relied on the American news media. The first reason, as discussed above, is to relay information on the Afghan government, because of Afghan government officials' penchant for U.S. coverage of them, and to relay information on the American government, since U.S. journalists have greater access to U.S. officials than Afghan journalists. The second reason is because Afghan journalists often cannot identify original news stories because of their relative professional immaturity and/or because they have become desensitized to bad news, and citing American news adds credibility to theirs. The third reason is that they often choose to self-censor for their own security.

First, Afghan journalists need U.S. news to be able to report on their own government, but also to understand U.S. policy toward their country. Farid Ahmad, a former broadcast journalist who runs the Payk Investigative Journalism Center, explained in 2016 that even though the volume of U.S. journalism about Afghanistan had sharply decreased by then, "There is still a sense that U.S. policy affects Afghans' lives."[104] Afghan journalists need U.S. news to understand what Washington is deciding about their country, and what the influential American elites think about it so that they can try to forecast future policy. U.S. journalism is credible inside Afghanistan because of the journalists' access to American, and other Western, officials and because few Afghan journalists have bureaus inside the United States.[105]

Second, as already established, a professional Afghan independent press is still emerging. While storytelling is an inherent dimension of Afghan culture, it is difficult for Afghan journalists to identify news beyond Afghan government reports. Decades of conflict have made the Afghan people desensitized to bad news.[106] As one Afghan print journalist explained in 2010, "War has made Afghan journalists numb about tragedy and [government] incompetence."[107] For instance, 2012 was a Summer Olympics year, and the stadium in Kabul where Afghan Olympic athletes, including women, were training had formerly been the location for Taliban public executions. What was remarkable to Western reporters was not to Afghan ones. It was only when Reuters reported the December 15, 2011, article "Taliban Death Stadium Reborn as Afghan Sporting Hope" that Afghan journalists recognized it as a story that could instill a sense of pride in the Afghan public.[108] The Western view of Afghanistan helps them to identify news, features, and investigative reporting opportunities they would often overlook.

In addition, Afghan journalists tend to think on a very local level, which is why they need the U.S. and Western press to find important national and regional stories.[109] The U.S. press, the *Times*' Mashal explained, can "zoom out a little bit and hit broader themes." The Afghan press may not be able to draw conclusions on various dynamics, or may be afraid that they will cause panic, he continued, "but we do draw those conclusions, because we have to tell the [American] reader why it matters, whereas if you are Afghan, you care about anything that is news because it is the Vice President and he said something."[110] The lack of resources and skills for long-term, in-depth investigative reporting among Afghan journalists means that they turn to U.S. reporters for guidance.[111] Their news is perceived to be legitimate and authoritative, and therefore adds credibility to the journalists' reportage.[112] "When the *New York Times* says something, it means something and the Afghan officials and powerbrokers react strongly," an Afghan radio journalist said in 2010.[113] The newness of Afghan media made Afghans interested in what Afghan journalists had to say, but Afghan elites continued to believe into 2016 that U.S. news is more mature and attuned to detail, and their appearance in those papers will confer global status on them.

The local reporters are increasingly taking risks, but they are stuck in a daily routine of rote reportage without analysis, according to the Afghan and U.S. journalists interviewed for this book. The *Times*' Nordland said this is particularly the case for social issues about Afghanistan, as the Afghan press often does not challenge conservative attitudes in society that can violate universal standards of human rights. When he completed his book, *The Lovers*, about an Afghan couple who fought to be together despite cultural mores against their inter-ethnic union and the threat of an honor killing, "Afghan journalists interviewed me and asked, 'Who gave you that story from the Afghan government? Why did they give it to you and not to Afghan journalists?'" Nordland explained that no one had given him the story. Afghan journalists were actually much better equipped to report on social issues or those of corruption than Western journalists: "They could find those kinds of stories easily. It happens all around them."[114] But the Afghan journalists could be desensitized to such news, or their cultural identity does not consider newsworthy an event that would shock Western norms. The Afghan journalists said they often report news on social issues and human rights violations in a benign, fairly inoffensive form. Television programming and talk shows on independent news have worked to promote human rights within the country, but while talking about it, they often do not expose individual acts of bad behavior and identify the abusers, especially when it comes to Afghan women's rights. They do not want to shame men's honor.

American news about the world often gains attention when it violates Western norms of human rights, and U.S. journalists have regularly sought stories about Afghan women's health, well-being, and advancement in Afghan government and society. The story of the gruesome murder of Farkhunda Malikzada, a 27-year-old scholar of Islam, is one example. In 2015, she was killed by a mob that believed she had burned the Koran in a Muslim shrine; an investigation later found that she had actually confronted four men who were using the shrine as a center to traffic Viagra and condoms. The four men, outraged a woman would challenge them, fabricated a story that they caught her desecrating the Koran, and the mob quickly formed. Men filmed each other stoning and clubbing her, while also yelling accusations that she worked for the American and French embassies. They drove a car over her, with Afghan police directing traffic around the scene to facilitate the act. She begged them to stop, but they continued, fueled by rage. When they could not set her on fire because her body was soaked in blood, they used their clothing to absorb the blood and tried again. The men then proudly posted videos to their social media accounts of the grisly scenes.

On Facebook, Hashmat Stanekzai, the spokesman for the Afghan National Police, praised the death, as did the Deputy Minister of Culture, Simin Ghazal Hasanzada, and some members of Parliament.[115] Once it was revealed that she did not desecrate the Koran, the Afghan nation became horrified. For days, there were mass protests for women's rights. President Ghani called it a heinous act and said that more focus should be on local policing to protect women and other citizens from such mobs; his Interior Ministry arrested 28 people and suspended 13 police officers. Stanekzai was fired.

Afghan journalists did not shy away from this story and reported in sync with their Western peers. They reported on the incident and the protests that followed, and they covered the trial of the accused men. Tolo News wrote in an editorial, "It is important that Farkhunda is not forgotten. Her story should not be lost in the nation's selective memory; it should be remembered as a national tragedy, as a taint on the national honor. Only then can we ensure that no such tragedy happens again."[116] The shocking nature and evidence of the murder also made this an important story for the U.S. press, which put it into the larger context of the plight of Afghan women and the unevenness of the justice system in Afghanistan, tying it to the weaknesses of U.S. foreign policy. Alissa Rubin, a longtime *New York Times* reporter in the country, received a Pulitzer Prize for her 2015 feature piece, "Flawed Justice After a Mob Killed an Afghan Women," which detailed Farkhunda's murder and the failed attempts at justice that came after. Rubin connected it to the botched $1 billion effort from the American government to remake the rule of law in the country:

> Like so many other Western attempts to remake Afghanistan, the efforts have foundered . . . Afghan society has resisted more than 150 years of such endeavors by outsiders, from the British to the Russians to the Americans. This remains a country where ties of kinship and clan trump justice, and where the money brought by the West has made corruption into a way of life. The rule-of-law programs were often designed in ignorance of Afghan legal norms, international and Afghan lawyers say. And Western efforts to lift women's legal status provoked fierce resentment from powerful religious figures and many ordinary Afghans.[117]

Farkhunda Malikzada's death captured Afghan and Western journalists' attention because it was a spectacularly horrifying event. There are many cases when Afghan journalists could have challenged social mores and/or their government but passed on reporting them because they feared for their lives or their relationships, as social capital in Afghanistan is essential for survival.

Once the news is reported, though, it is common property, a public good that can be repeated.[118] This leads to the third reason why U.S. news is so valuable to Afghan reporters: It helps them to distribute the news while also censoring their own reporting. U.S. news stories provide them with cover, the space they need to expose corruption and malfeasance by Afghan officials, warlords, religious leaders, and other strongmen. The "Afghan media does not have the authority or clout that American media has," one Afghan broadcast journalist explained in 2012. "Talking about the warlords, for instance, is essentially a job for the American journalists; the Afghan journalists can then translate the story and relay it."[119] U.S. journalists are essential to Afghan reporting because they have more freedom, strength, and influence, one Afghan broadcaster emphasized: "They have more freedom because there is no warlord in America to intimidate them. They are strong because they have more money, more resources. They have more influence because they are professional."[120] The American government also protects U.S. journalists, which enables them to acquire information without fear of persecution: They are off limits to various Afghan power brokers who are dependent on the United States for assistance, or who could be attacked by the U.S. military if they hurt an American citizen.[121]

The Afghan reporters said they would at times relinquish stories on powerful Afghan officials, extremist groups, and warlords to Western reporters due to the possible violence inflicted on them or their families if they reported it themselves.[122] A majority of the American journalists confirmed that, like Afghan officials, Afghan journalists—and media owners—come to them or their local staff with information that they feel they couldn't make public themselves.[123] Saad Mohseni said in an October 2016 interview that Tolo often gave corruption stories to the *Times* or the *Post* that they did not feel safe running themselves; they would then report the stories citing the American publications as the sources.[124] *Times* editor Schorzman acknowledged this as true: "Afghan reporters are subject to threats that we are not. The way the Afghan press interacts with the American press is fascinating. Sometimes you do get scoops that start with local journalists . . . their key issue is safety. They want a story to come out, but they are making a realistic analysis on their safety. We have the protection of the name of the *New York Times*."[125] But the identity of the *Times* can also get murky: It can simultaneously be seen as not just a U.S. newspaper that serves the American people, and maintains a general sense of shared identity, but as being chauvinistically nationalistic and patriotic toward the U.S. government. We'll explore this more in chapter 7.

Why U.S. Journalists Want Afghan News

U.S. journalists based in Kabul also use Afghan news, but differently. They and their local staff track dozens of Afghan news organizations, but the ones that are the most important to them are, as mentioned, Tolo TV, 1TV, Ariana, *Hashteh Sobh*, and Pajhowk newswire service.[126] The Afghan news media does not set the agenda for the U.S. journalists in the country, but Afghan journalists are the "go-to" sources for breaking news about attacks by the Taliban and other extremist groups; such reports are often broadcast via Twitter.

Often, Afghan local journalists provide fragments of information that lead to bigger feature and investigative pieces by their American counterparts. For instance, the U.S. news bureaus in Kabul often have their local reporters look for stories percolating in local news. The *Times'* Nordland explained that some of the social stories he covers "begin as small items in the Afghan press, like child marriage stories reported in the Afghan media but not in much detail and only when there is an arrest. But they are reactive, simple stories."[127] Sometimes, security news stories begin by watching interviews local reporters have with Afghan officials. In 2012, for instance, Tolo interviewed the governor of Wardak province, a volatile area less than 100 miles from Kabul. The governor told the Tolo journalist that the transfer of control from NATO to the Afghan National Army was too dangerous and needed more time. This sparked an idea at a U.S. bureau to call other provincial governors to see if they were also concerned about the military transfer. They were.

The warlord television stations can also be fertile ground for news. Abdul Rashid Dostum's "Aina," or mirror; Haji Mohammad Mohaqiq's "Rah-e-Farda," or future path; Burhanuddin Rabbani's "Noor," or light; and Karim Khoram's Kabul TV have been especially reliable resources for U.S. journalists to learn more about the warlords' priorities and actions throughout the country. For instance, Dostum—the warlord in Afghanistan's north who had declared victory over the Taliban on Radio Balkh in 2002 and served as Afghanistan's vice president from 2014 to 2017—holds large rallies in northern Afghanistan that are broadcast on his station to maintain his identity as a powerful strongman separate from his role in the Afghan government. Such assemblies are valuable indicators of Afghan public sentiment and the warlords' cult of personality. Yet they are stories that inspire other news stories, they don't necessarily set the agenda for Afghan or Western coverage of the country.

U.S. JOURNALISTS HAD MUCH greater access to Afghan government officials than Afghan journalists did for the first 15 years of the post-9/11 entanglement. The U.S. press set the agenda for Afghan news on issues about the American-led war, the region, the U.S. government, and the Afghan government. Therefore, U.S. reporters were not just informing

Americans, but were also speaking to a second, unintended audience: the Afghan nation. Because of Afghan journalists' perceived lack of professionalism, their lack of access to U.S. and Afghan officials, and their tendency toward self-censorship, U.S. news has been highly valued.[128] Yet by 2016, this was changing. As Tolo's news director Lotfullah Najafizada said, "The capacity among Afghan journalists to report on both local and international news has expanded dramatically the last few years. They continue to monitor the Western press, but they no longer rely on it."[129]

As long as U.S. troops are in Afghanistan and the elite news bureaus can afford it, U.S. news coverage there will continue.[130] At some point, the U.S. journalists believed, security would further deteriorate, which would make the foreign bureaus much more costly and difficult to manage, compelling the U.S. journalists to abandon them full time.[131] In 2016, 8,400 U.S. troops remained—and so did the AP, *New York Times*, NPR, *Wall Street Journal*, and *Washington Post* bureaus with full-time, Western correspondents. A few others, such as CBS and CNN, also remained with local correspondents in case there was breaking news.[132] The *Post*'s Pamela Constable, who had covered Afghanistan since the 1990s, said in 2016 that while the television networks are largely gone and the print bureaus have been reduced in size as well, "those of us still here still feel like this story is a big and important commitment."[133] Nordland predicted in October 2016 that his *Times* bureau would also stay in Afghanistan for the foreseeable future. The *Times*' mantra, he explained, is "Whatever it takes to cover the news," in the sense that "when all the other traditional media fold up and collapse, the *New York Times* is so indispensable it will still be here."[134]

However, the U.S. journalists, like the public, are exhausted by a war that has lasted more than 15 years.[135] In 2017, *Washington Post* reporter Joshua Partlow reflected:

> The sheer duration of the conflict dulls the senses to what's going on. It's not that interesting for readers and it's not that interesting for journalists to write the same story over and over. That's definitely something we were reckoning with, how to try to keep it interesting for people back in the U.S. and for ourselves. Particularly the violence-related stories are very similar often when you are writing a bombing story, after the tenth or twentieth or hundredth time—you kind of are going through the motions, you know what is required to write a bombing story. So there is some fatigue in that sense.[136]

Times editor Schorzman concurred in 2016, "People are tired of Afghanistan. There is even editorial fatigue [at the *Times*]. But we're committed to it because of American responsibility over what is happening there."[137] He continued, "Even if we think people are tired about reading about Afghanistan, it's my job to put it in their face."[138] And, as will be explored in Chapter 7, the *Times* has been changing how it is telling Afghanistan's story. Carlotta Gall believed that the exhaustion was normal for any protracted conflict but that "so many people's lives have been touched by Afghanistan there is going to be a permanent interest . . . It's like Vietnam now, it's a part of American history and it's going to be always there. There are going to be waves of people getting tired, and then people returning to it; that's normal."[139]

No matter how long the U.S. journalists are in Afghanistan, the Afghan journalists—like the Afghan government—deem U.S. news to have a large impact on U.S. public opinion and U.S. foreign policy, and that U.S. foreign policy officials largely influence the content of U.S. reportage. The negative view that U.S. journalists project about Afghanistan has an erosive effect on the American public, the Afghan elite journalists feared. With so many negative stories, U.S. journalists were "fixing the minds" of Americans with a resoundingly negative view about Afghanistan the country, giving the perception that it was consumed with violence.[140] "We have lost this war in your living rooms, in your pubs and bars," one Afghan broadcaster said in 2012.[141] Another sympathized with the American public: "If I was an American reading this news, I wouldn't support U.S. involvement in Afghanistan either."[142]

The Afghan elites seemed to be split on decoding the motive for this coverage. Like Karzai, some saw this negative depiction as proof that the United States wants to occupy the country in perpetuity and exploit its resources, while others saw it as giving a reason for the United States to stop supporting the country with military and development aid. But most of all, Afghan officials and reporters wanted equal praise and moral support from both Afghan reporters and officials, whom they saw as promoting the same agenda. And therein lies the tension: The journalists are attracted to U.S. news for status conferral and support in building a democratic news system in Afghanistan, and simultaneously resent the stories they tell of their nation through an American lens.

Your Country, Our War

When American journalists are talking about corruption, that is the country I experience.
When they are talking about the insurgency, that's not the country I experience
—An Afghan broadcaster in 2010[1]

WHILE MAINSTREAM U.S. NEWS about the world is largely ethnocentric, it is distributed globally. The telegraph, radio, and satellite television has allowed American news to be largely accessible to interested foreign audiences for more than a century. Digital technology has now accelerated a media boomerang pattern for foreign correspondence: News written abroad for an American audience travels back to the government officials, journalists, and citizens of the nation U.S. journalists are talking about. In Afghanistan, because of the compact network of U.S. news bureaus in the country, the Afghan journalists have become interwoven with them.

Since 2001, the Afghan journalists interviewed for this study have looked to their Western counterparts for professional guidance and self-censorship purposes. But how do they process seeing their country through an American lens? They agreed that U.S. journalists package the Afghan people as violent and corrupt and Afghanistan as an inherently failed state.[2] As discussed in Chapter 3, frames organize knowledge by assigning issues and events to recognizable categories, shaping one's understanding of them, and then suggesting how one should act toward or within them.[3] Filtering complexity by giving news a simple storyline within a frame is especially common for foreign events, as they do not readily resonate with audiences who have no prior experience with a place.[4] The frames are both mental images, "the pictures in our heads," as Walter Lippmann said, and social objects that are embedded in our discourses, routines, institutions, and cultural norms. They are often assumptions taken to be truth. They allow readers to quickly interpret, categorize, and evaluate issues without giving them due analysis.[5] Frames also allow journalists to maintain narratives that feel familiar and resonate with their home audiences.

In chapter 2, we discussed four conventional news frames for international news: security, diplomacy, the economy, and humanitarianism. With Afghanistan, there are two dominant and over-arching news story frames. First is the security frame, which assembles Afghan, U.S., and other international troops; warlords; the Taliban; Islamic State of the Levant; and other extremist factions operating in the country, and largely explains Afghanistan as a matter of U.S. national security. Second is the failed governance frame, which looks specifically at corruption and inefficiency in the Afghan government. This frame can also be categorized as a diplomacy frame, as the content is indexed to U.S. foreign policy since the U.S. government has spent billions of taxpayer dollars trying to build the Afghan government's capacity.

Afghan journalists are frustrated with American news' overwhelming use of the security frame, the Afghan journalists agreed, because the bulk of U.S. news coverage since 9/11 has been about the U.S.-led war, with a sharp focus on American troops.[6] Yet the Afghan journalists can appreciate the failed governance frame and its focus on corruption mostly because the journalists are still slowly developing investigative skills to uncover stories and/or because they do not feel safe reporting these stories themselves.

However, the fact that U.S. journalists report more bad news than good, and seemingly project Afghanistan as a country that needs American and Western saviors, can also be aggravating.[7] Similar to former President Hamid Karzai and other Afghan officials, Afghan journalists can be emotionally affected by the news stories they consume that narrowly constrict their country as a conflict-ridden wasteland. Consuming American news about Afghanistan can hurt their pride and stir nationalistic feelings within themselves. Sometimes they see journalists for U.S. news agencies as not just reporting for the American nation, but also as being advocates for the U.S. government's worldview and policies.

The journalists for U.S. news agencies in Kabul vehemently refuted this. As discussed in Chapter 6, they acknowledged their constraints. They also agree that they tend to report with Western biases of what makes attitudes and behaviors normative and acceptable. But that does not mean they work to intentionally amplify the American government's rhetoric and support U.S. policies. They balance support of American troops and other U.S. citizens with working to keep U.S. foreign policy and military officials—and, by extension, the Afghan government that depends on their support—accountable.

Afghanistan the War

The dozen correspondents for U.S. news agencies interviewed for this study concurred that U.S. reporting about the world is largely organized within a security frame, which validates the dominant military status of the United States in the international system.[8] The more frames are repeated, the more they create a norm, a consensual understanding among their consumers.[9] Since 9/11, the security frame has dominated U.S. news about Afghanistan mainly because U.S. troops are there. As an American print reporter explained: "We put high stock in stories about the American military, and they go on the front page often because they have a clear connection to the American reader."[10] American audiences primarily want to know about their fellow citizens who are in the country.

The U.S. journalists interviewed believed that their Afghan peers' criticism that U.S. news about the region is too narrowly focused on security is legitimate.[11] Nonetheless, reporting on the region within a security framework is a fixed part of their mission as correspondents for U.S. news organizations. As one American print journalist explained in 2012: "I'm not here to write a portrait of the nation of Afghanistan. I am here to write about the war. So the ebb and flow of security is definitely a guiding, major frame of how I look at this place."[12] It is only natural that Afghanistan is described through a security lens in U.S. news because the war began with the 9/11 attack on the United States, an American radio reporter said also in 2012: "The U.S. government didn't come here because they decided they needed to provide water for people."[13]

The Afghan journalists interviewed see U.S. journalists' use of the security frame as a crutch, a default mode for their reporting. They reduce Afghanistan to a violent country because it is easy, they believe, and because it already fits within Americans' worldview. Understanding a country can take a very long time, and it can be challenging for a foreign correspondent to fully understand the dynamics within one, let alone unpack and explain them to their audiences.[14] Yet, in Afghanistan, even the U.S. journalists who have been living there for multiple years face limitations.[15] As one Afghan broadcaster said in 2010, sometimes being from Afghanistan isn't enough to understand Afghanistan: "We're a very complex society. It's even difficult for us to be able to tell all issues and facts as Afghans."[16] But while Afghanistan might be complex, U.S. news about violence provides simple storylines that hook American and Afghan audiences alike.

The Afghans said they largely do not recognize the country described in the Western press as theirs.[17] They agreed U.S. news stories give Americans, and the world, a distorted view of their country with an exaggerated sense of its violence and their people's cruelty.[18] Some argued that by disproportionally reporting on the carnage instead of the character of the Afghan people, the U.S. journalists are making Afghans seem inhuman.[19] "If you look at U.S. news, it looks like Afghanistan is at war," Lotfullah Najafizada said in 2016. "If you live in Afghanistan, it doesn't feel that way."[20] U.S. news presents "a dark picture of Afghanistan" another broadcaster insisted in 2012, and "it's not real."[21] The focus on the lives of U.S. soldiers instead of Afghan civilians creates mainly negative and sensationalist news stories that they believe to be overwhelmingly American-centric.[22] One Afghan broadcaster conceded that Afghans' worldview is inherently different: "American see Afghanistan through the prism of war, and Afghans don't."[23] But the focus on "suicide bombings, the Taliban, and the U.S. military" distracts readers and viewers from who the Afghan people are. As one Afghan print reporter explained in 2012:

> We are people, we are normal human beings. War and suicide bombings and explosions is not all that we do—we are so many other things. Yes, we are poor and we are illiterate . . . but there are so many other things that need to be covered about Afghans, our traditions, our families and our social structures.[24]

While the Afghan journalists in Kabul saw the fighting as being sequestered in certain rural areas, American journalists, they said, make it seem as if the violence engulfs the entire country, staging American diplomats, generals, soldiers, and Marines as the heroes working to "save" their homeland.

When asked in 2012 for an example of a story that encapsulated their frustration, roughly a quarter of the Afghan journalists pointed to the July 2012 *New Yorker* article, "Will Civil War Hit Afghanistan When the U.S. Leaves?" by Dexter Filkins.[25] The article explored the possibility of Afghanistan returning to a state of civil war after the bulk of troops from the United States and the International Assistance Force (ISAF)/North Atlantic Treaty Organization (NATO) were originally scheduled to withdraw from the country in 2014, much like the horrifying civil war that ensued after Soviet troops withdrew in 1989. While a couple of Afghan journalists interviewed in 2012 agreed with the prospect, the majority thought the article was detrimental to Afghanistan's long-term prospects for peace, which was consistent with President Karzaï's frustrations: The U.S. press, they believed, was creating a poisonous environment for U.S. policy decision-making that could affect their future. By focusing on a likelihood of increased violence, the article could indicate to the American public and government that Afghanistan was not worth their time, sacrifice, and investment. Some Afghan journalists believed Filkins, who was not at the time based in Kabul but previously was with the *New York Times*, acted like a parachute journalist, choosing to speak with preselected sources rather than getting a more diverse view of the situation on the ground.[26] Nonetheless, the Afghan news media relayed the news story because they knew it would impact U.S. policymakers, and they wanted the Afghan public to know what America was thinking.[27]

Afghanistan the Failed State

The U.S. journalists also often frame Afghanistan as a corrupt and weakly governed country. News stories about the health of the Afghan government and the economy—and how they are affected by chronic corruption—are congruent with a security frame because it affects Afghanistan's overall stability, and whether or not U.S. security policy is succeeding. U.S. journalists agreed that the prospects for long-term stability in Afghanistan impact long-term American national interests.[28] Should Afghanistan become anarchic or fall to extremists because of weak governance, then the United States could become embroiled in a longer, even bloodier conflict. It is in American readers' interests to prepare for such a possibility, they said; this is why they focused so much on Afghanistan's elite class and their ability to govern the country.

The Afghan journalists had more complicated feelings about this frame than the security one. Some agreed that corruption is the most important story in Afghanistan and that it matters more to the country's stability than violence and terrorism.[29] As one Afghan television reporter explained in 2012, "When American journalists are talking about corruption, that is the country I experience. When they are talking about insurgency, that's not the country I experience."[30] This reporting is especially valuable to Afghans because, as established in Chapter 6, they do not feel safe in reporting these stories themselves. As Tolo's Sami Mahdi explained, the Afghan press "doesn't feel shackled—but when it comes to corruption, they do lean toward self-censorship. It's not the policy, but it's the influence that corrupt individuals can have."[31]

Failed governance and corruption became a major theme in U.S. news about Afghanistan during the 2009 Afghan presidential elections, a process that the U.S. media deemed to be fraudulent and that contributed to the souring of relations between the U.S. and Afghan governments.[32] President Karzai and Afghan officials insisted that U.S. news reports on the election were wrong, but they did not offer any evidence to refute them.[33] They, along with some Afghan reporters, believed that the U.S. government was encouraging U.S. correspondents, especially those from the *New York Times*, to report negatively about Karzai so that his legitimacy within Afghanistan and within international governments and institutions would be weakened. Other Afghan journalists believed that U.S. journalists had the right to criticize how Karzai's administration managed the country since U.S. taxpayer dollars were supporting him.[34]

In addition to the 2009 presidential election, the Afghan journalists pointed to *Washington Post* and *New York Times* stories of the Karzai family—especially his late brother, Ahmed Wali Karzai—and their alleged involvement in corruption and the opium trade.[35] While this was infuriating for Karzai, the majority of the Afghan journalists thought corruption stories were fair game. They wanted their U.S. peers to pressure Afghan officials and other elites to make their government and economy work better so that it could more efficiently leverage foreign donor funding. The *Post*'s 2012 Kabul Bank story was a prime example of this: It exposed the elites who used the bank for their own expense accounts and then blamed the American press, and not themselves, for the bank's destruction. But partly because of the elites' sense of entitlement and immunity, some Afghan journalists believed that the U.S. journalists do not go far enough in their corruption reporting. Since they are based in Kabul, U.S. news stories tend to overlook corruption at the provincial and local levels, where it can be even more pervasive and in need of exposure.[36]

While valued, corruption stories can also lower the Afghan journalists' morale. As one Afghan broadcaster said, U.S. news about poor governance issues in general was fair—which is exactly why it's so painful. "It's so sad for me," he said. "Why is Afghanistan always a controversial country?"[37] Another bemoaned in 2012 that the focus on Karzai's family's drug trafficking and corruption was making all Afghans look as if they were involved in a "mafia war."[38] As one explained, "I'm not frustrated about the American media's view of the country; I'm frustrated that these things exist in my country. I'm embarrassed. When I hear about corruption, I curse the officials. When I hear about drugs, I am sad that they exist."[39] For this reason, the independent Afghan journalists insisted that they infuse their coverage with more positive stories than the American and other Western news media do, as it is their duty to give the Afghan people good news to maintain a unified sense of the nation.[40]

Craving Good News

Stories of hope matter deeply to the Afghan journalists. They felt that too much reportage on politics and security could discourage the Afghan public about their future. Many interviewed felt it was their responsibility to instill in Afghans some optimism and confidence that their country and their quality of life was improving.[41]"Afghanistan's not a good place to live," an Afghan reporter explained in 2012. "But if you live here, you have to do something positive."[42] Journalists especially have a responsibility to bring about constructive change in Afghanistan and to be socially responsible. The news media, Sami Mahdi likewise said in 2016, needs to "maintain hope and to introduce a vision about modern Afghanistan, which is very important to keep people going."[43]

Afghan journalists are more likely to highlight Afghan bravery and resilience in the face of violence than the act itself. For instance, in June 2010, a significant news story was the Peace *Jirga*, an attempt by the Karzai administration to begin negotiations with the Taliban.[44] The *jirga*, or grand assembly, attracted hundreds of tribal representatives to discuss reconciliation in Kabul. The Taliban leadership, however, did not attend. On the *jirga*'s first day, two Taliban fighters dressed as women in burkas detonated suicide bombs at the entrance, located half a mile away from the main tent where 2,000 Afghan delegates were already gathered. Rockets were also fired haphazardly near the tent. No one except the Taliban suicide bombers, however, was killed. An Afghan print journalist said in 2012 that his news agency ran more than 30 news stories in the course of three days about the *jirga*. One of them was about the 400 young Afghans who were involved in making the event possible and how not one *jirga* representative fled from the event after the Taliban attack.[45] "When each rocket attack came, there was nobody scared from the *jirga*. What it showed was the strength of our people; they did not care that their lives were in danger," an Afghan broadcaster emphasized.[46] This enabled them to focus on the positive: the fortitude of the Afghan people and young, patriotic Afghans trying to make a constructive impact on Afghan politics and society. The American news, on the other hand, focused on the attack and the insecure environment surrounding the talks. For instance, Rod Nordland and Alissa Rubin of the *New York Times* had written of the June 2, 2010, attack on the Peace *Jirga*: "Regardless of whether delegates were supporters of Mr. Karzai or his critics, there was an overwhelming sense that the country's security was deteriorating and that Afghans had lost faith in pledges of peace."[47]

The Afghan journalists were frustrated that American journalists insist on painting such a picture for American and other global, unintended audiences. Even though they understand the factors that drive U.S. news about Afghanistan, they, like Afghan—and American—government officials, are frustrated that the U.S. reporters do not focus more on positive developments within the country.[48] "It is understandable that U.S. coverage about Afghanistan focuses on the U.S. role here since they are mainly writing for an American audience . . . But at the same time, that approach builds a narrative about Afghanistan that is always about war and nothing else," Sami Mahdi explained in 2016.[49] This is especially puzzling for Afghans since the United States has poured more than $100 billion into the country and supported an expansion of education and health initiatives, in addition to the dramatic increase of women's participation in government and society. It's not true that U.S. support for Afghanistan has been wasted, the Afghan journalists agreed.[50] As one described it, "We've had a lot of achievements in Afghanistan. They are historic. Never before have we had so much electricity, or paved roads, or telephones, or universities, or boys and girls going to school."[51] American reporting about the country isn't balanced, the Afghan journalists agreed, because the journalists do not look at the "commitment, morality, capacity, initiative, and potential that exists in Afghanistan."[52] As a result, the U.S. press affects perceptions of the credibility of not only the Afghan government but also the Western governments who have invested so much into the country.

The majority of U.S. news professionals interviewed saw this as a legitimate criticism.[53] Doug Schorzman, a foreign editor for the *New York Times*, agreed that U.S. news' global reporting relies on a security frame, which is a problem. "That most of the stories about the world are about security are absolutely true, and it is horrible and it is wrong," he said in 2016.[54] Other U.S. journalists interviewed believed that the American and Western publics deserved to have more context about Afghanistan and to hear the struggles of the Afghan people, appealing to their sense of humanitarianism and creating emotional appeals for more assistance to the country. Some of the U.S. journalists regretted not writing enough from the Afghan perspective and showing the U.S. public the toll the war has taken on the Afghan public.[55] The more interesting news stories, one American radio journalist emphasized in 2012, are about the Afghan nation—the culture and the Afghan public's attitudes, habits, and traditions. But at the same time, he explained, "we have a responsibility to cover the American presence here through the American military or the civilians' words and actions. And our readers have a particular interest in those stories because those could be their sons or daughters, or friends or colleagues."[56] The primary audience, Americans, want to read about the impact of the war on American troops, U.S. national security, and their taxpayer dollars.

The U.S. reporters insisted that they frame their stories in terms of violence and corruption because they accurately reflect the country's major challenges as it tries to build sound democratic and national security institutions. Kathy Gannon, a veteran AP reporter in Afghanistan and Pakistan, said in a 2017 interview:

> Violence and corruption. These are the two big stories, let's face it. There are lots of humanitarian stories too, but the big stories are violence and corruption. This isn't unreasonable. There are thousands of foreign troops in the country. And corruption is pervasive. A friend had to pay 100 Afghanis (roughly $1.50) just to get his registration of a small piece of property moving. You have to pay money to pay your utility bill . . . I write these stories because I go to the marketplace and people are angry. That's the reality of living in this country. It's not because of the narrative outside.

She acknowledged that it must be demoralizing for the Afghans to read about themselves in this way: "I'm sure it does hurt Afghans when they read these news stories, but it does not change the reality. You don't want the imagery of your country to be violent, but they're in a war and there's a lot of violence right now."[57] Other U.S. journalists said that it wasn't their job to balance bad news with good news and that Afghan journalists are more likely to know what is encouraging and hopeful for their societies than Americans. "It's very hard for us to justify [to editors] some of the good news stories that we would tell," one American print journalist explained in 2012, when she already had limited space to report on the region. Moreover, good news stories often do not qualify as news. "So you have to ask yourself if that is the best use of the space. Are you really showing people something real?"[58] Usually, she answers "no."

The *Times'* Rod Nordland said in an October 2016 interview, "If there was a good news story in Afghanistan, it would be so counter-intuitive that it would be newsworthy." He couldn't identify one positive news story he had filed about Afghanistan in the last year, but later remembered that he had written in 2016 "A 'Wall of Kindness' Against a Harsh Reality in Afghanistan."[59] It was about three Kabul teenagers who wanted to create a mural wall "with slogans about how giving to the poor enriches the giver as much as the receiver." They hammered nails into it for people to hang clothes for the city's neediest. That news story encapsulated the new generation that is trying to change Afghanistan, Afghan reporter Sami Mahdi pointed out, and they want the U.S. and Western press to acknowledge and legitimize them. Afghanistan's good news, he said, is how younger Afghans have had the courage to transform so much of their society since 2001:

> We have more than 8 million kids going to school. We have access to health services, we have freedom of expression, telecommunications, roads, we are connected to the international community. These are all positive stories. I think these positive achievements are going to change this country and this upcoming generation is going to make us more confident.[60]

Some Afghan journalists comprehend that, universally, bad news is often more newsworthy than good news, and that societies demand drama.[61] If Americans were reading about the Afghanistan these Afghan journalists knew, one broadcaster said in 2010, "then the American public may not take the news seriously."[62] But, they said, Afghanistan is in U.S. national security interests because of the 9/11 attacks. The immense loss of life that day is why so many U.S. news professionals supported the launch of the American-led war soon after. The Afghan journalists know that their counterparts report narrowly on U.S. actions in Afghanistan because their readership is primarily American, and American citizens have invested in the war with taxes and a volunteer military.[63]

But why not report back on the positive advancements in the country? Doesn't the American public want to know the constructive ways in which their taxpayer dollars are being used? Don't they want to know the good they have sacrificed American lives for? The U.S. officials in Afghanistan ask the same questions.

U.S. Reporters and Officials in Afghanistan

The core reason why U.S. news is often produced through an American, or Western, lens, is because the majority of the reporters are trying to connect primarily with home audiences. When U.S. journalists report from Afghanistan, they mostly think about what the American people need to know.[64] Their reporting is ethnocentric because they feel a responsibility to inform their fellow citizens.[65] While the Internet has widened audiences, the default one for U.S. news about the world includes Americans who take interest in international affairs—whether they be policymakers, educators, expatriates living abroad, or engaged citizens who want to know what actions are being taken on their behalf.[66] As a U.S. print reporter said simply in 2012, "The Afghans are not my main concern here; my country is."[67] In keeping American citizens in mind, the bulk of U.S. journalists often feel like they need to provide them with streamlined news that reflects their interests. Maria Abi-Habib, a former *Wall Street Journal* reporter in Kabul, explained in a 2017 interview how she felt that she had to write for Americans: "We would hit on themes of corruption quite a bit because people were so worried about the results the war was actually producing. And especially because the Americans were on such an anticorruption crusade."[68] The *Washington Post*'s Joshua Partlow agreed: "You recognize as a U.S. reporter that you write for a U.S. publication and a lot of people are interested in the fate of the U.S. effort there. You try to do a range of stories for the American public, about what the troops are doing, about the Afghan civilians, and economic and political stories so it is well rounded."[69]

Another U.S. newspaper reporter said in 2012 that coverage of Afghanistan is probably biased in U.S. coverage "in ways you don't even always understand" as sympathy toward fellow Americans can happen so naturally, especially when you see firsthand U.S. troops fighting for their country: "They are the protagonists in your story and the people they fight are the enemy, and that's the way your story is framed—as their success or failure against the enemy. So you are telling it from their side."[70] The news that matters to Americans, the U.S. journalists interviewed concurred, includes security stories that indicate how the war is going. As another print journalist explained in 2012:

> Part of our charge is that there are more than 75,000 American troops on the ground right now. When our readers think of

Afghanistan they are thinking of the soldiers who are here. So I feel like we have a responsibility to write what those 80,000 guys are doing and what their lives look like.[71]

Yet not every reporter for a U.S. news agency is an American. Kathy Gannon, a Canadian reporter for the AP, stated in a 2017 interview: "I don't write for an audience, I write for the story." She knows, however, that this is not the American news media's norm. In August 2001, weeks before 9/11, she gave a talk at the AP office in New York about Afghanistan. An editor asked her when she finished, "But what does that have to do with us?" The question frustrated her and, in her opinion, encapsulated the myopia of American news coverage about the world. However, she said her own editors have never asked her to change the direction of a news story or make it more palatable for an American or Western audience. Because she writes for a newswire, she said, she did not have to think about competition in the way her newspaper and broadcast colleagues did.[72] Carlotta Gall, a British reporter for the *New York Times*, said that her "audience has always been the international world," and not just Washington. She is thinking about anyone in the world who reads English, but also "the people in the countries that I cover who read it, and especially the local media who often pick up the stories and then run them," she said in a 2017 interview. Gall is sensitive to the self-censorship at play in societies that are suffering from protracted conflict and/or are authoritarian, and therefore considers how her news could influence the local news ecosystem.[73]

While not every journalist who writes for U.S. news agencies chooses to write primarily for Americans, those who do often employ symbols, frames, and language that will resonate with the American nation and project a national and/or Western liberal bias. But U.S. news articles about Afghanistan can often provoke suspicion among the Afghan journalists that they are also advocating for the U.S. government's policies and infusing their work with a sense of fidelity to their government.[74] Some of the Afghan journalists understood that U.S. journalists index their news coverage to U.S. government actions so it will resonate with Americans, who they need to attract for market purposes.[75] But others believed that U.S. reporters and officials regularly work together to coerce Afghan officials to change their behavior.[76] While U.S. journalists have no problem taking on the Afghan government, the Afghans believe their peers are more cautious when it comes to the U.S. government because they need to maintain strong relationships with officials and not isolate them—after all, without them, they will not have information to report.[77] They point out that U.S. reporters mostly socialize with American and other Western officials in the country, developing close ties that influence and shape the content of their reporting.

Citing the U.S. press's reaction to the 9/11 attacks and the buildup to the Iraq War, the Afghans believed that the U.S. government has enormous agenda-setting power for American journalism.[78] They saw the power of the American president to direct news agendas. In 2009, for instance, the security situation did not suddenly worsen in Afghanistan, but President Obama had directed his attention to the country and, as explained in Chapter 2, the U.S. journalists admittedly followed his lead.[79] Americans started to learn more about Afghanistan eight years after U.S. troops arrived there because the U.S. president cared.[80]

This closeness with U.S. officials may seem suspicious, but it is also what makes the news credible and useable, some Afghan journalists said, as it affords an authentic, intimate look at the U.S. government.[81] The Afghan journalists can turn to U.S. journalists to understand the words, actions, and motivations of U.S. officials. However, U.S. reporters are not seen to be credible watchdogs of the U.S. government regarding foreign policy issues. Most of the Afghan reporters admire the adversarial role American journalists play in the United States when it comes to domestic issues, but they do not see them play the same role on international issues, and certainly not on policy in Afghanistan.[82] When it comes to coverage about Afghanistan, as one Afghan broadcaster put it, "American journalists are more American than they are journalists and they want the U.S. government to succeed."[83] U.S. government officials can direct U.S. journalists on what to say and when to say it through strategic leaks, many Afghan reporters believed.[84] And when they do challenge U.S. officials, they do not go far enough.[85]

The majority of the Afghan reporters agreed with Hamid Karzai that U.S. reporters wanted to work with American officials to damage his reputation, especially when stories about the alleged corruption of Ahmed Wali Karzai, the president's now-deceased brother, began to appear in the *New York Times* in 2004, followed by corruption stories of another brother, Mahmood Karzai.[86] While they did not dispute the accuracy of U.S. news reports, they agreed with this notion. Another Afghan print journalist concurred with President Karzai that the U.S. press was an outright extension of the U.S. government: "CNN is run by the CIA and the *New York Times* is run by the White House," he said in 2012.[87] Other

journalists interviewed had less extreme ideas of U.S. media and government cooperation but agreed that U.S. journalists normally, naturally,
support U.S. foreign policy goals.[88] Their closeness is evident, they said,
when U.S. government officials come to Afghanistan and only speak with
U.S. reporters.[89]

The U.S. journalists strongly refuted most of the Afghan journalists'
belief that U.S. journalists actively work to support their government.
Reporters for U.S.-based news rarely had the kind of access to American
officials and their secret information that Afghan reporters and officials
assumed they had. They would often hear the criticism that they are complicit advocates of U.S. foreign policy from not just Karzai and his palace
staff, but other Afghan officials as well.[90] But the Afghan officials' and
journalists' widespread belief that U.S. officials leaked entire stories to the
U.S. press corps was not true, the U.S. journalists insisted.

In actuality, U.S. journalists' relationships with U.S. State Department
and military officials in Afghanistan are often cold and contentious.[91] After
all, one American print reporter explained in 2012, "The really great story
is showing how we [the United States] fucked up—not how the Afghans
fucked up . . . The best stories are the ones you don't expect, and the ones
you don't expect are the ones of total malfeasance from American military and officials."[92] The *Times'* Nordland similarly agreed in 2016 that
if "Karzai was a more careful reader, he would see that there are tons of
things we have done on the U.S. military, the night raids in general, and
any case where Afghan civilians have been killed and there have been
Americans involved in some way."[93] They are consistently critical of these
mistakes and want to show that the U.S. government has been complicit
in creating the precarious and failing state of the country.

The U.S. officials who focused on Afghanistan agreed. Daniel
Feldman, the former U.S. Deputy Special Representative to Afghanistan
and Pakistan, said it was "laughable to government officials to think the
press was an organ of a state apparatus, because it was anything but."
Yet inside Afghanistan, "Conspiracy theories are rife . . . and there is this
sense that people are out to screw them, so it makes sense that there is
this competent, all-knowing deep state." The results of U.S. foreign policy
and military action are normally a result of happenstance, not meticulous planning.[94] While some see U.S. government leaks as a way to control the press, the interplay of U.S. government officials and journalists
isn't always black and white and it isn't always clean. Leaks normally
happen, former Ambassador Zalmay Khalilzad explained, when there is

an exceptional relationship between a reporter and an official: "There is no such thing as a deep state; some individuals have a particular relationship, it's not a cabal sitting in the CIA thinking about leaking."[95]

While leaks are inevitable in foreign policy reporting, they usually do not merit an entire story on their own, unless they are about massive data dumps like the ones given to WikiLeaks by Chelsea Manning, or National Security Agency files provided by Edward Snowden. They also normally take place in Washington, an incredibly information-rich environment with thousands of U.S. government employees. Officials can leak information to try to steer a policy in a certain way, but those officials are often low- to mid-ranking and rarely have the full picture of the policy landscape they are part of.

In the field, it's more difficult for reporters to get information from officials. As Partlow said:

> Nine times out of 10, U.S. officials blow us off. We're always clawing for scraps for whatever information you can get, and usually it's very thin. You hear a scrap of something or a rumor of something and then you have to triangulate it a million different ways to get enough information to put it in the paper, by testing it with Afghan or American officials and trying to get evidence . . . You never go to the U.S. embassy and people hand you a document. Not in my experience. The idea [that you do] is laughable to me.[96]

U.S. officials worldwide rarely want to share information with foreign correspondents unless it is celebrating a major U.S. mission initiative. When officials, whether American or Afghan, approach journalists, it is usually because they are frustrated by their higher-ups.[97] They don't have a ready-made story to offer, just chatter.

Contrary to the Afghan journalists' opinions, the U.S. foreign correspondents said that they are legitimately skeptical of U.S. foreign policy in the country. "I don't think we ever wrote: 'Our guys are here to fix things, and isn't it great?' I never wrote that," Pamela Constable of the *Washington Post* said. "I remember writing, 'American policy is having problems in Afghanistan'" based on what the U.S. officials were telling her.[98] This includes the story on Afghanistan's national unity government, which was manufactured by the Obama administration and former Secretary of State John Kerry in particular in 2014.[99] *Times'* editor Schorzman explained in 2016 that the reporters have not just

been censorious of the Afghan government, but also very critical of the
U.S. government and European governments involved in Afghanistan's
reconstruction: "A steady line of our coverage is that the current government exists because of a fiat by Kerry. The solution for the government
was unconstitutional, and we've been really critical of the hand of foreign
influence in the election process." He continued:

> We are very aware and very critical. Another constant line of our re-
> porting is: How is the American presence in Afghanistan distorting
> values? When Karzai says we brought corruption, is he right? Is the
> U.S. inflating the impact of aid work? Is it imposing institutions that
> don't necessarily work for the Afghan culture? Karzai is right about
> that. Part of our reporting is where the U.S. gets it wrong, such as
> what is the U.S. government not seeing? Why does the U.S. mili-
> tary keep having to revise the rules of engagement? Officially we're
> not at war in Afghanistan, but we're obviously still at war.[100]

Like the Afghans, the U.S. officials resent this coverage, and they
certainly did not see the U.S. press as supporting them. "I certainly
don't recall looking at a story and thinking, 'Wow, that is so pro-U.S.!'"
Feldman said about his tenure.[101] Khalilzad also remembered during his
time as Ambassador from 2003–2005, "The U.S. media was criticizing
the U.S. more than the Afghans. There were a lot of stories critical of
the U.S. mission, mistakes we were making, being too heavy-handed,
not pushing as we should."[102] While Washington often does create the
larger international news agenda for the U.S. press, the American embassy in Kabul had little sway in setting the agenda for Afghanistan-based
reporters. American officials regularly pitch them narratives that positively depict U.S. foreign policy efforts and effects, but the journalists normally turn down invitations to cover school or hospital openings that the
U.S. military or the U.S. Agency for International Development (USAID)
funds. For David Ensor, who spent three decades as a journalist for NPR,
ABC, and CNN and later became the senior communications official at
the U.S. embassy from 2010 to 2011, it was maddening:

> Fifty new health clinics opened in a day and all the sudden maternal
> health was transformed in multiple cities. But the same day a bomb
> went off. Guess what made it in the news? . . . Good news tended to
> be overshadowed by a bomb or two, or a shooting between soldiers.

I understand that; I used to do it myself. But it was frustrating from the point of view from a government official. And it was certainly frustrating for the president of Afghanistan.[103]

The U.S. correspondents interviewed agreed that reporting what the U.S. government wants would give Americans an exaggerated idea of the U.S. mission's accomplishments in Afghanistan. The narrative that the journalists construct for Americans about the war is closer to reality, they agreed, and therefore in the American public's interest to consume. The idea that U.S. journalists are affiliated with or beholden to the U.S. government is especially absurd, the reporters said, when you consider their relationship with the American diplomats.[104]

While as noted above some low- to mid-level officials will provide chatter, the reporters largely described the embassy as being increasingly closed off to reporters. This was especially the case as the Obama surge played out from 2010 to 2014. "The embassy officials distrusted us quite a bit," Abi-Habib recalled, and they rarely wanted to know what the U.S. reporters were seeing in the country.[105] Nordland described the relationship between U.S. reporters and officials as "politely hostile." Most of the stories the U.S. embassy wants him to cover, he emphasized, "are bullshit, self-serving puffery." He said, "I have a terrible relationship with them and I'm proud of it. I don't want to have a good relationship with the American government. I'll respect confidences and so on, but I'm certainly not in any way a tool of theirs."[106] Gall described "a great nervousness" around her whenever she visited the embassy. "There's a feeling of hiding things which I don't think is necessary," and the hesitancy to engage reporters worked against the officials. This was especially the case with USAID representatives, Gall explained: "We could have always done stories on what they were doing, but they had a great fear that we were going to write critical stuff. Every briefing was off the record, which meant we couldn't use it."[107]

Not just the U.S. embassies but the entire State Department works from a defensive posture, on the crisis of the day, Feldman explained. In Afghanistan, they felt subject to a constant barrage of criticism: "Criticized in the SIGAR [Special Inspector General for Afghanistan Reconstruction] report, criticized because of civilian casualties, criticized because money isn't flowing fast enough."[108] They are normally writing talking points to react to a news story and rarely to proactively shape one. The embassy's public affairs section arranges interviews between reporters and officials, but they also often insist on their right to edit and approve embassy officials' quotes before journalists can publish them. Most of the interviews are off the record or on background, meaning that the journalist often cannot use any of the information and cannot quote the official by name. On-the-record interviews are only allowed if they are with the American ambassador or at a press conference. And even then there is little candor. The only honest moments they have with American officials are off the record, the U.S. journalists stressed.[109] Eileen O'Connor, the Director for Communications and Public Diplomacy at the U.S. embassy from 2011 to 2012 and a former reporter for CNN, agreed it was a difficult line to walk. Her philosophy on working with the press was: "Tell the truth and tell as much as you can, but always be honest when you can't tell them anymore." She would say to reporters, "I can wave you off of a false story, but there will be times when I can't talk to you." But she always believed the embassy should be a resource for U.S. and Afghan journalists.[110]

The *Post*'s Constable was more conciliatory to the U.S. embassy's position: "As a journalist, I never doubted the good intentions of the American government in Afghanistan. But I certainly and my colleagues, just as much if not more, investigated and raised questions about whether or not those intentions were working out."[111]

FOR NEARLY A year, Maria Abi-Habib of the *Wall Street Journal* investigated the horrifying neglect of Afghan soldiers and policemen who were patients at the Dawood National Military Hospital in Kabul, which holds prestige comparable to that of the Walter Reed National Military Medical Center. Most of the hospital staff's salaries and supplies were funded by U.S. taxpayer dollars. Abi-Habib had heard pieces of this story for months and slowly collected evidence that decorated Army General William B. Caldwell thwarted an investigation of the hospital by the Department of Defense Inspector General. "We're so busy as journalists; your attention would be jerked around constantly. But I would always make sure to ask about it when I sat with someone who may know about the situation," she explained.[112]

She eventually identified a key source, Colonel Schuyler Geller, a U.S. Army doctor who brought the dire state of the hospital to General Caldwell's attention in 2010 and wanted the Inspector General to conduct an investigation. Caldwell and his deputy, Brigadier General Gary Patton, said they were concerned about the effect it could have on the upcoming midterm congressional elections in the United States, and they did not want to embarrass President Obama. Caldwell told Geller to keep quiet about it, and then he demoted him. "He tried to do the right thing by going up his chain of command, and his chain of command quickly destroyed him," Abi-Habib explained. "It did nothing to serve the country. He was a good soldier. He didn't feel the need to leak that to anybody, but I found him and I think that set off a light switch in his mind." He agreed to speak with her in the courtyard of the ISAF headquarters in Kabul. "I was so nervous," Abi-Habib recalled. "I used to meet so many sources there and a lot of military people knew me pretty well. I didn't even bring a notebook because I didn't want them to try to put a kibosh on my reporting before I was done." Geller and Abi-Habib sat there and spoke for hours.

It took Abi-Habib roughly eight months to get a critical mass of evidence; she then worked on the story exclusively for three months. On September 3, 2011, "At Afghan Military Hospital, Graft and Deadly Neglect," was published in the *Journal*. She wrote that after U.S. officials discovered the patient neglect, the Afghan officials refused to take action for months.[113] For patients to get care, they had to bribe Afghan nurses and doctors. Many died from "malnourishment, starvation . . . and willful neglect." The victims were poor Afghan National Army (ANA) soldiers and members of the Afghan National Police (ANP), often far from home in Kabul. That distance made some families feel as if what happened to their sons was a singular incident, not a systematic pattern of neglect and abuse.[114] Abi-Habib quoted Sher Hazrat, who watched his veteran brother die at the hospital and asked, "If there's no service for us, why should we serve our country?" It was exactly the kind of sentiment the U.S. military had feared as they tried to build the capacity of the Afghan National Security Forces. She recalled in a 2017 interview:

> General Caldwell and his entire machine had tried to make my editors very nervous . . . They could tell I had a lot on them. They sent this very long email to my editors saying, "It's clear Maria is coming in here with an agenda; she's not giving us a fair shake." Which is all bullshit; I was giving them a fair shake. I didn't tell them what I was writing, like, "This is paragraph five and it is going to say . . ." [but] I told them, "This is what I heard and I need you to comment." They knew that I was young and they tried to take advantage of that . . . That was extraordinary, the lengths that they went to. He knew it was career-ending and what he did was illegal. He tried to thwart an IG [Inspector General] inspection and intimidate Dr. Geller, the whistleblower and my source.[115]

The story continued to develop for more than a year, setting the agenda for multiple other U.S. and Afghan news outlets. In July 2012, Colonel Geller testified to the House Oversight subcommittee in Washington on the neglect, and in 2013, General Caldwell retired. Roughly one-third of the Afghan journalists interviewed cited Abi-Habib's investigation as an example of when U.S. journalists are independent and critical of the U.S. government.[116] It's also a story, they say, they could not report on their own due to the powerful U.S. Army and ANA forces.

Like Abi-Habib, other U.S. journalists said they would often be shunned by military public affairs people who didn't approve of their reporting. Gall recalled a story she wrote in March 2003 about a 22-year-old taxi driver named Dilawar who had been detained at Bagram Air Force Base and died. The U.S. Army told the press that he had coronary artery disease and had died of a heart attack, but Gall and her Afghan colleagues at the *New York Times* tracked down the death certificate, which clearly stated that the cause of death was homicide.[117] This was in 2003, more than a year before the story broke about the torture at the Abu Ghraib prison in Iraq, and no one was thinking that U.S. soldiers and officials were torturing prisoners. Later, the story gained more traction, and eventually an Academy Award–winning documentary, "Taxi to the Dark Side," was made about the case and the U.S. military's torture of detainees.

Gall's access to the military suffered as a result of her reporting: "I didn't get blackballed, but I got dubbed inside the American military as being 'difficult' and 'anti-military'," she said. The military's press officers reportedly kept a file on her that was referenced each time she requested an interview or an embed with the troops, and she was often denied both, even though she was a senior correspondent for the *Times*.[118] It was only after she had lived and worked in Afghanistan for many years that her relationship with individual soldiers and generals improved.

Navigating the U.S. military and ISAF bureaucracies, with multiple press offices, can be confusing. Identifying the right people to speak with and investigating the veracity of their statements can be exhausting. Some U.S. journalists concurred that U.S. military spokespeople don't honestly answer their questions and can be openly hostile. This could be because of their insecurity about how the war is progressing, some journalists offered: They don't know if they are actually winning, even though they insist that they are. Gannon explained that the common narrative of the U.S. military seems to be that American military is having great success, but the inability to maintain that success is the fault of the ANA and the

Afghan government. She blames this in part to the lack of critical examination of the conflict by U.S. journalists, but also because American military officials can block journalists' access to information when they want to keep an issue under wraps, and then pester them to cover the stories they want covered.[119] Journalists often are forced to give up on reporting information when military officials do not confirm it before their deadlines.[120] Another print reporter explained in 2012 how U.S. Special Forces actively ridiculed her pursuit of a story, refused to cooperate with her, and then berated her after she published it with multiple sound sources. She said: "If Afghan journalists have any illusions that we have better access to the U.S. military than they do, those are illusions. It is not reality."[121]

U.S. journalists are, however, more likely to be embedded with American troops. Nordland explained in 2016 that if the military wants to work with journalists, there is a certain affinity they have for their fellow Americans: "The U.S. military are always going to be more forthcoming with the American press than with the Afghan press, which they don't always necessarily trust as much. That's just normal."[122] Once the U.S. journalists travel with American troops, they see at close range how they risk their lives, but the experience is rife with attempts at manipulation. They are aware that they are entertaining a form of military censorship, since officials can control what the journalists see. As one U.S. print journalist explained:

> I'm pretty cynical about the U.S. military agenda with reporters . . . their mission is really to steer you towards whatever they want. They want you to write about success, so they go out of their way to shield you from seeing something that would depict them as losing the war or doing a bad job. It feels like propaganda because they make such an active effort to send you to certain units. They don't want you to see soldiers with bad morale or the units that have lost a lot of people.[123]

Yet military embeds are also one of the few ways in which U.S. journalists can keep the U.S. military accountable, and to also fill a demand by the American public to know how "our boys" are doing. The embed system functions when it allows the journalists to interact with soldiers, who are often candid, and when the higher-ranking officials do not try to control the narrative.[124] This is often the case in the most dangerous locations, where the military does not send a public affairs minder to manage the journalists. Therefore, the most volatile places are the ones the journalists prefer. "No one is telling you what things mean. You're seeing it," one print journalist explained in 2012.[125] Still, there is so much message discipline within the U.S. military that it can be difficult to uncover truth.[126] As the *Post*'s Constable explained, "I would say that being embedded with troops is a particular and unique form of reporting . . . We couldn't really get the other side of the story; we were only getting what the military wanted us to see and to say. That was hard. It was something I didn't like, but that was the deal you made. You write what happens to them, what their problems are and what their perspectives are. That's what your job is." The embeds are not the norm, though, she and others emphasized.[127] They provide a time-limited peephole into the frontlines but don't provide much insight into the larger conflict and the political and economic dynamics at play.

While U.S. journalists in the region do not conspire with the U.S. government, they do concur that they benefit from its power and its policy of protecting American citizens overseas (just as the journalists with Canadian, U.K., or other Western countries benefit from the protection of their governments). Because they are American citizens, they can take more risks in their reporting and investigate the country's most powerful people.[128] "I think everyone [in the Afghan government] knows that it's a pretty serious line to cross to kill an American journalist, and the other power brokers know that too," one American print journalist said in 2012.[129] "The U.S. journalists are associated with American's power, and the U.S. military could retaliate should an American citizen be targeted." The journalists know that their embassy will support them regardless of how they report on American and other Western officials' efforts.

The U.S. officials interviewed agreed that the journalists play an important role in American democracy and that it was their responsibility to protect them as citizens and to work to help them explain policy. Ambassadors Khalilzad, Neumann, Crocker, and Grossman, in addition to the other U.S. officials interviewed for this book, all said that they found U.S. reporting on Afghanistan to be largely well sourced and accurate. Sometimes there are mistakes, and they do not like every report, but the dynamic between reporters and officials, the tension for more transparency and accountability, is important to the health of the American democracy, and they respected it.[130]

Yet Afghans perceive U.S. journalists as valuing the word of U.S. officials or other Americans in Afghanistan more than Afghan officials or Afghans because they are biased toward the source, and they naturally see their fellow citizens as the source of truth.[131]

Nationalism as the Norm

For a journalist from one nation that is in conflict with another—whether it be trade wars, cold wars, combat wars, or others—looking at both sides of the story and challenging the national interests or aims of his or her country can sometimes be perceived as deviant.[132] This is universal, especially in the early period of conflict. One can disagree with policy, but a sense of automatic patriotism can activate when American lives are at risk.[133] Criticizing a war effort early on can also be commercial suicide for news outlets, as it can provoke a sense of outrage among consumers if a national news agency did not appear to be supporting its country.[134] It's an "undeniable historical fact," argued Phillip Taylor in 2000, that a country's "national media have helped the prosecution of wars far more than they have ever hindered them."[135] This is in part because governments have developed more sophisticated strategic communications techniques but also because, during conflict, journalists are just like their fellow citizens. They're occupationally disposed to pay more attention.

Nations, according to Silvio Waisbord, "culturally coordinate," meaning that they "simultaneously aggregate and separate people on the basis of cultural forms such as language, religion, history and symbols"; national institutions create, maintain, and transform that sense of cultural membership.[136] A nation's flag, monuments, leaders, songs, and/or pictures can have potent cognitive and emotional effects.[137] A nation is, as Benedict Anderson famously said, "imagined" because its members "will never know most of their fellow-members, meet them, or even hear of them, yet in the minds of each lives the image of their communion."[138] It is, in other words, socially constructed. To belong to a nation means that one participates in maintaining narratives around these symbols and cultural forms to bestow meaning to the nation and its place in the world. One's national narrative can resonate with them, often deeply and powerfully, and help provide a foundation for their identity.

Nationalism is a term with many connotations. It can be used to refer to an inherent loyalty and affection one has for their nation, and/or a belief that they should have political autonomy. The negative connotation is a chauvinistic nationalism, a sense of superiority that can lead to jingoism, the belief that "one's own group is better than others, and therefore has the right to dominate or displace them."[139] Being nationalistic means that you can at once feel solidarity with one group and be intolerant of another. Yet national identity, and the degree to which one feels a sense of nationalism, can be politically and socially constructed and reconstructed in order to align citizens with their leaders' agendas, particularly when it comes to a country's role in the international system.[140] Although this identity can be plastic and reshaped to fit modern times, where you are from is fundamental to who you are and how you see the world.[141]

The news media are a critical institution to a nation; they help to construct and sustain the nation daily by disseminating these narratives and symbols. As Anderson said in *Imagined Communities*, while the standardization of time and calendars "synchronized time and space," the emergence of a capitalist print industry ensured that newspapers served as platforms for citizens to communicate and debate issues important to the nation in step with one another.[142] The news media set the rhythm of daily life. They can also make citizenship meaningful by serving as a means of expression and education.[143] The media can oscillate between providing a sort of everyday sense of nationalism to maintain cultural identity and a sense of national unity, and chauvinistic nationalism or patriotism when it comes to its reporting about the world, especially during conflict.[144] The press can articulate the priorities of the state, give definition to modern cultural and political events, and legitimize them.

So what happens when a national narrative—one that helps the citizens of a nation feel solidarity, cohesion, and purpose with each other— travels internationally? National bias can become more pronounced. There are, according to Waisbord, "Globalophobes, Globalophiles, and Cosmopolitanists." Globalophobes can be defined as those who applauded the efforts of UNESCO in the 1970s and 1980s. They equate globalization with Westernization. They insist that the mass media, mainly coming from the West, strip other nations of their cultural autonomy. Globalophiles believe in the power of technology to inspire cultural diversity and increase understanding abroad. They are so optimistic about technology, Waisbord says, that they "ignore persistent power inequalities in cultural production and consumption" and do not acknowledge that cultural production is Western-dominated and that technology cannot change the political-economic structures responsible for those inequalities. Cosmopolitanists believe that we can transcend our nation and can become global citizens.[145] But while people can share a common cause with someone who lives in a different nation, that commonality alone doesn't challenge the bond of the nation. And there is no evidence that the mass media can induce and maintain long-term cultural transformations. To the contrary, the international media can actually intensify national feelings, making cultural, political, religious, and philosophical differences more pronounced.

Even with globalization, "the national" still matters. The international news media do not activate cross-border solidarity. Nationalistic feelings are powerful. And by setting their own agenda or following those of their national leaders, the media greatly contribute to stirring them. Journalism normally is targeted toward national audiences and "coordinates the life of a nation." National media promote a sense of collective memory and give people a sense of place. While the global news media can help some audiences recognize commonality in others, they do not manufacture and preserve common symbols that can help people transcend their national identity.

Each country has its own unique brand of nationalism, and the degree of it changes with the times.[146] While some news media brands aim to have international reach, they are normally tethered to one country.[147] Like their fellow citizens, journalists are naturally "culture-bound" and influenced by their nation's own political context.[148] In the mid-1990s, for instance, Philo Wasburn found that the language and explanatory frameworks that made up Japanese news reports on trade disputes with the United States were staunchly pro-Japanese and served the objectives of the Japanese state.[149] C. C. Lee and J. Yang similarly discovered that journalists from five countries—Australia, Canada, China, Japan, and the United Kingdom—who covered the United Kingdom's return of Hong Kong to China in 2000 employed their own national lenses to tell the story to their audiences.[150] Betwa Sharma interviewed journalists covering the 2009 Copenhagen Climate Summit and discovered that journalists from India and Nigeria acknowledged that they used the filters of their national interests in their reportage. The U.S. correspondent interviewed, however, insisted he was detached from the U.S. in his reporting.[151]

For this study, the majority of the U.S. journalists reporting from Afghanistan interviewed plainly accepted the fact that they could not separate their nationality from their work. Most journalists writing for American news agencies are American; they have a worldview and a sense of American identity that is difficult to abandon when they are writing primarily for home audiences. They agreed that they are sympathetic to their fellow countrymen. They may be independent and free to report anything, but they naturally gravitate toward U.S. economic and security concerns around the world.[152] They examine what matters to U.S. national interests and to American citizens.[153]

The Afghan reporters saw this. They perceived U.S. journalists as putting their nationality above their profession, as being "more American than they are journalists."[154] One U.S. print reporter agreed that this was "inevitably true . . . We are Americans and we do see the world through a lens imbued with America."[155] Another U.S. reporter concurred that it is probably true "in ways you don't even always understand" as sympathy toward fellow Americans can happen so naturally.[156]

The virtue of nationalism, of appealing to symbols and narratives their target audience shares, is indeed part of U.S. journalism. But the reporters are not automatic cheerleaders for the government.[157] Just because reporters are attached to their nationhood does not mean they are blindly supportive of their government. There is a difference between maintaining American's sense of identity and projecting American superiority. "We might hope America wins in general, but we want to document the reality along the way," an American newspaper reporter said in 2012. U.S. journalists can be supportive of their country without supporting U.S. policy, which officials will almost always frame as being successful.

The U.S. reporters interviewed knew that their reportage could be taken personally inside Afghanistan, and they knew it could also be viewed as narrowly focusing on security and failed governance frames. They were not, however, concerned about their storytelling's impact on those Afghan perceptions. The problem, another American print reporter said in 2012, is that it is easy to "confuse having an American worldview with having a specific Western government agenda."[158] They primarily felt a sense of responsibility toward their American audiences. They regarded themselves as watchdogs, but primarily as *national* watchdogs: They track how U.S. tax dollars are spent; monitor the efficiency of American diplomatic efforts; and highlight the welfare, achievements, and mistakes of American soldiers fighting in Afghanistan. In this way, the journalists worked to hold U.S. power in Afghanistan accountable and to criticize them when criticism was merited. They wanted to hold the U.S. government accountable so that it is successful in maintaining the country's material strength, in addition to its international credibility on issues like human rights and the value of liberal democratic governance.

While a sense of ethnocentrism and national bias may be inevitable, the news professionals interviewed insist that they don't seek to be advocates. As *Times* editor Schorzman explained, "Afghan journalists are correct when they are talking about a sense of American bias, but they are not correct about it when they talk about that being intentional." He continued, "When they say that we parrot American officials . . . is there an intent to serve as an official arm of the U.S. government? Absolutely not. There is no way I want to be an arm of the U.S. government."[159] Schorzman said, "Fairness in foreign affairs reporting is not necessarily about finding balance, but about making an honest, good-faith effort to understand where people are coming from and why they might feel that way, and to reflect that accurately . . . [it] is a willingness to have your mind changed when you come across facts" and to seek out sources beyond the normal officials. "When we're doing it right, we're doing it with humility and an awareness of our own biases.[160] A sense of American partiality can inevitably creep in, even for those correspondents who think they can objectively interpret foreign events and cultures. The trick is to consciously and deliberately question and challenge those sympathies. While it may be easy to look at the United States as a monolithic entity with enormous power, strip away its political complexities, and see all citizens as being subservient to the government, it is a gross oversimplification.

The U.S. journalists acknowledged their own ethnocentric biases, but they also pointed out that Afghan reporters, editors, and pundits likewise reduce the U.S. to fit their own worldviews. "Just as we are Americans, they are Afghans," one American reporter said in 2012. They "complain about their country being too simplified in our coverage, but they do the same with simplifying America."[161] Another agreed that Afghans are fiercely proud of their place in history, positioned at the nexus of Iran, China, and Russia and along the historic Silk Road from China to North Africa, which significantly shaped the global economy. It is a land that the Mongols, Persians, British, and Soviets wanted to occupy, and the United States has settled there for more than a decade. This geopolitical importance naturally inclines them toward this view.[162]

The independent Afghan journalists interviewed seek to use their positions to build and modernize their nation. An Afghan broadcaster concurred that his national identity comes before his profession: "I am more Afghan than I am a journalist." It is likely that Afghans reporting from foreign countries would be just as Afghanistan-centric, another said: "If Afghanistan sent Afghan troops to Syria, then the Afghan people would want to know that their media was recognizing the sacrifice of Afghan troops."[163] Another Afghan print journalist acknowledged, "I'm interested in everything in my country because I am an Afghan," but why would Americans be interested in everything about Afghanistan?[164] They see U.S. news as largely pro-American mostly because they are pro-Afghanistan. To see themselves through American news filters can be displacing and jarring, and it can injure their honor.[165] They react emotionally because they want to be perceived more positively abroad among international institutions and the community of donor nations supporting Afghanistan. They know that U.S. journalists have authority in a global news system in which they define and project Afghanistan as a violent, failed, hopeless place.[166] They want to be supported by and within the international system, not demoralized and shunned by it.

The U.S. government also wants to see their efforts in Afghanistan viewed more positively. They do not see an American press corps that is chauvinistically nationalistic and serving to the government. They want U.S. reporters to validate their military, diplomatic, and development agendas in the country and report the truth as the U.S. officials see it. It is because U.S. journalists frame Afghanistan as a violent, failed, and corrupt nation that they are not supporting the U.S. military and diplomatic corps in their mission to help Afghanistan become a peaceful and prosperous nation.

So how do we reconcile this?

Former president Karzai believed that the U.S. news media framed Afghanistan negatively—and wrote stories about corruption and drug trafficking by his family—to help the U.S. government put pressure on him to be subservient to the Western agenda in his country. Some Afghan journalists agreed with him as they tried to make sense of the perceived closeness between U.S. reporters and officials. But the worldview of Afghan reporters and officials has also been affected by a history of heavy government interference with their news media. The Afghan journalists almost expect U.S. news media to be deferential to the American government because that has been their experience under decades of authoritarianism. Perhaps the compromise in this thought is that when the U.S. government has bad news to share about the Afghan government, the U.S. press often reports it, but when it is positive, the U.S. press often does not. If they were to report good news at the scale U.S. government officials wanted them to, the journalists would feel as if they were government agents.

The Afghan journalists were conflicted. They valued the opportunity to serve as watchdogs on their government with the support of the U.S. government and press, but their own ethnocentrism caused them to resent the fact that Afghanistan's triumphs are not routinely highlighted in

U.S. news. Many understand that the U.S. news content on Afghanistan focuses on American "enduring values" and on providing news for an American audience. Afghan journalists have been too dependent on U.S. journalism about Afghanistan thus far to reject it. While the Afghan journalists were becoming increasingly professional, they all appreciated their U.S. colleagues' reporting, especially how they expose Afghan politicians' and strongmen's malfeasances. With more than 30 years of conflict, few leaders are innocent of human rights violations and corruption. Nominally, Afghan journalists have been unleashed from authoritarian controls, yet they still operate within a norm of fear and oppression. While this is the frame within which U.S. journalists report Afghanistan, Afghan journalists are still Afghan, and they resent that the West considers their country to be a violent failure.

Despite the inherent and personal frustrations with negative news frames, in addition to the suspicions of U.S. government hegemony over the press, the Afghan independent journalists are largely willing to accept it because America gives them the space they need to professionally contribute to an emerging democratic society. Without U.S. economic support and news bureaus, Afghan journalism and the independent press might limp along, but insights and revelations about Afghanistan's most powerful would largely go unreported. According to the Afghan journalists interviewed, U.S. journalists have a responsibility to tell the American people that there will be destructive security implications if the United States leaves Afghanistan too early; a responsibility to encourage the world to look at Afghanistan positively; and a responsibility to help build the confidence of the Afghan government and people.

Afghanistan the Country: A Changing Paradigm for American News

Growing up in western Kabul during the civil war and Taliban years, Mujib Mashal would often create magazines to pass the time. They'd include a mix of art, poetry, and verses from the Koran. He would give them to his uncle when he visited from Pakistan so that he could "publish" them. Mashal didn't know what publishing meant, but he liked the idea of his stories and work transcending his space. When he wasn't writing and curating content, he would read Iranian detective novels, which he devoured continuously throughout the U.S. airstrikes on Kabul in October 2001. Stories were his lifeline; later they became his livelihood.

In 2017, he became a senior correspondent for the *New York Times* in Kabul, one of the first ones who was native to the country in which they were reporting. As a teenager in 2004, Mashal had gone to the Seeds of Peace Camp in Otisfield, Maine, as part of a first cohort of Afghan youth to spend time with their Pakistani peers and try to deconstruct the poisonous narratives they had told of one another. He won a scholarship to Deerfield Academy, and then another to Columbia College in New York, where he studied history.[167] In 2010, Mashal fell into a summer job with the *New York Times* in Kabul after his brother connected him with *Times* bureau chief Alissa Rubin. She told Mashal that the *Times* didn't take interns in conflict zones; Mashal replied that Kabul was his home, and he would be there anyway.

Rubin let him join the bureau as a seasonal paid translator, but he also would occasionally report on breaking news. He said in an October 2016 interview, "I realized that what I wrote down could become part of a story, and there was a world out there that would see the details of whatever it was I wrote down in that moment." He continued, "What I see will shape what the larger audience understands whatever happened. That was a powerful moment for me."[168]

Upon college graduation in 2011, Mashal became a contractor with Al Jazeera in Doha before returning to Kabul in 2012 as a freelance feature writer. Magazine writing allowed him to profile influential figures and to explain to Americans their impact from the Afghan point of view. He had an especially prolific year in 2014, when he wrote several articles for *Harper's Magazine* and *The Atlantic*, including one on the end of Karzai's tenure in 2014. "The Karzai story in particular was very fulfilling," he said in 2016, "because it was an opportunity for my voice to emerge more . . . I was a product of his rule. Fourteen years of his government is who I was also."[169]

Now, Mashal writes from the Afghan point of view nearly every day for *Times* readers. When he joined the bureau in 2015, Karzai began to warm up to the newspaper. Karzai gave an interview to Rod Nordland in 2015, the first one since 2008—and since Karzai had expelled Matthew Rosenberg in 2014. Mashal brought a nuanced understanding to Afghanistan that other Western reporters inherently could not.[170] "The way I am seen in the room is not just as a *New York Times* reporter, but as an Afghan also," Mashal explained.[171] He constantly confronts the perception that he writes for a newspaper that is pro-American: "My role becomes using a lot of personal and social networking skills and energy to try to minimize the ramifications of a hard story that I do which, from their [Afghan] view, is seen as being unpatriotic or against their national interests."[172] Once a story runs, he often spends time with the story's subjects and sources, trying to lessen the potential damage to a relationship by listening to them vent. To report what he is expected to by Americans and to maintain expected cultural norms from Afghans, he has to walk a fine line of humility and avoid sensationalism. "If we want a deeper understanding of current events in Afghanistan," he explained, "it is difficult to get those without relationships."[173] His Afghan cohort agrees with him, often stating how proud they are that one of them is now explaining Afghanistan to America and the world. Between April 2015 and December 2016, he filed more than 200 news stories that look at life and politics in Afghanistan from a local's point of view.

Mashal is far from a parachute, Western reporter, and his understanding of his audience, which drives the stories he selects and how he frames them, is more complicated: "I might tilt to an American audience, but I need to aim broader as the *New York Times* is moving on from an American-centric paper." He continued, "That will be a slow transition in Afghanistan, because of the presence of the American troops here. My life and background here ends up toning down the American lens of the story and makes it into a more open-ended lens."[174] While this is not yet a norm, it is a significant change for a Western news agency that many believe can draw the most authoritative picture of a nation for foreign audiences. As the war has dragged on, Afghanistan is increasingly being represented as a multidimensional country to the American and global publics who remain interested.[175]

8

The Diplomatic Dimension
of News

A NATION'S NEWS media illuminate the nation itself. How news
professionals determine newsworthiness, how they construct narratives,
and how they present them indicate their nation's priorities, its agreements,
divisions, and role in the world. The news media have a special role in
creating and maintaining a nation: reinforcing its symbols, its shared
narratives, its language, its culture, and the frameworks in which one can
understand the world.[1] Journalists have astounding power to construct a
sense of reality for people, but despite the transnational reach of news
today, the bulk of editors, producers, and reporters select and construct
media messages and images to cater to their targeted audiences.[2] They
often aim to deliver a worldview that feels comfortable for their audiences
and/or governments and to give them evidence that the "pictures in their
heads" are accurate.

The picture of U.S.–Afghan relations during this historically long
war, no matter your vantage point, has been infused by more than three
decades of tunnel vision, distortion, mutual dependency, and resentment.
Journalists from both countries try to make sense of the conflict and everyday life, yet whatever clarity they arrive at comes mainly from their sense
of ethnocentrism and nationalism: It is equipment that reporters use to
make sense of conflict. A lens that puts your standards and country at the
center can bring war into sharp focus, but it can also radically oversimplify
the chaos, complexity, and surreal nature of war.[3]

The principle of objectivity might be necessary for professional
journalists, but it is much easier to supply, even simulate, in the examination of domestic issues. When reporting about their own governments,

journalists can take up a certain familiar distance from a political party and take advantage of that distance to critique officials and politicians vying for influence. They can employ a plausible mental grid with which to understand, and sometimes clarify, the various positions and conflicts. Yet detaching themselves from their government is different than detaching themselves from their nation, in this case, the shared history, culture, language, and place that makes one American and another Afghan.

When it comes to the question of their country's role in the world, journalists do not disengage themselves from their national identity. As we have seen, Afghan and American journalists identify with their fellow citizens and aim to communicate with them first. In part this is cultural, virtually automatic—a case of emotional identification. In part it is strategic—a need to make their story comprehensible to their primary readers. But by reporting for a primary audience, they unintentionally package their nations in an efficient form for outsiders to consume. They rehearse what it means to be Afghan or American or "Western." The journalists play the role of representatives, or de facto diplomats, for their nations. This is the case for U.S. journalists who work for elite American news organizations at home and abroad.

How does U.S. news about Afghanistan reverberate inside Afghanistan? Afghan journalists have steadily relied on it for content, guidance, and moral support, depending on the topic. The Afghan news media are still young, and the country's security is deeply dependent on American and Western alliances for economic and military investment. Afghan journalists look to U.S. news because the Afghan government deems the content to be important, and they study it closely. For these journalists, U.S. news also provides a window on a government that—because thousands of U.S. troops remain stationed in the country and billions of U.S. dollars have flooded the Afghan economy—affects Afghans' daily lives. As we have seen, they have a generally weak relationship with Afghan government officials. But Afghan journalists also have little, if any, relationship with U.S. government officials. They see American news as primary source material for relaying facts about the conflict, American policy, and general chatter in Washington. They also, however, look to it for insight on their government through investigative reports and analysis that the American journalists conduct more easily than they can.

Afghan journalists habitually look to them in order to understand a country that has loomed so large in their daily affairs.[4] Yet they seek to understand the United States in its relation to their own nation. They do not want to understand America in all of its complexity; they want to know what the American government and people think about *them*. Afghan officials and reporters can find validation in these news stories, but they are also frustrated when such validation is not provided in a steady stream. Just as U.S. journalists talk about America in global news, Afghan journalists focus on themselves, on their nation, when talking about America. National interest is universal.

Ethnocentricity in journalism is also universal. News agencies that have transnational reach still have a physical headquarters in a country, where they make editorial decisions on content often based on their geopolitical location.[5] Bella Mody found in her study of news representations of the conflict in Darfur that how different news agencies describe cross-national foreign events depends on the locations and characteristics of the news organizations that create the news: National news agencies tell stories that will make sense to their audiences.[6] If "objectivity were humanely possible, reporting on an event would be identical in all news media around the world," she stated.[7] But it's not possible; ideas and events look drastically different depending on where you stand worldwide. While some had hope that transnational news stations could help bring about a global civil society, the news content can have a decisively national feel.[8] The CNN that one watches in Kabul is not the CNN one watches in Washington: CNN distinctly tailors its programming for American and international audiences. As does the BBC World Service, which is the news agency that comes closest to reaching all corners of the globe through radio, since it is the medium that can access the largest swaths of populations worldwide.[9] Al Jazeera, too, M. Ayish argued in 2002, diverts from the principle of objectivity when it comes to issues that have a pan-Arab, public consensus.[10] When given the choice, audiences are more likely to choose news agency brands that are national than international and report news that is local and real to them.[11] National interest is the most frequently determined influence on media coverage throughout the world.[12]

Journalists are not merely observers of international relations; they are active participants in it, especially in developing countries. American and Western journalists have the power to shape and fix identities for them. Their content often travels beyond intended audiences to secondary or unintended ones. Foreign government and civil society leaders read it not just to get a reflection of U.S. government and society, but also to forecast

U.S. behaviors and actions. The news provides a common, open source of intelligence for global leaders and publics alike. Through the U.S. news media, they receive a sort of instruction manual, a guide on how to move forward in bilateral, regional, and international relations.

Therefore, American ethnocentricity and nationalism in journalism has a special weight and significance. At least for the time being, the United States is a global power, and American journalists, as citizens, can have a natural loyalty to their country. Since those journalists dominate the international media market and news flows, they can accentuate images and the brands of other leaders, people, and countries. Since the late 1970s and the New World Information and Communication Order movement via UNESCO, developing countries have complained about this one-way flow of communication from the United States and other Western countries. Leaders in Asian, African, and Middle Eastern countries referred to this information imbalance as a form of neocolonialism in which Westerners were serving as image-makers for others.[13] They saw it as a form of suppression: The Western media should be supporting these countries' development, not focusing on their failures. This especially applied to the United States.[14]

Three decades later, this sentiment has been palpable in Afghanistan. The influence the American and Western press has on international and local dynamics is profound. Shortly after 9/11, when the United States was still reeling from trauma, Afghanistan was constructed in the U.S. news media as a country full of hope and Karzai as an elegant, heroic figure. Over time, though, the Afghans saw a U.S. press that insisted on American superiority, with a strong sense of nationalism that permeated its coverage, reporting a recurring picture of a failed state seething with violence and instability, and America as their savior. The intense reactions of former president Karzai, other Afghan government officials, and Afghan journalists is logical. The U.S. reporters interviewed for this study cannot blame them. This visceral reaction comes from their own sense of ethnocentricity and nationalism, constructed and reconstructed over time through their shared stories of battles against foreign forces and the civil struggle they've endured.

Afghan Journalists

Elite Afghan journalists are extraordinarily proud of their culture, religion, and heritage. Yet they also look to Western news for affirmation about their country's potential for economic and political progress. While they are frustrated that the U.S. news media focuses on the war when they attempt to explain Afghanistan to the United States, they also accept the criticisms of their government and value the information U.S. reporters give them about the wrongdoings of their country's most powerful people.[15] They want the U.S. news media to support their professional development and they also value U.S. funding that supports Afghan journalism and civil society, in addition to the educational role that American journalists have played in their country.

Afghan journalists feel pressure from many directions: the government, warlords, Iranians, Pakistanis, and the West (mainly Americans). The government-sponsored news media continue their century-long tradition of uncritical reportage about official policies and actions; warlord television promotes the political agendas of strongmen who destroyed the country in the early 1990s; and the Iranian- and Pakistani-sponsored press wants to bend the Afghan public in favor of their visions for the region. The Western-backed news media, the most popular in the country, also reflect an agenda for a liberal society with a free press. But within that free press, the journalists for this study can be reluctant to hold power accountable. They want to be responsible stewards of a relatively open society, but they fear for their livelihoods and lives. After decades of war, one cannot blame them for wanting to put their personal security first.

Even though they should be able to set the agenda and frame of their country's story, Afghans still felt in 2016 too overwhelmed by their situation to do so. Nominally, their press system is free, but the degree of that freedom is narrow. Doing investigative stories and finding objective information are especially difficult. The Afghan population is only fitfully emerging from periods of harsh authoritarian rule where people were supposed to be subservient to the government. The Afghan government may trumpet a free press as a sign of their liberalization and progress in international society, but in reality, it's only tolerated.

Yet Afghan journalists deeply value their roles in their society. They see themselves as public guides to democracy and modernity. They want to create order out of chaos, to make sense of issues and events for themselves and their fellow citizens. There is a sense of national vulnerability and a penchant for conspiracy tales in the Afghan news media system, yet the Afghan journalists who work for independent news organizations are rightly proud of their evolution. They want to report the good news of their country, of which there is much. They are largely hopeful that they can continue to contribute to a robust, democratic society for the long term. Tolo News Director Lotfullah Najafizada attributed much of the Afghan news media's success to following their Western colleagues' lead. He said:

> We could easily be similar to the media in the Central Asian coun-
> tries . . . the only thing we have better than these countries is our
> freedom, is our courage to speak our minds and raise our voices and
> talk about whatever we can. Apart from that we don't have much.
> We have a weaker economy, we have war, we are still suffering. But
> we are more outspoken, we are more engaged, we are more social.[16]

While they are most critical of the lack of professionalism in Afghan news, their free news system is young and journalists are still evolving.

Afghan journalists largely do not independently and actively pursue the major malfeasances of their government, warlords, and overall society. Decades of authoritarianism have habituated them to following government dictates. They tend to accept conflict, corruption, poverty, warlordism, and inefficiency as normal. This dysfunction is remarkable and fascinating to outsiders like U.S. reporters, but to the Afghans it is routine. They are just beginning to learn to recognize that they can challenge the people and institutions responsible for wreaking such havoc in the country, and the U.S. journalists who are based in Kabul have been their tutors. In their reporting, they also reflect a culture that is eager for change in security, human rights, and the economy but is reticent to push for it too quickly as the powerful forces that ran the country for decades still linger. Roughly 20 Afghan journalists were killed between 2001 and 2016 (another 15 international journalists covering Afghanistan were killed), with the majority of the murders not resulting in conviction.[17] This helps to explain Afghan journalists' norm of self-censorship.

While the U.S. and other Western governments urge the Afghan government to protect free speech, American and Western journalists both indirectly and directly advise Afghan journalists on how to hold power accountable. They also serve as conduits for information that the Afghans do not feel safe reporting. In this way, Afghan journalists see a distinction between their personal relationships with Western journalists and the actual press coverage those journalists produce. Without a steady U.S. presence in the country to support a free and functional press, warlords and Iranian and Afghan government officials—all of whom are eager to make journalists their spokespeople—will more easily overpower the Afghan news media. The Afghan journalists will have to try to continue to lead, as long as security conditions and a democratic government allow them to.

U.S. News in Afghanistan

In Afghanistan, the general public assumption has been that the United States controls their fate. To them, America is all-powerful, brutally efficient, and constantly conspiring. And there is enough evidence to believe this: The more-than-15-year presence of U.S. troops in Afghanistan shows them the insistence of the United States on treating their country as battleground space to advance their national security goals, and perhaps to expand its power. This is a narrative consistent with Hamid Karzaï's. Afghan officials and journalists alike react viscerally to American news about their countries, and understandably so: American political, economic, and security apparatuses have directly affected Afghans' lives for decades, long before 9/11.

The U.S. news media amplify that power as American news professionals have considerable reach and authority in the world. A nation's soft power, by Joseph Nye's definition, is, "its ability to attract others by the legitimacy of U.S. policies and the values that underlie them."[18] The U.S. news media in principle encompass the value of free speech and a free press, which can be attractive to many abroad. But the image of a free press that is impartial and critical of the U.S. government doesn't always hold up overseas. For foreign citizens digesting U.S.-produced international news, it helps them to see more starkly how different they and their worldviews are from those of Americans. The narrow, violent picture that U.S. journalists have helped construct for Americans about Afghanistan is frightening, and Afghans do not accept it as accurate or fair. In their eyes, American news judges their country harshly yet fails to apply the same standard toward the United States and its actions abroad.

The Afghan journalists are therefore correct: U.S. journalists do focus on U.S. national interests and frame the world through lenses of conflict, disaster, and crisis. A focus on conflict and violence is an "enduring news value," a significant or even decisive factor in determining the newsworthiness of events.[19] Another value at work in American journalism is the assumption that the United States is the most important and valued nation in the world order.[20] The framework in which Americans understand U.S. involvement in Afghanistan is overwhelmingly one of security rooted in al Qaeda's 9/11 attacks. U.S. journalists who report from

Afghanistan try to give their American readers context about the country, but a disproportionate amount of coverage has been on Afghanistan as a theater with U.S. troops as the lead players. As individuals, U.S. foreign correspondents have gained empathy for the plight of the people and the persistent uncertainty they live with. But they normally describe those struggles in the context of America's role in them. After all, the majority of U.S. journalists feel a primary responsibility to report and analyze issues and events for Americans, not Afghans.

Despite this focus on the American nation, the journalists who report for U.S. news organizations from Kabul insist that they strive to hold U.S. government officials accountable, and this is undeniably true. The American news media have told a story of this war that is frustrating, exhausting, and endlessly complicated. Some of the most sobering stories have been about the limits of American power in the region, such as the fact that the United States has not won this war, which, by 2017, killed 2,300 American soldiers, more than 30,000 Afghan National Security Forces, and tens of thousands of civilians. [21] Stories by the AP, NPR, *Wall Street Journal, Washington Post,* and *New York Times,* among others, about the U.S. government's fumbled interference in the 2009 and 2014 presidential elections, the journalists insisted, also reflect their intent to keep U.S. officials accountable. But the Afghans still largely do not see any humility in American news; they see a reflection and propagation of power.

Perhaps this is changing. The *New York Times* journalists in particular believe that their allegiance to American audiences in their foreign correspondence is evolving as they see their website as a global digital platform. They have launched Spanish and Chinese editions to attract more digital advertising dollars (with the goal of doubling their digital revenue to $800 million by 2020) and are hiring more local reporters to give deeper, less American-centric reportage. As the public editor stated in February 2016, Mexican reporters have suffered significantly from death threats but, like their American reporters in Afghanistan, "working under the umbrella of *The Times* can mean a little more protection."[22] *Times* foreign editor Doug Schorzman explained that while "recognition of global readership for the *New York Times* is necessary for its survival in the market, the American audience will always be our primary audience." He continued, "We do, however, need to do a better job in understanding it is not our only audience."[23] Rod Norland, former chief of the *Times'* Kabul bureau, agreed, saying, "We're increasingly thinking of ourselves not as an American news organization but as a news organization. It will take a long time to transition out of that." *Times* Carlotta Gall said in 2017, "We're really changing in the way we write, but also in the way we react to our audience."[24] After 15 years of conflict, the hiring of an Afghan, Mujib Mashal, as a senior correspondent in the bureau will likely be transformational in how one of America's most-read newspapers will be viewed inside Afghanistan, and could perhaps change how Americans understand the country.

The Diplomatic Dimension of News

While the norm has been that U.S. journalists largely report for American, or at least Western, audiences, they have also been major purveyors of information for anyone invested in this conflict. Once reported, information from U.S. news organizations becomes a global force. The international news net is interwoven, with the American product the single most influential strand. Technology has accelerated the media boomerang effect: Words and images about a foreign country produced for a U.S. audience can simultaneously be received by the government officials, journalists, and citizens of the subject nation.

Until "we know what others think they know," Walter Lippmann said in 1922, "we cannot truly understand their acts." Consuming American news about them is a ritual for Afghan journalists, officials, and other elites. It has been an addiction to understanding their place in America's world. Worldwide, the news media provide a common sense of intelligence for leaders so that they can forecast behaviors and attitudes. Research has shown that global elites, like Afghan elites, see the *New York Times* as the agenda-setter for American policy, and arguably the most important news organization in the world, with the *Washington Post, Wall Street Journal* and AP coming after.[25] All countries are not equal in the international news space, and global publics definitely sense that when they look at U.S. and Western journalism.[26] Afghans, however, have seen themselves relatively frequently in American news in the past 15 years, especially when presidents Obama and Bush focused their attention on Afghanistan. They set the news agenda with the influx of U.S. troops in the country. By the end of President Obama's second term in 2017, five major U.S. news agencies maintained bureaus in Kabul: the *New York Times, Washington Post*, AP, NPR, and the *Wall Street Journal.*

Journalists are actors in international diplomacy, mediating communications between governments and publics, and between governments

and governments.[27] Governments can share information through traditional diplomatic channels, but a nation's news systems can reach both
governments and citizens, playing an unofficial diplomatic role. In one
way, Afghan journalists are proud that American elite news agencies continue to find Afghanistan newsworthy, because it confers legitimacy on
Afghanistan's importance in the world. Since U.S. journalists' work is
regularly consumed by American and foreign government officials, it can
help shape their opinions and therefore become part of the dynamics that
affect the conduct of international relations.

U.S. journalists can play a diplomatic role in the sense that they help
Americans, who elect leaders who can shape the world, to understand international politics and conflict. They also become stand-ins, surrogates,
conveying to non-Americans a plausible replica of their nation's politics
and views. They signal to Afghans and their neighbors how the U.S. government sees the region and what it wants to happen there. In the developing world, where there has long been outrage about the global power
the Western news media have, journalists are also teachers, instructors
on how to be journalists through indirect and direct contact. This is partly
why Afghan journalists are fearful of the day when the U.S. news bureaus
are shuttered and the American press stops talking with them because it
will impede their own development. Yet they simultaneously resent the
story the American press is projecting to the world as it is not instilling
confidence in Western powers that their country is worth their long-term
investment.

Many commentators have argued that the diplomatic dimension
of journalism is that reporters can write news stories that foster understanding and that they play an unofficial, mediator role between nations
and are therefore "journalists of consequence" in international relations.[28] In 1964, for instance, John Hohenberg, a professor at Columbia
University and the former administrator of the Pulitzer Prize, wrote that
foreign correspondents could create "understanding between peoples by
bringing them more meaningful news of each other."[29] Yet this view never
took into account the asymmetric power of U.S. news, and it does not
stand in today's context. Through international communications, national
identity can become more pronounced.

Many Afghans assume that U.S. journalists are advocates for the
U.S. government's foreign policies and largely let government officials set
the news agenda on foreign matters. They then project foreign issues and
events through an American worldview frame, as they largely write for

American audiences. They established news bureaus in Afghanistan in 2001 because the U.S. government was suddenly there, and they will likely stay until the American military's presence disappears. Rarely does the U.S. news media challenge the norm of U.S. power in the world, but they want to keep the government accountable so that it maintains that power as a force for good and one that keeps America safe.

U.S. journalists do not, however, work in tandem with U.S. officials to propagate the views of the U.S. government. They do not set out to please officials; they set out to tell the truth.

But that doesn't really matter in an international context. When it comes to diplomacy and global public opinion, perception can weigh heavier than reality. In Afghanistan, the stories U.S. journalists choose to pursue and how they frame them have contributed to the tensions and rapprochements between the U.S. and Afghan administrations. It has certainly been a factor in the low support among Americans for American involvement there. While the U.S. press has helped to directly and indirectly support the development of the Afghan news system, it has not mediated understanding between American and Afghan leaders, nor between their two societies. Karzai saw U.S. journalists as co-conspirators with U.S. government officials, with the American press as a means to publicly register complaints against him and the Afghan nation. When President Ghani asked the *New York Times'* Matthew Rosenberg to return to Kabul shortly after Karzai had banished him, and conveyed his gratitude in March 2015 during his trip to the United States via remarks to the U.S. Congress, the U.S. press relayed it, almost grateful for the recognition that Ghani seemingly gave them for their service in covering the conflict. The long duration of this conflict has changed the tenor of U.S. news, with less of a focus on U.S. troops at war and more on the internal affairs of the country. Yet Ghani continues to be frustrated with the negative reporting of his administration. By publishing and producing stories, the journalists are actively shaping the environment in which U.S.–Afghan diplomacy, development, and war are conducted.

Fundamentally, what frustrates Afghans about U.S. news is what frustrates them about America. The Afghan journalists and officials believe U.S. news should consider their perspective more, be more empathetic, give them hope, and stop serving itself. The U.S. reporters represent their nation and they abide by a norm that explains the contours of American power and its impact abroad, seeing the world through an American-centric, security lens. This does not bridge understanding or broker goodwill between the United States and Afghanistan, or any other country. For the U.S. reporters, just because their reportage is transnational does not mean their identity is. We all make sense of the world through our senses of nationalism—our shared cultures, worldviews, narratives, symbols, and frameworks. Transcending it is not easy.

Epilogue: 16 Years and Counting

On August 20, 2017, President Donald J. Trump did what his two predecessors had before him: He delivered a speech to the American people about why their security was intricately tied to Afghanistan's. With words that nearly echoed President Bush's statement in 2001 and President Obama's in 2009, he said: "A hasty withdrawal would create a vacuum that terrorists, including ISIL and al-Qaeda, would instantly fill."[30]

President Trump was reportedly reluctant to double down on what he considered to be a failing war, but he also didn't want to be the American president who saw Afghanistan overrun by terrorists. He insisted he would bring a dramatically different approach to the war but gave few details on how he'd do so. Indicating that his administration did not want to send signals to the enemy, he did not disclose troop levels or how long they would be there, saying that future decisions would not be forced by preset timetables but by conditions on the ground. He reiterated the previous administration's calls to focus on Pakistan's responsibility in the conflict; instead of calling it an "Af-Pak" strategy as the Obama administration had in 2009, he chose to frame it as the "South Asian" strategy. Further vexing the Pakistanis, he said that much more resolve and support needed to come from India.[31]

"In the end," he promised the American people, "we will win."

An ironclad truth in communications scholarship is that the U.S. press follows the agenda of the U.S. president regarding issues of national security, and that it is largely deferential toward the president. At least in the beginning. Months before Trump announced his decision about Afghanistan, he launched dozens of cruise missiles into a Syrian military airfield on April 6, 2017. It was in retaliation for a chemical weapons attack Syrian President Bashar Assad had directed against his own people, killing more than 70 civilians. In the United States, there was political consensus among Republicans and Democrats; former Secretary of State—and his opponent in the 2016 election—Hillary Clinton, Senator Chuck Schumer, and Representative Nancy Pelosi all agreed that it was the right action to take.

The American news media largely did not counter the president's judgment either, largely calling it a defining moment in his presidency. David Sanger of the *New York Times* wrote as his lede, "In launching a military strike just 77 days into his administration, President Trump has the opportunity, but hardly a guarantee, to change the perception of disarray in his administration."[32] Cable news networks played B-roll footage on repeat of the Tomahawks leaving the aircraft carrier in the Mediterranean Sea. MSNBC news anchor Brian Williams called the weapons "beautiful" three times in 30 seconds. He said at one point, "We see these beautiful pictures at night from the decks of these two U.S. Navy vessels in the eastern Mediterranean. I am tempted to quote the great Leonard Cohen: 'I am guided by the beauty of our weapons'."[33] Fareed Zakaria later said on CNN, "I think Donald Trump became President of the United States" last night."[34]

But this was a startling development in a conflict President Obama had been reluctant to enter, not a 16-year-old war born from 9/11. Trump's Afghanistan decision didn't contribute to a large uptick in coverage on Afghanistan, and it didn't generate much debate in Congress. With no contentious political climate for the U.S. national security reporters to peg coverage to, the story faded from headline American news. As a White House official told Politico, the decision to increase troops to Afghanistan "wasn't a debate . . . It was an attempt to convince the president."[35] The news media that had continued to cover Afghanistan at the end of 2016— *New York Times, Washington Post*, AP, NPR, *Wall Street Journal*—were well prepared to cover the president's speech, and then resume normal coverage on the country. There was a slight uptick in network and cable news coverage, but it was fleeting. Only 28 million Americans watched the president's speech in August. Five million more Americans had watched his announcement of Supreme Court nominee Neil Gorsuch in February. And perhaps irksome to a reality-star-turned-president who closely follows his ratings, 40.8 million Americans watched Obama make his similar Afghanistan policy decision in December 2009.[36]

The most remarkable aspect about the continuance of these official and reporter dynamics regarding U.S. national security is that there is nothing else normal about President Trump's relationship with the press.

As a candidate and now president, Trump uses anti-press rants as a rallying cry. He has actively worked to discredit the news media he does not agree with by dismissing it as "fake news"; he has the same disdain for the U.S. elite news media that President Karzai had. In the first six months of his presidency, he tweeted about "fake news" more than 70 times; by the end of his first year, he had done so more than 160 times.[37] And that was just on Twitter. During speeches, interviews, and press conferences, he often rails about the press being willfully dishonest, promoting an agenda to advance profits and/or a "deep state." A common refrain is, "I have a running war with the media. They are among the most dishonest human beings on earth." And it seems as if the Republican Party he leads agrees with him. As a sign of political polarization, according to the Pew Research Center, Democrats are 47 points more likely than Republicans to support the U.S. news media's watchdog role, the largest gap since they started asking the question in 1985.[38]

President Ashraf Ghani and other Afghan elites were reportedly relieved about Trump's decision to keep U.S. troops in the Afghanistan. Tolo News reported Ghani's statement shortly after the president's speech: "I am grateful to President Trump and the American people for this affirmation of support for our efforts to achieve self-reliance and for our joint struggle to rid the region from the threat of terrorism."[39] Trump had insisted that in his "Operation Resolute Support" plan, "We are not nation-building again. We are killing terrorists."[40] The focus would be on training, advising, and assisting the Afghan National Security Forces. There was no talk about development and economic assistance to create the conditions for long-term security, and there certainly was no talk about supporting civil society and the Afghan news media.

One of the most alarming concerns about Trump's anti-press rhetoric is the signal he is potentially sending to foreign leaders on how they can treat their journalists and news professionals. As explored in this book, since the 1990s, media assistance has been a pillar of development support for the United States abroad; the United States has morally rooted this work in Article 19 of the Universal Declaration of Human Rights. While media assistance efforts under the U.S. Agency for International Development (USAID) and State Department programs have managed to continue despite the Trump administration's efforts to gut the international affairs budget, the U.S. president is no longer personally concerned with exporting the First Amendment and press freedoms.

According to Freedom House, press freedom worldwide hit its lowest point in 2016 since 2003, and the sharpest declines occurred in democracies:

> Political leaders and other partisan forces in many democracies— including the United States, Poland, the Philippines, and South Africa—attacked the credibility of the independent and mainstream media through alarmingly hostile rhetoric, personalized abuse on-line, and indirect editorial pressure. They sought to delegitimize critical or impartial sources of information and reshape news coverage to their advantage, apparently rejecting the traditional watchdog role of a free press in democratic societies . . . Meanwhile, pressure on journalists in more restrictive environments continued unabated.[41]

By the same metrics, however, Afghanistan, moved from "not free" to "partly free." The increase was due to a more systemic commitment by Ghani and his CEO, Abdullah Abdullah, to protect the rights of journalists and improve press–state relations. And by 2017, 65.7 percent of Afghans trusted their news media, second now only to religious leaders at 67.3 percent, according to the Asia Foundation's annual survey, and more than their government at 56 percent.[42]

This book reviewed the themes, frames, tenor, and senses of ethno-centrism and nationalism in U.S. news in the post-9/11 era, from 2001 to 2016. Indeed, much of the current scholarship is drawn from the media's experience with 9/11 and the Iraq War. Under Trump, we have a new era where the data for political communications, national security reportage, press–state relations, and even media development assistance promise to be incredibly rich. While we need more data, context, and time to rigorously analyze it, some questions could include: Has our knowledge about agenda-setting, framing, and hegemony shifted? Are the "enduring values" of U.S. news coverage of the world still enduring? How did the words of a so-called leader of the free world who does not value free speech and/or a free press travel abroad? What did nationalism and/or chauvinistic nationalism look like in the U.S. news media? How did it change, if it did?

There will also continue to be the question of Afghanistan's future, which is increasingly being driven by a generation who came of age under President Hamid Karzai and the U.S.-led war and diplomatic and development missions. Many of the country's change-makers are journalists who, unlike their American counterparts, have the majority of their public's confidence. More than 16 years after al Qaeda attacked New York, Washington, and Shanksville, Pennsylvania, the United States will continue to be intertwined with this country for an undefined period of time. With the changes in how U.S. elite news writes the world for global, not just American, audiences and the rising strength of the Afghan journalists, it may be that Americans finally start to learn more about Afghanistan the country, and not just the war.

If we can remove ourselves from the dizzying haze of Washington.

APPENDIX I

Methodology

In this qualitative study I sought to explain Afghan and American journalists' philosophies through the analysis of interviews. In-depth interviewing is an intensive method that is tailored to the individual respondent. It seeks to understand the background of the participants, allows for the observation of nonverbal responses, and can be influenced by the dynamic between the interviewer and the interviewee. I might have used ethnography, participant observation, or a quantitative analysis of Afghan news products. But possible biases and interpretations can be subtle in print or broadcast transcripts, and these are not always available. In-depth qualitative interviews, however, allow journalists to explore, in their own words, their approaches to their work and their use of U.S. news narratives about their countries. In his book *Political Ideology*, Robert Lane noted that in-depth interviewing provides the opportunity for discursiveness, rambling, anecdote, argument, moral comment, and rationalization. It also provides the opportunity for extensive probing, testing, and reflecting, and thus insight into connotative meanings. This method allows the journalists to reflect at length on their habits and philosophies toward journalism, and how they justify and make meaning of the current conflict for national audiences.

Scholarship on the news media in Afghanistan is rare. Reports from nongovernmental organizations and think tanks lack in-depth interviews. Conducting such interviews enabled me to develop a detailed description of journalistic life in Kabul by integrating multiple perspectives, describing the journalists' thinking processes, learning their interpretations, and giving inside accounts of their experiences. Afghan and U.S. journalists, who are creating habits and relaying interpretations almost daily, are in position to observe themselves, their peers, government officials, and the publics they reach.

I was able to gain access to their experiences and views through interviews that lasted between 45 minutes and three hours. I wanted to know how these journalists understood their situations, and the conceptual frameworks they used to make sense of their role as journalists, their relationships with their governments, and their relationships with the other nations' press corps. I kept to a structured interview schedule but also allowed respondents to deviate. I worked to steer the conversations toward topics relevant to my study, but my subjects at times provided unexpected insight or color that enriched it. Whenever possible, I dug to understand where these understandings came from. Many of the interviews were imperfect. Some were more detailed than others.

THE SAMPLE

In 2003, I began traveling to Afghanistan for jobs in media and public affairs. My capacity as a State Department official and a staff member with the nongovernmental organization the Asia Foundation enabled me to create relationships that were helpful to me with my research. I began my fieldwork in 2010 with relative ease.

In May and June 2010, I was able to interview 15 Afghan journalists in Kabul. In the summer of 2012, I returned to Kabul to interview 15 more, in addition to seven American journalists who have covered the country. In January 2015 I conducted one interview in Washington with an American journalist and in October 2016, I returned to Kabul to interview five Afghan journalists on the record and three U.S. ones. That month I also spoke with two Afghan journalists that month in Washington, DC, and another American journalist in New York in December. In fall 2017, after receiving the contract for the book, I spoke with five U.S. journalists and eight U.S. officials who had experience with Afghanistan policy.

Creating a meaningful sample, however, meant targeting American and Afghan journalists who represented the most popular news outlets in their countries and could be assumed to wield the most influence with local publics. These were "elite" journalists, those who have "an impact with intellectuals and opinion leaders," are respected within their communities, and have "the biggest impact on the serious thinking of a nation." Between 2010 and 2012, each participant signed a Columbia University institutional review board (IRB) form that promised confidentiality; therefore, this book withholds some information that could lead the reader to identify the respondent. Pseudonyms were chosen for all respondents and are noted in the endnotes but not the text. While IRB protocols limited me from describing the journalists and the institutions they represent, they are well-known figures to news consumers in their respective societies.

My 2015–2017 interviews were held on the record, meaning that the journalists and U.S. officials were identified. I interviewed some U.S. journalists who had been reporting on Afghanistan for years, in addition to some U.S. officials who served there and/or had significant responsibility for U.S.–Afghan bilateral relations and the development effort.

Finding elite journalists to speak with meant using the technique of purposive sampling, which aims to strategically collect participants who have direct relevance to the research questions and have specific characteristics or qualities that will enhance the study. Purposive sampling helped me target journalists who represented both print and broadcast outlets who reported in the Dari or Pashto languages in Afghanistan. Because I was also conducting research in a space in which I had previously worked professionally, I was also partaking in convenience sampling and snowball sampling. In other words, I was approaching former colleagues and acquaintances first, and then contacting the people they recommended I speak with. By choosing selectively among the people I knew and the people they referred me to, I found the most robust samples of elite journalists.

My samples of elite journalists show considerable variance in how they approach journalism, how they perceive other journalists' work, and how they construct reality. They are grappling with their own journalistic and national cultures, and with a seemingly ever-proliferating electronic and digital media landscape. Afghan journalists especially have seen staggering growth within electronic media, putting new demands on a nascent press corps with little experience.

INTERVIEW ANALYSIS

The interview schedule included 15 primary questions to let the journalists give their impressions of the media spaces they worked in; their general habits and philosophies of newsgathering, especially during wartime; their limitations; what they deem the future of the work to be; how they see their role in the conflict; how they work with government officials; and how they perceive their Afghan or American peers' work.

Transcribing, sorting, sifting, and integrating the material into a wider analysis took months. Each of the respondents provided a great deal of information, so significant time was required to interpret, summarize, and integrate their viewpoints. Once the interviews were transcribed, I coded them into the meta-categories of common themes, deviations, and journalists' backgrounds. I then re-examined the data and coded them into more detailed sub-categories. Mapping these journalists' thoughts allowed for both coherence and inconsistency, but it put them in a "wider web of beliefs" that exist within elite journalism communities.

RESEARCH LIMITATIONS

There are good reasons for the lack of sociological scholarship on Afghanistan in general, although it certainly has increased in the past decade. Due to years of war that ravaged the country, Afghan intellectuals fled, and then Taliban control of the country dictated that education focus on religion. For foreigners trying to advance research on the country, there are multiple barriers to doing so. The language barrier, security precautions, and the difficulty of travel to remote locations make social inquiry inherently difficult—and all of these factors played a role in why and how I created this study.

I focused on elite journalists not just because they are influential but also because they could speak English. While I speak intermediate-level Farsi, of which Dari is a dialect, and I do not speak Pashto, which made conversing in English necessary. The journalists' level of education made them appreciate the contribution they were making to scholarship and willing to speak at length about their experiences and opinions. These English-speaking, elite journalists would often report in two languages and, because they could speak English, they were most affected by Western media development programs and regularly used U.S. journalism as source material for their reportage.

I would be remiss, however, if I did not acknowledge the limitations of my own identity as a researcher in these countries as well as the biases journalists may have had toward me because of my nationality, gender, and past professional history as an American government official. While I believe that I captured their unfiltered, candid opinions on the issues I asked about during the interview, it is not entirely unlikely that they expected my research to have administrative value for the U.S. government. From 2010–2012, despite signing a form that clearly communicated their protection of privacy, they might not have believed that I would make every effort to protect their identity. In the 2016 and 2017 interviews, the journalists were happy to speak on the record, and I felt that they were surprisingly candid.

The concept of "parachute journalism" is discussed in parts of the dissertation. The idea is that journalists spend limited time in a country to get the legitimacy they need to publish or broadcast a story; often their reporting is criticized as having been more or less predetermined in their home country. It is a constant critique of Western foreign correspondents that they give precedence to their home-country views over any reporting they undertake abroad. But given the costs of on-the-ground reporting, and the perception that there is little taste for foreign news, parachute journalism is normal. This practice lends itself to episodic journalism. Instead of a developing "film" of a country, we get "snapshots" of specific events and issues. Because these are normally disasters or war, the image of the country is distorted. The Western audience encounters the country only as a field of chaos.

To a certain extent, my own research was a sort of parachute journalism. For the sake of this research project, my time in Afghanistan amounted to approximately six months. Collectively, however, I have spent 2 years in the country over the course of 13 years, which gives me some long-term perspective on the places and the ability to identify the most salient issues worthy of exploration.

Interview Subjects

AFGHAN JOURNALISTS INTERVIEWED, 2010–2012 (ANONYMOUS, IRB-PROTECTED)

These interviews were conducted by the author in Kabul, Afghanistan, and were tape-recorded: Aalem, June 2010; Abdullah, June 2010; Atash, June 2012; Babur, June 2010; Badi, July 2012; Behnam, July 2012; Delewar, June 2010; Faisal, June 2010; Farhang, June 2010; Farzin, June 2012; Fazia, June 2010; Feda, June 2010; Ghazanfar, June 2010; Hakim, July 2012; Houshmand, July 2012; Jabar, July 2012; Jahandar, July 2012; Jamshid, June 2010; Jawid, June 2010; Kambas, July 2012; Khaleeq, June 2010; Mansoor, July 2012; Matteen, June 2012; Mitra, June 2010; Morad, June 2010; Nasir, July 2012; Omaid, June 2012; Parsa, July 2012; Sarwar, July 2012; Sina, June 2010.

AFGHAN JOURNALISTS INTERVIEWED, 2016 (ON THE RECORD)

These interviews were conducted by the author and were tape-recorded: Farid Ahmad, Kabul, Afghanistan, October 2016; Mujib Khalvatgar, Kabul, Afghanistan, October 2016; Saad Mohseni, Washington, DC, October 2016; Ahmad Mukhtar, Kabul, Afghanistan, October 2016; Sami Mahdi, Kabul, Afghanistan, October 2016; Lotfullah Najafizada, Washington, DC, October 2016; Bilal Sarwary, Kabul, Afghanistan, October 2016.

U.S. JOURNALISTS INTERVIEWED, 2012 (ANONYMOUS, IRB-PROTECTED)

These interviews were conducted in July 2012 by the author in Kabul, Afghanistan, and were tape-recorded: James, Jason, Maya, Nathan, Nikki, Roger, and Tom.

U.S. JOURNALISTS INTERVIEWED, 2015–2017 (ON THE RECORD)

These interviews were conducted by the author and were tape-recorded: Matthew Rosenberg, Washington, DC, January 2015; Pamela Constable, Kabul, Afghanistan, October 2016; Mujib Mashal, Kabul, Afghanistan, October 2016 (Mashal is an Afghan national who reports for an American news agency); Rod Nordland, Kabul, Afghanistan, October 2016; Douglas Schorzman, Kabul, Afghanistan, December 2016; Joshua Partlow, Washington, DC, September 2017; Maria Abi-Habib, Washington, DC, September 2017; Kathy Gannon, Washington, DC, October 2017 (Gannon is a Canadian national who reports for an American news agency); Carlotta Gall, Washington, DC, October 2017 (Gall is a British national who reports for an American news agency); David Rohde, Washington, DC, October 2017.

U.S./FORMER OFFICIALS INTERVIEWED (ON THE RECORD)

All of these interviews were conducted by the author in Washington, DC, and were tape-recorded: Michael Hammer, September 2017; Marc Grossman, October 2017; David Ensor, October 2017; Eileen O'Connor, October 2017; Daniel Feldman, October 2017; John Dempsey, October 2017; Zalmay Khalilzad, September 2017; Ryan Crocker, October 2017.

Notes

PREFACE

1. In 2003, Afghanistan still had 32 provinces. Two new ones, Daykundi and Panjshir, were established by the Karzai administration in 2004.
2. "Evening News," December 2003 Broadcast Index, Vanderbilt Television News Archive, accessed November 11, 2017, https://tvnews.vanderbilt.edu/siteindex/2003-12
3. Biby Sowry, "Today in History—February 16," *Vogue UK*, February 16, 2010, http://www.vogue.co.uk/article/tom-ford-described-hamid-karzai-as-the-chicest-man-on-the-planet; "The Best Dressed Men in the World, 2007," *Esquire*, August 23, 2007, http://www.esquire.com/style/a3302/bestdressed0907/
4. Mujib Mashal, "Afghanistan Is in Chaos. Is That What Hamid Karzai Wants?" *New York Times*, August 6, 2016, http://www.nytimes.com/2016/08/06/world/asia/afghanistan-hamid-karzai.html?_r=0
5. Interview with Hamid Karzai by the author, October 23, 2016, Kabul, Afghanistan.

CHAPTER 1

1. Agence France-Presse, "Afghanistan Orders US Reporter to Leave over Election Story," August 21, 2014, http://www.jamaicaobserver.com/news/Afghanistan-orders-US-reporter-to-leave-over-election-story_17388693
2. Hamid Karzai press conference aired live by state television on October 4, 2012. Translation from the Pashto by BBC Monitoring South Asia service. BBC Monitoring provided an English transcript of both Dari and Pashto remarks by President Karzai from this press conference. Quoted in Joshua Partlow, "Podium Wars: President Hamid Karzai, the Foreign Press, and the Afghan War," Harvard University Shorenstein Center on Media, Politics and Public Policy, Fall 2012, http://shorensteincenter.org/podium-wars-president-hamid-karzai-the-foreign-press-and-the-afghan-war/

3. Interview with Hamid Karzai by the author, October 24, 2016, Kabul, Afghanistan.

4. Carlotta Gall, "Afghan Poppy Growing Reaches Record Level, U.N. Says," *New York Times*, November 19, 2004, http://www.nytimes.com/2004/11/19/ world/asia/afghan-poppy-growing-reaches-record-level-un-says

5. Interview with Carlotta Gall by the author, October 28, 2017, Washington, DC.

6. Interview with Hamid Karzai by the author, October 24, 2016, Kabul, Afghanistan.

7. Alissa Rubin and Thom Shanker, "Afghan Leader Says U.S. Abets Taliban's Goal," *New York Times*, March 10, 2013, http://www.nytimes.com/2013/03/ 11/world/asia/karzai-accuses-us-and-taliban-of-colluding-in-afghanistan. html; in November 2012, the *New York Times* editorial board wrote: "It would be impossible to overstate the challenges facing Afghanistan and the urgency of addressing them while American troops are still in the country. Instead of doing that, President Hamid Karzai is again conjuring up scapegoats and false alarms and diverting attention from what really matters. . . . Such arguments are a convenient canard for governments seeking to discredit anyone who asks tough questions." "President Karzai's Misplaced Priorities," *New York Times*, November 6, 2012, http://www.nytimes.com/2012/11/07/opinion/president-hamid-karzais-misplaced-priorities.html

8. "A Timeline of U.S. Troop Levels in Afghanistan Since 2001," Associated Press, July 6, 2016, http://www.militarytimes.com/story/military/2016/07/06/ timeline-us-troop-levels-afghanistan-since-2001/86755782/

9. Rubin and Shanker, "Afghan Leader Says."

10. Interview with Hamid Karzai by the author, October 24, 2016, Kabul, Afghanistan.

11. Matthew Rosenberg, "Amid Election Impasse, Calls for an Afghan Interim Government," *New York Times*, August 18, 2014, http://www.nytimes.com/2014/ 08/19/world/asia/amid-election-impasse-calls-in-afghanistan-for-an-interim-government.html

12. Ibid.

13. Interview with Matthew Rosenberg by the author, January 2015, Washington, DC.

14. Sangar Rahimi, "Afghan Attorney General bans Matthew Rosenberg of the New York Times from leaving the country after a story he wrote on AFG election. TOLOTV," Twitter, August 19, 2014, https://twitter.com/SangarRahimi/status/ 501720750790041601

15. Interview with Douglas Schorzman by the author, December 2, 2016, Washington, DC.

16. Interview with Rod Nordland by the author, October 25, 2016, Kabul, Afghanistan.

17. Rod Nordland, "Afghan Officials Interrogate Matthew Rosenberg," *New York Times*, August 19, 2014, http://www.nytimes.com/2014/08/20/world/asia/afghan-officials-interrogate-matthew-rosenberg.html

18. Matthew Rosenberg, Twitter, August 21, 2014, https://twitter.com/ mrosenbergNYT/status/502423052190113795

19. Interview with Hamid Karzai by the author, October 24, 2016, Kabul, Afghanistan.

20. Ibid.

21. Dennis Wu, "Systemic Determinants of International News Coverage: A Comparison of 38 Countries," *Journal of Communication*, Vol. 50, No. 2 (Spring 2000): 110–130.

22. Stephen Hess, *Through Their Eyes: Foreign Correspondents in the United States* (Washington, DC: Brookings Institution Press, 2005), 129; Philo Wasburn, *The Social Construction of International News: We're Talking About Them, They're Talking About Us* (Westport, CT: Praeger Publishers, 2002), 20.

23. Wasburn, *The Social Construction*, 45.

24. For instance, U.S. news on the Falklands War described the Soviet Union as a key antagonist that wanted to increase its military and commercial connections with Latin America. It's unlikely that Argentines saw the situation that way. The British, too, likely rejected the view of American news outlets that their actions in the Falklands reflected British imperialism and that they were trying to resolve a political dispute with force, Wasburn argued. U.S. news, on the other hand, described the U.S.'s deep involvement throughout the Western Hemisphere during the 1980s—in El Salvador, Guatemala, Nicaragua, and Grenada—only rarely as being about American imperialism but rather a struggle for "freedom" and "democracy." With Iran, many Americans become aware of the country through the Iran hostage crisis and not the Iran–Iraq war or, for that matter, the American-sponsored overthrow of a democratically elected government in Iran in 1953. The revolution was explained by Ayatollah Khomeini's taste for tension and martyrdom, not the dynamics of Iranian opinion (Wasburn, *The Social Construction*, 43–44).

25. This book's focus is on the *elite* U.S. news media, defined as that "which has an impact with intellectuals and opinion leaders," is respected within their communities, and has "the biggest impact on the serious thinking of a nation." For the United States, normally, it is just the elite brands—*New York Times, Washington Post, Wall Street Journal*, and *Los Angeles Times*, among the highest—that establish which international issues are the most significant for the country and explain how those issues should be explained to the American public. The elite U.S. press has long been seen as the dominant news media in the international system not only because they are linked to the world's largest military power, with dozens of bases around the world, but also because of their transnational reach. However, this global impact is disproportionate to the amount of information that Americans consume about the world. Traditionally, foreign news makes up less than 10 percent of total news content. But U.S. citizens and their elected officials depend on it for information about the world, as they can rarely rely on personal experience and interpersonal communication to understand events in the global arena. Less than one-third of Americans have a passport. and most citizens use that passport to travel to neighboring Canada and Mexico. The news media therefore serve as a vital intermediary between the American public and the state on issues of national security and foreign policy.

26. "Afghanistan—Freedom of the Press in 2017," Freedom House, June 2017, accessed November 19, 2017, https://freedomhouse.org/report/freedom-press/2017/afghanistan.

27. Matthew Rosenberg, "Ashraf Ghani Thanks U.S. for Support in First Visit as Afghan Leader," *New York Times*, March 23, 2015, http://www.nytimes.com/2015/03/24/world/asia/an-afghans-sentiment-for-an-ally-gratitude.html?_r=0

CHAPTER 2

1. Danielle Kurtzleben, "Journalists Remember 9/11: For Many Journalists, No War or Crisis Will Ever Compare to That Day," *U.S. News and World Report*, September 11, 2011, http://www.usnews.com/news/articles/2011/09/09/journalists-remember-911

2. Eric Lipton, "Death Toll Is Near 3,000 but Some Uncertainty Over the Count Remains," *New York Times*, September 11, 2002, https://www.nytimes.com/2002/09/11/us/death-toll-is-near-3000-but-some-uncertainty-over-the-count-remains.html

3. Elinor Kelley Grusin and Sandra H. Utt, "The Challenge: To Examine Media's Role, Performance on 9/11 and After," In *Media in an American Crisis: Studies of September 11, 2001* (New York: University Press of America, 2005), 1; Pat Aufderheide, "All-Too-Reality TV: Challenge for Television Journalists after September 11," *Journalism*, Vol. 3, No. 1 (2002): 11.

4. Michael Schudson, *Sociology of News* (New York: W.W. Norton, 2003), 188.

5. Ibid.

6. Grusin and Utt, "The Challenge," 6.

7. Caryn James, "The New York Times. Sept. 12, 2001," quoted in *What We Saw*, eds. CBS News (New York: Simon and Schuster, 2002), 83.

8. Howard Kurtz, "The Washington Post. Sept. 20, 2001," quoted in *What We Saw*, eds. CBS News (New York: Simon and Schuster, 2002), 86.

9. Pippa Norris, Montague Kern, and Marion Just, *Framing Terrorism: The News Media, the Government and the Public* (London: Routledge, 2003), 290. Also see: Brigitte Nacos, *Mass-Mediated Terrorism* (Lanham, MD: Rowman & Littlefield, 2002); Bradley S. Greenberg and Marcia Thomson, *Communication and Terrorism: Public and Media Responses to 9/11* (New York: Hampton Press, 2002).

10. Pippa Norris, Montague Kern, and Marion Just, *Framing Terrorism*, 290. They concluded that "The power of the War on Terrorism frame in America was such that, although there was no published intelligence of a proven link connecting President [Saddam] Hussein directly to the events of 9/11, in early March 2003, prior to military intervention, when a representative sample of the American public was asked by Gallup polls whether they thought that Saddam Hussein was involved in supporting terrorist groups that had plans to attack the United States, most people agreed."

11. Norris, Kern, and Just, *Framing Terrorism*, 4; Brigitte Nacos and Torres Reyna pointed out that before 9/11, national news coverage—but especially news in New York—employed negative news frames about Arabs and Muslims. Brigitte Nacos and Torres Reyna, "Framing Muslim-Americans Before and After 9/11," in *Framing Terrorism: The News Media, the Government and the Public*, eds. Pippa Norris, Montague Kern, and Marion Just (London: Routledge, 2003), 154.

12. According to the Global Terrorism Index, terrorism did later increase in 2014 and 2016, with 2000, 2014, and 2016 being the deadliest years worldwide. "Global Terrorism Index 2017," Institute for Economics and Peace, last accessed November 15, 2017, https://reliefweb.int/sites/reliefweb.int/files/resources/Global%20Terrorism%20Index%202017%20%284%29.pdf

13. Norris, Kern, and Just, *Framing Terrorism*, 291.

14. Herbert Gans, *Deciding What's News: A Study of CBS Evening News, NBC Nightly News, Newsweek, and Time* (New York: Vintage Books, 2004), 31.

15. James Carey, *Communications as Culture: Essays on Media and Society* (New York: Routledge, 1992); Giovanna Dell'Orto, "Foreign Policy and Foreign Correspondence: Integrating IR and Communication Theories to Examine the History of Press Involvement in International Affairs," Paper Presented at the International Studies Association Annual Conference (Montreal, 2011).

16. Gans, *Deciding What's News*, 2004, 18; Christopher E. Beaudoin and Esther Thorson, "Value Representation in Foreign News," *International Communication Gazette*, Vol. 63, No. 6 (December 2001): 486.

17. Gans, *Deciding What's News*, 19, 37.

18. Simon Cottle, *Global Crisis Reporting* (Berkshire, England: Open University Press, 2009); W. Russell Neuman, Marion R. Just, and Ann N. Crigler, *Common Knowledge: News and the Construction of Political Meaning* (Chicago: University of Chicago Press, 1992); Gans, *Deciding What's News*, 31, 42.

19. Donald Matheson and Stuart Allan, *Digital War Reporting* (Malden, MA: Polity Press, 2009), 12.

20. Daniel Riffe, Charles F. Aust, Ted C. Jones, Barbara Shoemake, and Shyam Sundar, "The Shrinking Foreign Newshole of the New York Times," *Newspaper Research Journal*, Vol. 15, No. 3 (Summer 1994): 74–89; Michael Emery, "An Endangered Species: The International Newshole," *Freedom Forum Media Studies Journal*, Vol. 3 (Fall 1989): 151–164; John Maxwell Hamilton and George A. Krimsky, "'Juju' News from Abroad," *Freedom Forum Media Studies Journal*, Vol. 20, No. 9 (November 1998): 50–67; Ed Seaton, "The Diminishing Use of Foreign News Reporting (Remarks)," *International Press Institute*, May 26, 1998, http://www.asne.org/ideas/seatonmoscow.htm

21. James B. Weaver, Christopher J. Porter, and Margaret E. Evans, "Patterns of Foreign News Coverage on U.S. Network TV: A Ten-Year Analysis," *Journalism Quarterly*, Vol. 61 (1984): 356–363; Seaton, "The Diminishing Use of Foreign News"; Emery, "An Endangered Species"; William A. Hachten and James

Scotton, *The World News Prism* (Ames: Iowa State University, 2002), 116; "The decline in coverage of international news in the magazines *Time* and *Newsweek*, particularly, was significant. Throughout 1995, *Time* devoted 14 percent of its coverage to international news; and *Newsweek* 12 percent of its coverage. But in 1985, *Time* dedicated 24 percent to foreign news; *Newsweek* 22 percent." By 1995, foreign news represented only 13.5 percent of total coverage; budgets and staff were cut, foreign bureaus were closed, and media began to emphasize economic concerns.

22. Norris, Kern, and Just, *Framing Terrorism*, 15.

23. Matheson and Allan, *Digital War Reporting*, 12.

24. Max Frankel, "The Shroud," *New York Times Magazine*, November 17, 1994; Dan Rather was also quoted as telling Harvard students: "Foreign coverage requires the most space and the most air time because you are dealing with complicated situations, in which you have to explain a lot. And then there's always somebody around who says people don't give a damn about this stuff anyway." Quoted in Stephen Hess, *International News and Foreign Correspondents* (Washington, DC: Brookings Institution Press, 1996), 61.

25. See: Hess, *International News and Foreign Correspondents*, xiii and 99; Beaudoin and Thorson, "Value Representation in Foreign News," 486; Beverly Horvit, "Combat, Political Violence Top International Categories," *Newspaper Research Journal*, Vol. 24, No. 2 (Spring 2003): 23–35; Morton Rosenblum's "coups and earthquakes" theory showed that news from the Third World is only important when it is a crisis. Morton Rosenblum, *Coups and Earthquakes* (New York: Harper and Row, 1979).

26. See: Tsan-Kuo Chang, Tuen-yu Lan, and Hao Xiaoming, "From the United States with News and More: International Flow, Television Coverage and the World System," *International Communication Gazette*, Vol. 62, No. 6.(December 2000): 505–522; John Lent, "Foreign News in American Media," *Journal of Communication*, Vol. 27 (Winter 1977): 46–51; George Gerbner and George Marvanyi, "The Many Worlds of the World's Press," *Journal of Communications*, Vol. 27, No. 1 (Winter 1977): 52–66; Melissa Johnson, "Predicting News Flow from Mexico," *Journalism and Mass Communication Quarterly*, Vol. 74, No. 2 (1997): 315–331; Denis H. Wu, "Systemic Determinants of International News Coverage: A Comparison of 38 Countries," *Journal of Communication*, Vol. 50, No. 2 (Spring 2000): 110–130.

27. See: Guy Golan and Wayne Wanta, "International Elections on the U.S. Network News: An Examination of Factors Affecting Newsworthiness," *International Communication Gazette*, Vol. 65 (2003): 25–39; Denis W. Wu, "Investigating the Determinants of International News Flow: A Meta-Analysis," *International Journal for Communication Studies*, Vol. 60 (1998): 493–512; Wayne Wanta and Yu-Wei Hu, "International News Coverage: An Examination of Differing News Frames," *International Journal of Public Opinion Research*, Vol. 5 (1993): 250–264;

K. Kim and G. A. Barnett, "The Determinants of International News Flow: A Network Analysis," *Communications Research*, Vol. 23 (1996): 323–352; T. K. Chang, "All Countries Not Created Equal to be News: World System and International Communication," *Communication Research*, Vol. 25 (1998): 528–566. In the 1970s, ABC, CBS, and NBC dedicated 32.4 percent of their international news coverage to the Middle East, 21.1 percent to Western Europe, 10.8 percent to Eastern Europe, 9.5 percent to Asia, and only 6.2 percent to Latin America. James B. Weaver, Christopher J. Porter, and Margaret E. Evans, "Patterns of Foreign News Coverage on U.S. Network TV: A Ten-Year Analysis," *Journalism Quarterly*, Vol. 61 (1984): 356–363.

28. See: Zixue Tai, "Media of the World and World of the Media: A Cross-National Study of the Rankings of the 'Top 10 World Events' from 1988 to 1998," *International Communication Gazette*, Vol. 62, No. 5 (October 2000): 331–353.

29. Wayne Wanta, Guy Golan, and Cheolhan Lee, "Agenda Setting and International News: Media Influence on Public Perceptions of Foreign Nations," *Journalism and Mass Communication Quarterly*, Vol. 81, No. 2 (2004): 364–377; Guy Golan and Wayne Wanta, "Second-Level Agenda Setting in the New Hampshire primary: A comparison of coverage in three newspapers and public perceptions of candidates," Journalism & Mass Communication, Vol. 78, No. 2 (2001): 247–259.

30. Philip J. Powlick and Andrew Z. Katz, "Defining the American Public Opinion/Foreign Policy Nexus," *Mershon International Studies Review*, Vol. 42 (1998): 30–35.

31. Philo Wasburn, *The Social Construction of International News: We're Talking about Them, They're Talking About Us* (Westport, CT: Praeger Publishers, 2002), 154.

32. See: Dietram Scheufele, "Agenda-Setting, Priming, and Framing Revisited: Another Look at Cognitive Effects of Political Communication," *Mass Communication & Society*, Vol. 3 (2000): 297–316; Wanta, Golan, and Lee, "Agenda Setting and International News," 364–377; Golan and Wanta, "Second-level Agenda Setting," 247–259.

33. Wasburn, *The Social Construction*, 163.

34. For more on the function of American news in U.S. foreign policy see: W. Lance Bennett, "Toward a Theory of Press-State Relations in the United States," *Journal of Communication*, Vol. 40 (1990): 103–125; Eytan Gilboa, "Global Communication and Foreign Policy," International Communication Association, 2002; Ole Holsti, *Public Opinion and American Foreign Policy* (Ann Arbor: University of Michigan Press, 2004); M. Linsky, *Impact: How the Press Affects Federal Policymaking* (New York: W.W. Norton & Company, 1986); Chanan Naveh, "The Role of the Media in Foreign Policy Decision-Making: A Theoretical Framework," *Conflict & Communication Online*, Vol. 1, No. 2 (2002); David L. Paletz and Robert Entman, *Media, Power, and Politics* (New York: Free Press, 1991); David L. Paletz, *The Media in American Politics* (New York: Longman, 2002); James Reston, *The Artillery of the Press: Its Influence on American Foreign Policy* (New York: Harper & Row, 1966); Piers Robinson, *The CNN Effect: The*

Myth of News, Foreign Policy and Intervention (London: Routledge, 2002); Richard Sobel, *The Impact of Public Opinion on U.S. Foreign Policy Since Vietnam* (New York: Oxford University Press, 2001).

35. See: Todd Gitlin, *The Whole World Is Watching: Mass Media in the Making and Unmaking of the New Left* (Berkeley: University of California Press, 1980).

36. See: John Zaller and Dennis Chiu, "Government's Little Helper: U.S. Press Coverage of Foreign Policy Crises, 1945–1991," *Political Communication*, Vol. 13, No. 2 (1996): 385–405. A typical refrain in Noam Chomsky's work is that news framing normally reflects the interests of the government and dominant ideology of the nation where the news agency is based. See: Edward S. Herman and Noam Chomsky, *Manufacturing Consent: The Political Economy of Mass Media* (New York: Random House, 1988). Similarly, Piers Robinson's review of U.S. press–state relations found that the U.S. press has consistently supported the U.S. government during times of war, most notably the Vietnam War, the 1991 Gulf War, and U.S. actions in Somalia in 1992. See: Piers Robinson, "Researching U.S. Media-State Relations and Twenty-First Century Wars," in *Reporting War: Journalism in Wartime*, eds. Stuart Allen and Barbie Zelizer (Oxford: Routledge, 2004).

37. See: Timothy Cook, *Governing With the News, Second Edition: The News Media as a Political Institution* (Chicago: University of Chicago Press, 1996); Doris A. Graber, *Mass Media and American Politics* (5th ed.) (Washington, DC: Congressional Quarterly, 1997), 271.

38. See: Leon V. Sigal, *Reporters and Officials: The Organization and Politics of Newsmaking* (Lexington, MA: D. C. Heath, 1973); Cook, *Governing with the News*. A governmental agenda here is defined by John W. Kingdon as "the list of subjects or problems to which government officials, and people outside of government closely associated with those officials, are paying some serious attention at any given time." John W. Kingdon, *Agendas, Alternatives and Public Policies* (Boston: Little, Brown, 1984), 3; Gitlin, *The Whole World*; Daniel Hallin, *The Uncensored War: The Media and Vietnam* (Berkeley: University of California Press, 1989); N. O. Berry, *Foreign Policy and the Press: An Analysis of The New York Times' Coverage of U.S. Foreign Policy* (New York: Greenwood Press, 1996); William A. Dorman and Mansour Farhang, *The U.S. Press and Iran: Foreign Policy and the Journalism of Deference* (London: University of California Press, 1987); R.L. Behr and S. Iyengar, "Television News, Real World Cues and Changes in the Public Agenda," *Public Opinion Quarterly*, Vol. 49: 38–57.

39. See: Timothy Cook, "Domesticating a Crisis: Washington Newsbeats and Network News after the Iraq Invasion of Kuwait," in *Taken by Storm: The Media, Public Opinion, and U.S. Foreign Policy in the Gulf War*, eds. Lance W. Bennett and David L. Paletz (Chicago: University of Chicago Press, 1994).

40. Cook, "Domesticating a Crisis"; W. Lance Bennett, "Toward a Theory of Press-State Relations in the United States," *Journal of Communication*, Vol. 40 (1990): 103–125.

41. Bennett, "Toward a Theory," 103–125.

42. Robert Entman, "Framing U.S. Coverage of International News: Contrasts in Narratives of the KAL and Iran Air Incidents," *Journal of Communication*, Vol. 41, No. 4 (1991): 6–27.

43. Holsti, *Public Opinion and American Foreign Policy*, 289, 316.

44. Reston, *The Artillery of the Press*; Berry, *Foreign Policy and the Press*.

45. Patrick O'Heffernan, *Insider Perspectives on Global Journalism and the Foreign Policy Process* (Westport, CT: Alex Publishing, 1991), 232–233.

46. W. Lance Bennett, Regina G. Lawrence, and Steven Livingston, *When the Press Fails. Political Power and the News Media from Iraq to Katrina* (Chicago: University of Chicago Press, 2007), 467–485.

47. See: Meg Greenfield, *Washington* (New York: Public Affairs, 2001); Bennett, "Toward a Theory," 103–125. This is also reflected in Bennett's assessment of the U.S. news media's handling of the 2004 Abu Ghraib news story. Bennett found that while the event provided the news media an opportunity to act independently from the government and to raise the difficult issue of torture, the media framed the story as an isolated event—consistent with the Bush administration's rhetoric on this issue—and did not provide an independent counter-frame to challenge the administration despite all the imagery and evidence that pointed toward torture. Bennett's summary was that mainstream news organizations' deference to political power drives episodic reporting and constrains news stories that are consequential to U.S. foreign policy. Bennett, Lawrence, and Livingston, *When the Press Fails.*

48. Hallin, *The Uncensored War*, 116–117.

49. David Samuels, "The Aspiring Novelist Who Became Obama's Foreign Policy Guru: How Ben Rhodes Rewrote the Rules of Diplomacy for the Digital Age," *New York Times*, May 5, 2016, http://www.nytimes.com/2016/05/08/magazine/the-aspiring-novelist-who-became-obamas-foreign-policy-guru.html?_r=0

50. Susan L. Carruthers, *The Media at War: Communication and Conflict in the Twentieth Century* (New York: Palgrave Macmillan, 2000), 5.

51. Interview with Michael Hammer by the author, September 15, 2007, Washington, DC.

52. Interview with Marc Grossman by the author, October 5, 2007, Washington, DC.

53. Interview with Michael Hammer by the author, September 15, 2017, Washington, DC.

54. Interview with David Ensor by the author, October 20, 2017, Washington, DC.

55. Interview with Michael Hammer by the author, September 15, 2017, Washington, DC.

56. See: Erving Goffman, *Frame Analysis: An Essay on Organization and Experience* (Cambridge, MA: Harvard University Press, 1974); Severine Autesserre, "Hobbes and the Congo—Frames, Local Violence, and International Intervention in the Congo," *International Organization*, Vol. 63 (2009): 249–280.

57. Bernard Cohen, *The Press and Foreign Policy* (Princeton, NJ: Princeton University Press, 1963); Ulf Hannerz, *Foreign News: Exploring the World of Foreign Correspondents* (Chicago: University of Chicago Press), 2004: 211; Gitlin, *The Whole World*, 7.

58. Autessere, "Hobbes and the Congo."

59. See: Robert Entman, "Cascading Activation: Contesting the White House's Frame After 9/11," *Political Communication*, Vol. 20, Issue 4 (2003): 413–432; Arie S. Soesilo and Philo C. Wasburn, "Constructing a Political Spectacle: American and Indonesian Media Accounts of the 'Crisis in the Gulf'," *Sociological Quarterly*, Vol. 35, No. 2 (1994): 367–381; Karl E. Weick, *Sense-making in Organizations* (Ann Arbor: University of Michigan Press, 1995).

60. See: Robert Entman, *Projections of Power: Framing News, Public Opinion, and U.S. Foreign Policy* (Chicago: University of Chicago, 2004); Norris, Kern, and Just, *Framing Terrorism*, 11; Gitlin, *The Whole World*; Maxwell McCombs, Esteban Lopez-Escobar, and Juan Pablo Llamas, "Setting the Agenda of Attributes in the 1996 Spanish General Election," *Journal of Communication*, Vol. 50, No. 2 (2000): 77–92; Dietram Scheufele, "Agenda-Setting, Priming, and Framing Revisited: Another Look at Cognitive Effects of Political Communication," *Mass Communication & Society*, Vol. 3 (2000): 297–316.

61. Hess, *International News and Foreign Correspondents*, xiii and 99; Beaudoin and Thorson, "Value Representation," 486; Beverly Horvit, "Combat, Political Violence Top International Categories," *Newspaper Research Journal*, Vol. 24, No. 2 (Spring 2003): 23–35.

62. Hess, *International News and Foreign Correspondents*, xiii and 99.

63. Entman, "Cascading Activation."

64. Ibid.

65. Norris, Kern and Just, *Framing Terrorism*, 11.

66. Ibid., 15.

67. George W. Bush, "Address to a Joint Session of Congress and the American People," The White House, September 20, 2001, http://georgewbush-whitehouse.archives.gov/news/releases/2001/09/20010920-8.html

68. Andrew Calabrese and Barbara Burke, "American Identities: Nationalism, the Media and the Public Sphere," *Journal of Communication Inquiry*, Vol. 16, No. 2 (Summer 1992): 52–73; John Hutchinson, *Modern Nationalism* (Glasgow: Harper Collins, 1994); Vanessa Beasely, "The Rhetoric of Ideological Consensus in the United States: American Principles and American Prose in Presidential Inaugurals," *Communications Monographs*, Vol. 68, No. 2 (June 2001): 169–183; Nancy K. Rivenburgh, "Social Identity and News Portrayals of Citizens Involved

in International Affairs," *Media Psychology*, Vol. 2, No. 4 (November 2000): 303–329; Philip Schlesinger, "Media, the Political Order and National Identity," *Media, Culture and Society*, Vol. 13, No. 3 (July 1991): 297–308; David Katz, "Nationalism and Conflict Resolution," *International Behavior: A Social Psychological Analysis*, ed. Herbert C. Kelman (New York: Holt, Rinehart and Winston, 1965).

69. George W. Bush, "Address to a Joint Session of Congress and the American People," The White House, September 20, 2001, http://georgewbush-whitehouse. archives.gov/news/releases/2001/09/20010920-8.html. "Strategic communications" is defined as "in which leaders craft their public language and communications with the goal to create, control, distribute and use mediated messages as a political resource." Jarol B. Manheim, *All the People, All the Times: Strategic Communication and American Politics* (Armonk, NY: M.E. Sharpe, 1991); Jarol B. Maheim, "Strategic Public Diplomacy," in *Taken by Storm: The Media, Public Opinion, and U.S. Foreign Policy in the Gulf Wars*, eds. W. Lance Bennett and David L. Paletz (Chicago: University of Chicago Press, 1994), 131–148.

70. Interview with Zalmay Khalilzad by the author, September 10, 2017, Washington, DC.

71. Changho Lee, "Post, Times Highlight Government's War Efforts," *Newspaper Research Journal*, No. 1 (Winter 2003): 190–203.

72. Elizabeth Perse, *Media Effects and Society* (Florence, KY: Psychology Press, 2001), 73; Elinor Kelley Grusin and Sandra H. Utt, "The Challenge: To Examine Media's Role, Performance on 9/11 and After," in *Media in an American Crisis: Studies of September 11, 2001* (New York: University Press of America, 2005), 11

73. Elizabeth Perse, *Media Effects and Society*, 87.

74. Elizabeth Perse, *Media Effects and Society*, 86.

75. The Editors, "Rules of Engagement," *Washington Post*, September 23, 2001.

76. Jack Lule, "Myth and Terror on the Editorial Page: The New York Times Responds to September 11, 2001," *Journalism and Mass Communication Quarterly*, Vol. 79, No. 2 (Summer 2002): 286. Jack Lule's analysis of *New York Times* editorials also identified four myths promulgated in their content: the end of innocence, the victims, the heroes, and the foreboding future. He wrote: "The Times lamented a loss of innocence and grieved over a world in which everything had changed. It offered the myth of the victim, called out for vengeance, and built support for survivors. It constructed and celebrated heroes and bolstered leaders as they responded to the crisis. It mobilized for war and warned of a foreboding future, or suffering and sacrifice to come."

77. The Editors, "Calibrating the Use of Force," *New York Times*, September 22, 2001.

78. Ibid.

79. Andre Billeaudeaux, David Dinke, John S. Hutcheson, and Philip Garland, "Newspaper Editorials Follow Lead of Bush Administration," *Newspaper Research Journal*, Vol. 24, No. 1 (Winter 2003): 73.

80. Ibid.

81. The Editors, "The American Offensive Begins," *New York Times*, October 8, 2001.
82. Ibid.
83. Ibid. The U.S. media received just a 43 percent approval rating.
84. See: Entman, *Projections of Power*; Robert Entman, "Doomed to Repeat: Iraq News, 2002–2007," *American Behavioral Scientist*, Vol. 52, No. 5 (2009): 689–708; Paul Manning, *News and News Sources: A Critical Introduction* (London: Sage, 2001).
85. Interview with Zalmay Khalilzad by the author, September 5, 2017, Washington, DC.
86. See: Entman, "Cascading Activation"; Bennett, "Toward a Theory of Press-State Relations"; John Zaller, "Elite Leadership of Mass Opinion: New Evidence from the Gulf War," in *Taken by Storm: The Media, Public Opinion, and U.S. Foreign Policy in the Gulf War*, eds. W. Lance Bennett and David L. Paletz (Chicago: University of Chicago Press, 1994), 186–209.
87. Richard F. Grimmett, "Authorization for Use of Military Force in Response to the 9/11 Attacks (P.L. 107-40): Legislative History," *CRS Report for Congress*, January 16, 2007.
88. Entman, "Cascading Activation."
89. Frank Newport, "Overwhelming Support for War Continues," Gallup, November 29, 2001, http://www.gallup.com/poll/5083/overwhelming-support-war-continues.aspx. His Secretary of State, Colin Powell, received 87 percent.
90. Ibid.
91. David W. Moore, "Support for War on Terrorism Rivals Support for WWII," Gallup News Service, October 3, 2001, http://www.gallup.com/poll/4954/support-war-terrorism-rivals-support-wwii.aspx

CHAPTER 3

1. Interview with Kathy Gannon by the author, October 11, 2017, Washington, DC.
2. Barry Bearak and James Risen, "Reports Disagree on Fate of Anti-Taliban Rebel Chief," *New York Times*, September 11, 2001, http://www.nytimes.com/2001/09/11/world/reports-disagree-on-fate-of-anti-taliban-rebel-chief.html?rref=collection%2Ftimestopic%2FMassoud%2C%20Ahmed%20Shah
3. Serge Schmemann, "U.S. ATTACKED; President Vows to Exact Punishment for 'Evil'," *New York Times*, September 12, 2001.
4. Bearak and Risen, "Reports Disagree."
5. Steve Coll, *Ghost Wars: The Secret History of the CIA, Afghanistan, and Bin Laden, from the Soviet Invasion to September 10, 2001* (New York: Penguin Press, 2004).
6. William A. Hachten and James Scotton, *The World News Prism* (Ames: Iowa State University, 2002), 40.
7. Ibid., 33.
8. See: Stephen Hess, *International News and Foreign Correspondents* (Washington, DC: Brookings Institution Press, 1996), xiii and 99; Christopher E. Beaudoin

and Esther Thorson, "Value Representation in Foreign News," *International Communication Gazette*, Vol. 63, No. 6 (December 2001): 486; Beverly Horvit, "Combat, Political Violence Top International Categories," *Newspaper Research Journal*, Vol. 24, No. 2 (Spring 2003): 23–35; Tsan-Kuo Chang, Pamela Shoemaker, and Nancy Bredlinger, "Determinants of International News Coverage in the U.S. Media," *Communications Research*, Vol. 14, No. 4 (August 1987): 396–414; Zixue Tai, "Media of the World and World of the Media: A Cross-National Study of the Rankings of the 'Top 10 World Events' from 1988 to 1998," *International Communication Gazette*, Vol. 62, No. 5 (October 2000): 331–353; Rosemary Righter, *Whose News: Politics, the Press and the Third World* (New York: Times Books, 1978); Sally Bedall Smith, "Why TV News Can't Be A Complete View of the World," *New York Times*, August 8, 1982. Hodding Carter, a media critic, said in 1982 that American news networks, by focusing on violence, showed an "extraordinary lack of continuity and perspective, which is the shadow of all television news." This is because, Gerald Long of Reuters said in 1978, the rule is to show the exception, not the norm in a country: "In other words, you don't report that everything is fine in Pakistan. You report that there has been an air crash."

9. Barry Bearak, "Over World Protests, Taliban Are Destroying Ancient Buddhas," *New York Times*, March 4, 2001.

10. Ibid.

11. Barry Bearak, "Accused Aid Workers Face Islamic Judges in Afghanistan," *New York Times*, September 9, 2001.

12. Kathy Gannon, "Aid Workers Arrested in Afghanistan," Associated Press, August 8, 2001, http://www.washingtonpost.com/wp-srv/aponline/20010808/aponline045410_000.htm

13. "1998 Missile Strikes on Bin Laden May Have Backfired: Extensive 1999 Report on Al-Qaeda Threat Released by U.S. Department of Energy, Taliban Told U.S. They Wanted to Bomb Washington," *National Security Archive, Electronic Briefing Book No. 253*, August 20, 2008, http://www2.gwu.edu/~nsarchiv/NSAEBB/NSAEBB253/, last accessed April 28, 2018.

14. Barry Bearak, "A DAY OF TERROR: THE AFGHANS; Condemning Attacks, Taliban Says bin Laden Not Involved," *New York Times*, September 12, 2001.

15. Quoted in Sven Kraemer, *Inside the Cold War From Marx to Reagan: An Unprecedented Guide to the Roots, History, Strategies, and Key Documents* (Lanham, MD: UPA, 2015).

16. Susan B. Epstein and K. Alan Kronstadt, "Pakistan: U.S. Foreign Assistance," Congressional Research Service, June 7, 2011; "About Those Billions," *Newsweek*, October 20, 2009, http://www.thedailybeast.com/newsweek/2009/10/21/about-those-billions.html

17. Elisabeth Bumiller, "Remembering Afghanistan's Golden Age," *New York Times*, October 17, 2009, http://www.nytimes.com/2009/10/18/weekinreview/18bumiller.html?_r=0

18. Interview with Kathy Gannon by the author, October 11, 2017, Washington, DC.

19. Rhoda Margesson, "Afghan Refugees: Current States and Future Prospects," Congressional Research Service, January 26, 2007.

20. Interview with Kathy Gannon by the author, October 11, 2017, Washington, DC.

21. Jayshree Bajoria, "The Taliban in Afghanistan," Council on Foreign Relations, October 6, 2011, http://www.cfr.org/afghanistan/taliban-afghanistan/p10551

22. Mary Habeck, "What Does Al-Qaeda Want?" *Foreign Policy*, March 6, 2012, http://foreignpolicy.com/2012/03/06/what-does-al-qaeda-want/

23. See: Beverly Horvit, "Some Papers Gave Scant Space to Taliban, Afghanistan Pre-9/11," in *Media in an American Crisis: Studies of September 11, 2001*, eds. Elinor Kelley Grusin and Sandra H. Utt (New York: University Press of America, 2005), 131–142. The papers included were the elite newspapers the *Los Angeles Times, New York Times*, and *Washington Post* and five lesser-read newspapers, the *Boston Globe, Columbus* (Ohio) *Dispatch*, (Cleveland) *Plain Dealer, San Francisco Chronicle*, and *Tampa Tribune*.

24. Philo Wasburn, *The Social Construction of International News: We're Talking about Them, They're Talking About Us* (Westport, CT: Praeger Publishers, 2002), 20. Also see: Colin Cherry, *World Communication: Threat or Promise?* (New York: Wiley, 1978); Thomas L. McPhail, *Electronic Colonialism: The Future of International Broadcasting and Communication* (Beverly Hills, CA: Sage, 1978); Herbert I. Schiller, *Communication and Cultural Domination* (White Plains, NY: International Arts and Sciences Press, 1976); Jeremy Tunstall, *The Media are American* (London: Constable, 1977); Stephen Reese, "Theorizing a Globalized Journalism," in *Global Journalism Research: Theories, Methods, Findings, Future*, eds. Martin Loffelholz and David Weaver (Boston: Blackwell Publishing, 2008).

25. "Afghanistan: Media round-up Monday 3 December 2001," *BBC Monitoring World Media*, December 3, 2001.

26. Herbert Gans, *Deciding What's News: A Study of CBS Evening News, NBC Nightly News, Newsweek, and Time* (New York: Vintage Books, 2004), 55.

27. See: Daniel C. Hallin and Todd Gitlin, "The Gulf War as Popular Culture and Television Drama," in *Taken by Storm: The Media, Public Opinion, and U.S. Foreign Policy in the Gulf War*, eds. Lance W. Bennett and David L. Paletz (Chicago: University of Chicago Press, 1994), 149; Susan Carruthers, *The Media at War: Communication and Conflict in the Twentieth Century* (New York: Palgrave Macmillan, 2000), 7, 4.

28. Hallin and Gitlin, "The Gulf War as Popular Culture and Television Drama," 149.

29. See: Carruthers, *The Media at War*, 7.

30. Carruthers, *The Media at War*, 4. Also see: Harold Lasswell, *Propaganda Technique in the World War* (Cambridge, MA: MIT Press, 1927), 192.

31. See: Karl E. Weick, *Sense-making in Organizations* (Ann Arbor: University of Michigan Press, 1995); Michael Barnett and Martha Finnemore, *Rules for*

the World: International Organizations in Global Politics (Ithaca, NY: Cornell University Press, 2004), 32–33.

32. Giovanna Dell'Orto, Giving Meanings to the World: The First U.S. Foreign Correspondents, 1838–1859 (London: Greenwood Press, 2002), 122. The "enduring value" is reflective in Entman's 1991 study that showed that U.S. journalists explained the Soviets' downing of Korean Air Lines Flight 007 in 1983 as murder, but when the United States downed an Iranian airplane in 1988, it was explained as a technical accident. Robert Entman, "Framing U.S. Coverage of International News: Contrasts in Narratives of the KAL and Iran Air Incidents," Journal of Communication, Vol. 41, No. 4 (1991): 6–27.

33. Interview with Kathy Gannon by the author, October 11, 2017, Washington, DC.

34. Interview with David Rohde by the author, October 25, 2017, Washington, DC.

35. Interview with Carlotta Gall by the author, October 28, 2017, Washington, DC.

36. "Murders in Afghanistan Send Chill Through Media," Press Gazette, November 21, 2001, http://www.pressgazette.co.uk/story.asp?storyCode=21157&sectioncode=1

37. "Journalists and Media Staff Killed in 2001," International Federation of Journalists, 2002, http://www.ifj.org/fileadmin/images/Killed_List/IFJ_Report_on_Journalists_Killed_2001.pdf

38. Interview with Pamela Constable by the author, October 23, 2016, Kabul, Afghanistan.

39. Ibid.

40. Ibid.

41. Interview with David Rohde by the author, October 25, 2017, Washington, DC.

42. Interview with Carlotta Gall by the author, October 28, 2017, Washington, DC.

43. George W. Bush, "State of the Union," Washington Post, January 28, 2003, http://www.washingtonpost.com/wp-srv/onpolitics/transcripts/bushtext_012803.html

44. See: Sean Aday, "Chasing the Bad News: An Analysis of 2005 Iraq and Afghanistan War Coverage on NBC and Fox News Channel," Journal of Communication, Vol. 60 (2003): 144–164.

45. "Tyndall Report Weekly Archives 2003," Tyndall Report, http://tyndallreport.com/weekly/archive/2003, last accessed April 28, 2018.

46. Jim Lobe, "Iraq Blotted Out Rest of the World in 2003 TV News," Global Policy Forum, January 6, 2004, http://www.globalpolicy.org/empire/media/2004/0106blotted.htm, last accessed April 28, 2018.

47. Brian Stelter, "Goodbye Baghdad, Hello Kabul," New York Times, October 19, 2009, https://www.nytimes.com/2009/10/19/business/media/19coverage.html.

48. Marc Seamon and Matt Peters, "News Mix Reflects Media's Gatekeeping Role in Crises," in Media in an American Crisis: Studies of September 11, 2001, eds. Elinor Kelley Grusin and Sandra H. Utt (New York: University Press of America, 2005), 265–273.

49. Michael Sweeney, *The Military and the Press: An Uneasy Truce* (Evanston, IL: Northwestern University Press, 2006), 182. In an age of digital and satellite media, the news was instantaneous, causing the players within the war theater to "live it and watch it at the same time."

50. Terry McDermott, "Review: Judith Miller's 'The Story: A Reporter's Journey'," *New York Times*, April 7, 2015, https://www.nytimes.com/2015/04/08/books/review-judith-millers-the-story-a-reporters-journey.html?_r=0

51. "The Times and Iraq," *New York Times*, May 26, 2004, https://www.nytimes.com/2004/05/26/world/from-the-editors-the-times-and-iraq.html

52. Sweeney, *The Military and the Press*, 209; Michelle Ferrari, *Reporting America at War: An Oral History* (New York: Hyperion, 2003), 213. Some journalists recognized that they had neglected the war in Afghanistan, but others blamed the U.S. military for restricting journalists' access to the country. The chief foreign affairs correspondent for CNN, Christiane Amanpour, blamed the U.S. military's restrictions on access to Afghanistan in 2003 for limited coverage of the country, and the failure to provide a total account of U.S. reconstruction efforts there. She said, "We have gotten a very empty view of what is happening in Afghanistan, and it is a dangerous view, because you get the impression that all America is about is bombing and high tech and bulldozing." This narrow sense of the war was negative for the U.S. image, too, she said: "I think America needs to have its other side shown to the world—its human side, the good things, the constructive things it is doing."

53. W. Russell Neuman, "The Threshold of Public Attention," *Public Opinion Quarterly*, Vol. 54, No. 2 (Summer 1990): 159–176; Anthony Downs, "Up and Down with Ecology: The Issue-Attention Cycle," *Public Interest*, Vol. 28 (Summer 1972): 28–50; Joe Bob Hester, "New York Times' Coverage Before, During and After 9/11," in *Media in an American Crisis: Studies of September 11, 2001*, eds. Elinor Kelley Grusin and Sandra H. Utt (New York: University Press of America, 2005), 40–41. W. Russell Neuman's 1990 work, "The Threshold of Public Attention," used Anthony Downs's "Issue-Attention Cycle" to show that the public's perception of most crises is more about a systematic cycle of increased public interest, followed by a saturation/boredom effect, and then a general decline of public attention. It's therefore not so much about the issue than just a general cycle in people's attention. There are specifically five stages: (1) the pre-problem stage, where the problem exists but has yet to be recognized by the public; (2) a discovery stage, where the problem is suddenly part of public consciousness and gets much attention, which Downs calls "the threshold"; (3) the plateau stage, when the public realizes the problem is complex and will not be easy to solve; (4) the decline stage, when the public becomes frustrated with the problem and more inattentive to it; and (5) the post-problem stage, where the problem still exists, but there is a period of inattention. All of this occurs even though the fundamental issue never changes itself.

54. Interview with Ronald Neumann by the author, September 26, 2017, Washington, DC.

55. Ibid. Also see: Stephen Hess, "Media Mavens," *Society*, Vol. 33, No. 3 (March/April 1996): 70.

56. David Rohde and David Sanger, "How a 'Good War' in Afghanistan Went Bad," *New York Times*, August 12, 2007, http://www.nytimes.com/2007/08/12/world/asia/12afghan.html?pagewanted=all; Hester, "New York Times' Coverage Before, During and After 9/11," 45–46. This, Hester argued, is prevalent in the *Times*' own coverage: The paper had covered terrorism sparsely, averaging 23.3 stories per week, as an issue before September 11, 2001. For the first 16 weeks after September 10, 2001, the *Times* averaged 578.9 stories per week. By December 31, 2001, the news had hit a plateau, averaging 170.8 stories a week.

57. Rohde and Sanger, "How a 'Good War' in Afghanistan."

58. Maura Reynolds, "Bush Presses NATO to Send More Troops to Afghanistan," *Los Angeles Times*, February 16, 2007, http://articles.baltimoresun.com/2007-02-16/news/0702160410_1_nato-offensive-in-afghanistan-troops-to-afghanistan

59. "Iraq News: Less Dominant, Still Important," Pew Center for the People and the Press, November 9, 2007, http://www.people-press.org/2007/11/09/iraq-news-less-dominant-still-important/

60. Stelter, "Goodbye Baghdad, Hello Kabul."

61. "Obama Calls Iraq War a 'Dangerous Distraction'," CNN, July 15, 2008, http://www.cnn.com/2008/POLITICS/07/15/obama.iraq/index.html?iref=nextin

62. "Network TV News—State of the News Media in 2010," Pew Project for Excellence in Journalism, 2011, http://www.stateofthemedia.org/2010/network_tv_news_investment.php. "Since 2008, there have been an average of 12 foreign bureaus for each news network. In 2009, ABC had 10 overseas news bureaus—2 in Latin America, 3 in Europe, 2 in the Middle East, and 3 in Asia. CBS had 14—1 in Latin America, 4 in Europe, 3 in the Middle East, 1 in Africa, and 5 in Asia (including Afghanistan and Pakistan). NBC had 12—1 in Latin America, 2 in Europe, 3 in the Middle East, and 6 in Asia (including Afghanistan and Pakistan). In 2009 CBS partnered with the international news website GlobalPost, which expanded its reach to 70 affiliated correspondents in 50 countries."

63. "Hours Devoted to Stories with a Foreign Dateline—State of the News Media in 2010," Pew Project for Excellence in Journalism, March 2011, http://www.stateofthemedia.org/2010.

64. After the economy and health care, however, there were six other stories that accounted for 2% of the newshole or more in 2009: the new Obama administration (5%), Afghanistan (5%), U.S. efforts to combat terrorism (4%), Iran (2%), the swine flu outbreak (2%), and the Iraq War (2%).

65. Barack Obama, "Transcript of Obama Speech on Afghanistan," CNN, December 2, 2009, http://www.cnn.com/2009/POLITICS/12/01/obama.afghanistan.speech.transcript/index.html; J. Taylor Rushing, "Goal

of Kerry-Lugar Legislation Is to 'Deepen' U.S. Ties with Pakistan," *The Hill*, May 4, 2009, http://thehill.com/homenews/news/19490-goal-of-kerry-lugar-legislation-is-to-deepen-us-ties-with-pakistan.

66. Interview with Michael Hammer by the author, September 15, 2017, Washington, DC.

67. Obama, "Transcript of Obama Speech on Afghanistan."

68. The Editors, "The War Up Close," *Time*, October 12, 2009, http://www.time.com/time/covers/0,16641,20091012,00.html

69. Stelter, "Goodbye Baghdad, Hello Kabul."

70. Ibid.

71. Ibid.

72. "Afghanistan—State of the News Media in 2009," Pew Project for Excellence in Journalism, 2010, http://www.stateofthemedia.org/2010/year_overview.php

73. "Time Devoted to the Wars in Afghanistan and Iraq Over Time—State of the News Media in 2010," Pew Project for Excellence in Journalism, March 2011, http://www.stateofthemedia.org/2010: in 2004, 1.76 hours; in 2005, 1.71 hours; in 2006, 1.73 hours; in 2007, 1.68 hours; and in 2008; 2.1 hours.

74. "2010 in Review—State of the News Media in 2010," Pew Project for Excellence in Journalism, 2011, http://www.stateofthemedia.org/2010/year_overview.php

75. "2012 in Review—State of the News Media in 2012," Pew Project for Excellence in Journalism, 2012, http://stateofthemedia.org/2012/mobile-devices-and-news-consumption-some-good-signs-for-journalism/year-in-2011/

76. "Top Ten Stories Ranked by Time on U.S. Foreign Policy Focus 2015," *Tyndall Report*, 2015.

77. In 2016, there had been a modest decline in foreign bureaus for cable news stations compared to 2010, from 53 to 48. CNN remained the leader in terms of the sheer number of bureaus it operated around the world and domestically. "As of March 2016, the organization listed 31 "editorial operations" internationally and 11 domestically; that compares with 3 foreign and 11 domestic bureaus operated by Fox News. NBC News (whose resources are shared with MSNBC) did not provide updated figures for bureaus in 2016, but as of 2015, the network operated 11 foreign and 9 domestic bureaus, in addition to 10 international locations in which it had a presence, but no bureau"; "2016 in Review—State of the News Media in 2016," Pew Project for Excellence in Journalism, 2016, http://www.journalism.org/files/2016/06/State-of-the-News-Media-Report-2016-FINAL.pdf

78. Jeremy Tunstall and David Machin, *The Anglo-American Media Connection* (Oxford: Oxford University Press, 1999); Bella Mody, *The Geopolitics of Representation in Foreign News: Explaining Darfur* (Boulder, CO: Lexington Books, 2010), 14.

79. Daya Kishan Thussu, "Managing the Media in an Era of Round-the-Clock News: Notes from India's First Tele-War," *Journalism Studies*, Vol. 3, No. 2 (2002): 203–212.

80. "CNN Fact Sheet," CNN, http://cnnpressroom.blogs.cnn.com/cnn-fact-sheet/; "BBC's Global Audience Rises to 372m," BBC Media Centre, http://www.bbc.co.uk/mediacentre/latestnews/2017/global-audience-measure

81. Hachten and Scotton, *The World News Prism*. The normative framework of the Western news media is often emulated overseas. The Western media, Nisbet et al. argued in 2004, have had a large impact on how news organizations are structured in the Muslim world, and how publics consume news, as emerging news networks have been pushed to be globally competitive. Al Jazeera created a new model for countries in the Middle East and South Asia based on Western global news networks: "Even though the Muslim public has had limited exposure to Western media, the diversity, structure, and format of Western media coverage has provided an alternative image of what Muslim news media could provide." Erik C. Nisbet, Matthew C. Nisbet, Dietram A. Scheufele, and James E. Shanahan, "Public Diplomacy, Television News and Muslim Opinion," *Harvard International Journal of Press/Politics*, Vol. 9, Issue 2 (2002): 11–37.

82. Werner A. Meier, "Media Ownership—Does It Matter?" in *Networking Knowledge for Information Societies*, eds. Robin Mansell, Rohan Samarajiwa, and Amy Mahan (Delft: Delft University Press, 2003); Mody, *The Geopolitics of Representation*, 25.

83. "Freedom of the Press 2017: Press Freedom's Dark Horizon," Freedom House, April 28, 2017, https://freedomhouse.org/report/freedom-press/freedom-press-2017, last accessed November 12, 2017.

84. Simon Cottle, *Global Crisis Reporting* (Berkshire, England: Open University Press, 2009); W. Russell Neuman, Marion R. Just, and Ann N. Crigler, *Common Knowledge: News and the Construction of Political Meaning* (Chicago: University of Chicago Press, 1992); Gans, *Deciding What's News*, 31, 42.

85. Ibid.

86. Wasburn, *The Social Construction of International News*, 101. See also: C. Anthony Gifford, "Developed and Developing Nation News in the U.S. Wire Service Files to Asia," *Journalism Quarterly*, Vol. 61 (1984): 14–19; Mustapha Masmoudi, "The New World Information Order," Document 21, UNESCO International Commission for the Study of Social Problems (Paris: UNESCO, 1978); McPhail, *Electronic Colonialism*; Rita Cruise O'Brien, "The Political Economy of Information: A North-South Perspective," in *World Communications: A Handbook*, eds. George Gerbner and Marsha Siefert (New York: Longman, 1984), 37–44; Morton Rosenblume, "The Western Wire Services and the Third World," in *The Third World and Press Freedom*, ed. P. C. Horton (New York: Praeger, 1978), 104–126; Elizabeth Fox, *Media and Politics in Latin America: The Struggle for Democracy* (Newbury Park, CA: Sage, 1988); Goran Hedebro, *Communication and Social Change in Developing Nations: A Critical View* (Ames: Iowa State University Press, 1982).

87. Giovanna Dell'Orto, "Foreign Policy and Foreign Correspondence: Integrating IR and Communication Theories to Examine the History of Press Involvement

in International Affairs," Paper Presented at the International Studies Association Annual Conference, Montreal, 2011; Hachten and Scotton, *The World News Prism*, 34–35.

88. See: Wasburn, *The Social Construction of International News*, 124. This is reflected in the coverage of the 1991 Gulf War, when the West and rich oil states were aligned against a relatively poor Third World country, Iraq.

89. Craig LaMay, *Exporting Press Freedom* (New York: Routledge, 2007), 77.

90. "Universal Declaration of Human Rights," United Nations, Paris, December 10, 1948, http://www.un.org/en/universal-declaration-human-rights/, last accessed November 25, 2017.

91. William H. Meyer, "Structures of North–South Information Flows: An Empirical Test of Galtung's Theory," *Journalism Quarterly*, Vol. 68, No. 1–2 (Spring–Summer 1991): 230–237.

92. Dell'Orto, "Foreign Policy and Foreign Correspondence."

93. Stephen D. McDowell, "Theory and Research in International Communication: A Historical and Institutional Account," in *Handbook of International and Intercultural Communication, Second Edition*, eds. William B. Gudykunst and Bella Mody (London: Sage Publications, 2002), 302.

94. Quoted in W. Phillips Davidson, Donald R. Shanor, and Frederick T. C. Yu, *News from Abroad and the Foreign Policy Public* (New York: Foreign Policy Association, 1980), 12–15.

95. Mustapha Masmoudi, "The New World Information Order."

96. LaMay, *Exporting Press Freedom*, 80.

97. Robert G. Picard, "Global Communication Controversies," in *Global Journalism*, ed. John C. Merrill (New York: Longman, 1991).

98. Roxanne Doty, *Imperial Encounters: The Politics of Representation in North-South Relations* (Minneapolis: University of Minnesota Press, 1996).

99. A. Sreberny-Mohammadi, Kaarle Nordenstreng, R. L. Stevesnon, and Frank Ugboajah, "Foreign News in the Media: International Reporting in 29 Countries." Final Report of the "Foreign Images" Study Undertaken for UNESCO by the IAMCR, 1985.

100. David Campbell, *Writing Security: U.S. Foreign Policy and the Politics of Identity* (Minneapolis: University of Minnesota Press, 1992).

101. Mody, *The Geopolitics of Representation*, 20.

102. Susan L. Carruthers, "Tribalism and Tribulation: Media Constructions of 'African Savagery' and 'Western Humanitarianism' in the 1990s," in *Reporting War*, eds. Stuart Allan and Barbie Zelizer (New York: Routledge, 2004).

103. Stuart J. Kaufman, *Modern Hatreds: The Symbolic Politics of Ethnic War* (Ithaca: Cornell University Press, 2001), 1–44.

104. See: Dell'Orto, "Foreign Policy and Foreign Correspondence."

105. Hachten and Scotton, *The World News Prism*, 34.

106. See: Hess, *International News and Foreign Correspondents*.

107. See: Wasburn, *The Social Construction of International News.*

108. Interview with Michael Hammer by the author. September 15, 2017, Washington, DC.

109. Peter Bergen, *The Longest War: The Enduring Conflict Between America and Al-Qaeda* (New York: Simon and Schuster, 2011).

110. Interview with Ronald Neumann by the author, September 26, 2017, Washington, DC.

111. Interview with Ronald Neumann by the author, September 26, 2017, Washington, DC.

112. Dexter Filkins, "Iran Is Said to Give Top Karzai Aide Cash by the Bagful," *New York Times*, October 23, 2010, http://www.nytimes.com/2010/10/24/world/asia/24afghan.html

113. Deb Reichman, "Karzai Says His Office Gets Cash from Iran, US," Associated Press, October 25, 2010, http://www.sandiegouniontribune.com/sdut-karzai-says-his-office-gets-cash-from-iran-us-2010oct25-story.html

114. Interview with David Ensor by the author, October 20, 2017, Washington, DC.

115. Interview with Marc Grossman by the author, October 7, 2017, Washington, DC.

116. Interview with Marc Grossman by the author, October 7, 2017, Washington, DC.

117. Interview with Ronald Neumann by the author, September 26, 2017, Washington, DC.

118. Interview with Zalmay Khalilzad by the author, September 10, 2017, Washington, DC.

CHAPTER 4

1. Mujib Mashal, "After Karzai," *The Atlantic*, July 2014, https://www.theatlantic.com/magazine/archive/2014/07/after-karzai/372294/

2. Ken Auletta, "The Networker: Afghanistan's First Media Mogul," *New Yorker*, July 5, 2010, http://www.newyorker.com/reporting/2010/07/05/100705fa_fact_auletta

3. "Afghanistan: Media Round-Up 12 Oct 2001," *BBC Monitoring World Media*, October 12, 2001. As the article notes, on October 9, 2001, the radio station's two control buildings were damaged in a U.S. air raid, according to the Pentagon.

4. Ibid.

5. "Afghanistan: Media Round-Up 13 Nov 2001," *BBC Monitoring World Media*, November 13, 2001.

6. Ibid.

7. "Afghanistan: Media Round-Up 24 Oct 2001," *BBC Monitoring World Media*, October 24, 2001.

8. "Afghanistan: Media Round-Up 10 Nov 2001," *BBC Monitoring World Media*, November 10, 2001.

9. "Afghanistan: Media Round-Up 11 Nov 2001," *BBC Monitoring World Media*, November 11, 2001.

10. "Afghanistan Press, Media, TV, Radio, Newspapers," *Press Reference*, 2003, http://www.pressreference.com/A-Be/Afghanistan.html

11. Lisa Anne Hartenberger, *Mediating Transition in Afghanistan, 2001–2004*, Doctoral Dissertation, University of Texas at Austin, 2005; V. Brossel, "Press Freedom One Year After the Fall of the Taliban," *Reporters sans Frontières*, 2002, http://www.rsf.org/article.php3?id_article=4278; B. Girard and J. Van der Spek, "The Potential for Community Radio in Afghanistan," *Comunica*, 2002, www.comunica.org.

12. Auletta, "The Networker."

13. George Szalai, "Afghan Media Mogul Saad Mohseni on Taking His Moby Group to New Markets and His Hollywood Connections (Q&A)," *Hollywood Reporter*, October 2016, http://www.hollywoodreporter.com/news/afghan-media-mogul-saad-mohseni-937657

14. Interview with Saad Mohseni by the author, October 2016, Washington, DC.

15. Szalai, "Afghan Media Mogul."

16. Interview with Sami Mahdi by the author, October 2016, Kabul, Afghanistan.

17. Hartenberger, *Mediating Transition in Afghanistan*; M. Ewans, *Afghanistan: A Short History of its People and Politics* (New York: Harper Collins, 2002); S. N. Nawid, *Religious Response to Social Change in Afghanistan 1919–29: King Aman-Allah and the Afghan Ulama* (Costa Mesa, CA: Mazda Publishers, 1999); S. M. Rawan, "Modern Mass Media and Traditional Communication in Afghanistan," *Political Communication*, Vol. 19 (2002): 155–170; Barnett Rubin, *The Fragmentation of Afghanistan: State Formation and Collapse in the International System* (New Haven and London: Yale University Press, 2002).

18. S. M. Rawan, "Modern Mass Media and Traditional Communication in Afghanistan," *Political Communication*, Vol. 19 (2002): 155–170; Barnett Rubin, *The Fragmentation of Afghanistan: State Formation and Collapse in the International System* (New Haven and London: Yale University Press, 2002).

19. See: Stuart J. Kaufman, *Modern Hatreds: The Symbolic Politics of Ethnic War* (Ithaca: Cornell University Press, 2001), 1–44; Silvio Waisbord, "Media and the Reinvention of the Nation," in *The SAGE Handbook of Media Studies*, eds. John D. H. Downing, Denis McQuail, Philip Schlesinger, and Ellen Wartella (Thousand Oaks, CA: Sage Publishers, 2004), 375–389.

20. "Afghanistan Press, Media, TV, Radio, Newspapers," *Press Reference*.

21. Hartenberger, *Mediating Transition in Afghanistan*.

22. Ibid.; Rawan, "Modern Mass Media." Radio Afghanistan was not officially given the name until 1964. Germany continued to support Afghanistan's radio system by giving King Zahir Shah (1933–1973) news transmitters in 1966 and 1970.

23. Rawan, "Modern Mass Media," 155–170.

24. "Afghanistan Press, Media, TV, Radio, Newspapers," *Press Reference*.

25. M. H. Razi, "Afghanistan," in *Mass Media in the Middle East: A Comprehensive Handbook*, eds. Y. R. Kamalipour and H. Mowlana (Westport, CT: Greenwood Press, 2002).

26. "Afghanistan Press, Media, TV, Radio, Newspapers," *Press Reference*.

27. Hartenberger, *Mediating Transition in Afghanistan*.

28. Diego Cordovez and Selig S. Harrison, *Out of Afghanistan: The Inside Story of the Soviet Withdrawal* (New York: Oxford University Press, 1995), 15.

29. Hartenberger, *Mediating Transition in Afghanistan*; Rawan, "Modern Mass Media," 155–170.

30. Seth Jones, *In the Graveyard of Empires* (New York: W.W. Norton & Company, Inc., 2009), 15–17.

31. Nabi Misdaq, *Afghanistan: Political Frailty and External Interference* (New York: Taylor and Francis, 2006), 125.

32. Hartenberger, *Mediating Transition in Afghanistan*.

33. Bill Keller, "Last Soviet Soldiers Leave Afghanistan," *New York Times*, February 15, 1989, http://partners.nytimes.com/library/world/africa/021689afghan-laden.html

34. Vanessa Gezari, "Unlikely Stories, or the Making of an Afghan News Agency," Pulitzer Center of Crisis Reporting, November 19, 2010, http://pulitzercenter.org/blog/untold-stories/afghanistan-journalism-pajhwok-afghan-news-taliban

35. Raymond Whitaker, "Kabul Falls to the Tide of the Taliban," *The Independent*, September 28, 1996, http://www.independent.co.uk/news/world/kabul-falls-to-the-tide-of-the-taliban-1365343.html

36. "Afghan Media Assessment and Development," International Media Support, 2001, http://www.i-m-s.dk/pic/Afgh-Media%20assessment.pdf

37. "Afghanistan Press, Media, TV, Radio, Newspapers," *Press Reference*.

38. Ibid.

39. Ibid.

40. Vanessa Gezari, "Reporting from Afghanistan," Pulitzer Center on Crisis Reporting, December 10, 2010, http://pulitzercenter.org/video/pajhwok-afghan-news-afghanistan-journalism

41. Interview with Carlotta Gall by the author, October 28, 2017, Washington, DC.

42. Interview with Mujib Mashal by the author, October 21, 2016, Kabul, Afghanistan.

43. "Filling the Vacuum: The Bonn Conference," *PBS Frontline*, 2003, http://www.pbs.org/wgbh/pages/frontline/shows/campaign/withus/cbonn.html

44. "Agreement on Provisional Arrangements in Afghanistan Pending the Re-Establishment of Permanent Government Institutions," United Nations, December 5, 2001, http://www.un.org/News/dh/latest/afghan/afghan-agree.htm

45. "Filling the Vacuum: The Bonn Conference."

46. Ibid.; David Rohde, "A Nation Challenged: Transfer of Power; Afghan Leaders Is Sworn In, Asking for Help to Rebuild," *New York Times*, December 23, 2001, http://www.nytimes.com/2001/12/23/world/nation-challenged-transfer-power-afghan-leader-sworn-asking-for-help-rebuild.html. In that article was this point on corruption: "The line in his speech that had received especially loud applause was a call to end the corruption that plagues the country and could threaten the

efficient use of an estimated $16 billion in reconstruction and development aid. "The significance of this day in Afghan history really depends on what happens in the future," Mr. Karzai said in fluent English. "If we deliver, this will be a great day. If we don't deliver, this will go into oblivion."

47. Rohde, "A Nation Challenged."
48. Interview with David Rohde by the author, October 25, 2017, Washington, DC.
49. Interview with Hamid Karzai by the author, October 24, 2017, Kabul, Afghanistan.
50. Girard and Van der Spek, "The Potential for Community Radio in Afghanistan."
51. Ibid.; "Internews Radio Summary 2003," http://www.internews.org/regions/afghanistan/afghan_radioreport_2003-07.htm; B. N. Bonde, "The Afghan Media Landscape," Baltic Media Centre, 2003, www.bmc.dk
52. Brossel, "Press Freedom One Year After the Fall of the Taliban"; Girard and Van der Spek, "The Potential for Community Radio in Afghanistan."
53. Brossel, "Press Freedom One Year After the Fall of the Taliban."
54. C. Levine, "Afghanistan Project Formulation Mission Report," Institute for Media, Policy and Civil Society, 2002, http://www.impacs.org/pdfs/afghanprojmissionrep.pdf
55. D. Widiastuti and R. Sulaiman, *Situation of Freedom of Expression and the Media in Afghanistan* (London: Article 19, 2003).
56. Carlotta Gall, "THREATS AND RESPONSES: KABUL; Afghan Editors Test Freedom's Boundaries With Cartoons," *New York Times*, January 12, 2003, http://www.nytimes.com/2003/01/12/world/threats-responses-kabul-afghan-editors-test-freedom-s-boundaries-with-cartoons.html
57. Interview with Hamid Karzai by the author, October 24, 2016, Kabul, Afghanistan.
58. Ibid.
59. Interview with Ahmad Mukhtar by the author, October 2016, Kabul, Afghanistan.
60. Craig LaMay, *Exporting Press Freedom* (New York: Routledge, 2007), 2, 81.
61. Ibid., 2.
62. Ibid., 23.
63. Ibid., 90–91.
64. Ibid., 23, 82.
65. Quoted in "Seeking Free & Responsible Media," *Global Issues*, Vol. 8, No. 1 (February 2003).
66. LaMay, *Exporting Press Freedom*, 151.
67. Ibid., 3–30.
68. Interview with Saad Mohseni by the author, October 10, 2016, Washington, DC.
69. Ibid.
70. Ibid.
71. Ibid.
72. Brossel, "Press Freedom One Year After the Fall of the Taliban"; A. Tarzi, "The State of the Media in Afghanistan," *Radio Free Europe/Radio Liberty*, 2003, http://www.rferl.org/afghanreport/2003/02/6-130203.asp; Bonde, "The Afghan Media Landscape."

73. Eran Fraenkel, Sheldon Himelfarb, and Emrys Schoemaker, "Afghanistan Media Assessment: Opportunities and Challenges for Peacebuilding," U.S. Institute for Peace (Washington, DC: Peaceworks, 2010).

74. Ibid.; "Afghan Media in 2010: A Comprehensive Assessment of the Afghan Media Landscape, Audience Preferences and Impact on Opinions," Altai Consulting, October 13, 2010; "Afghanistan: Media and Telecoms Landscape Guide," Info AusAid, March 2011.

75. Fraenkel, Himelfarb, and Schoemaker, "Afghanistan Media Assessment." Afghans also largely saw television as a tool to educate and open minds and a positive force in Afghan society since it tackled key issues such as corruption, the economy, and crime. The Afghan people, however, seem split on what content on Afghan media they prefer. The BBC Survey explained that the largest point of contention among Afghans was over pop culture on television—specifically music videos and soap operas imported mainly from India. Private stations, especially those from Tolo TV, ran them throughout the day to acquire higher ratings. As a result, television has become a symbol of conflict between those who want to modernize Afghanistan, politicians who want to advance their own interests, and conservatives who want to regulate television.

76. Tom Peter, "Afghanistan Funding: Local Media Already Feeling the Pinch," *Christian Science Monitor*, July 8, 2012.

77. Interview with Bilal Sarwary by the author, October 20, 2016, Kabul, Afghanistan.

78. The United States also funded the launch of Pajhwok, Afghanistan's first independent newswire, in 2004 (Pajhwok means "echo" in both Dari and Pashto). The Institute for War and Peace Reporting (IWPR), a media development non-governmental organization, guided its development. The profound weakness of Afghanistan's economy severely affects the media's long-term prospects. For instance, Pajhwok, which was originally supported by USAID, had planned to become financially independent by charging subscriber fees, but people found ways to acquire its news content without subscribing and, by the summer of 2012, Pajhwok was forced to reduce its staff by 38 percent. Pajhwok's owners expect even less revenue as subscribers lose interest in Afghanistan after NATO troops leave and the economy falters with less international support. Gezari, "Unlikely Stories."

79. Interview with Farhang by the author, June 2010, Kabul, Afghanistan.

80. Interview with Eileen O'Connor by the author, October 31, 2017, Washington, DC.

81. Nick Hopkins, "Afghanistan's Jack Bauer Says He is Under Pressure to Give Up TV Cop Show," *The Guardian*, January 11, 2012, https://www.theguardian.com/global/defence-and-security-blog/2012/jan/11/afghanistan-and-jack-bauer-and-tv-show-and-taliban; Interview with Ryan Crocker by the author, October 25, 2017, Washington, DC; interview with Eileen O'Connor by the author, October 31, 2017, Washington, DC; interview with David Ensor by the author, October 20, 2017, Washington, DC.

82. Interview with David Ensor by the author, October 20, 2017, Washington, DC.

83. Interview with Babur by the author, June 2010, Kabul, Afghanistan; interview with Sina by the author, June 2010, Kabul, Afghanistan; interview with Atash by the author, June 2012, Kabul, Afghanistan; interview with Mansoor by the author, July 2012, Kabul, Afghanistan; interview with Hakim by the author, July 2012, Kabul, Afghanistan. Hakim acknowledged that his news outlet needs to become more multimedia online and needs more content so that it can become more modern and international in its reach. But the style of news also needs developing, to challenge power more but to also be constructive for the government and the Afghan public. He sees the model as being more British news than American.

84. Interview with Faisal by the author, June 2010, Kabul, Afghanistan; interview with Delewar by the author, June 2010, Kabul, Afghanistan; interview with Aalem by the author; interview with Jahandar by the author, July 2012, Kabul, Afghanistan; interview with Jawid by the author, June 2010, Kabul, Afghanistan.

85. Interview with Babur by the author, June 2010, Kabul, Afghanistan; interview with Houshmand by the author, July 2012, Kabul, Afghanistan; interview with Delewar by the author, June 2010, Kabul, Afghanistan; interview with Omaid by the author, June 2012, Kabul, Afghanistan; interview with Farhang by the author, June 2010, Kabul, Afghanistan.

86. Tom Peter, "Afghanistan Funding."

87. Interviews with Mujib Mashal by the author, October 19 and 22, 2016, Kabul, Afghanistan.

88. LaMay, *Exporting Press Freedom*, 21.

89. Interview with Khaleeq by the author, June 2010, Kabul, Afghanistan; interview with Kambas by the author, July 2012, Kabul, Afghanistan; interview with Mitra by the author, June 2010, Kabul, Afghanistan.

90. Interview with Mansoor by the author, July 2012, Kabul, Afghanistan; interview with Behnam by the author, July 2012, Kabul, Afghanistan. Behnam predicted that, if security and the economy really deteriorated, the warlords would flee the country with their money: "If I'm a warlord and I have $100 million, why would I waste my neck? That's enough for generations." The people who can leave Afghanistan will leave, he predicted.

91. Szalai, "Afghan Media Mogul."

92. Interview with Saad Mohseni by the author, October 10, 2016, Washington, DC.

93. "Afghanistan Demographics Profile," IndexMundi, July 2016, https://www.indexmundi.com/afghanistan/demographics_profile.html, last accessed November 12, 2017

94. Interview with Maria Abi-Habib by the author, September 24, 2017, Washington, DC.

CHAPTER 5

1. Interview with Sardar Ahmad by the author, June 2012, Kabul, Afghanistan.
2. Saad Mohseni, "Statement on the January 20, 2016 Attack," *Tolo News*, January 20, 2016,http://www.tolonews.com/en/afghanistan/23401-seven-tolo-tv-employees-killed-in-wednesday-attack. "Murdering those who work to enlighten, educate, and entertain will not stop Afghans from exercising their universal human right to freedom of expression," according to a statement issued by the American Embassy in Kabul on Wednesday evening. "A vibrant media is one of the great successes of the Afghan people over the past 14 years."
3. Taliban press release, October 12, 2015.
4. Ibid.
5. Ibid.
6. Mohseni, "Statement on the January 20, 2016 Attack"
7. Mujib Mashal, "Vibrant Lives of Afghan TV Crew, Erased in a Taliban Bombing," *New York Times*, January 22, 2016, http://www.nytimes.com/2016/01/22/world/asia/afghanistan-tolo-tv-bombing.html
8. Emma Graham-Harrison, "Serena Hotel Attack, March 21, 2014—Sardar Ahmad," *The Guardian*, March 21, 2014, http://www.theguardian.com/world/2014/mar/21/taliban-gunmen-kill-nine-kabul-serena-hotel
9. Rod Nordland and Habib Zahori, "Killing of Afghan Journalist and Family Members Stuns Media Peers," *New York Times*, March 26, 2014, https://www.nytimes.com/2014/03/27/world/asia/killing-of-afghan-journalist-and-family-members-stuns-media-peers.html?_r=0
10. Interview with Bilal Sarwary, October 20, 2016, Kabul, Afghanistan.
11. Nordland and Zahori, "Killing of Afghan Journalist."
12. Hamid Karzai, "Condolence Message by President Karzai Statement on the Loss of Afghan Journalist," Presidential Palace of Afghanistan, March 21, 2014, http://president.gov.af/en/news/president-karzais-condolence-message-on-the-loss-of-afghan-journalist?version=meter+at+6&module=meter-Links&pgtype=article&contentId=&mediaId=&referrer=https%3A%2F%2Fwww.google.com%2F&priority=true&action=click&contentCollection=meter-links-click
13. Vanessa Gezari, "Unlikely Stories, or the Making of an Afghan News Agency," Pulitzer Center of Crisis Reporting, November 19, 2010, http://pulitzercenter.org/blog/untold-stories/afghanistan-journalism-pajhwok-afghan-news-taliban
14. Eran Fraenkel, Sheldon Himelfarb, and Emrys Schoemaker, "Afghanistan Media Assessment: Opportunities and Challenges for Peacebuilding," U.S. Institute for Peace (Washington, DC: Peaceworks, 2010).
15. The Regional Stabilization Strategy for Afghanistan and Pakistan aimed to focus on the training of new journalists, enable more communities to receive information through mobile phones, and help public and private radio stations gain a wider reach throughout the region (BBC 2010 Survey).

16. "Afghanistan," Reporters without Borders, 2016, https://rsf.org/en/afghanistan

17. "Afghan Media in 2010: A Comprehensive Assessment of the Afghan Media Landscape, Audience Preferences and Impact on Opinions," Altai Consulting, October 13, 2010; "Afghanistan: Media and Telecoms Landscape Guide," Info AusAid, March 2011.

18. Freedom of speech is enshrined in the 2004 constitution, and the Media Law has been updated twice since 2002, in 2006 and 2009.

19. "Afghanistan: Media and Telecoms," Info AusAid.

20. Ibid.; Amie Ferris-Rotman, "New Afghan Law Ignites Fear over Shrinking Press Freedoms," Reuters, July 1, 2012, http://www.reuters.com/article/2012/07/01/afghanistan-media-law-idUSL3E8HR4R120120701

21. "Afghanistan: Media and Telecoms," Info AusAid.

22. Ibid.; Benawa.com protested that the mistake had been rectified within half an hour and accused Information Minister Sayed Makhdum Raheen of imposing the ban because the website had published unflattering stories about him.

23. "Afghanistan: Draft Law Threatens Media Freedom," Human Rights Watch, July 2, 2012, http://www.hrw.org/news/2012/07/02/afghanistan-draft-law-threatens-media-freedom; Ferris-Rotman, "New Afghan Law," 2012. In July 2012, the Ministry of Information and Culture circulated a new media law to Afghan government officials for their comment before they sent it to Parliament. The minister would become the director of the High Media Council—a 13-member body that includes a religious scholar and civil society representatives—that would have vast control over ethics and legal procedures for the media. It would reduce the number of journalists on the nongovernmental Mass Media Commission, curtailing the current role of experienced and independent journalists in providing media oversight. And it would remove several of the commission's key functions, including reviewing complaints and violations, and instead creating a powerful new Media Violation Assessments Commission controlled by government representatives. The draft law would also establish a costly and unnecessary new system of prosecutors and courts specifically to bring and hear civil cases regarding media abuses—and create civil sanctions for a long new list of vaguely defined media violations. One major violation would be broadcasting foreign programming, such Turkish soap operas and Bollywood films that have become particularly popular with the Afghan public, without the Council's "acknowledgement." The foreign programs are seen to promote liberal views of women and romance and are criticized by conservative elements in the country. Print media and websites would also be required to observe a "guideline of phraseology and orthography" determined by Afghan officials.

24. Interview with Saad Mohseni by the author, October 2016, Washington, DC. Tolo often engaged in disputes with the National Directorate of Security and the Ministry of Interior over the content of news stories.

25. Mujib Mashal, "After Karzai," *The Atlantic*, July 2014, http://www.theatlantic.com/magazine/archive/2014/07/after-karzai/372294/

26. Freedom House, "Afghanistan—Freedom of the Press in 2015," 2016, https://freedomhouse.org/report/freedom-press/2015/afghanistan

27. Ibid.

28. "Afghanistan: Draft Law Threatens," 2012; Ferris-Rotman, "New Afghan Law." At first, the Ministry did not seek comment from the journalism community and civil society. Abdul Mujeeb Khalvatgar, the executive director of media advocacy group Nai, told Reuters that the revised media law was attempting to prepare for the withdrawal of NATO troops from Afghanistan and the resurfacing of conservative elements.

29. Freedom House, "Afghanistan—Freedom of the Press in 2015."

30. Ibid. Worldwide, press freedoms were on the decline, hitting the lowest point in 12 years. Only 13 percent of the world enjoyed a free press due to such factors as increased political polarization, physical violence, and extralegal intimidation.

31. Interview with Sami Mahdi by the author, October 19, 2016, Kabul, Afghanistan.

32. "Afghanistan: Media and Telecoms," Info AusAid.

33. "Afghanistan," Committee to Protect Journalists, 2017, https://www.cpj.org/killed/asia/afghanistan/

34. "Violence Against Journalists in Afghanistan," Nai, 2017, http://data.nai.org.af/

35. "Growing Fears as More Afghan Journalists and Media Workers Come Under the Gun," Committee to Protect Journalists, February 2016. In February 2016, Afghan broadcast journalist Mohammad Zubair Khaksar was fatally shot and freelance reporter Yahya Jawahari beaten.

36. "Impunity Index," Committee to Protect Journalists, 2016, https://www.cpj.org/reports/2016/10/impunity-index-getting-away-with-murder-killed-justice.php

37. Interview with Sami Mahdi by the author, October 19, 2016, Kabul, Afghanistan.

38. Interview with Lotfullah Najafizada by the author, October 12, 2016, Washington, DC.

39. "A Survey of the Afghan People, 2016," The Asia Foundation, 2016, http://asiafoundation.org/wp-content/uploads/2016/12/2016_Survey-of-the-Afghan-People_full-survey.Jan2017.pdf; "A Survey of the Afghan People, 2012," The Asia Foundation, 2012, http://asiafoundation.org/country/afghanistan/2012-poll.php; interview with Jamshid by the author, June 2010, Kabul, Afghanistan; interview with Sina by the author, June 2010, Kabul, Afghanistan.

40. Interview with Lotfullah Najafizada by the author, October 12, 2016, Washington, DC.

41. Interview with Bilal Sarwary by the author, October 20, 2016, Kabul, Afghanistan.

42. Interview with Sami Mahdi by the author, October 19, 2016, Kabul, Afghanistan.

43. "Afghan Media in 2010," Altai Consulting.

44. Interview with Abdullah by the author, June 2010, Kabul, Afghanistan.

45. Interview with Lotfullah Najafizada by the author, October 12, 2016, Washington, DC.

46. Ibid.

47. Interview with Sami Mahdi by the author, October 19, 2016, Kabul, Afghanistan.

48. Interview with Lotfullah Najafizada by the author, October 12, 2016, Washington, DC.

49. Interview with Saad Mohseni by the author, October 10, 2016, Washington, DC.

50. Interview with Delewar by the author, June 2010, Kabul, Afghanistan.

51. Interview with Sarwar by the author, July 2012, Kabul, Afghanistan; interview with Delewar by the author, June 2010, Kabul, Afghanistan.

52. Interview with Sarwar by the author, July 2012, Kabul, Afghanistan.

53. Interview with Khaleeq by the author, June 2010, Kabul, Afghanistan; interview with Kambas by the author, July 2012, Kabul, Afghanistan.

54. Interview with Khaleeq by the author, June 2010, Kabul, Afghanistan.

55. Interview with Morad by the author, June 2010, Kabul, Afghanistan; interview with Abdullah by the author, June 2010, Kabul, Afghanistan. Abdullah, who also directs news in the Pashto-language at his news agency, said that news programming is not necessarily conservative, but it is sensitive to Pashtun traditions. It is focused on government issues, corruption, and the presence of international troops in Pashtun areas. Journalists based in Kandahar and Helmand—two large, Pashto-speaking cities—offer original content. He insisted that his fellow reporters at his agency provided investigative reporting.

56. Interview with Morad by the author, June 2010, Kabul, Afghanistan.

57. Interview with Behnam by the author, July 2012, Kabul, Afghanistan; Gezari, "Crossfire in Kandahar," 2011.

58. Interview with Babur by the author, June 2010, Kabul, Afghanistan. Parsa also pointed out that there is much corruption among the journalists themselves: Ministers of Parliament often pay cameramen and reporters "to keep them in a close shot so they get more publicity." Interview with Parsa by the author, July 2012, Kabul, Afghanistan.

59. Interview with Mujib Mashal by the author, October 19, 2016, Kabul, Afghanistan.

60. Gezari, "Crossfire in Kandahar."

61. Ibid.

62. Interview with Abdullah by the author, June 2010, Kabul, Afghanistan; interview with Babur by the author, June 2010, Kabul, Afghanistan

63. Interview with Hamid Karzai by the author, October 24, 2016, Kabul, Afghanistan.

64. Interview with Faisal by the author, June 2010, Kabul, Afghanistan; interview with Babur by the author, June 2010, Kabul, Afghanistan; interview with Atash by the author, June 2012, Kabul, Afghanistan; interview with Parsa by the author, July 2012, Kabul, Afghanistan; interview with Abdullah by the author, June 2010, Kabul, Afghanistan; interview with Aalem by the author, June 2010, Kabul, Afghanistan.

65. Parsa agrees that the Afghan government gives him some protection, which is why he can criticize it. Interview with Parsa by the author, July 2012, Kabul, Afghanistan; interview with Feda by the author, June 2010, Kabul, Afghanistan; interview with Faisal by the author, June 2010, Kabul, Afghanistan; interview with Kambas by the author, July 2012, Kabul, Afghanistan.

66. Interview with Sami Mahdi by the author, October 2016, Kabul, Afghanistan.

67. Ibid.

68. Ibid.

69. Interview with Babur by the author, June 2010, Kabul, Afghanistan; interview with Atash by the author, June 2012, Kabul, Afghanistan; interview with Mitra by the author, June 2010, Kabul, Afghanistan.

70. Interview with Morad by the author, June 2010, Kabul, Afghanistan; interview with Fazia by the author, June 2010, Kabul, Afghanistan.

71. Interview with Babur by the author, June 2010, Kabul, Afghanistan.

72. Interview with Babur by the author, June 2010, Kabul, Afghanistan.

73. Interview with Houshmand by the author, July 2012, Kabul, Afghanistan; interview with Jabar by the author, July 2012, Kabul, Afghanistan; interview with Babur by the author, June 2010, Kabul, Afghanistan.

74. Interview with Sina by the author, June 2010, Kabul, Afghanistan.

75. Interview with Mitra by the author, June 2010, Kabul, Afghanistan.

76. Interview with Mitra by the author, June 2010, Kabul, Afghanistan.

77. Interview with Farhang by the author, June 2010, Kabul, Afghanistan; interview with Mitra by the author, June 2010, Kabul, Afghanistan; interview with Feda by the author, June 2010, Kabul, Afghanistan; interview with Morad by the author, June 2010, Kabul, Afghanistan; interview with Sina by the author, June 2010, Kabul, Afghanistan.

78. Interview with Ghazanfar by the author, June 2010, Kabul, Afghanistan.

79. Interview with Jahandar by the author, July 2012, Kabul, Afghanistan; interview with Behnam by the author, July 2012, Kabul, Afghanistan; interview with Parsa by the author, July 2012, Kabul, Afghanistan; interview with Ghazanfar by the author, June 2010, Kabul, Afghanistan; interview with Farhang by the author, June 2010, Kabul, Afghanistan.

80. Interview with Farhang by the author, June 2010, Kabul, Afghanistan.

81. Ibid.; interview with Parsa by the author, July 2012, Kabul, Afghanistan; interview with Mansoor by the author, July 2012, Kabul, Afghanistan.

82. Joshua Partlow, *A Kingdom of Their Own: The Family Karzai and the Afghan Disaster* (New York: Knopf Doubleday, 2016).

83. Interview with Atash by the author, June 2012, Kabul, Afghanistan. For instance, government officials have not tried to stop special-interest money from Pakistan and Iran from hijacking a free press, Atash pointed out.

84. Interview with Abdullah by the author, June 2010, Kabul, Afghanistan; interview with Houshmand by the author, July 2012, Kabul, Afghanistan; interview with

Faisal by the author, June 2010, Kabul, Afghanistan; interview with Delewar by the author, June 2010, Kabul, Afghanistan; interview with Jamshid by the author, June 2010, Kabul, Afghanistan. Abdullah was the most vocal about the Afghan government's attempts to silence him. He said that his journalistic colleagues regularly receive threats from government officials via phone or face to face. He credits his news agency with being the first to be brave enough to discuss the story that President Karzai's brother, Ahmed Wali Karzai, was involved in the drug business and invited a parliamentarian from Kandahar to come to the news station and confirm it. Abdullah then received a call from a high-ranking official in the Karzai administration to complain; Abdullah invited him—or President Karzai—to come on the air to refute the allegation but they never did. Afterward, several of his fellow journalists received calls from government officials saying, "be careful." One time, Abdullah said, he was directly threatened by the Minister of Interior.

85. Interview with Abdullah by the author, June 2010, Kabul, Afghanistan.
86. Interview with Babur by the author, June 2010, Kabul, Afghanistan.
87. Interview with Houshmand by the author, July 2012, Kabul, Afghanistan.
88. Interview with Atash by the author, June 2012, Kabul, Afghanistan.
89. Interview with Houshmand by the author, July 2012, Kabul, Afghanistan; interview with Abdullah by the author, June 2010, Kabul, Afghanistan; interview with Ghazanfar by the author, June 2010, Kabul, Afghanistan; interview with Fazia by the author, June 2010, Kabul, Afghanistan; interview with Babur by the author, June 2010, Kabul, Afghanistan; interview with Bilal Sarwary by the author, October 20, 2016., Kabul, Afghanistan.
90. Interview with Babur by the author, June 2010, Kabul, Afghanistan; interview with Parsa by the author, July 2012, Kabul, Afghanistan; interview with Farhang by the author, June 2010, Kabul, Afghanistan.
91. Interview with Behnam by the author, July 2012, Kabul, Afghanistan; interview with Parsa by the author, July 2012, Kabul, Afghanistan; interview with Ghazanfar by the author, June 2010, Kabul, Afghanistan.
92. Interview with Kambas by the author, July 2012, Kabul, Afghanistan; interview with Behnam by the author, July 2012, Kabul, Afghanistan; interview with Parsa by the author, July 2012, Kabul, Afghanistan; interview with Ghazanfar by the author, June 2010, Kabul, Afghanistan; interview with Nader Nadery, October 2016, Kabul, Afghanistan.
93. Interview with Atash by the author, June 2012, Kabul, Afghanistan.
94. Interview with Sami Mahdi by the author, October 19, 2016, Kabul, Afghanistan.
95. Interview with Kambas by the author, July 2012, Kabul, Afghanistan.
96. Interview with Ahmad Mukhtar by the author, October 24, 2016, Kabul, Afghanistan.
97. Interview with Atash by the author, June 2012, Kabul, Afghanistan; interview with Mitra by the author, June 2010, Kabul, Afghanistan.

98. Interview with Mitra by the author, June 2010, Kabul, Afghanistan.

99. Interview with Atash by the author, June 2012, Kabul, Afghanistan.

100. Interview with Jamshid by the author, June 2010, Kabul, Afghanistan; interview with Kambas by the author, July 2012, Kabul, Afghanistan.

101. Interview with Morad by the author, June 2010, Kabul, Afghanistan.

102. Interview with Ghazanfar by the author, June 2010, Kabul, Afghanistan.

103. Ibid.

104. Interview with Sami Mahdi by the author, October 2016, Kabul, Afghanistan.

105. Interview with Farhang by the author, June 2010, Kabul, Afghanistan. Ghazanfar said his reporters are often defenseless when it comes to breaking news on the Taliban. Interview with Ghazanfar by the author, June 2010, Kabul, Afghanistan. This is why some Afghan journalists work for U.S. news agencies: "They do 50 to 70 percent of the work—the reporting, arrange for the interviews, and find the materials. But then somebody else writes it. And if the Afghan journalists realize that any of those stories could put us in danger, then they don't ask for credit. Because we know they will come after us." Interview with Behnam by the author, July 2012, Kabul, Afghanistan.

106. Interview with Atash by the author, June 2012, Kabul, Afghanistan.

107. Interview with Sami Mahdi by the author, October 19, 2016, Kabul, Afghanistan.

108. "Afghan Media in 2010," Altai Consulting.

109. Interview with Abdullah by the author, June 2010, Kabul, Afghanistan.

110. Interview with Bilal Sarwary by the author, October 20, 2016, Kabul, Afghanistan.

111. "Quarterly Report to the U.S. Congress," Special Inspector General for Afghanistan Reconstruction, October 30, 2016, 86, https://www.sigar.mil/pdf/quarterlyreports/2016-10-30qr-section3.pdf

112. "Selected Public Diplomacy Awards Mostly Achieved Objectives, but Embassy Can Take Steps to Enhance Grant Management and Oversight," Special Inspector General for Afghanistan Reconstruction July 30, 2012, https://www.sigar.mil/pdf/audits/2012-07-30audit-12-13508.pdf, last accessed November 26, 2017; interview with Eileen O'Connor by the author, October 31, 2017, Washington, DC.; interview with David Ensor by the author, October 20, 2017, Washington, DC.

113. Interview with Ahmad Mukhtar by the author, October 2016, Kabul, Afghanistan.

114. Interview with Houshmand by the author, July 2012, Kabul, Afghanistan.

115. Interview with Jahandar by the author, July 2012, Kabul, Afghanistan; interview with Farzin by the author, June 2012, Kabul, Afghanistan.

116. Interview with Jahandar by the author, July 2012, Kabul, Afghanistan; interview with Farzin by the author, June 2012, Kabul, Afghanistan.

117. Interview with Jawid by the author, June 2010, Kabul, Afghanistan; interview with Farzin by the author, June 2012, Kabul, Afghanistan; interview with Jahandar by the author, July 2012, Kabul, Afghanistan.

118. Interview with Babur by the author, June 2010, Kabul, Afghanistan; interview with Farhang by the author, June 2010, Kabul, Afghanistan; Farzin; interview with Sina by the author, June 2010, Kabul, Afghanistan; interview with Atash by the author, June 2012, Kabul, Afghanistan; interview with Houshmand by the author, July 2012, Kabul, Afghanistan; interview with Jahandar by the author, July 2012, Kabul, Afghanistan.

119. Interview with Jahandar by the author, July 2012, Kabul, Afghanistan.

120. Interview with Behnam by the author, July 2012, Kabul, Afghanistan.

121. Interview with Jawid by the author, June 2010, Kabul, Afghanistan; interview with Houshmand by the author, July 2012, Kabul, Afghanistan; interview with Jahandar by the author, July 2012, Kabul, Afghanistan

122. Interview with Pamela Constable by the author, October 23, 2016, Kabul, Afghanistan; interview with Rod Nordland by the author, October 25, 2016, Kabul, Afghanistan; interview with Jason by the author, July 2012, Kabul, Afghanistan; interview with Maya by the author, July 2012, Kabul, Afghanistan; interview with Nikki by the author, July 2012, Kabul, Afghanistan; interview with Nathan by the author, July 2012, Kabul, Afghanistan; interview with Roger by the author, July 2012, Kabul, Afghanistan.

123. Interview with Nathan by the author, July 2012, Kabul, Afghanistan.

124. Interview with Nikki by the author, July 2012, Kabul, Afghanistan.

125. Interview with Tom by the author, July 2012, Kabul, Afghanistan; interview with Nikki by the author, July 2012, Kabul, Afghanistan.

126. Interview with Nathan by the author, July 2012, Kabul, Afghanistan. Nathan was not sure if the U.S. government would support him if he angered the Afghan government, but should something happen to him, it would likely get much media attention. "Good, bad or otherwise, Western journalists are going to cover what happens to other Western journalists in an environment like this. So you just know how much of a black eye it would be if the government detains you, beats you, etc.," he said. There's a high probability that Afghan and Pakistani officials could pick up, intimidate, or harass Afghan and Pakistani journalists, or insurgents can take them. They are often legitimately afraid to report stories of corruption or malfeasance, or on the inner network of the insurgencies for that reason.

127. Interview with Pam Constable by the author, October 23, 2016, Kabul, Afghanistan.

128. Interview with Josh Partlow by the author, September 5, 2017, Washington, DC.

129. Interview with Maria Abi-Habib by the author, September 24, 2017, Washington, DC.

130. Interview with Rod Nordland by the author, October 25, 2016, Kabul, Afghanistan.

131. Interview with Nikki by the author, July 2012, Kabul, Afghanistan; interview with Nathan by the author, July 2012, Kabul, Afghanistan.

132. Interview with Pam Constable by the author, October 23, 2016, Kabul, Afghanistan.

133. Interview with Khaleeq by the author, June 2010, Kabul, Afghanistan.

134. Interview with Mitra by the author, June 2010, Kabul, Afghanistan; interview with Houshmand by the author, July 2012, Kabul, Afghanistan; interview with Jawid by the author, June 2010, Kabul, Afghanistan; interview with Jamshid by the author, June 2010, Kabul, Afghanistan.

135. Interview with Khaleeq by the author, June 2010, Kabul, Afghanistan; interview with Abdullah by the author, June 2010, Kabul, Afghanistan.

136. Interview with Atash by the author, June 2012, Kabul, Afghanistan; interview with Jawid by the author, June 2010, Kabul, Afghanistan; interview with Sina by the author, June 2010, Kabul, Afghanistan; interview with Morad by the author, June 2010, Kabul, Afghanistan; interview with Jabar by the author, July 2012, Kabul, Afghanistan; interview with Mansoor by the author, July 2012, Kabul, Afghanistan; interview with Fazia by the author, June 2010, Kabul, Afghanistan.

137. Interview with Ahmad Mukhtar by the author, October 24, 2016, Kabul, Afghanistan.

138. Ibid.

139. Interview with Sami Mahdi by the author, October 19, 2016, Kabul, Afghanistan.

140. Ibid.

141. Yalda Hakim, "Threatened with Death for Working on TV," BBC News, April 29, 2016.

142. Ibid.

143. Antonio Olivo, "Afghanistan Is Losing Its Local Press Corps as Journalists Flee the Country," *Washington Post*, May 7, 2016, https://www.washingtonpost.com/news/worldviews/wp/2016/05/07/afghanistan-is-losing-its-local-press-corps-as-journalists-flee-the-country/?utm_term=.59e702fefe59

144. Interview with Rod Nordland by the author, October 25, 2016, Kabul, Afghanistan.

145. Interview with Zalmay Khalilzad by the author, September 10, 2017, Washington, DC.

146. Interview with Ryan Crocker by the author, October 25, 2017, Washington, DC.

147. Interview with Kathy Gannon by the author, October 22, 2017, Washington, DC.

CHAPTER 6

1. Kim Barker, *The Taliban Shuffle: Strange Days in Afghanistan and Pakistan* (New York: Anchor, 2012).

2. Andrew Higgins, "In Afghanistan, Signs of Crony Capitalism," *Washington Post*, February 22, 2010, http://www.washingtonpost.com/wp-dyn/content/article/2010/02/21/AR2010022104317.html?sid=ST2010090107315.

3. Ibid.

4. Ibid.

5. Interview with Joshua Partlow by the author, September 5, 2017, Washington, DC.

6. U.S. Embassy in Kabul, "Afghanistan Banking Sector Vulnerabilities: Exposure to Dubai's Collapsing Property Market and the Role of Lottery Accounts," WikiLeaks Cable: 2010Kabul551_a. Dated February 13, 2010, https://wikileaks.org/plusd/cables/10KABUL551_a.html

7. Interview with James by the author, July 2012, Kabul, Afghanistan.

8. Interview with Marc Grossman by the author, October 5, 2007, Washington, DC.

9. Matthew Rosenberg and Graham Bowley, "Intractable Afghan Graft Hampering U.S. Strategy," *New York Times*, March 7, 2012, https://www.nytimes.com/2012/03/08/world/asia/corruption-remains-intractable-in-afghanistan-under-karzai-government.html.

10. "Ghani Orders Reinvestigation into Kabul Bank Case," ToloNews, October 1, 2014, http://www.tolonews.com/afghanistan/ghani-orders-reinvestigation-kabul-bank-case

11. Priya Kumar, "Shuttered Bureaus," *American Journalism Review* (December/January 2011), http://ajrarchive.org/article.asp?id=4996

12. See: Stephen Hess, *International News and Foreign Correspondents* (Washington, DC: Brookings Institution Press, 1996), xiii and 99; Christopher E. Beaudoin and Esther Thorson, "Value Representation in Foreign News," *International Communication Gazette*, Vol. 63, No. 6 (December 2001): 486; Beverly Horvit, "Combat, Political Violence Top International Categories," *Newspaper Research Journal*, Vol. 24, No. 2 (Spring 2003): 23–35.

13. Pan and Kosicki suggested that frames can be byproducts of social norms and values, organizational constraints, interest group pressures, journalistic norms, and ideological or political orientations of journalists.Z. Pan and G. M. Kosicki, "Framing Analysis: An Approach to News Discourse," *Political Communication*, Vol. 10 (1993): 55–75; Dietram Scheufele, "Agenda-Setting, Priming, and Framing Revisited: Another Look at Cognitive Effects of Political Communication," *Mass Communication & Society*, Vol. 3 (2000): 297–316.

14. This is not just for foreign correspondents; Michael Schudson found that the constraints of journalistic practice, compounded by the demands of a 24-hour news cycle, limits the amount of explanation in news stories. Michael Schudson, "The Sociology of News Production (Again)," In *Mass Media and Society*, eds. James Curran and Michael Gurevitch (London: Arnold, 2003). Also see: Philip M. Taylor, "The Military and the Media Past, Present and Future," in *The Media and International Security*, ed. Stephen Badsey (London: Frank Cass, 2003), 179.

15. Mark Pedelty, *War Stories: The Culture of Foreign Correspondents* (New York: Routledge, 1995); Ulf Hannerz, *Foreign News: Exploring the World of Foreign Correspondents* (Chicago: University of Chicago Press, 2004), 211; Jaap Van Ginneken, *Understanding Global News: A Critical Introduction* (Thousand Oaks, CA: Sage Publications, 1998): 65–75.

16. Pedelty, *War Stories*, 48; Hannerz, *Foreign News*, 211; Greg McLaughlin, *The War Correspondent* (London: Pluto Press, 2002), 23; Taylor, "The Military and the Media," 184–185.

17. Susan L. Carruthers, *The Media at War: Communication and Conflict in the Twentieth Century* (New York: Palgrave Macmillan, 2000), 10.

18. Van Ginneken, *Understanding Global News*, 86.

19. Interview with Roger by the author, July 2012, Kabul, Afghanistan; interview with James by the author, July 2012, Kabul, Afghanistan; interview with Tom by the author, July 2012, Kabul, Afghanistan. Covering Afghanistan and Pakistan accurately is particularly difficult for journalists who "parachute" into the region for short stints, Tom emphasized. Many journalists come in and out of the region on short freelancing work, and they often completely misinterpret the facts. It also depends on the talent and persistence of the American press corps, James said. Fewer people want to sign up for the job, since the news stories are risky and take you away from your family,: "If you're young, it's an opportunity to launch your career as a foreign correspondent—but they're the only people who will step up." But if you stay in Afghanistan for too long, reporting can become too simplistic, he said.

20. "Staff Sgt. Robert Bales Identified in Afghan Killings," *Army Times*, March 17, 2012, http://www.armytimes.com/news/2012/03/army-staff-sgt-robert-bales-named-suspect-afghan-killings-031712w/

21. Interview with Nikki by the author, July 2012, Kabul, Afghanistan; interview with Tom by the author, July 2012, Kabul, Afghanistan. The journalists consistently feel constrained by the security environment and the lack of support. Ideally, Nikki said, her news organization would have one journalist who focuses only on investigative reporting and one who only covers the military, but it's not possible, and they regularly become absorbed with writing on daily events. Still, Tom pointed out, American journalists often have more resources and sources available to them to report than most Afghan journalists have.

22. Interview with Maya by the author, July 2012, Kabul, Afghanistan. Afghanistan stories written in Washington are mainly security ones, Maya emphasized, because journalists' main sources are contacts in the Pentagon or the White House. But stories with an Afghanistan dateline tend to be more focused on Afghanistan the country and have more nuance and context about Afghanistan the country, she said.

23. Van Ginneken, *Understanding Global News*, 65–75.

24. Hannerz, *Foreign News*, 212, 217.

25. Ibid.; Philip J. Powlick and Andrew Z. Katz, "Defining the American Public Opinion/Foreign Policy Nexus," *Mershon International Studies Review*, Vol. 42 (1998): 42; Stephen Hess, *International News and Foreign Correspondents* (Washington, DC: Brookings Institution Press, 1996): 101.

26. Interview with Rod Nordland by the author, October 25, 2016, Kabul, Afghanistan.

27. Interview with James by the author, July 2012, Kabul, Afghanistan; interview with Tom by the author, July 2012, Kabul, Afghanistan. James and Tom felt some pressure from their Washington bureau, but their editors have never told them not to write a story.

28. Interview with Nikki by the author, July 2012, Kabul, Afghanistan.

29. Interview with Douglas Schorzman by the author, December 2, 2016, Washington, DC.

30. Ibid.

31. Ibid.

32. Interview with Faisal by the author, June 2010, Kabul, Afghanistan; interview with Atash by the author, June 2012, Kabul, Afghanistan.

33. Interview with Sarwar by the author, July 2012, Kabul, Afghanistan.

34. Interview with Mansoor by the author, July 2012, Kabul, Afghanistan.

35. David Rohde and Kristin Mulvihill, *A Rope and a Prayer: A Kidnapping from Two Sides* (New York: Viking, 2010).

36. David Cray, "Wounded AP Reporter Vows to Return to Afghanistan," *Associated Press*, October 15, 2014, https://apnews.com/50df8491a25648ebad24da6d8196 96d8/wounded-ap-reporter-vows-return-afghanistan

37. Interview with Kathy Gannon by the author, October 22, 2017, Washington, DC.

38. Interview with Bilal Sarwary by the author, October 2016, Kabul, Afghanistan.

39. Interview with Atash by the author, July 2012, Kabul, Afghanistan.

40. Interview with Faisal by the author, June 2010, Kabul, Afghanistan.

41. Interview with Ghazanfar by the author, June 2010, Kabul, Afghanistan.

42. Interview with Carlotta Gall by the author, October 28, 2017, Washington, DC.

43. Ibid.

44. Interview with Josh Partlow by the author, September 5, 2017, Washington, DC.

45. Interview with Maria Abi-Habib by the author, September 24, 2017, Washington, DC.

46. Interview with Jabar by the author, July 2012, Kabul, Afghanistan; interview with Abdullah by the author, June 2010, Kabul, Afghanistan; interview with Jamshid by the author, June 2010, Kabul, Afghanistan; interview with Sarwar by the author, July 2012, Kabul, Afghanistan; interview with Farhang by the author, June 2010, Kabul, Afghanistan; interview with Atash by the author, June 2012, Kabul, Afghanistan; interview with Khaleeq by the author, June 2010, Kabul, Afghanistan; interview with Jawid by the author, June 2010, Kabul, Afghanistan; interview with Feda by the author, June 2010, Kabul, Afghanistan; interview with Behnam by the author, July 2012, Kabul, Afghanistan; interview with Kambas by the author, July 2012, Kabul, Afghanistan; interview with Farzin by the author, June 2012, Kabul, Afghanistan; interview with Morad by the author, June 2010, Kabul, Afghanistan; interview with Parsa by the author, July 2012, Kabul, Afghanistan; interview with Matteen by the author, June 2012, Kabul, Afghanistan; interview with Babur by the author, June 2010, Kabul, Afghanistan.

47. Interview with Morad by the author, June 2010, Kabul, Afghanistan; interview with Kambas by the author, July 2012, Kabul, Afghanistan; interview with Farzin by the author, June 2012, Kabul, Afghanistan; interview with Babur by the author, June 2010, Kabul, Afghanistan.

48. Interview with Khaleeq by the author, June 2010, Kabul, Afghanistan; interview with Kambas by the author, July 2012, Kabul, Afghanistan; interview with Babur by the author, June 2010, Kabul, Afghanistan; interview with Sarwar by the author, July 2012, Kabul, Afghanistan; interview with Farhang by the author, June 2010, Kabul, Afghanistan; interview with Atash by the author, June 2012, Kabul, Afghanistan; interview with Jawid by the author, June 2010, Kabul, Afghanistan; interview with Feda by the author, June 2010, Kabul, Afghanistan; interview with Behnam by the author, July 2012, Kabul, Afghanistan; interview with Houshmand by the author, July 2012, Kabul, Afghanistan.

49. Interview with Feda by the author, June 2010, Kabul, Afghanistan.

50. Interview with Atash by the author, June 2012, Kabul, Afghanistan.

51. Interview with Jamshid by the author, June 2010, Kabul, Afghanistan; interview with Farhang by the author, June 2010, Kabul, Afghanistan; interview with Khaleeq by the author, June 2010, Kabul, Afghanistan; interview with Kambas by the author, July 2012, Kabul, Afghanistan.

52. Interview with Farid Ahmad by the author. October 20, 2016. Kabul, Afghanistan; interview with Delewar by the author, July 2012, Kabul, Afghanistan.

53. Interview with Jawid by the author, June 2010, Kabul, Afghanistan.

54. Interview with Sina by the author, June 2010, Kabul, Afghanistan. Sina said he looks to American news for guidance on how to cover news stories, but he believes that U.S. news on Afghanistan serves as an agenda-setter for his own agency's news coverage only on what the international community thinks about Afghanistan. Interview with Aalem by the author, June 2010, Kabul, Afghanistan.

55. Interview with Jawid by the author, June 2010, Kabul, Afghanistan; interview with Jahandar by the author, July 2012, Kabul, Afghanistan; interview with Jamshid by the author, June 2010, Kabul, Afghanistan; interview with Atash by the author, June 2012, Kabul, Afghanistan; interview with Mansoor by the author, July 2012, Kabul, Afghanistan.

56. Interview with Feda by the author, June 2010, Kabul, Afghanistan.

57. Interview with Sarwar by the author, July 2012, Kabul, Afghanistan; interview with Kambas by the author, July 2012, Kabul, Afghanistan.

58. Interview with Sarwar by the author, July 2012, Kabul, Afghanistan; interview with Morad by the author, June 2010, Kabul, Afghanistan; interview with Farhang by the author, June 2010, Kabul, Afghanistan; interview with Houshmand by the author, July 2012, Kabul, Afghanistan; interview with Ghazanfar by the author, June 2010, Kabul, Afghanistan; interview with Parsa by the author, July 2012, Kabul, Afghanistan.

59. Interview with Morad by the author, June 2010, Kabul, Afghanistan; interview with Houshmand by the author, July 2012, Kabul, Afghanistan; interview with Farzin by the author, June 2012, Kabul, Afghanistan; interview with Farhang by the author, June 2010, Kabul, Afghanistan. Farzin speculated that this was possibly because Saad Mohseni heavily depended on U.S. funds for his broadcast stations.

60. Interview with Behnam by the author, July 2012, Kabul, Afghanistan; interview with Abdullah by the author, June 2010, Kabul, Afghanistan.

61. Interview with Sarwar by the author, July 2012, Kabul, Afghanistan.

62. Ibid.

63. Interview with Behnam by the author, July 2012, Kabul, Afghanistan; interview with Delewar by the author, June 2010, Kabul, Afghanistan; interview with Jawid by the author, June 2010, Kabul, Afghanistan; interview with Jabar by the author, July 2012, Kabul, Afghanistan.

64. Interview with Mansoor by the author, July 2012, Kabul, Afghanistan.

65. Interview with Sina by the author, June 2010, Kabul, Afghanistan; interview with Jamshid by the author, June 2010, Kabul, Afghanistan.

66. Interview with Aalem by the author, June 2010, Kabul, Afghanistan.

67. Interviews with Mujib Mashal by the author, October 19 and 22, 2016, Kabul, Afghanistan.

68. Interview with Sami Mahdi by the author, October 2016, Kabul, Afghanistan.

69. Ibid.

70. Interview with Nathan by the author, July 2012, Kabul, Afghanistan.

71. Interview with Tom by the author, July 2012, Kabul, Afghanistan; interview with Jason by the author, July 2012, Kabul, Afghanistan.

72. Interview with Joshua Partlow by the author, September 5, 2017, Washington, DC.

73. Interview with Khaleeq by the author, June 2010, Kabul, Afghanistan; interview with Faisal by the author, June 2010, Kabul, Afghanistan; interview with Babur by the author, June 2010, Kabul, Afghanistan. Babur gave the example of a member of Parliament who, during her travels to the United Kingdom, had been interviewed on the BBC and Al Jazeera. When she returned to Kabul, she insisted on doing only exclusive interviews with American media agencies because of her newfound international recognition. Eventually, however, she realized she was losing her place with the Afghan people and returned to the Afghan press.

74. Interview with Faisal by the author, June 2010, Kabul, Afghanistan.

75. Interview with Babur by the author, June 2010, Kabul, Afghanistan; interview with Atash by the author, June 2012, Kabul, Afghanistan.

76. Interview with Khaleeq by the author, June 2010, Kabul, Afghanistan; interview with Morad by the author, June 2010, Kabul, Afghanistan; interview with Aalem by the author, June 2010, Kabul, Afghanistan. Afghan officials, Aalem said, would not go to a warlord-owned news station because they would reach only

a small fraction of the Afghan public—and would lose their credibility with the rest of the Afghan public for the fact that it granted the interview. Since there is a general perception that each Afghan station is controlled by a warlord, a politician, or a donor country, it's easier for officials to protect their own reputations by going to the international media. Interview with Babur by the author, June 2010, Kabul, Afghanistan; interview with Atash by the author, June 2012, Kabul, Afghanistan. Ghazanfar said it's because foreign journalists are guests, and Afghan culture puts a high premium on hospitality; interview with Ghazanfar by the author, June 2010, Kabul, Afghanistan.

77. Interview with Aalem by the author, June 2010, Kabul, Afghanistan.
78. Interview with Jason by the author, July 2012, Kabul, Afghanistan; interview with Maya by the author, July 2012, Kabul, Afghanistan; interview with Nikki, July 2012, Kabul, Afghanistan.
79. Interview with Maya by the author, July 2012, Kabul, Afghanistan.
80. Interview with Nikki by the author, July 2012, Kabul, Afghanistan. The presidential palace and cabinet officials may use U.S. or European media to send signals to Western governments, but that's not the case in Parliament. With ministers, you can be received immediately—or you have to wait months. Once Afghan officials are named in corruption stories in U.S. media, they tend to shun the U.S. media altogether. It's strange, Nikki said, that they take so personally what an American newspaper writes about them, but "We can't change what's true . . . so we just keep going."
81. Interview with Maria Abi-Habib by the author, September 24, 2017, Washington, DC.
82. Interview with Hamid Karzai by the author, October 24, 2016, Kabul, Afghanistan.
83. Interview with Nikki by the author, July 2012, Kabul, Afghanistan.
84. Interview with Maya by the author, July 2012, Kabul, Afghanistan.
85. Interview with Jamshid by the author, June 2010, Kabul, Afghanistan.
86. Interview with Tom by the author, July 2012, Kabul, Afghanistan.
87. Interview with Houshmand by the author, July 2012, Kabul, Afghanistan; interview with Jawid by the author, June 2010, Kabul, Afghanistan; interview with Farhang by the author, June 2010, Kabul, Afghanistan; interview with Mansoor by the author, July 2012, Kabul, Afghanistan; interview with Fazia by the author, June 2010, Kabul, Afghanistan; interview with Faisal by the author, June 2010, Kabul, Afghanistan.
88. Interview with Tom by the author, July 2012, Kabul, Afghanistan. So does Karzai's cabinet. A top defense official complained to Tom that he was misquoted and threatened to arrest the local journalist if there was not an official apology. Tom had a recording of the quote so the situation defused, but it showed him how seriously the Afghan government took American news stories.
89. See: "Afghanistan—State of the News Media in 2009," Pew Project for Excellence in Journalism, 2010, http://www.stateofthemedia.org/2010/year_overview.php

90. Interview with Jahandar by the author, July 2012, Kabul, Afghanistan.

91. Interview with Parsa by the author, July 2012, Kabul, Afghanistan; interview with Abdullah by the author, June 2010, Kabul, Afghanistan; interview with Jawid by the author, June 2010, Kabul, Afghanistan; interview with Mansoor by the author, July 2012, Kabul, Afghanistan. Another reason, Mansoor said, is that the American reporters have more resources to woo sources. He said he knows of situations when Western news agencies gave equipment or money to government spokespeople in return for information.

92. Alissa Rubin, "Afghan President Rebukes West and U.N.," *New York Times*, April 1, 2010, http://www.nytimes.com/2010/04/02/world/asia/02afghan.html

93. Alissa Rubin and Habib Zohrai, "Karzai Accuses U.S. of Duplicity in Fighting Afghan Enemies," *New York Times*, October 4, 2012, http://www.nytimes.com/2012/10/05/world/asia/karzai-accuses-us-of-duplicity-in-fighting-afghan-enemies.html

94. Afghan print reporter Bilal Sarwary was sympathetic to this point of view. He said in a 2016 interview, "I have no doubt that the *New York Times* had an agenda going against President Karzai. In 2009, there was no doubt that President Obama [and his administration] were trying to unseat him. In 2010, there were many leaks coming to the *New York Times* . . . a barrage of leaks from the American embassy. . . . I felt that Karzai's point of view was not taken seriously." Interview with Bilal Sarwary by the author, October 20, 2016, Kabul, Afghanistan.

95. Amy Belasco, "The Cost of Iraq, Afghanistan, and Other Global War on Terror Operations," Congressional Research Service, March 29, 2011, http://www.fas.org/sgp/crs/natsec/RL33110.pdf

96. Interview with Douglas Schorzman by the author, December 2, 2016, Washington, DC.

97. Interview with Nikki by the author, July 2012, Kabul, Afghanistan.

98. Interview with Pamela Constable by the author, October 23, 2016, Kabul, Afghanistan.

99. Interview with Maya by the author, July 2012, Kabul, Afghanistan. Maya is convinced that whatever relationship she created with Afghan officials is because she is a woman, and they were more willing to speak with her because they did not find her threatening. "I really do think they think that women are stupider than men. So that helps sometimes because people don't expect much of you. I think they've learned that's not the case, since," she said.

100. Interview with Nikki by the author, July 2012, Kabul, Afghanistan.

101. Interview with Mujib Mashal by the author, October 19 and 22, 2016, Kabul, Afghanistan.

102. Interview with Farhang by the author, June 2010, Kabul, Afghanistan; interview with Atash by the author, June 2012, Kabul, Afghanistan; interview with Ghazanfar by the author, June 2010, Kabul, Afghanistan; interview

with Houshmand by the author, July 2012, Kabul, Afghanistan; interview with Abdullah by the author, June 2010, Kabul, Afghanistan; interview with Jahandar by the author, July 2012, Kabul, Afghanistan. Also, however, Abdullah said that Afghan officials who want to speak out on corruption go to American journalists rather than Afghan journalists because they know they cannot protect the Afghan journalists—but the U.S. journalists are untouchable. "They think if they offer this information to foreign media, somehow they will be safe because the international community will protect them"—but most of the time, they would prefer not to offer any information, Abdullah said.

103. Interview with James by the author, July 2012, Kabul, Afghanistan; interview with Nikki by the author, July 2012, Kabul, Afghanistan.

104. Interview with Farid Ahmad by the author, October 2016, Kabul, Afghanistan.

105. Interview with Farhang by the author, June 2010, Kabul, Afghanistan; interview with Atash by the author, June 2012, Kabul, Afghanistan; interview with Abdullah by the author, June 2010, Kabul, Afghanistan; interview with Khaleeq by the author, June 2010, Kabul, Afghanistan.

106. Interview with Mujib Mashal by the author, October 19 and 22, 2016. Kabul, Afghanistan.

107. Interview with Farhang by the author, June 2010, Kabul, Afghanistan.

108. Daniel Magnowski, "Taliban Death Stadium Reborn as Afghan Sporting Hope," Reuters, December 15, 2011, http://www.reuters.com/article/2011/12/15/us-afghanistan-stadium-taliban-idUSTRE7BE0LB20111215

109. Interview with Sina by the author, June 2010, Kabul, Afghanistan.

110. Interview with Mujib Mashal by the author, October 19 and 22, 2016, Kabul, Afghanistan.

111. Interview with Abdullah by the author, June 2010, Kabul, Afghanistan; interview with Khaleeq by the author, June 2010, Kabul, Afghanistan; interview with Behnam by the author, July 2012, Kabul, Afghanistan; interview with Sina by the author, June 2010, Kabul, Afghanistan; interview with Jahandar by the author, July 2012, Kabul, Afghanistan; interview with Parsa by the author, July 2012, Kabul, Afghanistan; interview with Kambas by the author, July 2012, Kabul, Afghanistan; interview with Aalem by the author, June 2010, Kabul, Afghanistan; interview with Sarwar by the author, July 2012, Kabul, Afghanistan; Especially when there are erroneous reports that make it into the international realm. Aalem was frustrated that the power of U.S. news is especially palpable when they make a mistake. The news agency may correct it later, but the original copy with the mistake is already unleashed to the world and picked up and relayed as truth by other global news agencies.

112. Interview with Sarwar by the author, July 2012, Kabul, Afghanistan. Some Afghan journalists said that they, too, are sources for Western reporters—especially American reporters. American journalists, Faisel said, come to him for clarification on issues and to get his point of view "almost every day."

Jamshid, too, said U.S. news agencies, especially NBC and Fox News, come to gather information from him. Interview with Jamshid by the author, June 2010, Kabul, Afghanistan; interview with Faisal by the author, June 2010, Kabul, Afghanistan; interview with Jawid by the author, June 2010, Kabul, Afghanistan.

113. Interview with Delewar by the author, June 2010, Kabul, Afghanistan.
114. Interview with Rod Nordland by the author, October 25, 2016, Kabul, Afghanistan.
115. Hamid Shalizi and Jessica Donati, "Afghan Cleric and Others Defend Lynching of Woman in Kabul," Reuters, March 20, 2015, https://www.reuters.com/article/us-afghanistan-woman/afghan-cleric-and-others-defend-lynching-of-woman-in-kabul-idUSKBN0MG1Z620150320
116. "Farkhunda's Murder: A National Tragedy," ToloNews, March 28, 2015, http://www.tolonews.com/opinion/farkhundas-murder-national-tragedy
117. Alissa Rubin, "Flawed Justice After a Mob Killed an Afghan Woman," *New York Times*, December 26, 2015, https://www.nytimes.com/2015/12/27/world/asia/flawed-justice-after-a-mob-killed-an-afghan-woman.html
118. Interview with Mansoor by the author, July 2012, Kabul, Afghanistan; interview with Jahandar by the author, July 2012, Kabul, Afghanistan; interview with Faisal by the author, June 2010, Kabul, Afghanistan; interview with Farzin by the author, June 2012, Kabul, Afghanistan; interview with Aalem by the author, June 2010, Kabul, Afghanistan.
119. Interview with Jahandar by the author, July 2012, Kabul, Afghanistan; interview with Morad by the author, June 2010, Kabul, Afghanistan; interview with Sarwar by the author, July 2012, Kabul, Afghanistan.
120. Interview with Ghazanfar by the author, June 2010, Kabul, Afghanistan; interview with Houshmand by the author, July 2012, Kabul, Afghanistan.
121. Interview with Behnam by the author, July 2012, Kabul, Afghanistan; interview with Khaleeq by the author, June 2010, Kabul, Afghanistan; interview with Matteen by the author, June 2012, Kabul, Afghanistan; interview with Mansoor by the author, July 2012, Kabul, Afghanistan; interview with Babur by the author, June 2010, Kabul, Afghanistan.
122. Interview with Mansoor by the author, July 2012, Kabul, Afghanistan; interview with Sarwar by the author, July 2012, Kabul, Afghanistan; interview with Aalem by the author, June 2010, Kabul, Afghanistan.
123. Interview with James by the author, July 2012, Kabul, Afghanistan; interview with Jason by the author, July 2012, Kabul, Afghanistan
124. Interview with Saad Mohseni by the author, October 2016, Washington, DC.
125. Interview with Douglas Schorzman by the author, December 2, 2016, Washington, DC.
126. Interview with Nikki by the author, July 2012, Kabul, Afghanistan; interview with Maya by the author, July 2012, Kabul, Afghanistan

127. Interview with Rod Nordland by the author, October 25, 2016, Kabul, Afghanistan.

128. Interview with Aalem by the author, June 2010, Kabul, Afghanistan; interview with Farhang by the author, June 2010, Kabul, Afghanistan; interview with Sarwar by the author, July 2012, Kabul, Afghanistan; interview with Mansoor by the author, July 2012, Kabul, Afghanistan; interview with Abdullah by the author, June 2010, Kabul, Afghanistan.

129. Interview with Lotfullah Najafizada by the author, October 2016, Washington, DC.

130. Interview with James by the author, July 2012, Kabul, Afghanistan; interview with Jason by the author, July 2012, Kabul, Afghanistan; interview with Nikki by the author, July 2012, Kabul, Afghanistan; interview with Maya by the author, July 2012, Kabul, Afghanistan

131. Interview with James by the author, July 2012, Kabul, Afghanistan; interview with Nathan by the author, July 2012, Kabul, Afghanistan; interview with Roger by the author, July 2012, Kabul, Afghanistan; interview with Nikki by the author, July 2012, Kabul, Afghanistan.

132. Danielle Kurtzleben, "CHART: How The U.S. Troop Levels In Afghanistan Have Changed Under Obama," National Public Radio, July 6, 2016, http://www.npr.org/2016/07/06/484979294/chart-how-the-u-s-troop-levels-in-afghanistan-have-changed-under-obama

133. Interview with Pamela Constable by the author, October 23, 2016, Kabul, Afghanistan.

134. Interview with Rod Nordland by the author, October 25, 2016, Kabul, Afghanistan.

135. Interview with Jason by the author, July 2012, Kabul, Afghanistan.

136. Interview with Josh Partlow by the author, September 5, 2017, Washington, DC.

137. Interview with Douglas Schorzman by the author, December 2, 2016, Washington, DC.

138. Ibid.

139. Interview with Carlotta Gall by the author, October 28, 2017, Washington, DC.

140. Interview with Faisal by the author, June 2010, Kabul, Afghanistan; interview with Ghazanfar by the author, June 2010, Kabul, Afghanistan; interview with Khaleeq by the author, June 2010, Kabul, Afghanistan.

141. Interview with Houshmand by the author, July 2012, Kabul, Afghanistan.

142. Interview with Aalem by the author, June 2010, Kabul, Afghanistan.

CHAPTER 7

1. Interview with Farhang by the author, June 2010, Kabul, Afghanistan.

2. Interview with Mitra by the author, June 2010, Kabul, Afghanistan; interview with Sarwar by the author, July 2012, Kabul, Afghanistan; interview with Jabar

by the author, July 2012, Kabul, Afghanistan; interview with Parsa by the author, July 2012, Kabul, Afghanistan; interview with Kambas by the author, July 2012, Kabul, Afghanistan; interview with Mansoor by the author, July 2012, Kabul, Afghanistan; interview with Khaleeq by the author, June 2010, Kabul, Afghanistan; interview with Babur by the author, June 2010, Kabul, Afghanistan; interview with Delewar by the author, June 2010, Kabul, Afghanistan; interview with Houshmand by the author, July 2012, Kabul, Afghanistan; interview with Jamshid by the author, June 2010, Kabul, Afghanistan.

3. See: Erving Goffman, *Frame Analysis: An Essay on Organization and Experience* (Cambridge, MA: Harvard University Press, 1974); Severine Autesserre, "Hobbes and the Congo—Frames, Local Violence, and International Intervention in the Congo," *International Organization*, Vol. 63 (2009): 249–280.

4. Bernard Cohen, *The Press and Foreign Policy* (Princeton, NJ: Princeton University Press, 1963); Ulf Hannerz, *Foreign News: Exploring the World of Foreign Correspondents* (Chicago: University of Chicago Press, 2004), 211; Todd Gitlin, *The Whole World Is Watching: Mass Media in the Making and Unmaking of the New Left* (Berkeley: University of California Press, 1980), 7.

5. Autessere, "Hobbes and the Congo," 256.

6. Interview with Jahandar by the author, July 2012, Kabul, Afghanistan; interview with Ghazanfar by the author, June 2010, Kabul, Afghanistan; interview with Jawid by the author, June 2010, Kabul, Afghanistan; interview with Jabar by the author, July 2012, Kabul, Afghanistan.

7. Interview with Jamshid by the author, June 2010, Kabul, Afghanistan.

8. Mark Pedelty, *War Stories: The Culture of Foreign Correspondents* (New York: Routledge, 1995), 126.

9. Autessere, "Hobbes and the Congo," 256; Karl E. Weick, *Sense-making in Organizations* (Ann Arbor: University of Michigan Press, 1995); Martha Finnemore, *National Interests in International Society* (Ithaca, NY: Cornell University Press, 1996), 15.

10. Interview with Nikki by the author, July 2012, Kabul, Afghanistan.

11. Interview with Tom by the author, July 2012, Kabul, Afghanistan; interview with Nikki by the author, July 2012, Kabul, Afghanistan; interview with Jason by the author, July 2012, Kabul, Afghanistan. Jason thought that, since I mainly interviewed Afghan journalists in Kabul, they likely see Afghanistan differently than Afghanis who live in the south or east who are regularly afflicted by poor security: "I wonder if you ask a person in Helmand or Kandahar or along the Pakistani border then they might feel differently. It's easy to say that security isn't everything when you're in Kabul because it doesn't affect your life as much. But there are large swaths of this country where security and the war and the Taliban are very real parts of the daily life."

12. Interview with Nikki by the author, July 2012, Kabul, Afghanistan.

13. Interview with Nathan by the author, July 2012, Kabul, Afghanistan.

14. Interview with Babur by the author, June 2010, Kabul, Afghanistan; interview with Faisal by the author, June 2010, Kabul, Afghanistan.
15. Interview with Jahandar by the author, July 2012, Kabul, Afghanistan.
16. Interview with Delewar by the author, June 2010, Kabul, Afghanistan.
17. Interview with Kambas by the author, July 2012, Kabul, Afghanistan. The U.S. media have also given the Taliban more publicity: "The more you give them publicity, the more you encourage supporters as well to help them." This was the U.S. press's biggest, and worst, contribution to Afghanistan, Delewar said. Interview with Delewar by the author, June 2010, Kabul, Afghanistan.
18. Interview with Kambas by the author, July 2012, Kabul, Afghanistan; interview with Khaleeq by the author, June 2010, Kabul, Afghanistan.
19. Interview with Khaleeq by the author, June 2010, Kabul, Afghanistan.
20. Interview with Lotfullah Najafizada by the author, October 2016, Washington, DC. When it comes to giving Afghanistan more depth to Western readers, Najafizada explained that he thinks the newspapers have tried to occasionally, but he is less sure about American television: "Each of them have done some good stories. They've tried to look into different things. But the main focus has been security," he said.
21. Interview with Faisal by the author, June 2010, Kabul, Afghanistan.
22. Interview with Babur by the author, June 2010, Kabul, Afghanistan.
23. Interview with Houshmand by the author, July 2012, Kabul, Afghanistan.
24. Interview with Behnam by the author, July 2012, Kabul, Afghanistan.
25. Dexter Filkins, "Will Civil War Hit Afghanistan When the U.S. Leaves?" *The New Yorker*, July 9, 2012, http://www.newyorker.com/reporting/2012/07/09/120709fa_fact_filkins
26. Interview with Mitra by the author, June 2010, Kabul, Afghanistan.
27. Ibid.
28. Interview with James by the author, July 2012, Kabul, Afghanistan; interview with Nathan by the author, July 2012, Kabul, Afghanistan; interview with Nikki by the author, July 2012, Kabul, Afghanistan.
29. Interview with Farhang by the author, June 2010, Kabul, Afghanistan; interview with Parsa by the author, July 2012, Kabul, Afghanistan; interview with Fazia by the author, June 2010, Kabul, Afghanistan; interview with Jabar by the author, July 2012, Kabul, Afghanistan; interview with Jamshid by the author, June 2010, Kabul, Afghanistan; interview with Atash by the author, June 2012, Kabul, Afghanistan; interview with Farzin by the author, June 2012, Kabul, Afghanistan; interview with Morad by the author, June 2010, Kabul, Afghanistan; interview with Babur by the author, June 2010, Kabul, Afghanistan; interview with Mitra by the author, June 2010, Kabul, Afghanistan; interview with Delewar by the author, June 2010, Kabul, Afghanistan. Delewar did not appreciate U.S. news stories that described Afghanistan as a backward society whose conservative traditions keep it from making progress along the lines of democratic governance and human rights.

30. Interview with Farhang by the author, June 2010, Kabul, Afghanistan.

31. Interview with Sami Mahdi by the author, October 2016, Kabul, Afghanistan.

32. Joshua Partlow and Pamela Constable, "Accusations of Vote Fraud Multiply in Afghanistan," *Washington Post*, August 27, 2009, http://www.washingtonpost.com/wp-dyn/content/article/2009/08/27/AR2009082704199.html; Sabrina Tavernise and Abdul Waheed Wafa, "U.N. Official Acknowledges 'Widespread Fraud' in Afghan Election," *New York Times*, October 11, 2009, http://www.nytimes.com/2009/10/12/world/asia/12afghan.html; interview with Jamshid by the author, June 2010, Kabul, Afghanistan.

33. Interview with Fazia by the author, June 2010, Kabul, Afghanistan.

34. Interview with Farhang by the author, June 2010, Kabul, Afghanistan; interview with Parsa by the author, July 2012, Kabul, Afghanistan; interview with Fazia by the author, June 2010, Kabul, Afghanistan; interview with Jabar by the author, July 2012, Kabul, Afghanistan. Jamshid. Interview by the author; interview with Atash by the author, June 2012, Kabul, Afghanistan; interview with Farzin by the author, June 2012, Kabul, Afghanistan; interview with Morad by the author, June 2010, Kabul, Afghanistan; interview with Babur by the author, June 2010, Kabul, Afghanistan; interview with Mitra by the author, June 2010, Kabul, Afghanistan.

35. Interview with Mansoor by the author, July 2012, Kabul, Afghanistan. Two in particular are from James Risen: James Risen, "Reports Link Karzai's Brother to Afghan Heroin Trade," *New York Times*, October 4, 2008, http://www.nytimes.com/2008/10/05/world/asia/05afghan.html?ref=ahmedwalikarzai and James Risen, "Karzai's Kin Use Ties to Gain Power in Afghanistan," *New York Times*, October 6, 2008, http://topics.nytimes.com/top/reference/timestopics/people/k/ahmed_wali_karzai/index.html?offset=10&s=newest

36. Interview with Morad by the author, June 2010, Kabul, Afghanistan; interview with Jabar by the author, July 2012, Kabul, Afghanistan; interview with Parsa by the author, July 2012, Kabul, Afghanistan; interview with Mitra by the author, June 2010, Kabul, Afghanistan. "When they talk about corruption, they talk about corruption in the Afghan government . . . but there is also corruption everywhere," one Afghan broadcaster explained.

37. Interview with Babur by the author, June 2010, Kabul, Afghanistan.

38. Interview with Atash by the author, June 2012, Kabul, Afghanistan.

39. Interview with Farzin by the author, June 2012, Kabul, Afghanistan.

40. Interview with Ghazanfar by the author, June 2010, Kabul, Afghanistan; interview with Jamshid by the author, June 2010, Kabul, Afghanistan; interview with Morad by the author, June 2010, Kabul, Afghanistan.

41. Interview with Mansoor by the author, July 2012, Kabul, Afghanistan; interview with Sarwar by the author, July 2012, Kabul, Afghanistan; interview with Faisal by the author, June 2010, Kabul, Afghanistan; interview with Sina by the author, June 2010, Kabul, Afghanistan; interview with Ghazanfar by the author,

June 2010, Kabul, Afghanistan; interview with Jamshid by the author, June 2010, Kabul, Afghanistan.

42. Interview with Sina by the author, June 2010, Kabul, Afghanistan; interview with Faisal by the author, June 2010, Kabul, Afghanistan

43. Interview with Sami Mahdi by the author, October 2016, Kabul, Afghanistan.

44. Interview with Mansoor by the author, July 2012, Kabul, Afghanistan; interview with Faisal by the author, June 2010, Kabul, Afghanistan; interview with Abdullah by the author, June 2010, Kabul, Afghanistan.

45. Interview with Mansoor by the author, July 2012, Kabul, Afghanistan.

46. Ibid.

47. Alissa Rubin and Rod Nordland, "Taliban Attacks Shake Afghan Peace Gathering," *New York Times*, June 2, 2010, http://www.nytimes.com/2010/06/03/world/asia/03afghan.html

48. Interview with Khaleeq by the author, June 2010, Kabul, Afghanistan; interview with Faisal by the author, June 2010, Kabul, Afghanistan; interview with Ghazanfar by the author, June 2010, Kabul, Afghanistan; interview with Farhang by the author, June 2010, Kabul, Afghanistan; interview with Feda by the author, June 2010, Kabul, Afghanistan; interview with Babur by the author, June 2010, Kabul, Afghanistan; interview with Morad by the author, June 2010, Kabul, Afghanistan; interview with Parsa by the author, July 2012, Kabul, Afghanistan.

49. Interview with Sami Mahdi by the author, October 2016, Kabul, Afghanistan.

50. Interview with Houshmand by the author, July 2012, Kabul, Afghanistan.

51. Interview with Khaleeq by the author, June 2010, Kabul, Afghanistan.

52. Interview with Faisal by the author, June 2010, Kabul, Afghanistan; interview with Farhang by the author, June 2010, Kabul, Afghanistan.

53. Interview with James by the author, July 2012, Kabul, Afghanistan; interview with Nathan by the author, July 2012, Kabul, Afghanistan; interview with Roger by the author, July 2012, Kabul, Afghanistan; interview with Nikki by the author, July 2012, Kabul, Afghanistan.

54. Interview with Douglas Schorzman by the author, December 2, 2016, Washington, DC.

55. Interview with Roger by the author, July 2012, Kabul, Afghanistan. The European news coverage about Afghanistan differs from the American coverage, Roger pointed out: They focus more on war crimes, atrocities, and human rights abuses.

56. Interview with Roger by the author, July 2012, Kabul, Afghanistan.

57. Interview with Kathy Gannon by the author, October 22, 2017, Washington, DC.

58. Interview with Nikki by the author, July 2012, Kabul, Afghanistan.

59. Rod Nordland, "A 'Wall of Kindness' Against a Harsh Reality in Afghanistan," *New York Times*, March 24, 2016, https://www.nytimes.com/2016/03/25/world/asia/afghanistan-wall-of-kindness.html?_r=0

60. Interview with Sami Mahdi by the author, October 2016, Kabul, Afghanistan.

61. Interview with Atash by the author, June 2012, Kabul, Afghanistan; interview with Abdullah by the author, June 2010, Kabul, Afghanistan.

62. Interview with Faisal by the author, June 2010, Kabul, Afghanistan.

63. Interview with Jahandar by the author, July 2012, Kabul, Afghanistan.

64. Interview with Nathan by the author, July 2012, Kabul, Afghanistan; interview with Roger by the author, July 2012, Kabul, Afghanistan; interview with James by the author, July 2012, Kabul, Afghanistan; interview with Jason by the author, July 2012, Kabul, Afghanistan; interview with Tom by the author, July 2012, Kabul, Afghanistan; interview with Nikki by the author, July 2012, Kabul, Afghanistan; interview with Maya by the author, July 2012, Kabul, Afghanistan.

65. Interview with Roger by the author, July 2012, Kabul, Afghanistan. Despite this, American journalists do not come to the region to protect U.S. interests, Roger emphatically said.

66. Interview with James by the author, July 2012, Kabul, Afghanistan; interview with Nathan by the author, July 2012, Kabul, Afghanistan; interview with Roger by the author, July 2012, Kabul, Afghanistan; interview with Nikki by the author, July 2012, Kabul, Afghanistan.

67. Interview with James by the author, July 2012, Kabul, Afghanistan. James was aware that in 2009, 46 percent of the U.S. news coverage on Afghanistan was indexed to the "Af-Pak" policy debate in Washington. But he attributes this to the fact that many foreign correspondents came from covering the war in Iraq and realized quickly that Afghanistan and Iraq were vastly different countries, and wars. "The two countries are both Muslim, but that's where the similarities end. It would be like saying, 'Well, I covered a war in England, so I could definitely cover a war in Bulgaria.' So you don't totally get Afghanistan—but the one thing you do know is Washington, you get that. So it was easier to write about that for a while in 2009."

68. Interview with Maria Abi-Habib by the author, September 24, 2017, Washington, DC.

69. Interview with Josh Partlow by the author, September 5, 2017, Washington, DC.

70. Interview with Jason by the author, July 2012, Kabul, Afghanistan. The Taliban could also invoke sympathy if they allowed American journalists to embed with them in the same way the mujahedeen allowed Americans to in their fight against the Soviets. "Then, the Americans had access to the rebels and saw the story through their heroic efforts to fight the evil Soviets. I think if the Taliban had a smarter media strategy they would let us in and embed with them, then I think they would get much more sympathetic coverage—much like the mujahedeen did—if they took in journalists. I think they missed an opportunity to portray themselves as human beings with a legitimate struggle. A lot of people would be more sympathetic to their cause if they explained it a different way, that they just wanted to get foreign troops out of their country," Jason said.

71. Interview with Tom by the author, July 2012, Kabul, Afghanistan.

72. Interview with Kathy Gannon by the author, October 22, 2017, Washington, DC.

73. Interview with Carlotta Gall by the author, October 28, 2017, Washington, DC.

74. Interview with Aalem by the author, June 2010, Kabul, Afghanistan.

75. Interview with Behnam by the author, July 2012, Kabul, Afghanistan; interview with Feda by the author, June 2010, Kabul, Afghanistan; interview with Farzin by the author, June 2012, Kabul, Afghanistan; interview with Babur by the author, June 2010, Kabul, Afghanistan; interview with Morad by the author, June 2010, Kabul, Afghanistan.

76. Interview with Parsa by the author, July 2012, Kabul, Afghanistan.

77. Interview with Behnam by the author, July 2012, Kabul, Afghanistan.

78. Interview with Atash by the author, June 2012, Kabul, Afghanistan; interview with Jabar by the author, July 2012, Kabul, Afghanistan. Jabar, however, credited the U.S. press with being reflective and acknowledging that they did largely follow the U.S. government's talking points.

79. Interview with Jabar by the author, July 2012, Kabul, Afghanistan.

80. However, the degree to which the U.S. press complied with presidential talking points, Jabar said, depended on the agenda of the editors for each newspaper or television agency. Each election year, editors decide whether or not to support Republican or Democratic candidates. Fox News is known to support conservatives; MSNBC is known to support liberals. He explained, "News and editorial is blurred in the United States, because when you cover the story then you do an analysis" and invite specific pundits to comment: "I'm not saying partisan media applies to all American media, but, I mean, if you see a big newspaper supporting one presidential candidate or the other." He acknowledged that the editorial board is different from the reporters but believes that, in the end, the editors' opinions impact the overall slant of the paper's reporting: "Everyone says: 'The *New York Times* is supporting Obama'."

81. Interview with Aalem by the author, June 2010, Kabul, Afghanistan. One example Aalem cited was from the June 2010 Peace *Jirga* in Kabul, which was organized to explore the possibility of reconciliation with the Taliban. Aalem explained, "When the *Jirga* was in progress, during the second day of the *Jirga*, something was published on international media. That publication was like a copycat of the final agreement of the *Jirga* and the reporter was claiming that he received it from one of the embassies."

82. Interview with Houshmand by the author, July 2012, Kabul, Afghanistan; interview with Feda by the author, June 2010, Kabul, Afghanistan.

83. Interview with Houshmand by the author, July 2012, Kabul, Afghanistan; interview with Khaleeq by the author, June 2010, Kabul, Afghanistan.

84. Interview with Atash by the author, June 2012, Kabul, Afghanistan.

85. Interview with Abdullah by the author, June 2010, Kabul, Afghanistan.

86. Interview with Atash by the author, June 2012, Kabul, Afghanistan.

87. Interview with Farzin by the author, June 2012, Kabul, Afghanistan.

88. Interview with Ghazanfar by the author, June 2010, Kabul, Afghanistan; interview with Feda by the author, June 2010, Kabul, Afghanistan; interview with Farhang by the author, June 2010, Kabul, Afghanistan; interview with Sarwar by the author, July 2012, Kabul, Afghanistan.

89. Interview with Jamshid by the author, June 2010, Kabul, Afghanistan. This is usually indicated by the fact that U.S. officials prefer U.S. news media to Afghan media. For instance, when American officials and politicians visit Afghanistan and hold press conferences, they routinely give the first question to American journalists. Jamshid found this utterly frustrating: "What is the reason for this? Why don't they let journalists belonging to Afghanistan get the first question?"

90. Interview with James by the author, July 2012, Kabul, Afghanistan "There's not a lot we can say to that criticism," James said. "We try to point to stories that show we are critical, but nothing seems to dissuade them."

91. Interview with Nathan by the author, July 2012, Kabul, Afghanistan. Nathan said he has never felt a responsibility to defend U.S. policies, but sometimes he will hear a U.S. policy depicted inaccurately by a local official or journalist. He will interject to correct them "because that's a responsibility to the audience—whether it be Afghan, Pakistani or American—that information is getting out there fairly and accurately." Often, this is interpreted, he said, as being defensive of the United States.

92. Interview with Maya by the author, July 2012, Kabul, Afghanistan.

93. Interview with Rod Nordland by the author, October 25, 2016, Kabul, Afghanistan.

94. Interview with Dan Feldman by the author, October 20, 2017, Washington, DC.

95. Interview with Zalmay Khalilzad by the author, October 10, 2017, Washington, DC.

96. Interview with Josh Partlow by the author, September 5, 2017, Washington, DC.

97. Interview with Maria Abi-Habib by the author, September 24, 2017, Washington, DC.

98. Interview with Pamela Constable by the author, October 23, 2016, Kabul, Afghanistan.

99. Interview with Nikki by the author, July 2012, Kabul, Afghanistan.

100. Interview with David Ensor by the author, October 20, 2017, Washington, DC.

101. Interview with Dan Feldman by the author, October 25, 2017, Washington, DC.

102. Interview with Zalmay Khalilzad by the author, September 10, 2017, Washington, DC.

103. Interview with Maria Abi-Habib by the author, September 24, 2017, Washington, DC.

104. Interview with Nathan by the author, July 2012, Kabul, Afghanistan. Access to U.S. government officials in Kabul is more difficult than it is in Washington, Nathan agreed. In Washington, reporters have access to a variety of legislators or White House, Pentagon, or State Department officials. But in Islamabad

and Kabul, there are far more physical and bureaucratic barriers in place for journalists to interface and develop relationships with them, he said.

105. Interview with Maria Abi-Habib by the author, September 24, 2017, Washington, DC.
106. Interview with Rod Nordland by the author, October 25, 2016, Washington, DC.
107. Interview with Carlotta Gall by the author, October 28, 2017, Washington, DC.
108. Interview with Dan Feldman by the author, October 25, 2017, Washington, DC.
109. Interview with James by the author, July 2012, Kabul, Afghanistan One of the stories that began with off-the-record comments was the Kabul Bank story, which the *Washington Post* broke in February 2010. One of the journalists who worked on the story told me it began with U.S. officials telling him that a lot of money was leaving Kabul to buy homes in Dubai. A *Post* journalist went to Dubai to speak with the housing authority and the Afghan community there to investigate where exactly the money was coming from. They brought that information to the U.S. embassy for commentary, but a WikiLeaks cable later showed that the embassy seemed surprised by the extent of information the *Post* had gathered.
110. Interview with Eileen O'Connor by the author, October 31, 2017, Washington, DC.
111. Interview with Pamela Constable by the author, October 23, 2016, Kabul, Afghanistan.
112. Interview with Maria Abi-Habib by the author, September 24, 2017, Washington, DC.
113. Maria Abi-Habib, "At Afghan Military Hospital, Graft and Deadly Neglect," *Wall Street Journal*, September 3, 2011, http://online.wsj.com/article/SB1000142405 3111904480904576496703389391710.html
114. Interview with Maria Abi-Habib by the author, September 24, 2017, Washington, DC.
115. Ibid.
116. Interview with Feda by the author, June 2010, Kabul, Afghanistan; interview with Mitra by the author, June 2010, Kabul, Afghanistan; interview with Atash by the author, June 2012, Kabul, Afghanistan; interview with Jahandar by the author, July 2012, Kabul, Afghanistan; interview with Mansoor by the author, July 2012, Kabul, Afghanistan; interview with Jawid by the author, June 2010, Kabul, Afghanistan; interview with Babur by the author, June 2010, Kabul, Afghanistan; interview with Houshmand by the author, July 2012, Kabul, Afghanistan; Abi-Habib, "At Afghan Military Hospital, Graft and Deadly Neglect."
117. Carlotta Gall, "U.S. Military Investigating Death of Afghan in Custody," *New York Times*, March 3, 2004, http://www.nytimes.com/2003/03/04/world/threats-responses-prisoners-us-military-investigating-death-afghan-custody.html

118. Interview with Carlotta Gall by the author, October 28, 2017, Washington, DC.

119. Interview with Kathy Gannon by the author, October 22, 2017, Washington, DC.

120. Interview with Tom by the author, July 2012, Kabul, Afghanistan. If Afghans and Pakistanis do see the U.S. media as being sycophantic or stuck on security frames, it is often the journalists who parachute into the country for short reports, Tom emphasized. The U.S. military makes it easy for American journalists to travel to Afghanistan for short time periods, and then has great control over the narrative they write. The stories those parachute journalists produce are weak, Tom said, and are definitely American-centric because the reporters interact only with Americans and no Afghans. "But if you look at the journalists who are based here, I think our coverage is fair," Tom said. They know the military officials—and the region—well enough to criticize the military strategy and policy separate from covering the troops whose lives are at stake.

121. Interview with Nikki by the author, July 2012, Kabul, Afghanistan.

122. Interview with Rod Nordland by the author, October 25, 2016, Kabul, Afghanistan.

123. Interview with James by the author, July 2012, Kabul, Afghanistan; interview with Maya by the author, July 2012, Kabul, Afghanistan. Maya copes with this by writing a story at variance with what the military pitched her, and she often turns the story the military wanted against them. For instance, on her first trip with U.S. soldiers to Ghazni, a volatile province in the east, the press officer wanted to show her 47 schools that the Taliban had shut down and American troops had subsequently reopened. "But I definitely wasn't going to write what they said," Maya explained. "I was going to take advantage of a four-day trip to Ghazni." Once she was there, she saw that the schools were open but empty. She spoke with the local education director and discovered that the students were terrified to attend schools that the Americans had constructed, fearing that the Taliban would kill them. This was not the celebratory news story the military had imagined. "It's pretty impossible to ever meet the U.S. military's expectations because the reality is never as rosy as they project it to be," she said. "But the facts always come out, it doesn't matter."

124. Interview with Nikki by the author, July 2012, Kabul, Afghanistan. The military, Nikki said, doesn't know how to work with the Western elite media: "They have this huge press operation and they don't know how to use us. And one way they could do it is to tell stories of things that aren't going well to their leadership back in Washington. Whether if it's that they need more time or backing for one thing or another, they should use the press to get their message. The press should be in their arsenal," Nikki said. "We're doing our job, which is to report what we see, and they are doing their job, which is to get people to hear what is difficult."

125. Interview with Tom by the author, July 2012, Kabul, Afghanistan. Tom said that covering the military, too, as an institution is fascinating: "To be able to write what is a very local story about a few Americans that also happens to be a global story because those Americans are in a far-off place that is of geopolitical importance—that's very neat. There are few other places in the world where you can report on that kind of intersection. A kid from a small town and the province that hangs in the balance—for those things to intersect are really interesting, and important."

126. Interview with Nathan by the author, July 2012, Kabul, Afghanistan.

127. Interview with Pamela Constable by the author, October 23, 2016, Washington, DC.

128. Interview with Nikki by the author, July 2012, Kabul, Afghanistan. Nikki said, "But what Afghan journalists don't realize is that protection will diminish as U.S. aid and the presence of the U.S. military diminishes. So it is true that Afghans will have to do it themselves because we won't be able to do it either, or we'll be able to do much less." Afghan power brokers and government officials often threaten the local staffs of the U.S. news bureaus; it's frightening to think what could happen to them if they did not work for an American news organization, Nikki said. "In the end, though, we do have the protection of the U.S. government and that helps us a great deal. And it's something that Afghan reporters don't have. They are much more vulnerable."

129. Interview with Jason by the author, July 2012, Kabul, Afghanistan. Given recent episodes of American journalists who had been taken hostage (David Rohde and Steve Farrell of the *Times*, for instance), Jason said, "It is nice to know how much effort [the U.S. government] puts into getting you out."

130. Interview with Dan Feldman by the author, October 25, 2017, Washington, DC; interview with Zalmay Khalilzad by the author, September 10, 2017, Washington, DC; interview with Ryan Crocker by the author, October 25, 2017, Washington, DC; interview with Ronald Neumann by the author, September 26, 2017, Washington, DC; interview with Marc Grossman by the author, October 5, 2007, Washington, DC.

131. Interview with Kathy Gannon by the author, October 22, 2017, Washington, DC.

132. J. Herbert Altschull, *Agents of Power* (New York: Longman, 1995).

133. Bella Mody, *The Geopolitics of Representation in Foreign News: Explaining Darfur* (Boulder, CO: Lexington Books, 2010).

134. Philip M. Taylor, "The Military and the Media Past, Present and Future," in *The Media and International Security*, ed. Stephen Badsey (London: Frank Cass, 2000), 179.

135. Ibid.

136. Silvio Waisbord, "Media and the Reinvention of the Nation," in *The SAGE Handbook of Media Studies*, eds. John D. H. Downing, Denis McQuail, Philip

Schlesinger, and Ellen Wartella (Thousand Oaks, CA: Sage Publishers, 2004), 375–389.

137. Stuart J. Kaufman, *Modern Hatreds: The Symbolic Politics of Ethnic War* (Ithaca, NY: Cornell University Press, 2001), 1–44.

138. Benedict Anderson, *Imagined Communities: Reflections on the Origin and Spread of Nationalism* (New York: Verso, 1983).

139. Kaufman, *Modern Hatreds*, 1–44.

140. James D. Fearon, "Separatist Wars, Partition, and World Order," *Security Studies*, Vol. 13, No. 4 (2004): 394–415.

141. Kaufman, *Modern Hatreds*, 1–44.

142. See Anderson, *Imagined Communities*.

143. Craig LaMay, *Exporting Press Freedom* (New York: Routledge, 2007), 2.

144. Waisbord, "Media and the Reinvention of the Nation," 388.

145. Ibid.

146. See: Arie S. Soesilo and Philo C. Wasburn. "Constructing a Political Spectacle: American and Indonesian Media Accounts of the 'Crisis in the Gulf'," *Sociological Quarterly*, Vol. 35, No. 2 (2004): 377; Gaye Tuchman, *Making News* (New York: The Free Press, 1978).

147. Chin-Chuan Lee, Joseph Man Chan, Zhongdang Pan, and Clement Y. K. So, "National Prisms of a Global 'Media Event'," in *Mass Media and Society*, eds. James Curran and Michael Gurevitch (London: Arnold, 2000).

148. Ingrid Lehmann, "Exploring the Transatlantic Media Divide over Iraq: How and Why U.S. and German Media Differed in Reporting on UN Weapons Inspections in Iraq, 2002–2003," *International Journal of Press/Politics*, Vol. 10, No. 1 (Winter 2003): 63–89; Daniela V. Dimitrova and Jesper Strömbäck, "Mission Accomplished? Framing of the Iraq War in the Elite Newspapers in Sweden and the United States," *International Communication Gazette*, Vol. 67, No. 5 (2004): 399–417.

149. Philo Wasburn, *The Social Construction of International News: We're Talking About Them, They're Talking About Us* (Westport, CT: Praeger Publishers, 2002), 124.

150. C. C. Lee and J. Yang, "Foreign News and National Interest: Comparing U.S. and Japanese Coverage of the Chinese Student Movement," *International Communication Gazette*, Vol. 56 (1995): 1–18; Lee, Man Chan, Pan, and So, "National Prisms of a Global 'Media Event'."

151. Betwa Sharma, "Good COP, Bad COP: Reflections on Covering the Copenhagen Climate Summit," *Columbia Journalism Review*, December 22, 2009, https://archives.cjr.org/the_observatory/good_cop_bad_cop.php.

152. Interview with Babur by the author, June 2010, Kabul, Afghanistan; interview with Jawid by the author, June 2010, Kabul, Afghanistan; interview with Mitra by the author, June 2010, Kabul, Afghanistan.

153. Interview with Morad by the author, June 2010, Kabul, Afghanistan; interview with Atash by the author, June 2012, Kabul, Afghanistan; interview with

Jahandar by the author, July 2012, Kabul, Afghanistan; interview with Parsa by the author, July 2012, Kabul, Afghanistan; interview with Mitra by the author, June 2010, Kabul, Afghanistan.

154. Interview with Jawid by the author, June 2010, Kabul, Afghanistan.

155. Interview with Nikki by the author, July 2012, Kabul, Afghanistan.

156. Interview with Jason by the author, July 2012, Kabul, Afghanistan.

157. Interview with Roger by the author, July 2012, Kabul, Afghanistan.

158. Interview with James by the author, July 2012, Kabul, Afghanistan.

159. Interview with Douglas Schorzman by the author, December 2, 2016, Washington, DC.

160. Ibid.

161. Interview with Tom by the author, July 2012, Kabul, Afghanistan.

162. Interview with Roger by the author, July 2012, Kabul, Afghanistan.

163. Interview with Jawid by the author, June 2010, Kabul, Afghanistan.

164. Interview with Farzin by the author, June 2012, Kabul, Afghanistan.

165. Interview with Khaleeq by the author, June 2010, Kabul, Afghanistan.

166. Interview with Houshmand by the author, July 2012, Kabul, Afghanistan.

167. Interviews with Mujib Mashal by the author, October 19 and 22, 2016, Kabul, Afghanistan.

168. Ibid.

169. Ibid.

170. Ibid.

171. Ibid.

172. Ibid.

173. Ibid.

174. Ibid.

175. Interview with Ryan Crocker by the author, October 25, 2017, Washington, DC; interview with Carlotta Gall by the author, October 28, 2017, Washington, DC.

CHAPTER 8

1. Silvio Waisbord, "Media and the Reinvention of the Nation," in *The SAGE Handbook of Media Studies*, eds. John D. H. Downing, Denis McQuail, Philip Schlesinger, and Ellen Wartella (Thousand Oaks, CA: Sage Publishers, 2004): 375–389.

2. Dwight Dewerth-Pallmeyer, *The Audience in the News* (Mahwah, NJ: LEAA, 1996).

3. C. C. Lee and J. Yang, "Foreign News and National Interest: Comparing U.S. and Japanese Coverage of the Chinese Student Movement," *International Communication Gazette*, Vol. 56 (1995): 1–18; Chin-Chuan Lee, Joseph Man Chan, Zhongdang Pan, and Clement Y. K. So, "National Prisms of a Global 'Media Event'," in *Mass Media and Society*, eds. James Curran and Michael Gurevitch (London: Arnold, 2000). Lee and Yang found that journalists from

five different countries—Australia, Canada, China, Japan, and the United Kingdom—who covered the return of Hong Kong to China in 2000 employed their own national lenses to tell the story to their audiences.

4. See: J. C. H. Downing, "Drawing a Bead on Global Communications Theories," in *Global Communication*, ed. Yahya R. Kamalipour (Belmont, CA: Wadsworth/Thomson Learning, 2002); William A. Hachten and James Scotton, *The World News Prism* (Ames: Iowa State University, 2002); Jiafei Yin, "Beyond Four Theories of the Press: A New Model for the Asian and the World Press," *Journalism Communication Monographs*, Vol. 10 (Spring 2008): 35. In *Four Theories of the Press*, Fred Siebert, Theodore Peterson, and Wilbur Shramm looked at how much freedom the news media had under authoritarian, communist, and democratic rule. But the degrees of press freedom vary when media are in development as their societies are ever-changing, Jiafei Yin argued in "Beyond Four Theories of the Press" in 2008. She proposed a "Freedom/Responsibility" coordinate system to identify the categories of press systems that don't clearly fall into authoritarian, communism, libertarian, or social responsibility. Press systems would fall in the categories of "free and responsible," which would require a public demand for responsible journalism; "free and not responsible" systems, which exist in "intensely competitive media markets, such as new democracies"; "responsible but not free," which would mean that the press supports the societal goals of the government or from public pressure; and "not free and not responsible," which includes press systems that are often controlled by the leaders and therefore glorify the leaders.

5. Kai Hafez, *The Myth of Media Globalization* (Cambridge, UK: Polity, 2007).

6. Bella Mody, *The Geopolitics of Representation in Foreign News: Explaining Darfur* (Boulder, CO: Lexington Books, 2010), 321.

7. Ibid., 322.

8. Ibid., 29.

9. World Bank, "The Information Age," World Development Report (New York: Oxford University Press, 2009).

10. M. Ayish, "Political Communication on Arab World Television: Evolving Patterns," *Political Communication*, Vol. 19 (2002): 137–154.

11. Joseph Straubhaar, *World Television: From Global to Local* (Thousand Oaks, CA: Sage, 2007).

12. Mody, *The Geopolitics of Representation*, 322.

13. William H. Meyer, "Structures of North–South Information Flows: An Empirical Test of Galtung's Theory," *Journalism Quarterly*, Vol. 68, No. 1–2 (Spring–Summer 1991): 230–237.

14. See: A. Sreberny-Mohammadi, Kaarle Nordenstreng, R. L. Stevesnon, and Frank Ugboajah, "Foreign News in the Media. International Reporting in 29 Countries. Final Report of the 'Foreign Images' Study Undertaken for

UNESCO by the IAMCR," UNESCO, 1985; Denis W. Wu, "Investigating the Determinants of International News Flow: A Meta-Analysis," *International Journal for Communication Studies*, Vol. 60 (1998): 493–512.

15. See: Eran Fraenkel, Sheldon Himelfarb, and Emrys Schoemaker, "Afghanistan Media Assessment: Opportunities and Challenges for Peacebuilding," U.S. Institute for Peace (Washington, DC: Peaceworks, 2010); Yin, "Beyond Four Theories of the Press."

16. Interview with Lotfullah Najafizada by the author, October 2016, Washington, DC.

17. "30 Journalists Killed in Afghanistan Since 1992," Committee to Protect Journalists, November 2016, https://www.cpj.org/killed/asia/afghanistan/

18. Joseph Nye, "The Decline of America's Soft Power," *Foreign Affairs*, May/June 2004, http://www.foreignaffairs.com/articles/59888/joseph-s-nye-jr/the-decline-of-americas-soft-power

19. Herbert Gans, *Deciding What's News: A Study of CBS Evening News, NBC Nightly News, Newsweek, and Time* (New York: Vintage Books, 2004), 19, 37.

20. Ibid., 42.

21. Maria Abi-Habib, "At Afghan Military Hospital, Graft and Deadly Neglect," *Wall Street Journal*, September 3, 2011, http://online.wsj.com/article/SB100014240 53111904480904576496703389391710.html; Kevin Sieff, "Next to U.S. Firing Range in Afghanistan, a Village of Victims," *Washington Post*, May 26, 2012, http://www.washingtonpost.com/world/asia_pacific/next-to-us-firing-range-in-afghanistan-a-village-of-victims/2012/05/26/gJQAeQEIsU_story.html

22. Margaret Sullivan, "Is Global Expansion Good for Times Readers?" *New York Times*, February 12, 2016, https://publiceditor.blogs.nytimes.com/2016/02/12/is-global-expansion-good-for-times-readers/?_r=0

23. Interview with Douglas Schorzman by the author, December 2, 2016, Washington, DC.

24. Interview with Carlotta Gall by the author, October 28, 2017, Washington, DC.

25. Philo Wasburn, *The Social Construction of International News: We're Talking About Them, They're Talking About Us* (Westport, CT: Praeger Publishers, 2002).

26. Tsan-Kuo Chang, "All Countries Not Created Equal to Be News: World System and International Communication," *Communication Research*, Vol. 25 (1998): 528–566; Giovanna Dell'Orto, "Foreign Policy and Foreign Correspondence: Integrating IR and Communication Theories to Examine the History of Press Involvement in International Affairs," International Studies Association Annual Conference, Montreal, 2011; William A. Hachten and James Scotton, *The World News Prism* (Ames: Iowa State University, 2002), 34–35.

27. Patricia A. Karl, "Media Diplomacy," *Proceedings of the Academy of Political Science*, Vol. 34 No. 4 (1982): 143–152.

28. John C. Merrill, *A Handbook of the Foreign Press* (Baton Rouge: Louisiana State University Press, 1959), 3.

29. John Hohenberg, *Foreign Correspondence: The Great Reporters and Their Times* (New York: Columbia University Press, 1965).

30. Steve Benen, "How Trump's Team Changed His Mind About the War in Afghanistan," MSNBC, August 22, 2017, http://www.msnbc.com/rachel-maddow-show/how-trumps-team-changed-his-mind-about-the-war-afghanistan

31. See: Max Boot, "Trump's Path to Indefinite Afghan War," Council on Foreign Relations, August 22, 2017, https://www.cfr.org/expert-brief/trumps-path-indefinite-afghan-war; Thomas Gibbons-Neff, Eric Schmitt, and Adam Goldman, "A Newly Assertive C.I.A. Expands Its Taliban Hunt in Afghanistan," *New York Times*, October 22, 2017, https://www.nytimes.com/2017/10/22/world/asia/cia-expanding-taliban-fight-afghanistan.html?emc=edit_th_20171023&nl=todayshe adlines&nlid=67583462&mtrref=undefined&gwh=065B760876AFCAE6D1B69 402E0CEDA38&gwt=pay

32. David Sanger, "Striking at Assad Carries Opportunities, and Risks, for Trump," *New York Times*, April 7, 2017, https://www.nytimes.com/2017/04/07/world/middleeast/airstikes-syria-trump-russia.html?smid=tw-share

33. Derek Hawkins, "Brian Williams Is 'Guided by the Beauty of Our Weapons' in Syria Strikes," *Washington Post*, April 7, 2017, https://www.washingtonpost.com/news/morning-mix/wp/2017/04/07/beautiful-brian-williams-says-of-syria-missile-strike-proceeds-to-quote-leonard-cohen/?utm_term=.35b63ca9cado

34. Mark Hensch, "CNN Host: 'Donald Trump Became President' Last Night," *The Hill*, April 7, 2017, http://thehill.com/homenews/administration/327779-cnn-host-donald-trump-became-president-last-night

35. Benen, "How Trump's Team Changed His Mind."

36. Brian Stelter, "About 28 Million TV viewers Watched Trump's Afghanistan Speech," CNN, August 22, 2017, http://money.cnn.com/2017/08/22/media/president-trump-afghanistan-speech-ratings/index.html

37. Christopher Rosen, "All the Times Donald Trump Has Called the Media 'Fake News' on Twitter," *Entertainment Weekly*, June 27, 2017, http://ew.com/tv/2017/06/27/donald-trump-fake-news-twitter/; Trump Twitter Archive, http://www.trumptwitterarchive.com/, last accessed May 10, 2018.

38. Michael Barthel and Amy Mitchell, "Americans' Attitudes About the News Media Deeply Divided Along Partisan Lines," Pew Research Center, May 10, 2017, http://www.journalism.org/2017/05/10/americans-attitudes-about-the-news-media-deeply-divided-along-partisan-lines/

39. "Ghani Welcomes Trump's Strategy On Afghanistan," ToloNews, August 21, 2017, http://www.tolonews.com/afghanistan/ghani-welcomes-trump%E2%80%99s-strategy-afghanistan

40. Eliana Johnson, "How Trump Swallowed a Bitter Afghanistan Pill," Politico, August 22, 2017, http://politi.co/2wsSVRg

41. "Freedom of the Press in 2017," Freedom House, April 2017, https://freedomhouse.org/report/freedom-press/freedom-press-2017.

42. "Afghanistan in 2017: A Survey of the Afghan People," The Asia Foundation, November 2017, https://asiafoundation.org/where-we-work/afghanistan/survey/.

References

"30 Journalists Killed in Afghanistan Since 1992." Committee to Protect Journalists, November 2016. https://www.cpj.org/killed/asia/afghanistan/

"51 Journalists Killed in Pakistan Since 1992/Motive Confirmed." Committee to Protect Journalists, 2013. https://cpj.org/killed/asia/pakistan/

"1998 Missile Strikes on Bin Laden May Have Backfired: Extensive 1999 Report on Al-Qaeda Threat Released by U.S. Dept of Energy, Taliban Told U.S. They Wanted to Bomb Washington." National Security Archive Electronic Briefing Book No. 253, August 20, 2008. http://www2.gwu.edu/~nsarchiv/NSAEBB/NSAEBB253/

"2010 in Review—State of the News Media in 2010." Pew Project for Excellence in Journalism, 2011. http://www.stateofthemedia.org/2010/year_overview.php

"2012 in Review—State of the News Media in 2012." Pew Project for Excellence in Journalism, 2013. http://stateofthemedia.org/2012/mobile-devices-and-news-consumption-some-good-signs-for-journalism/year-in-2011/

"2016 in Review—State of the News Media in 2016." Pew Project for Excellence in Journalism, 2016. http://www.journalism.org/files/2016/06/State-of-the-News-Media-Report-2016-FINAL.pdf

Abi-Habib, Maria. "At Afghan Military Hospital, Graft and Deadly Neglect." *Wall Street Journal*, September 3, 2011. http://online.wsj.com/article/SB10001424053111904480904576496703389171 0.html

"About Those Billions." *Newsweek*, October 20, 2009. http://www.thedailybeast.com/newsweek/2009/10/21/about-those-billions.html

Aday, Sean. "Chasing the Bad News: An Analysis of 2005 Iraq and Afghanistan War Coverage on NBC and Fox News Channel." *Journal of Communication*, Vol. 60 (2010): 144–164.

"Afghanistan." Committee to Protect Journalists, 2016. https://www.cpj.org/killed/asia/afghanistan/

"Afghanistan." Reporters Without Borders, 2016. https://rsf.org/en/afghanistan

"Afghanistan Demographics Profile." IndexMundi, July 2016. https://www.indexmundi.com/afghanistan/demographics_profile.html

"Afghanistan: Draft Law Threatens Media Freedom." Human Rights Watch, July 2, 2012. http://www.hrw.org/news/2012/07/02/afghanistan-draft-law-threatens-media-freedom

"Afghanistan—Freedom of the Press in 2015." Freedom House, June 2016. https://freedomhouse.org/report/freedom-press/2015/afghanistan

"Afghanistan—Freedom of the Press in 2017." Freedom House, June 2017. https://freedomhouse.org/report/freedom-press/2017/afghanistan

"Afghanistan in 2011: A Survey of the Afghan People." The Asia Foundation, October 2011. http://asiafoundation.org/publications/pdf/976

"Afghanistan in 2012: A Survey of the Afghan People." The Asia Foundation, November 2012. http://asiafoundation.org/country/afghanistan/2012-poll.php

"Afghanistan in 2016: A Survey of the Afghan People." The Asia Foundation, November 2016. http://asiafoundation.org/wp-content/uploads/2016/12/2016_Survey-of-the-Afghan-People_full-survey.Jan2017.pdf

"Afghanistan in 2017: A Survey of the Afghan People." The Asia Foundation, November 2017. https://asiafoundation.org/where-we-work/afghanistan/survey/

"Afghan Media in 2010: A Comprehensive Assessment of the Afghan Media Landscape, Audience Preferences and Impact on Opinions." Altai Consulting, October 13, 2010. http:// www.altaiconsulting.com/wp-content/uploads/2016/03/Afghan-Media-in-2010.pdf

"Afghanistan Media Development and Empowerment Project." U.S. Agency for International Development, August 7, 2012. http://afghanistan.usaid.gov/en/USAID/Activity/205/Afghanistan_Media_Develo pment_ and_Empowerment_Project_AMDEP

"Afghan Media Assessment and Development." International Media Support, March 2011. http://www.i-m-s.dk/pic/Afgh-Media%20assessment.pdf

"Afghanistan: Media Round-Up 12 Oct 2001." BBC Monitoring World Media, October 12, 2001. Lexis-Nexis Academic.

"Afghanistan: Media Round-Up 24 Oct 2001." BBC Monitoring World Media, October 24, 2001. Lexis-Nexis Academic.

"Afghanistan: Media Round-Up 10 Nov 2001." BBC Monitoring World Media, November 10, 2001. Lexis-Nexis Academic.

"Afghanistan: Media Round-Up 11 Nov 2001." BBC Monitoring World Media, November 11, 2001. Lexis-Nexis Academic.

"Afghanistan: Media Round-Up 13 Nov 2001." BBC Monitoring World Media, November 13, 2001. Lexis-Nexis Academic.

"Afghanistan: Media Round-up Monday 3 December 2001." BBC Monitoring World Media, December 3, 2001. Lexis-Nexis Academic.

"Afghanistan: Media and Telecoms Landscape Guide." Info AusAid, March 2011. http://www.cdacnetwork.org/contentAsset/raw-data/e9d1a830-9aa9-4e0e-b25c-556d0aad330d/attachedFile

"Afghanistan Orders US Reporter to Leave Over Election Story." Agence France-Presse, August 21, 2014. http://www.jamaicaobserver.com/news/Afghanistan-orders-US-reporter-to-leave-over-election-story_17388693

"Afghan President Pleased by Al-Qa'idah leader's death (Radio Television Afghanistan)." BBC Monitoring Service, May 2, 2011. Lexis-Nexis Academic.

"Afghanistan Press, Media, TV, Radio, Newspapers." *Press Reference*, 2003. http://www.pressreference.com/A-Be/Afghanistan.html

"Afghanistan—State of the News Media in 2009." Pew Project for Excellence in Journalism, 2010. http://www.stateofthemedia.org/2010/year_overview.php

"Afghanistan Transition: Missing Variables." International Council on Security and Development, November 2010. http://www.icosgroup.net/2010/report/afghanistan-transition-missing-variables/

"Agreement on Provisional Arrangements in Afghanistan Pending the Re-Establishment of Permanent Government Institutions." United Nations, December 5, 2001. http://www.un.org/News/dh/latest/afghan/afghan-agree.htm

Akhtar, Hasan. "Khalilzad's Remarks Irresponsible: FO." *Dawn*, April 20, 2004. http://archives.dawn.com/2004/04/20/top6.htm

Akhtar, Rai Shakil. *Media, Religion, and Politics in Pakistan.* New York: Oxford University Press, 2004.

Altschull, J. Herbert. *Agents of Power.* New York: Longman, 1995.

Anderson, Benedict. *Imagined Communities: Reflections on the Origin and Spread of Nationalism.* New York: Verso, 1983.

"Apparatus of Lies: Saddam's Disinformation and Propaganda:1990–2003." The White House, January 2003. http://www.gwu.edu/~nsarchiv/.../docs/Underground-Apparatus.pdf

Aufderheide, Pat. "All-Too-Reality TV: Challenge for Television Journalists after September 11." *Journalism*, Vol. 3, No. 1 (2002): 11.

Auletta, Ken. "The Networker: Afghanistan's First Media Mogul." *The New Yorker*, July 5, 2010. http://www.newyorker.com/reporting/2010/07/05/100705fa_fact_auletta

Autesserre, Severine. "Hobbes and the Congo—Frames, Local Violence, and International Intervention in the Congo." *International Organization*, Vol. 63 (2009): 249–280.

Ayish, Muhammad. "Political Communication on Arab World Television: Evolving Patterns." *Political Communication*, Vol. 19 (2002): 137–154.

Bajoria, Jayshree. "The Taliban in Afghanistan." *Council on Foreign Relations*, October 6, 2011. http://www.cfr.org/afghanistan/taliban-afghanistan/p10551

Balz, Dan. "A Moment of National Unity at a Time of Deep Divisions." *Washington Post*, May 2, 2011. https://www.washingtonpost.com/politics/a-moment-of-national-unity-at-a-time-of-deep-divisions/2011/05/02/AF3hqJWF_story.html?utm_term=.87adc052ac03

Barakat, Sultan. "Setting the Scene for Afghanistan's Reconstruction: The Challenges and Critical Dilemmas." *Third World Quarterly*, Vol. 23, No. 5 (2002): 801–816.

Barker, Kim. *The Taliban Shuffle: Strange Days in Afghanistan and Pakistan.* New York: Anchor, 2012.

Barry, Dan. "A Singular Moment, and a Mix of Emotion Stored for a Decade." *New York Times*, May 2, 2011. https://www.nytimes.com/2011/05/03/us/03mood.html

Barnett, Michael, and Martha Finnemore. *Rules for the World: International Organizations in Global Politics.* Ithaca, NY: Cornell University Press, 2004.

Barthel, Michael, and Amy Mitchell. "Americans' Attitudes About the News Media Deeply Divided Along Partisan Lines." Pew Research Center, May 10, 2017. http://www.journalism.org/2017/05/10/americans-attitudes-about-the-news-media-deeply-divided-along-partisan-lines/

"BBC's Global Audience Rises to 372m." BBC Media Centre, date unknown. http://www.bbc.co.uk/mediacentre/latestnews/2017/global-audience-measure

Bearak, Barry. "Over World Protests, Taliban Are Destroying Ancient Buddhas." *New York Times,* March 4, 2001. https://www.nytimes.com/2001/03/04/world/over-world-protests-taliban-are-destroying-ancient-buddhas.html

Bearak, Barry. "Accused Aid Workers Face Islamic Judges in Afghanistan." *New York Times,* September 9, 2001. https://www.nytimes.com/2001/09/09/world/accused-aid-workers-face-islamic-judges-in-afghanistan.html

Bearak, Barry. "A DAY OF TERROR: THE AFGHANS; Condemning Attacks, Taliban Says bin Laden Not Involved." *New York Times,* September 12, 2001. https://www.nytimes.com/2001/09/12/us/day-terror-afghans-condemning-attacks-taliban-says-bin-laden-not-involved.html

Bearak, Barry, and James Risen. "Reports Disagree on Fate of Anti-Taliban Rebel Chief." *New York Times,* September 11, 2001. http://www.nytimes.com/2001/09/11/world/reports-disagree-on-fate-of-anti-taliban-rebel-chief.html?rref=collection%2Ftimestopic%2FMassoud%2C%20Ahmed%20Shah

Beasely, Vanessa. "The Rhetoric of Ideological Consensus in the United States: American Principles and American Prose in Presidential Inaugurals." *Communications Monographs,* Vol. 68, No. 2 (June 2001): 169–183.

Beaudoin, Christopher E., and Esther Thorson. "Value Representation in Foreign News." *Gazette,* Vol. 63, No. 6 (December 2001): 481–503.

Beckerman, Gal. "Let's Report More, Take Credit Less." *Columbia Journalism Review,* May 6, 2006. https://archives.cjr.org/behind_the_news/lets_report_more_take_credit_l.php

Behr, Roy L., and Shanto Iyengar. "Television News, Real World Cues and Changes in the Public Agenda." *Public Opinion Quarterly,* Vol. 49, Issue 1 (January 1985): 38–57.

Belasco, Amy. "The Cost of Iraq, Afghanistan, and Other Global War on Terror Operations." Congressional Research Service, March 29, 2011. http://www.fas.org/sgp/crs/natsec/RL33110.pdf,

Benen, Steve. "How Trump's Team Changed His Mind About the War in Afghanistan." MSNBC, August 22, 2017. http://www.msnbc.com/rachel-maddow-show/how-trumps-team-changed-his-mind-about-the-war-afghanistan

Bennett, W. Lance. "Toward a Theory of Press–State Relations in the United States." *Journal of Communication,* Vol. 40 (1990): 103–125.

Bennett, W. Lance, Regina G. Lawrence, and Steven Livingston, *When the Press Fails. Political Power and the News Media from Iraq to Katrina*. Chicago: University of Chicago Press, 2007.

Bergen, Peter. *The Longest War: The Enduring Conflict Between America and Al-Qaeda*. New York: Simon and Schuster, 2011.

Berry, N. O. *Foreign Policy and the Press: An Analysis of The New York Times' Coverage of U.S. Foreign Policy*. New York: Greenwood Press, 1996.

"The Best Dressed Men in the World, 2007." *Esquire*, August 23, 2007. http://www.esquire.com/style/a3302/bestdressed0907/

"Between Radicalization and Democratization in an Unfolding Conflict: Media in Pakistan." International Media Support, September 15, 2009. http://www.i-m-s.dk/article/war-terror%E2%80%9D-cripples-media-pakistan-said-new-ims-report

Bevir, Mark. "How Narratives Explain." In *Interpretation and Method: Empirical Research Methods and the Interpretive Turn*, edited by Dvora Yanow and Peregrine Schwartz-Shea. London: M. E. Sharpe, 2006.

Billeaudeaux, Andre, David Dinke, John S. Hutcheson, and Philip Garland. "Newspaper Editorials Follow Lead of Bush Administration." *Newspaper Research Journal*, Vol. 24, No. 1 (Winter 2003): 166–184.

"Bin-Ladin's Death "Good News" for Afghanistan—Opposition Leader (Tolo TV)." BBC Monitoring Service, May 2, 2011. Lexis-Nexis Academic.

Bonde, B. N. "The Afghan Media Landscape." Baltic Media Centre, 2003. http://www.bmc.dk

Boot, Max. "Trump's Path to Indefinite Afghan War." Council on Foreign Relations, August 22, 2017. https://www.cfr.org/expert-brief/trumps-path-indefinite-afghan-war

Brewer, Paul R., Joseph Graf, and Lars Wilnat. "Priming or Framing: Media Influence on Attitudes Toward Foreign Countries." *International Communication Gazette*, Vol. 65, No. 6 (2003): 493–508.

Brisbane, Arthur. "An American in Pakistan." *New York Times*, February 26, 2011. http://www.nytimes.com/2011/02/27/opinion/27pubed.html

Brossel, Vincent. "Press Freedom One Year After the Fall of the Taliban." Reporters Sans Frontières, 2002. http://www.rsf.org/article.php3?id_article=4278

Brown, Katherine. "For Afghanistan and Pakistan, Final Reflections of a Dark Anniversary." Bloomberg, September 16, 2011. http://www.bloomberg.com/news/2011-09-16/for-afghanistan-and-pakistan-final-reflections-on-a-dark-anniversary-brown.html

Brown, Katherine, and Tom Glaisyer. "Warlord TV." *Foreign Policy Magazine*, September 10, 2010. http://www.foreignpolicy.com/articles/2010/09/23/warlord_tv

Brulliard, Karen. "In Pakistan, Top Media Group Wields Clout Amid Controversy." *Washington Post*, August 19, 2011. http://www.washingtonpost.com/world/

asia-pacific/in-pakistan-top-media-group-wields-clout-amid-controversy/2011/ 08/12/gIQAZouUPJ_story.html

Bumiller, Elisabeth. "Remembering Afghanistan's Golden Age." *New York Times*, October. 17, 2009. http://www.nytimes.com/2009/10/18/weekinreview/ 18bumiller.html?_r=0

Bush, George W. "Address to a Joint Session of Congress and the American People." The White House, September 20, 2001. http://georgewbush-whitehouse. archives.gov/news/releases/2001/09/20010920-8.html

Bush, George W. "Address to the Joint Session of Congress, 20 Sept. 2001." The White House, September 20, 2001. https://www.c-span.org/video/?c4498346/ george-w-bush-address-congress-september-20-2001

Bush, George W. "The State of the Union." *Washington Post*, January 28, 2003. http:// www.washingtonpost.com/wpsrv/onpolitics/transcripts/bushtext_012803.ht ml

Calabrese, Andrew, and Barbara Burke. "American Identities: Nationalism, the Media and the Public Sphere." *Journal of Communication Inquiry*, Vol. 16, No. 2 (Summer 1992): 52–73.

Campbell, David. *Writing Security: U.S. Foreign Policy and the Politics of Identity.* Minneapolis: University of Minnesota Press, 1992.

Carey, James. *Communications as Culture: Essays on Media and Society.* New York: Routledge, 1992.

Carey, James. "The Dark Continent of American Journalism." In *Reading the News*, edited by Robert Manoff and Michael Schudson. New York: Pantheon, 1986.

Carey, Peter. "An Explosion of News: The State of Media in Afghanistan." Center for International Media Assistance, February 23, 2012. http://cima.ned.org/ publications/explosion-news-state-media-afghanistan

Carruthers, Susan L. *The Media at War: Communication and Conflict in the Twentieth Century.* New York: Palgrave Macmillan, 2000.

Carruthers, Susan L. "Tribalism and Tribulation: Media Constructions of 'African Savagery' and 'Western Humanitarianism' in the 1990s." In *Reporting War*, edited by Stuart Allan and Barbie Zelizer. New York: Routledge, 2004.

Chang, Tsan-Kuo. "All Countries Not Created Equal to Be News: World System and International Communication." *Communication Research*, Vol. 25 (1998): 528–566.

Chang, Tsan-Kuo, Tuen-yu Lan, and Hao Xiaoming, "From the United States with News and More: International Flow, Television Coverage and the World System." *International Communication Gazette*, Vol. 62, No. 6 (December 2000): 505–522.

Chang, Tsan-Kuo, Pamela Shoemaker, and Nancy Brendlinger. "Determinants of International News Coverage in the U.S. Media." *Communications Research*, Vol. 14, No. 4 (August 1987): 396–414.

Cherry, Colin. *World Communication: Threat or Promise?* New York: Wiley, 1978.

"CNN Fact Sheet." CNN, 2017. http://cnnpressroom.blogs.cnn.com/cnn-fact-sheet/

Cobb, Roger W., and Charles D. Elder. "The Politics of Agenda-Building: An Alternative Perspective for Modern Democratic Theory." *Journal of Politics*, Vol. 33, No. 4 (November 1971): 892–915.

Cohen, Bernard. *The Press and Foreign Policy*. Princeton, NJ: Princeton University Press, 1963.

Coll, Steve. *Ghost Wars: The Secret History of the CIA, Afghanistan, and Bin Laden, from the Soviet Invasion to September 10, 2001*. New York: Penguin, 2004.

Cook, Tim. "Domesticating a Crisis: Washington Newsbeats and Network News After the Iraq Invasion of Kuwait." In *Taken by Storm: The Media, Public Opinion, and U.S. Foreign Policy in the Gulf War*, edited by Lance W. Bennett and David L. Paletz. Chicago: University of Chicago Press, 1994.

Cordovez, Diego, and Selig S. Harrison. *Out of Afghanistan: The Inside Story of the Soviet Withdrawal*. New York: Oxford University Press, 1995.

Cornwell, Susan. "Factbox: U.S. Has Allocated $20 billion for Pakistan." Reuters, April 11, 2011. http://www.reuters.com/article/2011/04/21/us-pakistan-usa-aid-factbox-idUSTRE73K7F420110421

Cottle, Simon. *Global Crisis Reporting*. Berkshire, UK: Open University Press, 2009.

Cray, David. "Wounded AP Reporter Vows to Return to Afghanistan." Associated Press, October 15, 2014. https://apnews.com/50df8491a25648ebad24da6d819696d8/wounded-ap-reporter-vows-return-afghanistan,

Davidson, W. Phillips, Donald R. Shanor, and Frederick T. C. Yu. *News from Abroad and the Foreign Policy Public*. New York: Foreign Policy Association, 1980.

Dell'Orto, Giovanna. "Foreign Policy and Foreign Correspondence: Integrating IR and Communication Theories to Examine the History of Press Involvement in International Affairs." International Studies Association Annual Conference, Montreal, 2011.

Dell'Orto, Giovanna. *Giving Meaning to the World: The First U.S. Foreign Correspondents, 1838–1859*. London: Greenwood Press, 2002.

Dewerth-Pallmeyer, Dwight. *The Audience in the News*. Mahwah, NJ: LEAA, 1996.

Dimitrova, Daniela V., and Jesper Strömbäck. "Mission Accomplished? Framing of the Iraq War in the Elite Newspapers in Sweden and the United States." *International Communication Gazette*, Vol. 67, No. 5 (2005): 399–417.

"Direct Overt U.S. Aid Appropriations for and Military Reimbursements to Pakistan, FY2002–FY2014." Congressional Research Service, April 11, 2013. http://www.fas.org/sgp/crs/row/pakaid.pdf

Dorman, William A., and Mansour Farhang. *The U.S. Press and Iran: Foreign Policy and the Journalism of Deference*. London: University of California Press, 1987.

Doty, Roxanne. *Imperial Encounters: The Politics of Representation in North–South Relations*. Minneapolis: University of Minnesota Press, 1996.

Downing, J. C. H. "Drawing a Bead on Global Communications Theories." In *Global Communication*, edited by Yahya R. Kamalipour. Belmont, CA: Wadsworth/Thomson Learning, 2002.

Downs, Anthony. "Up and Down with Ecology: The Issue-Attention Cycle." *Public Interest*, Vol. 28 (Summer 1972): 28–50.

Editors. "Calibrating the Use of Force." *New York Times*, Sept. 22, 2001.

Editors. "Rules of Engagement." *The Washington Post*, Sept. 23, 2001.

Editors. "The American Offensive Begins." *The New York Times*, Oct. 8, 2001.

Editors. "The Times and Iraq." *The New York Times*, May 26, 2004.

Editors. "The War Up Close." *Time*, Oct. 12, 2009.

Editors. "President Karzai's Misplaced Priorities." *New York Times*, November 6, 2012. http://www.nytimes.com/2012/11/07/opinion/president-hamid-karzais-misplaced-priorities.html

Elliot, Andrea. "Militant's Path From Pakistan to Times Square." *New York Times*, June 22, 2011. http://www.nytimes.com/2010/06/23/world/23terror.html?pagewanted=all

Emadi, Hafizullah. *State, Revolution and Superpowers in Afghanistan*. New York: Praeger, 1990.

Emery, Michael. "An Endangered Species: The International Newshole." *Freedom Forum Media Studies Journal*, Vol. 3 (Fall 1989): 151–164.

Entman, Robert M. "Cascading Activation: Contesting the White House's Frame After 9/11." *Political Communication*, Vol. 20, Issue 4 (2003): 413–432.

Entman, Robert. "Doomed to Repeat: Iraq News, 2002–2007." *American Behavioral Scientist*, Vol. 52, No. 5 (2009): 689–708.

Entman, Robert. "Framing U.S. Coverage of International News: Contrasts in Narratives of the KAL and Iran Air Incidents." *Journal of Communication*, Vol. 41, No. 4 (1991): 6–27.

Entman, Robert. *Projections of Power: Framing News, Public Opinion, and U.S. Foreign Policy*. Chicago: University of Chicago, 2004.

Epatko, Larisa. "10 Years Later, 9/11 Conspiracy Theories Linger in Pakistan." *PBS NewsHour*, September 2, 2011. http://www.pbs.org/newshour/rundown/2011/09/view-from-pakistan-on-911.html

Epstein, Susan B., and K. Alan Kronstadt. "Pakistan: U.S. Foreign Assistance." Congressional Research Service, June 7, 2011.

"Evening News." December 2003 Broadcast Index, Vanderbilt Television News Archive. https://tvnews.vanderbilt.edu/siteindex/2003-12.

Ewans, M. *Afghanistan: A Short History of Its People and Politics*. New York: HarperCollins, 2002.

"Factbox: Pakistan, India troop strength, deployments." Reuters, February 25, 2010. http://www.reuters.com/article/2010/02/25/us-pakistan-india-militaries-factbox-idUSTRE61O0BJ20100225, last accessed April 20, 2018.

"Fact Sheet: The U.S.-Afghanistan Strategic Partnership Agreement." The White House, May 1, 2012. http://www.whitehouse.gov/the-press-office/2012/05/01/fact-sheet-us-afghanistan-strategic-partnership-agreement, last accessed April 20, 2018.

"Farkhunda's Murder: A National Tragedy." *Tolo News*, March 28, 2015. http://www.tolonews.com/opinion/farkhundas-murder-national-tragedy

Fawad Ali Shah, Syed. "Mysterious US Nationals." *The Nation (Pakistan)*, November 20, 2009. http://www.nation.com.pk/pakistan-news-newspaper-daily-english-online/Politics/20-Nov-2009/Mysterious-US-nationals

"FBIS Media Guide: Pakistan." Foreign Broadcast Information Service, January 16, 1996, p. 1.

Fearon, James D. "Separatist Wars, Partition, and World Order." *Security Studies*, Vol. 13, No. 4 (2004): 394–415.

Ferrari, Michelle. *Reporting America at War: An Oral History*. New York: Hyperion, 2003.

Ferris-Rotman, Amie. "Insight: Iran's 'Great Game' in Afghanistan." Reuters, May 24, 2012. http://www.reuters.com/article/2012/05/24/us-afghanistan-iran-media-idUSBRE84N0CB20120524, last accessed April 20, 2018.

Ferris-Rotman, Amie. "New Afghan law ignites fear over shrinking press freedoms." Reuters, July 1, 2012. http://www.reuters.com/article/2012/07/01/afghanistan-media-law-idUSL3E8HR4R120120701, last accessed April 20, 2018.

Filkins, Dexter. "Iran Is Said to Give Top Karzai Aide Cash by the Bagful." *New York Times*, October 23, 2010. http://www.nytimes.com/2010/10/24/world/asia/24afghan.html

Filkins, Dexter. "The Journalist and the Spies." *The New Yorker*, September 19, 2011. http://www.newyorker.com/reporting/2011/09/19/110919fa_fact_filkins?currentP age=all

Filkins, Dexter. "Will Civil War Hit Afghanistan When the U.S. Leaves?" *The New Yorker*, July 9, 2012. http://www.newyorker.com/reporting/2012/07/09/120709fa_fact_filkins

Filkins, Dexter, and Mark Mazetti. "Secret Joint Raid Captures Taliban's Top Commander." *New York Times*, February 15, 2010. http://www.nytimes.com/2010/02/16/world/asia/16intel.html?pagewanted=all

"Filling the Vacuum: The Bonn Conference." *PBS Frontline*, 2003. http://www.pbs.org/wgbh/pages/frontline/shows/campaign/withus/cbonn.html

Finnemore, Martha. *National Interests in International Society*. Ithaca, NY: Cornell University Press, 1996.

Flanagan, Ben. "News Corps Takes Stake in Dubai Company." *The National* (United Arab Emirates), January 12, 2012. http://www.thenational.ae/business/media/news-corp-takes-stake-in-dubai-media-company

Fox, Elizabeth. *Media and Politics in Latin America: The Struggle for Democracy*. Newbury Park, CA: Sage, 1988.

Fraenkel, Eran, Sheldon Himelfarb, and Emrys Schoemaker. "Afghanistan Media Assessment: Opportunities and Challenges for Peacebuilding." U.S. Institute for Peace. Washington, DC: Peaceworks, 2010.

Frankel, Max. "The Shroud." *New York Times Magazine*, November 27, 1994.

"Freedom of the Press 2017: Press Freedom's Dark Horizon." *Freedom House*, April 28, 2017. https://freedomhouse.org/report/freedom-press/freedom-press-2017

Gall, Carlotta, "Afghan Poppy Growing Reaches Record Level, U.N. Says." *New York Times*, November 19, 2004. http://www.nytimes.com/2004/11/19/world/asia/afghan-poppy-growing-reaches-record-level-un-says.html

Gall, Carlotta. "THREATS AND RESPONSES: KABUL; Afghan Editors Test Freedom's Boundaries With Cartoons." *New York Times*, January 12, 2003. http://www.nytimes.com/2003/01/12/world/threats-responses-kabul-afghan-editors-test-freedom-s-boundaries-with-cartoons.html

Gall, Carlotta. "U.S. Military Investigating Death of Afghan in Custody." *New York Times*, March 3, 2004. http://www.nytimes.com/2003/03/04/world/threats-responses-prisoners-us-military-investigating-death-afghan-custody.html.

Gannon, Kathy. "Aid Workers Arrested in Afghanistan." Associated Press, August 8, 2001. http://www.washingtonpost.com/wpsrv/aponline/20010808/aponline045410_000. htm

Gans, Herbert. *Deciding What's News: A Study of CBS Evening News, NBC Nightly News, Newsweek, and Time.* New York: Vintage Books, 2004.

Gans, Herbert. "The Message Behind the News." *Columbia Journalism Review*, Vol. 17, No. 1 (1979).

Gerbner, George. "Ideological Perspectives and Political Tendencies in News Reporting." *Journalism Quarterly*, Vol. 41 (Fall 1964): 495–508.

Gerbner, George, and George Marvanyi. "The Many Worlds of the World's Press." *Journal of Communications*, Vol. 27, No. 1 (Winter 1977): 52–66.

Gezari, Vanessa. "Crossfire in Kandahar." Pulitzer Center on Crisis Reporting, January 6, 2011. http://pulitzercenter.org/articles/afghanistan-journalists-nato-taliban-mohammad-nader

Gezari, Vanessa. "Reporting from Afghanistan." Pulitzer Center on Crisis Reporting, December 10, 2010. http://pulitzercenter.org/video/pajhwok-afghan-news-afghanistan-journalism

Gezari, Vanessa. "Unlikely Stories, or the Making of an Afghan News Agency." Pulitzer Center of Crisis Reporting, November 19, 2010. http://pulitzercenter.org/blog/untold-stories/afghanistan-journalism-pajhwok-afghan-news-taliban

"Ghani Orders Reinvestigation into Kabul Bank Case." *Tolo News*, October 1, 2014. http://www.tolonews.com/afghanistan/ghani-orders-reinvestigation-kabul-bank-case

"Ghani Welcomes Trump's Strategy on Afghanistan." *Tolo News*, August 21, 2017. http://www.tolonews.com/afghanistan/ghani-welcomes-trump%E2%80%99s-strategy-afghanistan

Gibbons-Neff, Thomas, Eric Schmitt, and Adam Goldman. "A Newly Assertive C.I.A. Expands Its Taliban Hunt in Afghanistan." *New York Times*, October 22, 2017. https://www.nytimes.com/2017/10/22/world/asia/cia-expanding-taliban-fightafghanistan.html?emc=edit_th_20171023&nl=todaysheadlines&nlid=675834 62&mtrref=undefined&gwh=065B760876AFCAE6D1B69402E0CEDA38&gwt= pay,

Gifford, C. Anthony. "Developed and Developing Nation News in the U.S. Wire Service Files to Asia." *Journalism Quarterly*, Vol. 61 (1984): 14–19.

Gilboa, Eytan. "The CNN Effect: The Search for a Communication Theory of International Relations." *Political Communication*, Vol. 22 (2005): 27–44.

Gilboa, Eytan. "Global Communication and Foreign Policy." International Communication Association Conference, 2002.

Girard, B., and J. Van der Spek. "The Potential for Community Radio in Afghanistan." Comunica, 2002. http://www.comunica.org

Gitlin, Todd. *The Whole World Is Watching: Mass Media in the Making and Unmaking of the New Left*. Berkeley: University of California Press, 1980.

Glanz, James, and Alissa Rubin. "Blackwater Shootings 'Murder', Iraq Says." *New York Times*, October 8, 2007. http://www.nytimes.com/2007/10/08/world/middleeast/o8blackwater.html?pagew anted=all

"Global Terrorism Index 2017." Institute for Economics and Peace, November 15, 2017. https://reliefweb.int/sites/reliefweb.int/files/resources/Global%20Terrorism%20In dex%202017%20%284%29.pdf

Goffman, Erving. *Frame Analysis: An Essay on Organization and Experience*. Cambridge, MA: Harvard University Press, 1974.

Golan, Guy, and Wayne Wanta. "International Elections on the U.S. Network News: An Examination of Factors Affecting Newsworthiness." *International Communication Gazette*, Vol. 65 (2003): 25–39.

Golan, Guy, and Wayne Wanta. "Second-Level Agenda Setting in the New Hampshire Primary: A Comparison of Coverage in Three Newspapers and Public Perceptions of Candidates." *Journalism and Mass Communication Quarterly*, Vol. 78 (2001): 247–259.

Goodhand, J. "Aiding Violence or Building Peace? The Role of International Aid in Afghanistan." *Third World Quarterly*, 23. Vol. 5 (2002): 837–859.

Goshko, John M. "UN Chief Stresses Need for Money." *Washington Post*, November 22, 1992. A1, A33, Quoted in Alleyne, Mark D. *International Power and International Communication*. New York: St. Martin's Press, 1995.

Graber, Doris. A. *Mass Media and American Politics* (5th ed.). Washington, DC: Congressional Quarterly, 1997.

Graham-Harrison, Emma. "Serena Hotel Attack, March 21, 2014—Sardar Ahmad." *The Guardian*, March 21, 2014. http://www.theguardian.com/world/2014/mar/21/taliban-gunmen-kill-nine-kabul-serena-hotel

Greenberg, Bradley S., and Marcia Thomson. *Communication and Terrorism: Public and Media Responses to 9/11*. New York: Hampton Press, 2002.

Greenfield, Meg. *Washington*. New York: Public Affairs, 2001.

Grimmett, Richard F. "Authorization for Use of Military Force in Response to the 9/11 Attacks (P.L. 107-40): Legislative History." Congressional Research Service, January 16, 2007.

"Growing Fears as More Afghan Journalists and Media Workers Come Under the Gun." Committee to Protect Journalists, February 2016.

Grusin, Elinor Kelley, and Sandra H. Utt. "The Challenge: To Examine Media's Role, Performance on 9/11 and After." In *Media in an American Crisis: Studies of September 11, 2001*. New York: University Press of America, 2005.

Habeck, Mary. "What Does Al-Qaeda Want?" *Foreign Policy*, March 6, 2012. http://foreignpolicy.com/2012/03/06/what-does-al-qaeda-want/

Hachten, William A., and James Scotton. *The World News Prism*. Ames: Iowa State University, 2002.

Hafez, Kai. *The Myth of Media Globalization*. Cambridge, UK: Polity, 2007.

Hakim, Yalda. "Threatened with Death for Working on TV." BBC News, April 29, 2016.

Hall, Stuart. "The Rediscovery of 'Ideology': Return of the Repressed in Media Studies." In *Culture, Society and the Media*, edited by Tony Bennett, James Curran, Michael Gurevitch, and Janet Woollacott. London: Methuen, 1982.

Hallin, Daniel C. "Hegemony: The American News Media from Vietnam to El Salvador, a Study of Ideological Change and Its Limits." In *Political Communication Research*, edited by David Paletz. Norwood, NJ: Albex, 1987.

Hallin, Daniel C. *The Uncensored War: The Media and Vietnam*. Berkeley: University of California Press, 1989.

Hallin, Daniel C., and Todd Gitlin. "The Gulf War as Popular Culture and Television Drama." In *Taken by Storm: The Media, Public Opinion, and U.S. Foreign Policy in the Gulf War*, edited by Lance W. Bennett and David L. Paletz. Chicago: University of Chicago Press, 1994.

Hamilton, John Maxwell. *Journalism's Roving Eye: A History of American Foreign Reporting*. Baton Rouge: Louisiana State University Press, 2011.

Hamilton, John Maxwell, and George A. Krimsky. "'Juju' News from Abroad." *Freedom Forum Media Studies Journal*, Vol. 20, No. 9 (November 1998): 50–67.

Hannerz, Ulf. *Foreign News: Exploring the World of Foreign Correspondents*. Chicago: University of Chicago Press, 2004.

Hartenberger, Lisa Anne. "Mediating Transition in Afghanistan, 2001–2004." Doctoral dissertation, University of Texas at Austin, 2005.

Hawkins, Derek. "Brian Williams Is 'Guided by the Beauty of Our Weapons' in Syria Strikes." *Washington Post*, April 7, 2017. https://www.washingtonpost.com/news/morning-mix/wp/2017/04/07/beautiful-brian-williams-says-of-syria-missile-strike-proceeds-to-quote-leonard-cohen/?utm_term=.35b63ca9cad0

Hedebro, Goran. *Communication and Social Change in Developing Nations: A Critical View*. Ames: Iowa State University Press, 1982.

Hensch, Mark. "CNN Host: 'Donald Trump Became President' Last Night." *The Hill*, April 7, 2017. http://thehill.com/homenews/administration/327779-cnn-host-donald-trump-became-president-last-night

Herman, Edward S., and Noam Chomsky. *Manufacturing Consent: The Political Economy of Mass Media*. New York: Random House, 1988.

Hess, Stephen. *International News and Foreign Correspondents*. Washington, DC: Brookings Institution Press, 1996.

Hess, Stephen. "Media Mavens." *Society*, Vol. 33, No. 3 (March/April 1996): 1–10.

Hess, Stephen. *Through Their Eyes: Foreign Correspondents in the United States.* Washington, DC: Brookings Institution Press, 2005.

Hester, Joe Bob. "New York Times' Coverage Before, During and After 9/11." In *Media in an American Crisis: Studies of September 11, 2001*, edited by Elinor Kelley Grusin and Sandra H. Utt. New York: University Press of America, 2005.

Higgins, Andrew. "In Afghanistan, Signs of Crony Capitalism." *Washington Post*, February 22, 2010. http://www.washingtonpost.com/wp-dyn/content/article/2010/02/21/AR2010022104317.html?sid=ST2010090107315

Hohenberg, John. *Foreign Correspondence: The Great Reporters and Their Times.* New York: Columbia University Press, 1965.

Holsti, Ole. *Public Opinion and American Foreign Policy.* Ann Arbor: University of Michigan Press, 2004.

Hopkins, Nick. "Afghanistan's Jack Bauer Says He is Under Pressure to Give Up TV Cop Show." *The Guardian*, January 11, 2012. https://www.theguardian.com/global/defence-and-security-blog/2012/jan/11/afghanistan-and-jack-bauer-and-tv-show-and-taliban

Hopkirk, P. *The Great Game: The Struggle for Empire in Central Asia.* New York: Kodansha International, 1994.

Horvit, Beverly. "Combat, Political Violence Top International Categories." *Newspaper Research Journal*, Vol. 24, No. 2 (Spring 2003): 23–35.

Horvit, Beverly. "Some Papers Gave Scant Space to Taliban, Afghanistan Pre-9/11." In *Media in an American Crisis: Studies of September 11, 2001*, edited by Elinor Kelley Grusin and Sandra H. Utt. New York: University Press of America, 2005.

"Hours Devoted to Stories with a Foreign Dateline." Pew Project State of the News Media 2010, March 2011. http://www.stateofthemedia.org/2010

Hutchinson, John. *Modern Nationalism.* Glasgow: Harper Collins, 1994.

"Impunity Index." Committee to Protect Journalists, 2016 https://www.cpj.org/reports/2016/10/impunity-index-getting-away-with-murder-killed-justice.php

"Influences on News Work—Internal Influences." *Worlds of Journalism*, 2010. http://www.worldsofjournalism.org

"Internews Radio Summary 2003." Internews, 2003. http://www.internews.org/regions/afghanistan/afghan_radioreport_2003-07.htm

"Iraq News: Less Dominant, Still Important." Pew Center for the People and the Press, November 9, 2007. http://www.people-press.org/2007/11/09/iraq-news-less-dominant-still-important/

James, Caryn. "The New York Times. Sept. 12, 2001." Quoted in *What We Saw*. New York: Simon and Schuster, 2002.

Jasperson, Amy E., and Mansour O. El-Kikhia. "CNN and al Jazeera's Media Coverage of America's War in Afghanistan." In *Framing Terrorism: The News Media, the Government and the Public*, edited by Pippa Norris, Montague Kern, and Marion Just. London: Routledge, 2003.

Johnson, Eliana. "How Trump Swallowed a Bitter Afghanistan Pill." Politico, August 22, 2017. http://politi.co/2wsSVRg

Johnson, Melissa. "Predicting News Flow from Mexico." *Journalism and Mass Communication Quarterly*, Vol. 74, No. 2 (1997): 315–331.

Jones, Seth. *In the Graveyard of Empires*. New York: W.W. Norton & Company, 2009.

"Journalists and Media Staff Killed in 2001." International Federation of Journalists, 2002.http://www.ifj.org/fileadmin/images/Killed_List/IFJ_Report_on_Journalists_Killed_2001.pdf

Karl, Patricia A. "Media Diplomacy." *Proceedings of the Academy of Political Science. The Communications Revolution in Politics*, Vol. 34 No. 4 (1982): 143–152.

Karzai, Hamid. "Condolence Message by President Karzai Statement on the Loss of Afghan Journalist." March 21, 2014. http://president.gov.af/en/news/president-karzais-condolence-message-on-the-loss-of-afghan-journalist

Katz, David. "Nationalism and Conflict Resolution." In *International Behavior: A Social Psychological Analysis*, edited by Herbert C. Kelman. New York: Holt, Rinehart and Winston, 1965.

Kaufman, Stuart J. *Modern Hatreds: The Symbolic Politics of Ethnic War*. Ithaca, NY: Cornell University Press, 2001.

Keck, Margaret E., and Kathryn Sikkink. *Activists Beyond Borders: Advocacy Networks in International Politics*. Ithaca, NY: Cornell University Press, 1998.

Keller, Bill. "Being There." *New York Times*, December 2, 2012. http://www.nytimes.com/2012/12/03/opinion/keller-being-there.html?pagewanted=2&_r=0

Keller, Bill. "Last Soviet Soldiers Leave Afghanistan." *New York Times*, February 15, 1989. http://partners.nytimes.com/library/world/africa/021689afghan-laden.html

Kern, Montague, and Marion Just. *Framing Terrorism: The News Media, the Government and the Public*. London: Routledge, 2003.

Kim, K., and G. A. Barnett. "The Determinants of International News Flow: A Network Analysis." *Communications Research*, Vol. 23 (1996): 323–352.

Kingdon, John W. *Agendas, Alternatives and Public Policies*. Boston: Little Brown, 1984.

Kishan Thussu, Daya, "Managing the Media in an Era of Round-the-Clock News: Notes from India's First Tele-War." *Journalism Studies*, Vol. 3, No. 2 (2002): 203–212.

Kraemer, Sven. *Inside the Cold War From Marx to Reagan: An Unprecedented Guide to the Roots, History, Strategies, and Key Documents*. Lanham, MD: UPA, 2015.

Kumar, Priya. "Shuttered Bureaus." *American Journalism Review*, December/January 2011. http://ajrarchive.org/article.asp?id=4996

Kurtz, Howard. "The Washington Post. Sept. 20, 2001." Quoted in *What We Saw*. New York: Simon and Schuster, 2002.

Kurtzleben, Danielle. "CHART: How the U.S. Troop Levels In Afghanistan Have Changed Under Obama." National Public Radio, July 6, 2016. http://www.npr.org/2016/07/06/484979294/chart-how-the-u-s-troop-levels-in-afghanistan-have-changed-under-obama

Kurtzleben, Danielle. "Journalists Remember 9/11: For Many Journalists, No War or Crisis Will Ever Compare to That Day." *U.S. News and World Report*, September 11, 2011. http://www.usnews.com/news/articles/2011/09/09/journalists-remember-911

LaMay, Craig. *Exporting Press Freedom*. New York: Routledge, 2007.

Lang, G. E., and K. Lang. *Watergate: An Exploration of the Agenda-Building Process*. Beverly Hills, CA: Sage Publications, 1981.

Lasswell, Harold. *Propaganda Technique in World War I*. Cambridge, MA: MIT Press, 1927.

Lee, C. C., and J. Yang. "Foreign News and National Interest: Comparing U.S. and Japanese Coverage of the Chinese Student Movement." *International Communication Gazette*, Vol. 56 (1995): 1–18.

Lee, Changho. "Post, Times Highlight Government's War Efforts." *Newspaper Research Journal*, No. 1 (Winter 2003): 190–203.

Lee, Changho. "Washington Post, New York Times Highlight Government's War Efforts." In *Media in an American Crisis: Studies of September 11, 2001*, edited by Elinor Kelley Grusin and Sandra H. Utt. New York: University Press of America, 2005.

Lee, Chin-Chuan, Joseph Man Chan, Zhongdang Pan, and Clement Y. K. So. "National Prisms of a Global 'Media Event'." In *Mass Media and Society*, edited by James Curran and Michael Gurevitch. London: Arnold, 2000.

Lehmann, Ingrid. "Exploring the Transatlantic Media Divide over Iraq: How and Why U.S. and German Media Differed in Reporting on UN Weapons Inspections in Iraq, 2002–2003." *International Journal of Press/Politics*, Vol. 10, No. 1 (Winter 2005): 63–89.

Lent, John. "Foreign News in American Media." *Journal of Communication*, Vol. 27 (Winter 1977): 46–51.

Levine, C. "Afghanistan Project Formulation Mission Report." Institute for Media, Policy and Civil Society, 2002. http://www.impacs.org/pdfs/afghanprojmissionrep.pdf

Lieven, Anatol. *Pakistan: A Hard Country*. Washington, DC: Public Affairs Books, 2011.

Linsky, M. *Impact: How the Press Affects Federal Policymaking*. New York: W.W. Norton & Company, 1986.

Lippman, Walter. *Public Opinion*. New York: Harcourt, Brace and Company, 1922.

Lipton, Eric. "Death Toll Is Near 3,000 but Some Uncertainty Over the Count Remains." *New York Times*, September 11, 2002, https://www.nytimes.com/2002/09/11/us/death-toll-is-near-3000-but-some-uncertainty-over-the-count-remains.html

Livingston, Steven. "Limited Vision: How Both the American Media and Government Failed Rwanda." In *The Media and The Rwanda Genocide*, edited by Allan Thompson. Ann Arbor, MI: Pluto Press, 2007.

Livingston, Steven, and Todd Eachus. "Rwanda: U.S. Policy and Television Coverage." In *The Path of a Genocide: The Rwanda Crisis from Uganda to Zaire*, edited by H. Adelman and A. Suhrke. New Brunswick, NJ: Transaction Publishers, 2000.

Lobe, Jim. "Iraq Blotted Out Rest of the World in 2003 TV News." Global Policy Forum, January 6, 2004. http://www.globalpolicy.org/empire/media/2004/0106blotted.htm

Lule, Jack. "Myth and Terror on the Editorial Page: The New York Times Responds to Sept. 11, 2001." *Journalism and Mass Communication Quarterly*, Vol. 79, No. 2 (Summer 2002): 275–293.

Magnowski, Daniel. "Taliban Death Stadium Reborn as Afghan Sporting Hope." Reuters, December 15. 2011. http://www.reuters.com/article/2011/12/15/us-afghanistan-stadium-taliban-idUSTRE7BE0LB20111215, last accessed April 20, 2018.

Majority Staff Report. "Evaluating U.S. Foreign Assistance to Afghanistan." Committee on Foreign Relations at the United States Senate, June 8, 2011. http://www.foreign.senate.gov/press/chair/release/?id=f157bdb1-9544-4d4c-ae1f-e02929086730

Maley, W. *Fundamentalism Reborn? Afghanistan and the Taliban*. New York: New York University Press, 1998.

Mamdani, Mahmoud. "Beyond Settler and Native as Political Identities: Overcoming the Political Legacy of Colonialism." *Comparative Studies in Society and History*, Vol. 43, No. 4 (October 2001): 651–664.

Manheim, Jarol B. *All the People, All the Times: Strategic Communication and American Politics*. Armonk, NY: M.E. Sharpe, 1991.

Manheim, Jarol B. "Strategic Public Diplomacy." In *Taken by Storm: The Media, Public Opinion, and U.S. Foreign Policy in the Gulf Wars*, edited by W. Lance Bennett and David L. Paletz. Chicago: University of Chicago Press, 1994.

Manning, Paul. *News and News Sources: A Critical Introduction*. London: Sage, 2001.

Margesson, Rhoda. "Afghan Refugees: Current States and Future Prospects." Congressional Research Service, January 26, 2007.

Marsden, P. "Afghanistan: The Reconstruction Process." *International Affairs*, Vol. 79, No. 1 (2003): 91–105.

Mashal, Mujib. "Afghanistan Is in Chaos. Is That What Hamid Karzai Wants?" *New York Times*, August 6, 2016. http://www.nytimes.com/2016/08/06/world/asia/afghanistan-hamid-karzai.html?_r=0

Mashal, Mujib. "After Karzai," *The Atlantic*, July 2014. http://www.theatlantic.com/magazine/archive/2014/07/after-karzai/372294/

Mashal, Mujib. "Vibrant Lives of Afghan TV Crew, Erased in a Taliban Bombing." *New York Times*, January 22, 2016. http://www.nytimes.com/2016/01/22/world/asia/afghanistan-tolo-tv-bombing.html

Masmoudi, Mustapha. "The New World Information Order." UNESCO International Commission for the Study of Social Problems, Document 21. Paris: UNESCO, 1978.

Matheson, Donald, and Stuart Allan. *Digital War Reporting*. Malden, MA: Polity Press, 2009.

McAnany, Emile. "Television and Crisis: Ten Years of Network News Coverage of Central America, 1972–1981." *Media, Culture and Society*, Vol. 5, No. 3 (1983): 199–212.

McCarthy, Rory. "Biden Condemns Israel over Homes Plans." *The Guardian*, March 9, 2010. http://www.guardian.co.uk/world/2010/mar/09/israel-jerusalem-settlement-homes-biden

McCombs, Maxwell. *Setting the Agenda*. Cambridge, UK: Polity, 2004.

McCombs, Maxwell, Esteban Lopez-Escobar, and Juan Pablo Llamas. "Setting the Agenda of Attributes in the 1996 Spanish General Election." *Journal of Communication*, Vol. 50, No. 2 (2000): 77–92.

McCombs, Maxwell, and D. Shaw. "The Agenda-Setting Function of Mass Media." *Public Opinion Quarterly*, Vol. 36, No. 2 (1972): 176–187.

McDermott, Terry. "Review: Judith Miller's 'The Story: A Reporter's Journey'." *New York Times*, April 7, 2015. https://www.nytimes.com/2015/04/08/books/review-judith-millers-the-story-a-reporters-journey.html?_r=0

McDowell, Stephen D. "Theory and Research in International Communication: A Historical and Institutional Account." In *Handbook of International and Intercultural Communication* (2nd ed.), edited by William B. Gudykunst and Bella Mody. London: Sage Publications, 2002.

McLaughlin, Greg. *The War Correspondent*. London: Pluto Press, 2002.

McNelly, John T., and Fausto Izcaray. "International News Exposure and Images of Nations." *Journalism and Mass Communication Quarterly*, Vol. 63 (1992): 546–553.

McPhail, Thomas L. *Electronic Colonialism: The Future of International Broadcasting and Communication*. Beverly Hills, CA: Sage, 1987.

Meier, Werner A. "Media Ownership—Does It Matter?" In *Networking Knowledge for Information Societies*, edited by Robin Mansell, Rohan Samarajiwa, and Amy Mahan. Delft: Delft University Press, 2003.

Mermin, Jonathan. "Television News and American Intervention in Somalia: The Myth of a Media-Driven Foreign Policy." *Political Science Quarterly*, Vol. 112, No. 3 (1997): 385–403.

Merrill, John C. "Global Elite: A Newspaper Community of Freedom." *Gannett Center Journal of World Media*, Vol. 4, No. 4 (Fall 1990): 91–101.

Merrill, John C. *Global Journalism*. New York: Longham, 1995.

Merrill, John C. *A Handbook of the Foreign Press*. Baton Rouge: Louisiana State University Press, 1959.

Meyer, William H. "Structures of North–South Information Flows: An Empirical Test of Galtung's Theory." *Journalism Quarterly*, Vol. 68, No. 1–2 (Spring–Summer 1991): 230–237.

Misdaq, Nabi. *Afghanistan: Political Frailty and External Interference*. New York: Taylor & Francis, 2006.

Mody, Bella. *The Geopolitics of Representation in Foreign News: Explaining Darfur.* Boulder, CO: Lexington Books, 2010.

Mohseni, Saad. "Statement on the January 20, 2016 Attack." Tolo News, January 20, 2016. http://www.tolonews.com/en/afghanistan/23401-seven-tolo-tv-employees-killed-in-wednesday-attack

Moore, David W. "Support for War on Terrorism Rivals Support for WWII." Gallup News Service, October 3, 2001. http://www.gallup.com/poll/4954/support-war-terrorism-rivals-support-wwii.aspx

Mowlana, Hamid. *Global Communication in Transition.* Thousand Oaks, CA: Sage Publications, 1996.

"Murders in Afghanistan Send Chill Through Media." *Press Gazette,* November 21, 2001. http://www.pressgazette.co.uk/story.asp?storyCode=21157&sectioncode=1

Nacos, Brigitte. *Mass-Mediated Terrorism.* Lanham, MD: Rowman & Littlefield, 2002.

Nacos, Brigitte, and Torres Reyna. "Framing Muslim-Americans Before and After 9/11." In *Framing Terrorism: The News Media, the Government and the Public,* edited by Pippa Norris, Montague Kern. and Marion Just. London: Routledge, 2003.

Naveh, Chanan. "The Role of the Media in Foreign Policy Decision-Making: A Theoretical Framework." *Conflict & Communication Online,* Vol. 1, No. 2 (2002): 1–14.

Nawid, S. N. *Religious Response to Social Change in Afghanistan 1919–29: King Aman Allah and the Afghan Ulama.* Costa Mesa, CA: Mazda Publishers, 1999.

"Network TV News—State of the News Media in 2010." Pew Project for Excellence in Journalism, 2011. http://www.stateofthemedia.org/2010/network_tv_news_investment.php

Neuman, W. Russell. "The Threshold of Public Attention." *Public Opinion Quarterly,* Vol. 54, No. 2 (Summer 1990): 159–176.

Neuman, W. Russell, Marion R. Just, and Ann N. Crigler. *Common Knowledge: News and the Construction of Political Meaning.* Chicago: University of Chicago Press, 1992.

Newport, Frank. "Overwhelming Support for War Continues." Gallup, November 29, 2001. http://www.gallup.com/poll/5083/overwhelming-support-war-continues.aspx

Nisbet, Erik C., Matthew C. Nisbet, Dietram A. Scheufele, and James E. Shanahan. "Public Diplomacy, Television News and Muslim Opinion." *Harvard International Journal of Press/Politics,* Vol. 9, Issue 2 (2004): 11–37.

Nordland, Rod. "Afghan Officials Interrogate Matthew Rosenberg." *New York Times,* August 19, 2014. http://www.nytimes.com/2014/08/20/world/asia/afghan-officials-interrogate-matthew-rosenberg.html

Nordland, Rod. "A 'Wall of Kindness' Against a Harsh Reality in Afghanistan." *New York Times,* March 24, 2016. https://www.nytimes.com/2016/03/25/world/asia/afghanistan-wall-of-kindness.html?_r=0

Nordland, Rod, and Habib Zahori. "Killing of Afghan Journalist and Family Members Stuns Media Peers." *New York Times*, March 27, 2014. http://www.nytimes.com/2014/03/27/world/asia/killing-of-afghan-journalist-and-family-members-stuns-media-peers.html

Norris, Pippa, Montague Kern, and Marion Just. *Framing Terrorism: The News Media, the Government and the Public*. London: Routledge, 2003.

Nye, Joseph. "The Decline of America's Soft Power." *Foreign Affairs*, May/June 2004. http://www.foreignaffairs.com/articles/59888/joseph-s-nye-jr/the-decline-of-americas-soft-power

Obama, Barack. "Obama's Remarks on bin Laden's Killing." *New York Times*, May 1, 2011, https://obamawhitehouse.archives.gov/blog/2011/05/02/osama-bin-laden-dead

Obama, Barack. "Transcript of Obama Speech on Afghanistan." CNN, December 2, 2009, http://www.cnn.com/2009/POLITICS/12/01/obama.afghanistan.speech.transcript/ index.html

"Obama Calls Iraq War a 'Dangerous Distraction'." CNN, July 15, 2008. http://www.cnn.com/2008/POLITICS/07/15/obama.iraq/index.html?iref=nextin

O'Brien, Rita Cruise. "The Political Economy of Information: A North–South Perspective." In *World Communications: A Handbook*, edited by George Gerbner and Marsha Siefert. New York: Longman, 1984.

Office of the Special Inspector General for Afghanistan Reconstruction. "Quarterly Report to the United States Congress." *Special Inspector General for Afghanistan Reconstruction*, October 30, 2016. https://www.sigar.mil/pdf/quarterlyreports/2016-10-30qr-section3.pdf

Office of the Special Inspector General for Afghanistan Reconstruction. "Selected Public Diplomacy Awards Mostly Achieved Objectives, but Embassy Can Take Steps to Enhance Grant Management and Oversight." Special Inspector General for Afghanistan Reconstruction, July 30, 2012. https://www.sigar.mil/pdf/audits/2012-07-30audit-12-13508.pdf

O'Heffernan, Patrick. *Insider Perspectives on Global Journalism and the Foreign Policy Process*. Westport, CT: Alex Publishing, 1991.

Olivo, Antonio. "Afghanistan Is Losing Its Local Press Corps as Journalists Flee the Country." *Washington Post*, May 7, 2016. https://www.washingtonpost.com/news/worldviews/wp/2016/05/07/afghanistan-is-losing-its-local-press-corps-as-journalists-flee-the-country/?utm_term=.59e702fefe59

Paletz, David L. *The Media in American Politics*. New York: Longman, 2002.

Paletz, David L. and Robert Entman. *Media, Power, and Politics*. New York: Free Press, 1991.

Pan, Z. and G. M. Kosicki. "Framing Analysis: An Approach to News Discourse." *Political Communication*, Vol. 10 (1993): 55–75.

"Participants of Afghan TV Debate Welcome Usamah Bin-Ladin's Killing (Radio Television Afghanistan)." BBC Monitoring Service, May 2, 2011. Lexis-Nexis Academic.

Partlow, Joshua. *A Kingdom of Their Own: The Family Karzai and the Afghan Disaster.* New York: Knopf Doubleday, 2016.

Partlow, Joshua. "Podium Wars: President Hamid Karzai, the Foreign Press, and the Afghan War." Harvard University Shorenstein Center on Media, Politics and Public Policy, Fall 2012. http://shorensteincenter.org/podium-wars-president-hamid-karzai-the-foreign-press-and-the-afghan-war/

Partlow, Joshua, and Pam Constable. "Accusations of Vote Fraud Multiply in Afghanistan." *Washington Post*, August 27, 2009. http://www.washingtonpost.com/wpdyn/content/article/2009/08/27/AR20090827 04199.html

"Passport Statistics." U.S. Department of State, 2012. http://travel.state.gov/passport/ppi/stats/stats_890.html

Pattanaik, Smruti S. *Elite Perceptions in Foreign Policy: Role of Print Media in Influencing India-Pakistan Relations, 1989–1999.* Colombo, Sri Lanka: Regional Centre for Strategic Studies, 2004.

"The Pearl Project: The Truth Left Behind, Inside the Kidnapping and Murder of Daniel Pearl." Center for Public Integrity, January 20, 2011. http://www.washingtonpost.com/wp-srv/world/documents/daniel-pearl-project/

Pedelty, Mark. *War Stories: The Culture of Foreign Correspondents.* New York: Routledge, 1995.

Perse, Elizabeth. *Media Effects and Society.* Florence, KY: Psychology Press, 2001.

Peter, Tom. "Afghanistan Funding: Local Media Already Feeling the Pinch." *Christian Science Monitor*, July 8, 2012. http://www.csmonitor.com/World/Asia-South-Central/2012/0708/Afghanistan-funding-Local-media-already-feeling-the-pinch

Picard, Robert G. "Global Communication Controversies." In *Global Journalism*, edited by John C. Merrill. New York: Longman, 1991.

Powlick, Philip J. "The Sources of Public Opinion for American Foreign Policy Officials." *International Studies Quarterly*, Vol. 39, No. 4 (1995): 427–451.

Powlick, Philip J., and Andrew Z. Katz. "Defining the American Public Opinion/Foreign Policy Nexus." *Mershon International Studies Review*, Vol. 42 (1998): 29–61.

"Press Freedom Index 2011–2012." Reporters Without Borders, 2013. http://en.rsf.org/press-freedom-index-2011-2012,1043.html

"Profile: Asif Ali Zardari." BBC News Asia, December 7, 2011. http://www.bbc.co.uk/news/world-asia-16066406

"Programme Summary of Afghan Tolo TV news in Dari 1330 GMT 2 May 11." BBC Monitoring Service, May 2, 2011. Lexis-Nexis Academic.

Rahimi, Sangar. Tolo News Twitter Account. August 19, 2014. https://twitter.com/SangarRahimi/status/501718909817716736

Ravi, Narsimhan. "Looking Beyond Flawed Journalism: How National Interests, Patriotism and Cultural Values Shaped the Coverage of the Iraq War." *Harvard Journal of Press/Politics*, Vol. 10. No. 1 (2005): 45–62.

Rawan, S. M. "Modern Mass Media and Traditional Communication in Afghanistan." *Political Communication*, Vol. 19 (2002): 155–170.

Razi, M. H. "Afghanistan." In *Mass Media in the Middle East: A Comprehensive Handbook*, edited by Y. R. Kamalipour and H. Mowlana. Westport, CT: Greenwood Press, 1994.

Reese, Stephen D. "Theorizing a Globalized Journalism." In *Global Journalism Research: Theories, Methods, Findings, Future*, edited by Martin Loffelholz and David Weaver. Boston: Blackwell Publishing, 2008.

Reese, Stephen D. "Understanding the Global Journalist: A Hierarchy-of-Influences Approach." *Journalism Studies*, Vol. 2, No. 2 (2001): 173–187.

Reichman, Deb. "Karzai Says His Office Gets Cash from Iran, US." Associated Press, October 25, 2010, http://www.sandiegouniontribune.com/sdut-karzai-says-his-office-gets-cash-from-iran-us-2010oct25-story.html

Reston, James. *The Artillery of the Press: Its Influence on American Foreign Policy*. New York: Harper & Row, 1966.

"Return to Normalcy? How the Media Covered the War on Terrorism." Project for Excellence in Journalism and Princeton Survey Research Associates, June 11, 2003.

Reynolds, Maura. "Bush Presses NATO to Send More Troops to Afghanistan." *Los Angeles Times*, February 16, 2007. http://articles.baltimoresun.com/2007-02-16/news/0702160410_1_nato-offensive-in-afghanistan-troops-to-afghanistan

Riffe, Daniel, Charles F. Aust, Ted C. Jones, Barbara Shoemake, and Shyam Sundar. "The Shrinking Foreign Newshole of the New York Times." *Newspaper Research Journal*, Vol. 15, No. 3 (Summer 1994): 74–89.

Righter, Rosemary. *Whose News: Politics, the Press and the Third World*. New York: Times Books, 1978.

Risen, James. "Karzai's Kin Use Ties to Gain Power in Afghanistan." *New York Times*, October 6, 2008. http://topics.nytimes.com/top/reference/timestopics/people/k/ahmed_wali_karzai/index.html?offset=10&s=newest

Risen, James. "Reports Link Karzai's Brother to Afghan Heroin Trade." *New York Times*, October 4, 2008. http://www.nytimes.com/2008/10/05/world/asia/05afghan.html?ref=ahmed walikarzai

Rivenburgh, Nancy K. "Social Identity and News Portrayals of Citizens Involved in International Affairs." *Media Psychology*, Vol. 2, No. 4 (November 2000): 303–329.

Roach, C. *Communication and Culture in War and Peace*. Newbury Park, CA: Sage Publications, 1993.

Robinson, Piers. *The CNN Effect: The Myth of News, Foreign Policy and Intervention*. London: Routledge, 2002.

Robinson, Piers. "Researching U.S. Media-State Relations and Twenty-First Century Wars." In *Reporting War: Journalism in Wartime*, edited by Stuart Allan and Barbie Zelizer. Oxford: Routledge, 2004.

Rohde, David. "A Nation Challenged: Transfer of Power; Afghan Leaders Is Sworn In, Asking for Help to Rebuild." *New York Times*, December 23, 2001. http://www.nytimes.com/2001/12/23/world/nation-challenged-transfer-power-afghan-leader-sworn-asking-for-help-rebuild.html

Rohde, David, and Kristin Mulvihill. *A Rope and a Prayer: A Kidnapping from Two Sides*. New York: Viking, 2010.

Rohde, David, and David Sanger. "How a 'Good War' in Afghanistan Went Bad." *New York Times*, August 12, 2007. http://www.nytimes.com/2007/08/12/world/asia/12afghan.html?pagewanted=all

Rosen, Christopher. "All the Times Donald Trump Has Called the Media 'Fake News' on Twitter." *Entertainment Weekly*, June 27, 2017. http://ew.com/tv/2017/06/27/donald-trump-fake-news-twitter/

Rosenberg, Matthew. "Amid Election Impasse, Calls for an Afghan Interim Government." *New York Times*, August 18, 2014. http://www.nytimes.com/2014/08/19/world/asia/amid-election-impasse-calls-in-afghanistan-for-an-interim-government.html

Rosenberg, Matthew. Personal Twitter Account, August 21, 2014. https://twitter.com/mrosenbergNYT/status/502423052190113795

Rosenberg, Matthew. "Ashraf Ghani Thanks U.S. for Support in First Visit as Afghan Leader." *New York Times*, March 23, 2015. http://www.nytimes.com/2015/03/24/world/asia/an-afghans-sentiment-for-an-ally-gratitude.html?_r=0

Rosenberg, Matthew, and Graham Bowley. "Intractable Afghan Graft Hampering U.S. Strategy." *New York Times*, March 7, 2012, https://www.worldhunger.org/intractable-afghan-graft-hampering-us-strategy-afghan-government-has-yet-to-prosecute-a-high-level-corruption-case/

Rosenblume, Morton. *Coups and Earthquakes*. New York: Harper and Row, 1979.

Rosenblume, Morton. "The Western Wire Services and the Third World." In *The Third World and Press Freedom*, edited by P. C. Horton. New York: Praeger, 1978.

Rubin, Alissa. "Afghan President Rebukes West and U.N." *New York Times*, April 1, 2010. http://www.nytimes.com/2010/04/02/world/asia/02afghan.html

Rubin, Alissa. "Flawed Justice After a Mob Killed an Afghan Woman." *New York Times*, December 26, 2015. https://www.nytimes.com/2015/12/27/world/asia/flawed-justice-after-a-mob-killed-an-afghan-woman.html

Rubin, Alissa, and Rod Nordland, "Taliban Attacks Shake Afghan Peace Gathering." *New York Times*, June 2, 2010. http://www.nytimes.com/2010/06/03/world/asia/03afghan.html

Rubin, Alissa, and Thom Shanker. "Afghan Leader Says U.S. Abets Taliban's Goal." *New York Times*, March 10, 2013. http://www.nytimes.com/2013/03/11/world/asia/karzai-accuses-us-and-taliban-of-colluding-in-afghanistan.html

Rubin, Alissa, and Habib Zohrai. "Karzai Accuses U.S. of Duplicity in Fighting Afghan Enemies." *New York Times*, October 4, 2012. http://www.nytimes.com/2012/10/05/world/asia/karzai-accuses-us-of-duplicity-in-fighting-afghan-enemies.html

Rubin, Barnett R. *The Fragmentation of Afghanistan: State Formation and Collapse in the International System*. New Haven, CT: Yale University Press, 2002.

Rusciano, Frank Louis. "Framing World Opinion in the Elite Press." In Pippa Norris, Montague Kern, and Marion Just. *Framing Terrorism: The News Media, the Government and the Public*. London: Routledge, 2003.

Saikal, A. "Afghanistan after the Loya Jirga." *Survival*, Vol. 44, No. 3 (2002): 47–56.

Salwen, Michael B., and Frances Matera. "Public Salience of Foreign Nations." *Journalism Quarterly*, Vol. 69 (1989): 623–632.

Samuels, David. "The Aspiring Novelist Who Became Obama's Foreign Policy Guru: How Ben Rhodes Rewrote the Rules of Diplomacy for the Digital Age." *New York Times Magazine*, May 5, 2016. http://www.nytimes.com/2016/05/08/magazine/the-aspiring-novelist-who-became-obamas-foreign-policy-guru.html?_r=0

Sanders, Edmund. "Israel's Netanyahu Seeks to Ease Tension After Biden's Mideast Trip." *Los Angeles Times*, March 15, 2010. http://articles.latimes.com/2010/mar/15/world/la-fg-israel-tensions15-2010mar15

Sanger, David. "Striking at Assad Carries Opportunities, and Risks, for Trump." *New York Times*, April 7, 2017. Z https://www.nytimes.com/2017/04/07/world/middleeast/airstikes-syria-trump-russia.html?smid=tw-share

Scheufele, Dietram. "Agenda-Setting, Priming, and Framing Revisited: Another Look at Cognitive Effects of Political Communication." *Mass Communication & Society*, Vol. 3 (2000): 297–316.

Schiller, Herbert I. *Communication and Cultural Domination*. White Plains, NY: International Arts and Sciences Press, 1976.

Schlesinger, Philip. "Media, the Political Order and National Identity." *Media, Culture and Society*, Vol. 13, No. 3 (July 1991): 297–308.

Schmemann, Serge. "U.S. ATTACKED; President Vows to Exact Punishment for 'Evil'." *New York Times*, September 12, 2001, https://www.nytimes.com/2001/09/12/us/us-attacked-president-vows-to-exact-punishment-for-evil.html

Schudson, Michael. *Sociology of News*. New York: W.W. Norton, 2003.

Schudson, Michael. "The Sociology of News Production (Again)." In *Mass Media and Society*, edited by James Curran and Michael Gurevitch. London: Arnold, 2001.

Schudson, Michael. "What's Unusual About Covering Politics as Usual?" In *Journalism After September 11th*, edited by Barbie Zelizer and Stuart Allan. London: Routledge, 2011.

Seamon, Marc, and Matt Peters. "News Mix Reflects Media's Gatekeeping Role in Crises." In *Media in an American Crisis: Studies of September 11, 2001*, edited by Elinor Kelley Grusin and Sandra H. Utt. New York: University Press of America. 2005.

Seaton, Ed. "The Diminishing Use of Foreign News Reporting (Remarks)." International Press Institute, May 26, 1998. http://www.asne.org/ideas/seatonmoscow.htm.

Shalizi, Hamid, and Jessica Donati. "Afghan Cleric and Others Defend Lynching of Woman in Kabul." Reuters, March 20, 2015. https://www.reuters.com/article/

us-afghanistan-woman/afghan-cleric-and-others-defend-lynching-of-woman-in-kabul-idUSKBN0MG1Z620150320

Sharma, Betwa. "Good COP, Bad COP: Reflections on Covering the Copenhagen Climate Summit." *Columbia Journalism Review*, December 22, 2009. https://archives.cjr.org/the_observatory/good_cop_bad_cop.php

Sieff, Kevin. "Next to U.S. Firing Range in Afghanistan, a Village of Victims." *Washington Post*, May 26, 2012. http://www.washingtonpost.com/world/asia_pacific/next-to-us-firing-range-in-afghanistan-a-village-of-victims/2012/05/26/gJQAeQEIsU_story.html

Sigal, Leon V. *Reporters and Officials: The Organization and Politics of Newsmaking.* Lexington, MA: D. C. Heath, 1973.

Smith, Craig. "The Intimidating Face of America." *New York Times*, October 13, 2004. http://www.nytimes.com/2004/10/13/international/asia/13letter.html

Smith, Sally Bedall. "Why TV News Can't Be A Complete View of the World." *New York Times*, August 8, 1982.

Sobel, Richard. *The Impact of Public Opinion on U.S. Foreign Policy Since Vietnam.* New York: Oxford University Press, 2001.

Soesilo, Arie S., and Philo C. Wasburn. "Constructing a Political Spectacle: American and Indonesian Media Accounts of the 'Crisis in the Gulf'." *Sociological Quarterly*, Vol. 35, No. 2 (2004): 367–381.

Soroka, Stuart N. "Media, Public Opinion, and Foreign Policy." *Press/Politics*, Vol. 8, No. 1 (2003): 27–48.

Soss, Joe. "Talking Our Way to Meaningful Explanations: A Practice-Centered View of Interviewing for Interpretive Research." In *Interpretation and Method: Empirical Research Methods and the Interpretive Turn*, edited by Dvora Yanow and Peregrine Schwartz-Shea. London: M.E. Sharpe, 2006.

Sowry, Biby. "Today in History—February 16." *Vogue UK*, February 16, 2010. http://www.vogue.co.uk/article/tom-ford-described-hamid-karzai-as-the-chicest-man-on-the-planet

Sreberny-Mohammadi, A., Kaarle Nordenstreng, R. L. Stevesnon. and Frank Ugboajah. "Foreign News in the Media. International Reporting in 29 Countries." In *Final Report of the "Foreign Images" Study Undertaken for UNESCO by the IAMCR.* Paris: UNESCO, 1985.

"Staff Sgt. Robert Bales Identified in Afghan Killings." *Army Times*, March 17, 2012. http://www.armytimes.com/news/2012/03/army-staff-sgt-robert-bales-named-suspect-afghan-killings-031712w/

Stelter, Brian. "About 28 Million TV Viewers Watched Trump's Afghanistan Speech." *CNN*, August 22, 2017. http://money.cnn.com/2017/08/22/media/president-trump-afghanistan-speech-ratings/index.html

Stelter, Brian. "Goodbye Baghdad, Hello Kabul." *New York Times*, October 19, 2009. https://www.nytimes.com/2009/10/19/business/media/19coverage.html

Straubhaar, Joseph. *World Television: From Global to Local.* Thousand Oaks, CA: Sage, 2007.

Suhrke, A., K. B. Harpviken, and A. Strand. "After Bonn: Conflictual Peace Building." *Third World Quarterly*, Vol. 23, No. 5 (2002): 875–891.

Sullivan, Margaret. "Is Global Expansion Good for Times Readers?" *New York Times*, February 12, 2016. https://publiceditor.blogs.nytimes.com/2016/02/12/is-global-expansion-good-for-times-readers/?_r=0

Sweeney, Michael S. *The Military and the Press: An Uneasy Truce*. Evanston, IL: Northwestern University Press, 2006.

Szalai, George. "Afghan Media Mogul Saad Mohseni on Taking His Moby Group to New Markets and His Hollywood Connections (Q&A)." *Hollywood Reporter*, October 2016. http://www.hollywoodreporter.com/news/afghan-media-mogul-saad-mohseni-937657

Tai, Zixue. "Media of the World and World of the Media: A Cross-National Study of the Rankings of the 'Top 10 World Events' from 1988 to 1998." *International Communication Gazette*, Vol. 62, No. 5. (October 2000): 331–353.

Taliban Press Release. *Tolo News*, October 12, 2015. http://www.mobygroup.com/news/99-news-2015/1214-press-statement

Tarzi, Amin. "The State of the Media in Afghanistan." Radio Free Europe/Radio Liberty, February 6, 2003. http://www.rferl.org/afghanreport/2003/02/6-130203.asp

Tavernise, Sabrina, and Abdul Waheed Wafa. "U.N. Official Acknowledges 'Widespread Fraud' in Afghan Election." *New York Times*, October 11, 2009. http://www.nytimes.com/2009/10/12/world/asia/12afghan.html

Taylor, Philip M. "The Military and the Media Past, Present and Future." In *The Media and International Security*, edited by Stephen Badsey. London: Frank Cass, 2000.

Thier, Alexander, and J. Chopra. "The Road Ahead: Political and Institutional Reconstruction in Afghanistan." *Third World Quarterly*, Vol. 23, No. 5 (2002): 893–907.

Thussu, Daya Kishan. "Managing the Media in an Era of Round-the-Clock News: Notes from India's First Tele-War." *Journalism Studies*, Vol. 3, No. 2 (2002): 203–212.

"Time Devoted to the Wars in Afghanistan and Iraq Over Time." The State of the News Media 2010, March 2011. http://www.stateofthemedia.org/2010

"Top Ten Stories Ranked by Time on U.S. Foreign Policy Focus 2015." *Tyndall Report*, 2015, http://tyndallreport.com/yearinreview2015/foreignpolicy/

Trump Twitter Archive, http://www.trumptwitterarchive.com/

Tuchman, Gaye. *Making News: A Study in the Construction of Reality*. New York: The Free Press, 1978.

Tunstall, Jeremy. *The Media Are American*. London: Constable, 1977.

Tunstall, Jeremy, and David Machin. *The Anglo-American Media Connection*. Oxford: Oxford University Press, 1999.

"Tyndall Report Weekly Archives 2003." *Tyndall Report*, 2004. http://tyndallreport.com/weekly/archive/2003/.

United Nations Educational, Scientific and Cultural Organization. *Many Voices, One World: Toward a More Just and More Efficient World Information and Communication Order.* Paris: UNESCO, 1980.

Universal Declaration of Human Rights. United Nations, Paris, December 10, 1948. http://www.un.org/en/universal-declaration-human-rights/

"U.S. Citizen Air Traffic to Overseas Regions, Canada and Mexico 2011." Office of Travel and Tourism Industries, 2012. http://tinet.ita.doc.gov/outreachpages/out-bound.general_information.outbound_ov erview.html

U.S. Embassy in Kabul, Afghanistan. "Afghanistan Banking Sector Vulnerabilities: Exposure to Dubai's Collapsing Property Market and the Role of Lottery Accounts." WikiLeaks Cable: 2010Kabul551_a., dated February 13, 2010. https://wikileaks.org/plusd/cables/10KABUL551_a.html

"U.S. Spending on the Afghan War." Center for Strategic and International Studies, May 15, 2012. http://csis.org/files/.../120515_US_Spending_Afghan_War_SIGAR

Van Ginneken, Jaap. *Understanding Global News: A Critical Introduction.* Thousand Oaks, CA: Sage Publications, 1998.

"Violence Against Journalists in Afghanistan." Nai, 2017. http://data.nai.org.af/

Waisbord, Silvio. "Media and the Reinvention of the Nation." In *The SAGE Handbook of Media Studies,* edited by John D. H. Downing, Denis McQuail, Philip Schlesinger, and Ellen Wartella (Thousand Oaks, CA: Sage Publishers, 2004), 375–389.

Wanta, Wayne, Guy Golan, and Cheolhan Lee. "Agenda Setting and International News: Media Influence on Public Perceptions of Foreign Nations." *Journalism and Mass Communication Quarterly,* Vol. 81, No. 2 (2004): 364–377.

Wanta, Wayne, and Yu-Wei Hu. "The Agenda-Setting Effects of International News Coverage: An Examination of Differing News Frames." *International Journal of Public Opinion Research,* Vol. 5 (1993): 250–264.

Wasburn, Philo. *The Social Construction of International News: We're Talking About Them, They're Talking About Us.* Westport, CT: Praeger Publishers, 2002.

Weaver, James B., Christopher J. Porter, and Margaret E. Evans. "Patterns of Foreign News Coverage on U.S. Network TV: A Ten-Year Analysis." *Journalism Quarterly,* Vol. 61 (1984): 356–363.

Weick, Karl E. *Sense-making in Organizations.* Ann Arbor: University of Michigan Press, 1995.

Weinbaum, Marvin G. "Civic Culture and Democracy in Pakistan." *Asian Survey,* Vol. 36, No. 7 (1996): 639–654.

Weiss, Robert. S. *Learning from Strangers: The Art and Method of Qualitative Interview Studies.* New York: The Free Press, 1994.

Whitaker, Raymond. "Kabul Falls to the Tide of the Taliban." *The Independent,* September 28. 1996. http://www.independent.co.uk/news/world/kabul-falls-to-the-tide-of-the-taliban-1365343.html

Widiastuti, D., and R. Sulaiman. *Situation of Freedom of Expression and the Media in Afghanistan*. London: Article 19, 2003.

Wilkinson, Sophia, and Shireen Sultan. "Audience Perceptions of Radio Programming in Afghanistan: An Evaluation of Listeners' Opinions." BBC World Service Trust, 2004.

Wimmer, R. D., and J. R. Dominick. *Mass Media Research: An Introduction* (6th ed.). Belmont, CA: Wadsworth, 2000.

World Bank. "The Information Age." World Development Report. New York: Oxford University Press, 2009.

Wu, Denis W. "Investigating the Determinants of International News Flow: A Meta-Analysis." *The International Journal for Communication Studies*, Vol. 60 (1998): 493–512.

Wu, Denis H. "Systemic Determinants of International News Coverage: A Comparison of 38 Countries." *Journal of Communication*, Vol. 50, No. 2 (Spring 2000): 110–130.

Yin, Jiafei. "Beyond Four Theories of the Press: A New Model for the Asian and the World Press." *Journalism Communication Monographs*, Vol. 10 (Spring 2008).

Zaller, John. "Elite Leadership of Mass Opinion: New Evidence from the Gulf War." In *Taken by Storm: The Media, Public Opinion, and U.S. Foreign Policy in the Gulf War*, edited by W. Lance Bennett and David L. Paletz. Chicago: University of Chicago Press, 1994.

Zaller, John, and Dennis Chiu. "Government's Little Helper: U.S. Press Coverage of Foreign Policy Crises, 1945–1991." *Political Communication*, Vol. 13, No. 2 (1996): 385–405.

Zehra, Nasim. "How a Vibrant Media Can Thwart a Coup." *South Asian News Agency*, January 12, 2012. http://www.sananews.net/english/2012/01/how-a-vibrant-media-can-thwart-a-coup/

Index